Windows® Sysinternals Administrator's Reference

Mark Russinovich

Aaron Margosis

PUBLISHED BY
Microsoft Press
A Division of Microsoft Corporation
One Microsoft Way
Redmond, Washington 98052-6399

Library of Congress Control Number: 2011931614

ISBN: 978-0-7356-5672-7

2 3 4 5 6 7 8 9 10 11 M 6 5 4 3 2 1

Printed and bound in the United States of America.

First Printing

Microsoft Press books are available through booksellers and distributors worldwide. If you need support related to this book, email Microsoft Press Book Support at mspinput@microsoft.com. Please tell us what you think of this book at http://www.microsoft.com/learning/booksurvey.

Acquisitions Editor: Devon Musgrave
Developmental Editor: Devon Musgrave
Project Editor: Devon Musgrave
Editorial Production: Waypoint Press
Technical Reviewer: Christophe Nassare; Technical Review services provided by Content Master, a member of CM Group, Ltd.
Copyeditor: Roger LeBlanc
Indexer: Christina Yeager
Cover: Twist Creative·Seattle

To my fellow Windows troubleshooters: Never give up! Never surrender!

— Mark Russinovich

To Elise, who makes great things possible and then makes sure they happen.
(And who is much cooler than I am.)

— Aaron Margosis

Contents at a Glance

Table of Contents

What do you think of this book? We want to hear from you!

Microsoft is interested in hearing your feedback so we can continually improve our books and learning resources for you. To participate in a brief online survey, please visit:

www.microsoft.com/learning/booksurvey/

What do you think of this book? We want to hear from you!

Microsoft is interested in hearing your feedback so we can continually improve our books and learning resources for you. To participate in a brief online survey, please visit:

www.microsoft.com/learning/booksurvey/

Foreword

I was honored when Mark and Aaron asked me to write the foreword for this book.

My association with Mark and his tools goes back to 1997 when I first heard him speak at a Windows developer conference in Santa Clara, California. Little did I know that two years later we would begin collaborating on *Inside Windows 2000* and the subsequent editions of *Windows Internals*.

In fact, because of working with Mark on both the Windows Internals books and later on the Windows Internals courses we authored and taught together, I often get thanked for the Sysinternals tools—something that irks Mark! While I'm tempted to graciously accept the praise and say "You're welcome," the truth is that, while I use the tools heavily in my training and consulting work, I have not authored any of them.

There has been a need for a Sysinternals book for many years now, though it's a testament to the design of the tools and their user interface that they have been used so widely and successfully *without* a book to explain them all. But the book opens the door even wider for more IT professionals to leverage the Sysinternals tools to peer beneath the surface of Windows to really understand what's going on. Aaron Margosis' careful, meticulous research resulted in many improvements in the tools—fixing inconsistencies, improving the help text, and adding new features.

I have personally solved innumerable client and server system and application problems with the tools, even in situations where I didn't think the tools would help. As a result, I coined the expression "When in doubt, run Filemon and Regmon" (now Procmon).

To help more IT professionals see how to apply the tools to real problems, this book has an entire section on case studies. These real-life examples show how your fellow IT professionals have used the Sysinternals tools to solve what would otherwise be unsolvable problems.

Finally, a word of warning—even though I talk to Mark on a regular basis, I can't count the number of times that I've reported a bug to him that he'd already fixed—so make sure you are running the latest versions before you send him email! The best way to do that is to follow the Sysinternals site blog RSS feed.

This book belongs on every IT professional's desk (or e-reader)—and if you see Mark, tell him you appreciate Dave's work on the Sysinternals tools.

David Solomon

President, David Solomon Expert Seminars, Inc.
www.solsem.com

Introduction

The Sysinternals Suite is a set of over 70 advanced diagnostic and troubleshooting utilities for the Microsoft Windows platform written by me—Mark Russinovich—and Bryce Cogswell. Since Microsoft's acquisition of Sysinternals in 2006, these utilities have been available for free download from Microsoft's Windows Sysinternals Web site (part of Microsoft TechNet).

The goal of this book is to familiarize you with the Sysinternals utilities and help you understand how to use them to their fullest. The book will also show you examples of how I and other Sysinternals users have leveraged the utilities to solve real problems on Windows systems.

Although I coauthored this book with Aaron Margosis, the book is written as if I am speaking. This is not at all a comment on Aaron's contribution to the book; without his hard work, this book would not exist.

Tools the Book Covers

This book describes all of the Sysinternals utilities that are available on the Windows Sysinternals Web site (*http://technet.microsoft.com/en-us/sysinternals/default.aspx*) and all of their features as of the time of this writing (summer, 2011). However, Sysinternals is highly dynamic: existing utilities regularly gain new capabilities, and new utilities are introduced from time to time. (To keep up, follow the RSS feed of the "Sysinternals Site Discussion" blog: *http://blogs.technet.com/b/sysinternals/.*) So, by the time you read this book, some parts of it may already be out of date. That said, you should always keep the Sysinternals utilities updated to take advantage of new features and bug fixes.

This book does not cover Sysinternals utilities that have been deprecated and are no longer available on the Sysinternals site. If you are still using RegMon (Registry Monitor) or FileMon (File Monitor), you should replace them with Process Monitor, described in Chapter 4. Rootkit Revealer, one of the computer industry's first rootkit detectors (and the tool that discovered the "Sony rootkit"), has served its purpose and has been retired. Similarly, a few other utilities (such as Newsid and EfsDump) that used to provide unique value have been retired because either they were no longer needed or equivalent functionality was eventually added to Windows.

The History of Sysinternals

The first Sysinternals utility I wrote, Ctrl2cap, was born of necessity. Before I started using Windows NT in 1995, I mostly used UNIX systems, which have keyboards that place the Ctrl key where the Caps Lock key is on standard PC keyboards. Rather than adapt to the new layout, I set out to learn about Windows NT device driver development and to write a driver that converts Caps Lock key presses into Ctrl key presses as they make their way from the keyboard into the Windows NT input system. Ctrl2cap is still posted on the Sysinternals site today, and I still use it on all my systems.

Ctrl2cap was the first of many tools I wrote to learn about the way Windows NT works under the hood while at the same providing some useful functionality. The next tool I wrote, NTFSDOS, I developed with Bryce Cogswell. I had met Bryce in graduate school at Carnegie Mellon University, and we had written several academic papers together and worked on a startup project where we developed software for Windows 3.1. I pitched the idea of a tool that would allow users to retrieve data from an NTFS-formatted partition by using the ubiquitous DOS floppy. Bryce thought it would be a fun programming challenge, and we divided up the work and released the first version about a month later.

I also wrote the next two tools, Filemon and Regmon, with Bryce. These three utilities— NTFSDOS, Filemon, and Regmon—became the foundation for Sysinternals. Filemon and Regmon, both of which we released for Windows 95 and Windows NT, showed file system and registry activity, becoming the first tools anywhere to do so and making them indispensible troubleshooting aids.

Bryce and I decided to make the tools available for others to use, but we didn't have a Web site of our own, so we initially published them on the site of a friend, Andrew Schulman, who I'd met in conjunction with his own work uncovering the internal operation of DOS and Windows 95. Going through an intermediary didn't allow us to update the tools with enhancements and bug fixes as quickly as we wanted, so in September 1996 Bryce and I created NTInternals.com to host the tools and articles we wrote about the internal operation of Windows 95 and Windows NT. Bryce and I had also developed tools that we decided we could sell for some side income, so the same month, we also founded Winternals Software, a commercial software company that we bootstrapped by driving traffic with a single banner ad on NTInternals.com. The first utility we released as Winternals Software was NTRecover, a utility that enabled users to mount the disks of unbootable Windows NT systems from a working system and access them as if they were locally attached disks.

The mission of NTInternals.com was to distribute freeware tools that leveraged our deep understanding of the Windows operating system in order to deliver powerful diagnostic, monitoring, and management capabilities. Within a few months, the site, shown below as it looked in December 1996 (thanks to the Internet Archive's Wayback Machine), drew 1,500 visitors per day, making it one of the most popular utility sites for Windows in the early days of the Internet revolution. In 1998, at the "encouragement" of Microsoft lawyers, we changed the site's name to Sysinternals.com.

Over the next several years, the utilities continued to evolve. We added more utilities as we needed them, as our early power users suggested enhancements, or when we thought of a new way to show information about Windows.

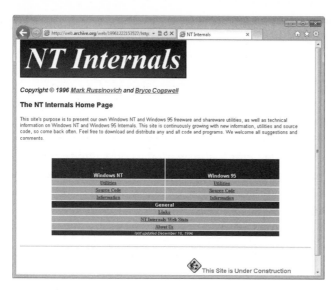

The Sysinternals utilities fell into three basic categories: those used to help programmers, those for system troubleshooting, and those for systems management. DebugView, a utility that captures and displays program debug statements, was one of the early developer-oriented tools that I wrote to aid my own development of device drivers. DLLView, a tool for displaying the DLLs that processes have loaded, and HandleEx, a process-listing GUI utility that showed open handles, were two of the early troubleshooting tools. (I merged DLLView and HandleEx to create Process Explorer in 2001.) The PsTools, discussed in Chapter 6, are some of the most popular management utilities, bundled into a suite for easy download. PsList, the first PsTool, was inspired initially by the UNIX "ps" command, which provides a process listing. The utilities grew in number and functionality, becoming a software suite of utilities that allowed you to easily perform many tasks on a remote system without requiring installation of special software on the remote system beforehand.

Also in 1996, I began writing for Windows IT Pro magazine, highlighting Windows internals and the Sysinternals utilities and contributing additional feature articles, including a controversial article in 1996 that established my name within Microsoft itself, though not necessarily in a positive way. The article, "Inside the Difference Between Windows NT Workstation and Windows NT Server," pointed out the limited differences between Windows NT Workstation and Windows NT Server, which contradicted Microsoft's marketing message.

As the utilities continued to evolve and grow, I began to contemplate writing a book on Windows internals. Such a book already existed, *Inside Windows NT* (Microsoft Press, 1992), the first edition of which was written by Helen Custer alongside the original release of Windows NT 3.1. The second edition was rewritten and enhanced for Windows NT 4.0 by David Solomon, a well-established operating system expert, trainer, and writer who had worked at DEC. Instead of writing a book from scratch, I contacted him and suggested that I coauthor the third edition, which would cover Windows 2000. My relationship with

Microsoft had been on the mend since the 1996 article as the result of my sending Windows bug reports directly to Windows developers, but David still had to obtain permission, which Microsoft granted.

As a result, David Solomon and I coauthored the third, fourth, and fifth editions of the book, which we renamed *Windows Internals* at the fourth edition. (The fifth edition of *Windows Internals* was published in 2009.) Not long after we finished *Inside Windows 2000* (Microsoft Press, 2000), I joined David to teach his Windows internals seminars, adding my own content. Offered around the world, even at Microsoft to the developers of Windows, these classes have long used the Sysinternals utilities to show students how to peer deep into Windows internals and learn more when they returned to their developer and IT professional roles at home. David still offers Windows internals classes at *http://www.solsem.com/*.

By 2006, my relationship with Microsoft had been strong for several years, Winternals had a full line of enterprise management software and had grown to about 100 employees, and Sysinternals had two million downloads per day. On July 18, 2006, Microsoft acquired Winternals and Sysinternals. Not long after, Bryce and I (there we are below in 2006) moved to Redmond to become a part of the Windows team. Today, I serve as one of Microsoft's small group of Technical Fellows, providing technical leadership to help drive the direction of the company. I'm now in the Windows Azure group, working on the "kernel" of Microsoft's cloud operating system.

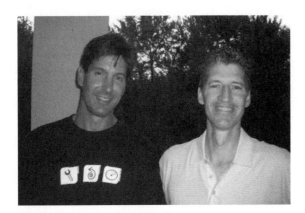

Two of the goals of the acquisition were to make sure that the tools Bryce and I developed would continue to be freely available and that the community we built would thrive, and they have. Today, the Windows Sysinternals site on technet.microsoft.com is one of the most frequently visited sites on TechNet, averaging 50,000 visitors per day and three million downloads per month. Sysinternals power users come back time and again for the latest versions of the utilities and for new utilities, such as the recently released RAMMap and VMMap, as well as to participate in the Sysinternals community, a growing forum with over 30,000 registered users at the time of this writing. I remain dedicated to continuing to enhance the existing tools and to add new tools, including ones focused on Windows Azure.

Many people suggested that a book on the tools would be valuable, but it wasn't until David Solomon suggested that one was way overdue that I started the project. My responsibilities at Microsoft did not permit me to devote the time necessary to write another book, but David pointed out that I could find someone to help. I was pleased that Aaron Margosis agreed to partner with me. Aaron is a Principal Consultant with Microsoft Public Sector Services who is known for his deep understanding of Windows security and application compatibility. I have known Aaron for many years and his excellent writing skills, familiarity with Windows internals, and proficiency with the Sysinternals tools made him an ideal coauthor.

Who Should Read This Book

This book exists for Windows IT professionals and power users who want to make the most of the Sysinternals tools. Regardless of your experience with the tools, and whether you manage the systems of a large enterprise, a small business, or the PCs of your family and friends, you're sure to discover new tools, pick up tips, and learn techniques that will help you more effectively troubleshoot the toughest Windows problems and simplify your system-management operations and monitoring.

Assumptions

This book expects that you have familiarity with the Windows operating system. Basic familiarity with concepts such as processes, threads, virtual memory, and the Windows command prompt, is helpful, though some of these concepts are discussed in Chapter 2, "Windows Core Concepts".

Organization of This Book

The book is divided into three parts. Part I, "Getting Started," provides an overview of the Sysinternals utilities and the Sysinternals Web site, describes features common to all of the utilities, tells you where to go for help, and discusses some Windows core concepts that will help you better understand the platform and the information reported by the utilities.

Part II, "Usage Guide," is a detailed reference guide covering all of the Sysinternals utilities' features, command-line options, system requirements, and caveats. With plentiful screen shots and usage examples, this section should answer just about any question you have about the utilities. Major utilities such as Process Explorer and Process Monitor each get their own chapter; subsequent chapters cover utilities by category, such as security utilities, Active Directory utilities, and file utilities.

Part III, "Troubleshooting—'The Case of the Unexplained...'," contains stories of real-world problem solving using the Sysinternals utilities from Aaron and me, as well as from administrators and power users from around the world.

Conventions and Features in This Book

This book presents information using conventions designed to make the information readable and easy to follow:

- Boxed elements with labels such as "Note" provide additional information or alternative methods for completing a step successfully.

- Text that you type (apart from code blocks) appears in bold.

- A plus sign (+) between two key names means that you must press those keys at the same time. For example, "Press Alt+Tab" means that you hold down the Alt key while you press the Tab key.

- A vertical bar between two or more menu items (for example, File | Close), means that you should select the first menu or menu item, then the next, and so on.

System Requirements

The Sysinternals tools work on the following versions of Windows, including 64-bit editions, unless otherwise specified:

- Windows XP with Service Pack 3
- Windows Vista
- Windows 7
- Windows Server 2003 with Service Pack 2
- Windows Server 2003 R2
- Windows Server 2008
- Windows Server 2008 R2

Some tools require administrative rights to run, and others implement specific features that require administrative rights.

Acknowledgments

First, Aaron and I would like to thank Bryce Cogswell, cofounder of Sysinternals, for his enormous contribution to the Sysinternals tools. Because of our great collaboration, what Bryce and I published on Sysinternals was more than just the sum of our individual efforts. Bryce retired from Microsoft in October 2010, and we wish him luck in whatever he pursues.

We'd like to thank David Solomon for spurring Mark to write this book, providing detailed review of many chapters, and writing the Foreword. Dave has also been one of Sysinternals most effective evangelists over the years and has suggested many valuable features.

Thanks to Curtis Metz and Karl Seng, who manage the Sysinternals Web site, forums, and code-publishing process. Otto Helweg had that role when Microsoft acquired Sysinternals, and we thank him for helping to preserve the spirit of Sysinternals during the integration.

We are grateful to the following people who provided valuable and insightful technical review, corrections, and suggestions for the book: Andreas Klein, Brian Matusz, Bruno Aleixo, Carsten Kinder, Chris Jackson, Ewan MacKellar, Fatih Colgar, Gautam Anand, Gowri Kumar Chandramouli, Greg Cottingham, John Dietrick, Mario Hewardt, Mario Raccagni, Mark Priem, Matt Garson, Pavel Lebedynskiy, Richard Diver, Scott Frunzi, Stephen Griffin, and Tim Reckmeyer. Andrew Richards deserves special mention for providing detailed feedback on more chapters than any other reviewer.

We also want to thank Carl Harrison for supplying a sidebar on using LiveKd to capture online kernel dumps.

We'd like to thank Martin DelRe from Microsoft Press for seeing the potential of the book; Devon Musgrave, also from Microsoft Press, for championing the book; and Steve Sagman from Waypoint Press for guiding the book through the editorial and production process. Thanks also to Christophe Nasarre for technical editing and Roger LeBlanc for copyediting.

Aaron's wife Elise deserves thanks for providing Aaron with enthusiastic encouragement at a crucial point in the book's development. Aaron thanks her and their children—Elana, Jonah, and Gabriel—for their love and support. Aaron also thanks Brenda Schrier for his author photo.

Mark thanks his wife, Daryl, and daughter, Maria, for supporting all his endeavors.

Errata & Book Support

We've made every effort to ensure the accuracy of this book and its companion content. Any errors that have been reported since this book was published are listed on our Microsoft Press site at oreilly.com:

http://go.microsoft.com/FWLink/?Linkid=220275

If you find an error that is not already listed, you can report it to us through the same page.

If you need additional support, e-mail Microsoft Press Book Support at *mspinput@microsoft.com.*

Please note that product support for Microsoft software is not offered through the addresses above.

We Want to Hear from You

At Microsoft Press, your satisfaction is our top priority, and your feedback our most valuable asset. Please tell us what you think of this book at:

http://www.microsoft.com/learning/booksurvey

The survey is short, and we read every one of your comments and ideas. Thanks in advance for your input!

Stay in Touch

Let's keep the conversation going. Follow Microsoft Press on Twitter: *http://twitter.com/ MicrosoftPress.*

Part I
Getting Started

Chapter 1
Getting Started with the Sysinternals Utilities

The Sysinternals utilities are free, advanced administrative, diagnostic, and troubleshooting utilities for the Microsoft Windows platform written by the founders of Sysinternals: me (Mark Russinovich) and Bryce Cogswell[1]. Since Microsoft's acquisition of Sysinternals in July 2006, these utilities have been available for download from Microsoft's TechNet Web site.

Among the hallmarks of a Sysinternals utility are that it

- Serves unmet needs of a significant IT pro or developer audience

- Is intuitive and easy to use

- Is packaged as a single executable image that does not require installation and can be run from anywhere, including from a network location or removable media

- Does not leave behind any significant incidental data after it has run

Because Sysinternals doesn't have the overhead of a formal product group, I can quickly release new features, utilities, and bug fixes. In some cases, I can take a useful and simple-to-implement feature from suggestion to public availability in under a week.

However, the other side of not having a full product group and formal testing organization is that the utilities are offered "as is" with no official Microsoft product support. The Sysinternals team maintains a dedicated community support forum—described later in this chapter—on the Sysinternals Web site, and I try to fix reported bugs as quickly as possible.

Overview of the Utilities

The Sysinternals utilities cover a broad range of functionality across many aspects of the Windows operating system. While some of the more comprehensive utilities such as Process Explorer and Process Monitor span several categories of operations, others can more or less be grouped within a single category, such as "process utilities" or "file utilities." Many of the utilities have a graphical user interface (GUI), while others are console utilities with rich command-line interfaces designed for automation or for use at a command prompt.

This book covers three major utilities (Process Explorer, Process Monitor, and Autoruns), each in its own chapter. Subsequent chapters cover several utilities each, grouped by category.

---

[1] Bryce left Microsoft in late 2010 and no longer contributes to the Sysinternals utilities.

Table 1-1 lists these chapters with a brief overview of each of the utilities covered within them.

TABLE 1-1 Chapter Topics

Utility	Description
Chapter 3, Process Explorer	
Process Explorer	Replaces Task Manager, and displays far more detail about processes and threads, including parent/child relationships, dynamic-link libraries (DLLs) loaded, and object handles opened such as files in use
Chapter 4, Process Monitor	
Process Monitor	Logs details about all file system, registry, network, process, thread, and image load activity in real time
Chapter 5, Autoruns	
Autoruns	Lists and categorizes software that is configured to start automatically when your system boots, when you log on, and when you run Internet Explorer, and lets you disable or delete those entries
Chapter 6, PsTools	
PsExec	Executes processes remotely and/or as Local System with redirected output.
PsFile	Lists or closes files opened remotely
PsGetSid	Displays the Security Identifier (SID) of a security principal, such as a computer, user, group, or service
PsInfo	Lists information about a system
PsKill	Terminates processes by name or by Process ID (PID)
PsList	Lists detailed information about processes and threads
PsLoggedOn	Lists accounts that are logged on locally and through remote connections
PsLogList	Dumps event log records
PsPasswd	Changes passwords for user accounts
PsService	Lists and controls Windows services
PsShutdown	Shuts down, logs off, or changes the power state of local and remote systems
PsSuspend	Suspends and resumes processes
Chapter 7, Process and Diagnostic Utilities	
VMMap	Displays details of a process' virtual and physical memory usage
ProcDump	Generates a memory dump for a process when it meets specifiable criteria, such as exhibiting a CPU spike or having an unresponsive window
DebugView	Monitors user-mode and kernel-mode debug output generated from the local computer or a remote computer
LiveKd	Runs a standard kernel debugger on a snapshot of the running local system or Hyper-V guest without having to reboot into debug mode, and also allows making a memory dump of a live system
ListDLLs	Displays information about DLLs loaded on the system in a console window
Handle	Displays information about object handles opened by processes on the system in a console window

Utility	Description
Chapter 8, Security Utilities	
SigCheck	Verifies file signatures, and displays version information
AccessChk	Searches for objects that grant permissions to specific users or groups, and provides detailed information on permissions granted
AccessEnum	Searches a file or registry hierarchy, and identifies where permissions might have been changed
ShareEnum	Enumerates file and printer shares on your network and who can access them
ShellRunAs	Restores the ability to run a program under a different user on Windows Vista
Autologon	Configures a user account for automatic logon when the system boots
LogonSessions	Enumerates active Local Security Authority (LSA) logon sessions on the computer
SDelete	Securely deletes files or folder structures, and erases data in unallocated areas of the hard drive
Chapter 9, Active Directory Utilities	
AdExplorer	Displays and enables editing of Active Directory objects
AdInsight	Traces Active Directory Lightweight Directory Access Protocol (LDAP) API calls
AdRestore	Enumerates and restores deleted Active Directory objects
Chapter 10, Desktop Utilities	
BgInfo	Displays computer configuration information on the desktop wallpaper
Desktops	Runs applications on separate virtual desktops
ZoomIt	Magnifies the screen, and enables screen annotation
Chapter 11, File Utilities	
Strings	Searches files for embedded ASCII or Unicode text
Streams	Identifies file system objects that have alternate data streams, and deletes those streams
Junctions	Lists and deletes NTFS directory junctions
FindLinks	Lists NTFS hard links
DU	Lists logical and on-disk sizes of a directory hierarchy
PendMoves	Reports on file operations scheduled to take place during the next system boot
MoveFile	Schedules file operations to take place during the next system boot
Chapter 12, Disk Utilities	
Disk2Vhd	Captures a VHD image of a physical disk
Diskmon	Logs sector-level hard disk activity
Sync	Flushes unwritten changes from disk caches to the physical disk
DiskView	Displays a cluster-by-cluster graphical map of a volume, letting you find what file is in particular clusters and which clusters are occupied by a given file
Contig	Defragments specific files, or shows how fragmented a particular file is
PageDefrag	Defragments system files at boot time that cannot be defragmented while Windows is running
DiskExt	Displays information about disk extents

Utility	Description
LDMDump	Displays detailed information about dynamic disks from the Logical Disk Manager (LDM) database
VolumeID	Changes a volume's ID (also known as its serial number)
Chapter 13, Network and Communication Utilities	
TCPView	Lists active TCP and UDP endpoints
Whois	Reports Internet domain registration information or performs reverse Domain Name System (DNS) lookups
Portmon	Monitors serial and parallel port I/O in real time
Chapter 14, System Information Utilities	
RAMMap	Provides detailed view of physical memory usage
CoreInfo	Lists mapping of logical processors to cores, sockets, Non-Uniform Memory Access (NUMA) nodes, and processor groups
ProcFeatures	Reports processor features such as No-Execute memory protection
WinObj	Displays Windows' Object Manager namespace
LoadOrder	Shows approximate order in which Windows loads device drivers and starts services
PipeList	Lists listening named pipes
ClockRes	Displays the current, maximum, and minimum resolution of the system clock
Chapter 15, Miscellaneous Utilities	
RegJump	Launches RegEdit, and navigates to the registry path you specify
Hex2Dec	Converts numbers from hexadecimal to decimal and vice versa
RegDelNull	Searches for and deletes registry keys with embedded NUL characters in their names
Bluescreen Screen Saver	Screen saver that realistically simulates a "Blue Screen of Death"
Ctrl2Cap	Converts Caps Lock keypresses to Control keypresses

The Windows Sysinternals Web Site

The easiest way to get to the Sysinternals Web site (Figure 1-1) is to browse to *http://www.sysinternals.com*, which redirects to the Microsoft TechNet home of Sysinternals, currently at *http://technet.microsoft.com/sysinternals*. In addition to all the Sysinternals utilities, the site contains or links to many related resources, including training, books, blogs, articles, webcasts, upcoming events, and the Sysinternals community forum.

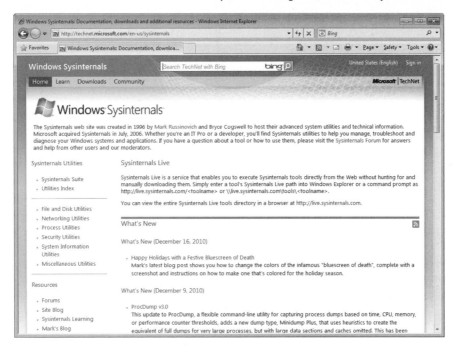

FIGURE 1-1 The Windows Sysinternals Web site.

Downloading the Utilities

You can download just the Sysinternals utilities that you need one at a time, or download the entire set in a single compressed (.zip) file called the *Sysinternals Suite*. Links on the Sysinternals home page take you to pages that link to individual utilities. The Utilities Index lists all the utilities on one page; links to categories such as "File and Disk Utilities" or "Networking Utilities" take you to pages that list only subsets of the utilities.

Each download is packaged as a compressed (.zip) file that contains the executable (or executables), an End User License Agreement (EULA) text file, and for some of the utilities, an online help file.

> **Note** The individual PsTool utilities are available for download only in bundles—either the PsTools suite or the full Sysinternals Suite.

My co-author, Aaron, makes it his habit to create a "C:\Program Files\Sysinternals" folder and extract the Sysinternals Suite into it, where it cannot be modified by non-administrative users. He then adds that location to the Path system environment variable so that he can easily launch the utilities from anywhere, including from the Windows 7 Start menu search box as shown in Figure 1-2.

FIGURE 1-2 Launching Procmon via Path search from the Start menu search box.

"Unblock" .zip Files Before Extracting Files

Before extracting content from the downloaded .zip files, you should first remove the marker that tells Windows to treat the content as untrusted and that results in warnings and errors like those shown in Figures 1-3 and 1-4. The Windows Attachment Execution Service adds an alternate data stream (ADS) to the .zip file indicating that it came from the Internet. When you extract the files with Windows Explorer, it propagates the ADS to all extracted files.

FIGURE 1-3 Windows displays a warning when files from the Internet are opened.

FIGURE 1-4 Compiled HTML Help (CHM) files fail to display content when marked as having come from the Internet.

One way to remove the ADS is to open the .zip file's Properties dialog box in Windows Explorer and click the Unblock button near the bottom of the General tab as shown in Figure 1-5. Another way is to use the Sysinternals Streams utility, which is described in Chapter 11, "File Utilities."

FIGURE 1-5 The Unblock button appears near the bottom of the downloaded file's Properties dialog box.

Running the Utilities Directly from the Web

Sysinternals Live is a service that enables you to execute Sysinternals utilities directly from the Web without first having to hunt for, download, and extract them. Another advantage of Sysinternals Live is that it guarantees you run the latest versions of the utilities.

To run a utility using Sysinternals Live from Internet Explorer, type **http://live.sysinternals. com/*utilityname*.exe** in the address bar (for example, http://live.sysinternals.com/procmon. exe). Alternatively, you can specify the Sysinternals Live path in Universal Naming Convention (UNC) as **\\live.sysinternals.com\tools*utilityname*.exe**. (Note the addition of the "tools" subdirectory, which is not required when you specify a utility's URL.) For example, you can run the latest version of Process Monitor by running **\\live.sysinternals.com\tools\ procmon.exe**.

> **Note** The UNC syntax for launching utilities using Sysinternals Live requires that the WebClient service be running. In newer versions of Windows, the service might not be configured to start automatically. Starting the service directly (for example, by running **net start webclient**) requires administrative rights. You can start the service indirectly without administrative rights by running **net use \\live.sysinternals.com** from a command prompt or by browsing to *live.sysinternals.com* with Windows Explorer.

You can also map a drive letter to \\live.sysinternals.com\tools or open the folder as a remote share in Windows Explorer, as shown in Figure 1-6. Similarly, you can view the entire Sysinternals Live directory in a browser at *http://live.sysinternals.com*.

FIGURE 1-6 Sysinternals Live displayed in Windows Explorer.

Single Executable Image

To simplify packaging, distribution, and portability without relying on installation programs, all of the Sysinternals utilities are single 32-bit executable images that can be launched directly. They embed any additional files they might need as resources and extract them either into the folder in which the program resides or, if that folder isn't writable (for example, if it's on read-only media), into the current user's %TEMP% folder. The program deletes extracted files when it no longer needs them.

Supporting both 32-bit and 64-bit systems is one example where the Sysinternals utilities make use of this technique. For utilities that require 64-bit versions to run correctly on 64-bit Windows, the main 32-bit program identifies the CPU architecture, extracts the appropriate x64 or IA64 binary, and launches it. When running Process Explorer on x64, for instance, you will see Procexp64.exe running as a child process of Procexp.exe.

> **Note** If the program file extracts to %TEMP%, the program will fail to run if the permissions on %TEMP% have been modified to remove Execute permissions.

Most of the Sysinternals utilities that use a kernel-mode driver extract the driver file to %SystemRoot%\System32\Drivers, load the driver, and then delete the file. The driver image remains in memory until the system is shut down. When running a newer version of a utility that has an updated driver, a reboot might be required to load the new driver.

The Windows Sysinternals Forums

The Windows Sysinternals Forums at *http://forum.sysinternals.com* (shown in Figure 1-7) are the first and best place to get answers to your questions about the Sysinternals utilities and to report bugs. You can search for posts and topics by keyword to see whether anyone else has had the same issue as you. There are forums dedicated to each of the major Sysinternals utilities, as well as a forum for suggesting ideas for new features or utilities. The Forums also host community discussion about Windows internals, development, troubleshooting, and malware.

You must register and log in to post to the Forums, but registration requires minimal information. After you register, you can also subscribe for notifications about replies to topics or new posts to particular forums, and you can send private messages to and receive messages from other forum members.

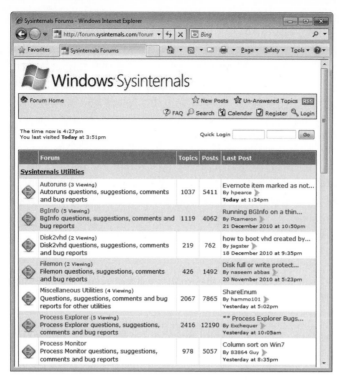

FIGURE 1-7 The Windows Sysinternals Forums.

Windows Sysinternals Site Blog

Subscribing to the Sysinternals Site Discussion blog is the best way to receive notifications when new utilities are published, existing utilities are updated, or other new content becomes available on the Sysinternals site. The site blog is located at *http://blogs.technet.com/b/ sysinternals*. Although the front page notes only major utility updates, the site blog reports all updates, including minor ones.

Mark's Blog

My own blog covers Windows internals, security, and troubleshooting topics. The blog features two popular article series related to Sysinternals: "The Case of..." articles, which document how to solve everyday problems with the Sysinternals utilities; and "Pushing the Limits," which describes resource limits in Windows, how to monitor them, and the effect of hitting them. You can access my blog by using the following URL:

http://blogs.technet.com/b/markrussinovich

You also can find a full listing of my blog posts by title by clicking on the Mark's Blog link on the Sysinternals home page.

Mark's Webcasts

You can find a full list of recordings of my presentations from TechEd and other conferences for free on-demand viewing—including my top-rated "Case of the Unexplained..." sessions, Sysinternals troubleshooting how-to sessions, my Channel 9 interviews and the Springboard Virtual Roundtables that I hosted—by clicking on the Mark's Webcasts link on the Sysinternals home page. The webcasts available at the time of this book's publication are included on this book's companion media.

Sysinternals License Information

The Sysinternals utilities are free. You can install and use any number of copies of the software on your computers and the computers owned by your company. However, your use of the software is subject to the license terms displayed when you launch a tool and at the Software License page linked to from the Sysinternals home page.

End User License Agreement and the *accepteula* Switch

As mentioned, each utility requires acceptance of an End User License Agreement (EULA) by each user who runs the utility on a given system. The first time a user runs a particular utility on a computer—even a console utility—the utility displays a EULA dialog box like the one shown in Figure 1-8. The user must click the Agree button before the utility will run.

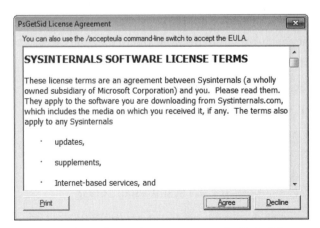

FIGURE 1-8 The End User License Agreement for PsGetSid.

Because the display of this dialog box interferes with automation and other noninteractive scenarios, most of the Sysinternals utilities take the command-line switch **/accepteula** as a valid assertion of agreement with the license terms. For example, the following command uses PsExec (described in Chapter 6) to run LogonSessions.exe (described in Chapter 8) in a noninteractive context on server1, where the **/accepteula** switch on the LogonSessions.exe command line prevents it from getting stuck waiting for a button press that will never come:

```
PsExec \\server1 logonsessions.exe /AcceptEula
```

Note that some Sysinternals utilities have not yet been updated to support the **/accepteula** switch. For these utilities, you might need to manually set the flag indicating acceptance. You can do this with a command line like the following, which creates a *EulaAccepted* registry value in the per-utility registry key in the HKEY_CURRENT_USER\Software\Sysinternals branch of the registry on server1:

```
psexec \\server1 reg add hkcu\software\sysinternals\pendmove /v eulaaccepted /t reg_dword /d
1 /f
```

Frequently Asked Questions About Sysinternals Licensing

- **How many copies of Sysinternals utilities can I freely load or use on computers owned by my company?**

  There is no limit to the number of times you can install and use the software on your devices or those you support.

- **Can I distribute Sysinternals utilities in my software, on my Web site, or with my magazine?**

  No. Microsoft is not offering any distribution licenses, even if the third party is distributing them for free. Microsoft encourages people to download the utilities from its download center or run them directly from the Web where they can be assured to get the most recent version of the utility.

- **Can I license or re-use any Sysinternals source code?**

  The Sysinternals source code is no longer available for download or licensing.

- **Will the Sysinternals tools continue to be freely available?**

  Yes. Microsoft has no plans to remove these tools or charge for them.

- **Is there technical support available for the Sysinternals tools?**

  All Sysinternals tools are offered "as is" with no official Microsoft support. Microsoft does maintain a Sysinternals dedicated community support forum (*http://forum.sysinternals.com*) where you can report bugs and request new features.

Chapter 2
Windows Core Concepts

The more you know about how Microsoft Windows works, the more value you can get from the Sysinternals utilities. This chapter offers an overview of select Windows concepts relevant to multiple Sysinternals utilities that can help you better understand these sometimes-misunderstood topics. The best and most comprehensive reference available today about Windows' core operating system components is *Windows Internals* (Microsoft Press, 2009)[1]. The Usage Guide of the book you are holding can offer at most only brief descriptions about aspects of complex subjects such as Windows memory management. After all, this book is about the Sysinternals utilities, not about Windows, and clearly cannot include all the rich detail provided by *Windows Internals*. It is also not a comprehensive overview of Windows architecture, nor does it cover basic concepts it's assumed you already understand, such as "What is the registry?" or "What is the difference between TCP and UDP?"

The topics covered in this chapter and the utilities to which they apply include

- Administrative Rights, and how to run a program with administrative rights on different versions of Windows (*Applies to most of the utilities*)

- Processes, Threads, and Jobs (*Process Explorer, Process Monitor, PsTools, VMMap, ProcDump, TCPView, RAMMap*)

- User Mode and Kernel Mode (*Process Explorer, Process Monitor, Autoruns, VMMap, ProcDump, DebugView, LiveKd, TCPView, RAMMap, LoadOrder*)

- Handles (*Process Explorer, Handle*)

- Call Stacks and Symbols, including what a call stack is, what symbols are, and how to configure symbols in the Sysinternals utilities (*Process Explorer, Process Monitor, VMMap*)

- Sessions, Window Stations, Desktops, and Window Messages *(Process Explorer, Process Monitor, PsExec, AdInsight, Desktops, LogonSessions, WinObj, RegJump)*

Administrative Rights

Windows NT has always had a rich access control model to protect sensitive system resources from modification by or disclosure to unauthorized entities. Within this model, user accounts are typically given Administrator rights or User rights. Administrators have complete and

---

[1] The latest edition as of this writing is *Windows Internals*, 5th Edition, by Mark E. Russinovich and David A. Solomon with Alex Ionescu (Microsoft Press, 2009). The 6th Edition, by the same authors, is in progress at the time of this writing.

unrestricted access to the computer and all its resources, while Users are restricted from making changes to operating system configuration or accessing data belonging to other users. For historical reasons, however, until recently end users on Windows computers were frequently granted administrative access, so many people have remained unaware that these distinctions exist. (Even today, the first local user account created on a Windows 7 computer is a member of the Administrators group.)

> **Note** Users can have *effective* administrative control over a computer without explicit member-ship in the Administrators group if they are given the ability to configure or control software that runs in a more powerful security context—for example: granting users control over systemwide file or registry locations used by administrators or services (as Power Users had before Windows Vista); granting users "admin-equivalent" privileges such as the Debug, Take-Ownership, Restore, or Load Driver privileges; or enabling the AlwaysInstallElevated Windows Installer policy, under which any MSI file launched by any user runs under the System account.

Recently, organizations wishing to improve security and reduce costs have begun moving toward a "non-admin" model for their end users. And with Windows Vista's introduction of User Account Control (UAC), most programs run by users—including those who are members of the Administrators group—execute with user rights, not administrative rights. However, it sometimes becomes necessary to run a program with administrative rights. While many people didn't know how to do this in Windows XP, Windows Vista changed those methods significantly.

Many of the Sysinternals utilities always require administrative rights, while many have full functionality without them. Some, however, are able to work correctly with standard user rights but have features that need administrative rights, and thus operate in a "partially degraded" mode when executed with standard user rights.

Running a Program with Administrative Rights on Windows XP and Windows Server 2003

If you log on to a Windows XP or Windows Server 2003 computer with an account that is a member of the Administrators group, no special steps are required to run a Sysinternals util-ity with administrative rights. *Every* program you run has full administrative rights.

But if you log on to that same computer with an account that does not have the required privileges to run a particular Sysinternals utility, you will need to get the administrative rights from a different user account. The Secondary Logon (Seclogon) service enables programs to start a new process as a different user on the current desktop by supplying alternative cre-dentials. Two programs that expose this functionality are Explorer's Run As dialog box and the Runas.exe command-line utility.

To use the Run As dialog box to start a program with administrative rights, right-click on any program or shortcut in Explorer or the Start menu and choose Run As from the context menu. In the Run As dialog box, choose the *second* radio button ("The Following User) as shown in Figure 2-1, type the credentials for an administrative account, and click OK. You can make Run As the default for a shortcut by opening its Properties dialog box, clicking the Advanced button, and selecting the "Run With Different Credentials check box.

FIGURE 2-1 The Windows XP Run As dialog box with the second radio button selected.

To start a program with administrative rights with the Runas.exe command-line utility, open a command prompt and start Runas.exe with this syntax:

```
runas /u:username program
```

For example, to run Process Monitor (Procmon.exe) with the local Administrator account, run the following command:

```
runas /u:administrator procmon.exe
```

After you press Enter, Runas.exe prompts you for the account's password. You must type the password at the prompt; Runas.exe does not accept a password on the command line nor piped to it from the standard input stream. You can use the **/savecred** command-line option to save the account's password the first time you enter it; subsequent use of **/savecred** with the same account will retrieve the saved password so that you don't have to enter it again. While this behavior is convenient, note that the standard user under whose account the administrator's password is saved can now use Runas.exe to launch *any* program without having to supply the password.

To use smartcard authentication instead of password authentication, add the **/smartcard** option to the command line. You will be prompted for a smartcard PIN instead of a password.

For more information and tips about using RunAs, see Aaron Margosis' "RunAs basic (and intermediate) topics" blog post at the following URL:

http://blogs.msdn.com/b/aaron_margosis/archive/2004/06/23/163229.aspx

If you need the Sysinternals utility to run with full administrative rights but under your nonadministrator account (for example, so that it can authenticate to domain resources), you can use Aaron Margosis' MakeMeAdmin script. It invokes Runas.exe twice to launch a command prompt that runs under your current account but with full administrative rights. (Note that you must have credentials for an administrative account to make this work.) For more information, see his "MakeMeAdmin — temporary admin for your Limited User account" blog post at the following URL:

http://blogs.msdn.com/b/aaron_margosis/archive/2004/07/24/193721.aspx

Running a Program with Administrative Rights on Windows Vista or Newer

Windows Vista and UAC changed everything when it came to running programs with administrative rights. Running as a standard user is now the default state for users' programs, even when run by a member of the Administrators group.

If you log on to a computer running Windows Vista or newer with an account that is a member of Administrators (the first account is the only one that defaults to Administrators group membership on computers not joined to a domain) or another powerful group such as Backup Operators or that has been granted "admin-equivalent" privileges, the Local Security Authority (LSA) creates two logon sessions for the user, with a distinct access token for each. (The LogonSessions utility enumerates these sessions and is described in Chapter 8, "Security Utilities.") One of these tokens represents the user's full rights, with all groups and privileges intact. The other is a *filtered* token that is roughly equivalent to one belonging to a standard user, with powerful groups disabled and powerful privileges removed. This filtered token is used to create the user's initial processes, such as Userinit.exe and Explorer.exe, and is inherited by their child processes. Starting a process with the user's full token requires UAC elevation, mediated by the Application Information (Appinfo) service. The Runas.exe command is still present, but it does not invoke the Appinfo service—so its effect is not quite the same as it was on Windows XP. If you start a program with Runas.exe and specify an administrative account, the target program runs under the "standard user" version of that account.[2]

---

2 With UAC enabled, there is one exception to this rule. By default, UAC token filtering and "admin approval mode" does not apply to the built-in Administrator account. Anything run under that account always runs with full administrative rights. However, the built-in Administrator account is disabled by default.

UAC elevation can be triggered for a new process in one of several ways:

- The program file contains a manifest that indicates that it requires elevation. Sysinternals GUI utilities such as Disk2Vhd and RAMMap that always require elevation contain such manifests. (You can view an image's manifest with the Sigcheck utility, described in Chapter 8.)

- The user explicitly requests that the program run elevated—for example, by right-clicking it and choosing Run As Administrator from the context menu.

- Windows heuristically determines that the application is a legacy installation program. (Installer detection is enabled by default, but it can be turned off through a security policy.)

- The application is associated with a compatibility mode or shim that requires elevation.

If the parent process is already running with an administrative token, the child process simply inherits that token and the UAC elevation sequence is not needed. By convention, console utilities that require administrative rights (for example, Sysinternals LogonSessions) do not request UAC elevation. Instead, you should start them from an elevated command prompt or Windows PowerShell console.

Once triggered, UAC elevation can be accomplished in three ways:

- **Silently**   The elevation occurs without end-user interaction. This option is available only if the user is a member of the Administrators group. By default in Windows 7, silent elevation is enabled for certain Windows commands. Silent elevation can be enabled for all elevation requests through security policy.

- **Prompt For Consent**   The user is prompted whether to permit the elevation to occur with a Yes/No dialog box. (See Figure 2-2.) This option is available only if the user is a member of the Administrators group and is the default (for elevations other than the default silent elevations of Windows 7).

- **Prompt For Credentials**   The user is prompted to provide credentials for an administrative account. (See Figure 2-3.) This is the default for nonadministrative accounts and is the only way that UAC elevation can be achieved by a nonadministrative user. You can also configure this option for administrative users with a security policy setting.

Note that UAC elevations can be disabled for standard users via security policy. When the policy is configured, users get an error message whenever an elevation is requested.

FIGURE 2-2 Windows 7 elevation prompt for consent.

FIGURE 2-3 Windows 7 elevation prompt for credentials.

When User Account Control is disabled, Windows reverts to a mode similar to that of Windows XP. In that case, the LSA does not create filtered tokens, and programs run by members of the Administrators group always run with administrative rights. Further, elevation prompts do not display, but Runas.exe can be used to start a program with administrative rights. Note that disabling UAC also disables Internet Explorer's Protected Mode, so Internet Explorer runs with the full rights of the logged-on user. Disabling UAC also turns off its file and registry virtualization, a feature that enables many applications that required administrative rights on Windows XP to work with standard user rights.

Processes, Threads, and Jobs

Although programs and processes appear similar on the surface, they are fundamentally different. A *program* is a static sequence of instructions, whereas a *process* is a container for a set of resources used to execute a program. At the highest level of abstraction, a Windows process comprises the following:

- A unique identifier called a *process ID* (PID).

- At least one thread of execution. Every thread in a process has full access to all the resources referenced by the process container

- A *private virtual address space*, which is a set of virtual memory addresses that the process can use to store and reference data and code

- An executable program, which defines initial code and data and is mapped into the process' virtual address space

- A list of open handles to various system resources, such as semaphores, communication ports, and files

- A security context called an *access token* that identifies the user, security groups, privileges, UAC virtualization state, LSA logon session ID, and terminal services session ID

Each process also has a record of the PID of its parent process. However, if the parent exits, this information is not updated. Therefore, it is possible for a process to reference a nonexistent parent or even a different process that has been assigned the original parent's PID. A process records its parent PID only for informational purposes, however.

Windows provides an extension to the process model called a *job.* A job object's main function is to allow groups of processes to be managed and manipulated as a unit. For example, a job can be used to terminate a group of processes all at once instead of one at a time and without the calling process having to know which processes are in the group. A job object also allows control of certain attributes and provides limits for the process or processes associated with the job. For example, jobs can enforce per-process or job-wide limits on user-mode execution time and committed virtual memory. Windows Management Instrumentation (WMI) loads its providers into separate host processes controlled by a job that limits memory consumption as well as the total number of WMI provider host processes that can run at one time.

As mentioned, a process is merely a container. Technically, it is not the process that runs—it is its *threads*. A *thread* is the entity within a process that Windows schedules for execution, and it includes the following essential components:

- The contents of a set of CPU registers representing the state of the processor. These include an instruction pointer that identifies the next machine instruction the thread will execute.

- Two stacks, one for the thread to use while executing in kernel mode and one for executing in user mode.

- A private storage area called thread-local storage (TLS) for use by subsystems, run-time libraries, and dynamic-link libraries (DLLs).

- A unique identifier called a *thread ID* (TID). Process IDs and thread IDs are generated from the same namespace, so they never overlap.

- Threads sometimes have their own security context that is often used by multithreaded server applications that impersonate the security context of the clients they serve.

Although threads have their own execution context, every thread within a process shares the process' virtual address space (in addition to the rest of the resources belonging to the process), meaning that all the threads in a process can write to and read from one another's memory. Threads cannot reference the address space of another process, however, unless the other process makes available part of its private address space as a *shared memory section* (called a *file mapping object* in the Windows API) or unless one process has the right to open another process to use cross-process memory functions.

By default, threads don't have their own access token, but they can obtain one, thus allowing individual threads to impersonate a different security context—including that of a process running on a remote Windows system—without affecting other threads in the process.

User Mode and Kernel Mode

To prevent user applications from accessing or modifying critical operating system data, Windows uses two processor access modes: *user mode* and *kernel mode*. All processes other than the System process run in user mode (Ring 3 on Intel x86 and x64 architectures), whereas device drivers and operating system components such as the executive and kernel run only in kernel mode. Kernel mode refers to a mode of execution (Ring 0 on x86 and x64) in a processor that grants access to all system memory and to all CPU instructions. By providing the low-level operating system software with a higher privilege level than user-mode processes have, the processor provides a necessary foundation for operating system designers to ensure that a misbehaving application can't disrupt the stability of the system as a whole.

 Note Do not confuse the user-mode vs. kernel-mode distinction with that of user rights vs. administrator rights. "User mode" in this context does not mean "has only standard user privileges."

Although each Windows process has its own private memory space, the kernel-mode operating system and device driver code share a single virtual address space that is also included in the address space of every process. The operating system tags each page of virtual memory with the access mode the processor must be in to read or write the page. Pages in system space can be accessed only from kernel mode, whereas all pages in the user address space are accessible from user mode.

Threads of user-mode processes switch from user mode to kernel mode when they make a system service call. For example, a call into the Windows *ReadFile* API eventually needs to call the internal Windows routine that actually handles reading data from a file. That routine, because it accesses internal system data structures, must run in kernel mode. The transition from user mode to kernel mode is accomplished by the use of a special processor instruction that causes the processor to switch to a system service dispatching function in kernel mode. The operating system executes the corresponding internal function, which for *ReadFile* is the *NtReadFile* kernel function. Kernel service functions validate parameters and perform appropriate access checks using the Security Reference Monitor before they execute the requested operation. When the function finishes, the operating system switches the processor mode back to user mode.

Thus, it is normal for a thread in a user-mode process to spend part of its time executing in user mode and part in kernel mode. In fact, because the bulk of the graphics and windowing system also runs in kernel mode, processes hosting graphics-intensive applications can spend more of their time in kernel mode than in user mode. You can see these two modes in the Process Explorer CPU usage graphs: the red portion of the graph represents time spent in kernel mode, and the green area of the graph represents time spent in user mode.

Handles

The kernel-mode core of Windows, which is implemented in Ntoskrnl.exe, consists of various subsystems such as the Memory Manager, Process Manager, I/O Manager, and Configuration Manager (registry), which are all parts of the Executive. Each of these subsystems defines one or more types with the Object Manager to represent the resources they expose to applications. For example, the Configuration Manager defines the *Key* object to represent an open registry key; the Memory Manager defines the *Section* object for shared memory; the Executive defines Semaphore, Mutant (the internal name for a mutex), and Event synchronization objects (which are objects that wrap fundamental data structures defined by the operating system's Kernel subsystem); the I/O Manager defines the *File* object to represent open instances of device-driver resources, which include file system files; and the Process Manager creates *Thread* and *Process* objects. Every release of Windows introduces new object types, with Windows 7 defining a total of 42. You can see the object types that a particular version of Windows defines by running the WinObj utility (described in Chapter 14,

"System Information Utilities") with administrative rights and navigating to the ObjectTypes directory in the Object Manager namespace.

When an application wants to use one of these resources, it first must call the appropriate API to create or open the resource. For instance, the *CreateFile* function opens or creates a file, the *RegOpenKeyEx* function opens a registry key, and the *CreateSemaphoreEx* function opens or creates a semaphore. If the function succeeds, Windows allocates a reference to the object in the process' handle table, which is maintained by the Executive, and returns the index of the new handle table entry to the application.

This handle value is what the application uses for subsequent operations on the resource. To query or manipulate the resource, the application passes the handle value to API functions such as *ReadFile*, *SetEvent*, *SetThreadPriority*, and *MapViewOfFile*. The system can look up the object the handle refers to by indexing into the handle table to locate the corresponding handle entry, which contains a pointer to the object. The handle entry also stores the accesses the process was granted at the time it opened the object, which enables the system to make sure it doesn't allow the process to perform an operation on the object for which it didn't ask permission. For example, if the process successfully opened a file for read access but tried to use the handle to write to the file, the function would fail.

When a process no longer needs access to an object, it can release its handle to that object, typically by passing the handle value to the *CloseHandle* API. (Note that some resource managers provide a different API to release its resources.) When a process exits, any handles it still possesses are closed.

Call Stacks and Symbols

Several Sysinternals utilities—including Process Explorer, Process Monitor, and VMMap—can display details about the code paths being executed at a particular point in time called *call stacks*. Associating symbols with the modules in a process' address space provides more meaningful context information about those code paths, particularly within Windows operating system code. Understanding call stacks and symbols, and how to configure them in the Sysinternals utilities, gives tremendous insight into a process' behavior and can often lead to the root cause of a problem.

What Is a Call Stack?

Executable code in a process is normally organized as a collection of discrete functions. To perform its tasks, a function can invoke other functions (subfunctions). When a function has finished, it returns control back to the function that called it.

A made-up example, shown in Figure 2-4, demonstrates this flow. MyApp.exe ships with a DLL named HelperFunctions.dll. That DLL includes a function named *EncryptThisText* that encrypts text passed to it. After performing some preparatory operations, *EncryptThisText* calls the Windows API *CryptEncryptMessage* in Crypt32.dll. At some point, *CryptEncryptMessage* needs to allocate some memory and invokes the memory-allocation function *malloc* in Msvcrt.dll. After *malloc* has done its work and allocated the requested memory, execution resumes at the point where *CryptEncryptMessage* had left off. And when *CryptEncryptMessage* has completed its task, control returns back to the point in *EncryptThisText* just after its call to *CryptEncryptMessage*.

Process Virtual Address Space

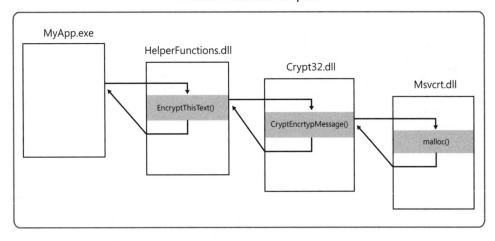

FIGURE 2-4 Example function calling sequence.

The *call stack* is the construct that allows the system to know how to return control to a series of callers, as well as to pass parameters between functions and to store local function variables. It's organized in a "last in, first out" manner, where functions remove items in the reverse order from how they add them. When a function is about to call a subfunction, it puts the memory address of the next instruction to execute upon returning from the subfunction (its "return address") at the top of the stack. When that subfunction calls yet another function, it adds its own return address to the stack. On returning from a function, the system retrieves whatever address is at the top of the stack and begins executing code from that point.

The convention for displaying a return address in a call stack is *module!function+offset*, where *module* is the name of the executable image file containing the function, and *offset* is the number of bytes (in hexadecimal) past the beginning of the function. If the function name is not available, the address is shown simply as *"module+offset"*. While *malloc* is executing in the fictitious example just given, the call stack might look like this:

```
msvcrt!malloc+0x2a
crypt32!CryptEncryptMessage+0x9f
HelperFunctions!EncryptThisText+0x43
MyApp.exe+0x25d8
```

As you can see, a call stack not only tells you what piece of code is executing, it also tells you how the program got there.

What Are Symbols?

When inspecting a thread start address or a return address on a call stack, a debugger can easily determine what module it belongs to by examining the list of loaded modules and their address ranges. However, when a compiler converts a developer's source code into computer instructions, it does not retain the original function names. The one exception is that a DLL includes an *export table* that lists the names and offsets of the functions it makes available to other modules. However, the export table does not list the names of the library's internal functions, nor does it list the names of COM entry points that are designed to be discovered at runtime.

> **Note** Executable files loaded in user-mode processes are generally either EXE files with which a new process can be started or DLL files that are loaded into an existing process. EXE and DLL files are not restricted to using those two file extensions, however. Files with COM or SCR extensions are actually EXE files, while ACM, AX, CPL, DRV, and OCX are examples of other file extensions of DLLs. And installation programs commonly extract and launch EXE files with TMP extensions.

When creating executable files, compilers and linkers can also create corresponding *symbol files* (with the default extension PDB). Symbol files hold a variety of data that is not needed when running the executable code but which can be useful during debugging, including the names and entry point offsets of functions within the module. With this information, a debugger can take a memory address and easily identify the function with the closest preceding address. Without symbols, the debugger is limited to using exported functions, if any, which might have no relation at all to the code being executed. In general, the larger the offset on a return address, the less likely the reported function name is to be accurate.

> **Note** The Sysinternals utilities are able to use only native (unmanaged) symbol files when reporting call stacks. They are not able to report function names within JIT-compiled .NET assemblies.

A symbol file must be built at the same time as its corresponding executable or it will not be correct and the debug engine might refuse to use it. Older versions of Microsoft Visual C++ created symbol files only for Debug builds unless the developer explicitly changed the build configuration. Newer versions now create symbol files for Release builds as well, writing them into the same folder with the executable files. Microsoft Visual Basic 6 can create symbol files, but it does not do so by default.

Symbol files can contain differing levels of detail. *Full symbol files* (sometimes called *private symbol files*) contain details that are not found in *public symbol files*, including the path to and the line number within the source file where the symbol is defined, function parameter names and types, and variable names and types. Software companies that make symbol files externally available typically release only public symbol files, while retaining the full symbol files for internal use.

The Debugging Tools for Windows make it possible to download correct symbol files on demand from a *symbol server*. The server can store symbol files for many different builds of a given executable file, and the Debugging Tools will download the one that matches the image you are debugging. (It uses the timestamp and checksum stored in the executable's header as a unique identifier.)

Microsoft has a symbol server accessible over the Web that makes Windows' public symbol files freely available. By installing the Debugging Tools for Windows and configuring the Sysinternals utilities to use the Microsoft symbol server, you can easily see what Windows functions are being invoked by your processes.

Figure 2-5 shows a call stack for an event captured with Process Monitor. The presence of MSVBVM60.DLL on the stack (frames 15 and 17–21) indicates that this is a Visual Basic 6 program because MSVBVM60.DLL is the Visual Basic 6 runtime DLL. The large offsets for the MSVBVM60 frames suggest that symbols are not available for that module and that the names shown are not the actual functions being called. Frame 14 shows a call into a function named *Form1::cmdCreate_Click* in the main executable (LuaBugs_VB6.exe). This frame also shows a source file path, indicating that we have full symbolic information for this third-party module. This function then calls *CWshShell::RegWrite* in Wshom.ocx (frame 13), indicating that this Visual Basic 6 program is using a Windows Script Host ActiveX to write to the registry. *CWshShell::RegWrite* calls an internal function in the same module (frame 12), which calls the documented *RegCreateKeyExA* Windows API in Kernel32.dll (frame 11). Execution passes through Kernel32 internal functions (frames 8–10) and then into the *ZwCreateKey* native API in Ntdll.dll (frame 7). So far, all of these functions have executed in user mode, as indicated by the *U* in the Frame column, but in frame 6 the program transitions to kernel mode, indicated by the *K*. The two-letter prefixes of the kernel functions (frames 0–6) identify the executive components to which they belong. For example, *Cm* refers to the Configuration Manager, which is responsible for the registry, and *Ob* refers to the Object Manager. It was during the processing of *CmpCallCallBacks* (frame 0) that this stack trace was captured. Note that the symbolic information shown in frames 0–13 was all derived from Windows public symbols downloaded on demand by Process Monitor from Microsoft's symbol server.

FIGURE 2-5 Process Monitor call stack with information from symbol files.

Configuring Symbols

The Sysinternals utilities that use symbols require two pieces of information, as shown in Figure 2-6: the location of the Dbghelp.dll to use, and the symbols path. The Sysinternals utilities that can use full symbolic information to display source files also request source code paths.

Dbghelp.dll is one of Microsoft's debug engine DLLs, and it provides the functionality for walking a call stack, loading symbol files, and resolving process memory addresses to names. Only the version of Dbghelp.dll that ships in the Debugging Tools for Windows supports the downloading of files from symbol servers. The Dbghelp.dll that ships with Windows in the %SystemRoot%\System32 directory can use only symbol files stored locally. The first time you run them, Sysinternals utilities check default installation locations for the Debugging Tools and use its Dbghelp.dll if found. Otherwise, it defaults to using the version in %SystemRoot%\System32.

FIGURE 2-6 Process Explorer's Configure Symbols dialog box.

The URL for the Debugging Tools for Windows is *http://www.microsoft.com/whdc/devtools/ debugging/default.mspx*. The Debugging Tools installer used to be a standalone download, but it is now incorporated into the Windows SDK. To get the Debugging Tools, you must run the SDK installer and select the Debugging Tools options you want. Among the options are the Debugging Tools redistributables, which are the standalone Debugging Tools installers, available for x86, x64, and IA64. The redistributables are handy for installing the debuggers to other machines in your environment without having to run the full SDK installer on each of them.

The symbols path tells the debugging engine where to search for symbol files if they cannot be found in default locations. The two default locations that the debugging engine searches for symbol files before checking the symbols path are the executable's folder and the folder where the symbol file was originally created, if that information is in the executable file.

The symbols path can consist of file system folders and symbol server directives. The first time you run it, the Sysinternals utility will set its symbol path to the value of the _NT_SYMBOL_PATH environment variable. If that variable is not defined, the utility sets its symbol path to *srv*http://msdl.microsoft.com/download/symbols*, which uses the Microsoft public symbol server but does not save the downloaded symbol files to a local cache.

File system folders and symbol server directives can be intermixed in the symbols path, separated with a semicolon. Each element is searched in the order it appears in the path. As implied earlier, symbol server directives are of the form srv*DownstreamStore*SymbolServer. Consider the following symbols path:

```
C:\MySyms;srv*C:\MSSymbols*http://msdl.microsoft.com/download/symbols
```

The debugging engine will first search the default locations and then C:\MySyms, which could be a good place to put your own applications' private symbol files. If it hasn't found the symbol file, it then searches C:\MSSymbols, and if the file isn't there it finally queries the symbol server. If the symbol server has the file, the debugging engine downloads the file to C:\MSSymbols.

See the Debugging Tools documentation for more information about symbol paths, symbol servers, source paths, and environment variables used by the debugging engine.

> **Tip** If the Microsoft public symbols are the only symbols you need, set the symbols path to the following:
>
> ```
> srv*c:\symbols*http://msdl.microsoft.com/download/symbols
> ```
>
> This directs the debugging engine first to search the cache under C:\Symbols and then to download symbol files as needed from the Microsoft public symbol server, saving them into the cache so that they won't need to be downloaded again. The debugging engine will create C:\Symbols if it doesn't already exist.

Sessions, Window Stations, Desktops, and Window Messages

The descriptions of several of the Sysinternals utilities—including Process Explorer, Process Monitor, PsExec, AdInsight, Desktops, and LogonSessions—refer to terminal services sessions, session IDs, the "console session," and "session 0"; interactive and noninteractive window stations; and other programs running on the "same desktop." These concepts, although not widely understood, can be critical to problem solving on the Windows platform.

Let's start with an overview of the hierarchy, an example of which is depicted in Figure 2-7, and then define the terms. At the outermost layer are terminal services (TS) sessions. Each session contains one or more window stations, which contain desktops. Each of these securable objects has resources allocated for its sole use. There is also a loose relationship between these and logon sessions created by the LSA. Although Windows documentation doesn't always make a clear distinction between LSA logon sessions and TS sessions, they are completely separate entities.

FIGURE 2-7 Relationship between sessions, window stations, and desktops.

Terminal Services Sessions

Terminal services support multiple interactive user sessions on a single computer. Introduced in Windows NT 4.0 Terminal Server Edition, they were not incorporated into the Windows client operating system family until Windows XP. Features they support include Fast User Switching, Remote Desktop, Remote Assistance, Remote Applications Integrated Locally (RAIL, a.k.a. RemoteApps), and virtual machine integration features. An important limitation of Windows clients (Windows XP, Windows Vista, and Windows 7) is that only one interactive session can be active at a time. That is, while processes can continue to run in multiple disconnected sessions simultaneously, only one session can update a display device and receive keyboard and mouse input. A further limitation is that a *domain-joined* Windows XP computer supports at most only one interactive session. For example, if a user is logged on at the console, you can log on to the computer via Remote Desktop using the same account and continue that session, but you cannot log on with a different user account unless the first user is logged off.

Terminal services sessions are identified by an incrementing numeric session ID, starting with session 0. Windows defines a global namespace in the Object Manager and a session-private "local" namespace for each session numbered 1 and higher to provide isolation between sessions. The global namespace serves as the local namespace for processes in session 0. (WinObj offers a graphical view of the Object Manager namespace and is described in Chapter 14.)

System processes and Windows services always run in terminal services session 0. In Windows XP and Windows Server 2003, the first interactive user to log on to a computer also uses terminal services session 0 and, consequently, uses the same local namespace as services. Windows XP and Windows Server 2003 create sessions 1 and higher only when needed; if the first user logs off before a second one logs on, the second user uses session 0 as well. Consequently, on a domain-joined Windows XP, session 0 is always the only session.

In Windows Vista and newer, services run in session 0, but for security reasons all interactive user sessions run in sessions 1 and higher. This increased separation between end-user processes and system processes is called *session 0 isolation*.

> **Note** The term *console session* is sometimes mistaken as a synonym for *session 0*. The console session is the terminal services session associated with the locally attached keyboard, video, and mouse. If all active sessions on a computer are remote desktop sessions, the console session remains connected and displays a logon screen. It might or might not happen to be session 0 on Windows XP/Windows 2003, but it is never session 0 on Windows Vista or newer.

Window Stations

Each terminal services session contains one or more named *window stations*. A window station is a securable object that contains a clipboard, an atom table, and one or more desktops. Every process is associated with one window station. Within a TS session, only the window station named *WinSta0* can display a user interface or receive user input. In TS sessions 1 and higher, Windows creates only a WinSta0 window station. (See Figure 2-8.) In session 0, in addition to WinSta0, Windows creates a separate window station for every LSA logon session associated with a service, with the locally unique identifier (LUID) of the logon session incorporated into the window station name. For example, service processes that run as System run in the *Service-0x0-3e7$* window station, while those that run as Network Service run in the *Service-0x0-3e4$* window station. These window stations cannot display UI.

FIGURE 2-8 WinObj showing the interactive window station in session 2's private namespace.

PsExec -s cmd.exe runs a command prompt in the *Service-0x0-3e7$* window station and redirects its console I/O to PsExec. PsExec's *-i* option lets you specify the terminal services session and runs the target process in its WinSta0 window station. PsExec is described in Chapter 6.

A service configured to run as System can also be configured to Allow Service To Interact With Desktop. When so configured, the service runs in session 0's *WinSta0* instead of *Service-0x0-3e7$*. When the interactive user was also in session 0, this allowed the service to display UI directly to the end user. In hindsight, this wasn't a good idea as I'll describe shortly, and Microsoft has recommended against using this technique—and with session 0 isolation, this no longer works. (The Interactive Services Detection service, UI0Detect, offers partial mitigation.)

Desktops

Each window station contains one or more desktops. A desktop is a securable object with a logical display surface on which applications can render UI in the form of windows.

 Note The desktops described here are unrelated to the Desktop abstraction at the top of the Windows Explorer shell namespace.

Multiple desktops can contain UI, but only one can be displayed at a time. There are typically three desktops in the interactive window station: Default, Screen-saver, and Winlogon. The Default desktop is where user applications run by default. (The Sysinternals Desktops utility creates up to three additional desktops on which to run applications. It is described in Chapter 10, "Desktop Utilities.") The Screen-saver desktop is where Windows runs the screen saver if password protection is enabled. The Winlogon desktop, also known as the *secure desktop*, is where Windows transfers control when you press Ctrl+Alt+Del and the default place to display UAC elevation dialog boxes. Permissions on the Winlogon desktop restrict access only to programs running as System, which protects secure operations involving password entry.

As a process is associated with a window station, each of its threads is associated with a desktop within the window station. Although individual threads of a process can be associated with different desktops, they are usually associated with a single desktop.

Several Sysinternals utilities, including Process Explorer (discussed in Chapter 3) and Process Monitor (covered in Chapter 4), identify the TS session ID to which a process belongs. Although none of the utilities reliably identify the window station or desktops that a process is associated with, Process Explorer's Handle View can offer hints in the form of open handles to window stations or desktop objects. For example, in Figure 2-9, Process Explorer shows a process running as System in session 0 with open handles to the \Default desktop and the \Windows\WindowStations\Service-0x0-3e7$ window station.

FIGURE 2-9 A process in session 0 with open handles to desktop and window station objects.

Window Messages

Unlike console applications, Windows-based applications are event driven. Each thread that creates window objects has a queue to which messages are sent. These *GUI threads* wait for and then process window messages as they arrive. These messages tell the window what to do or what occurred. For example, messages can tell the window "Redraw yourself," "Move to screen coordinates (x,y)," "Close yourself," "The Enter key was pressed," "The right mouse button was clicked at coordinates (x,y)," or "The user is logging off."

Window messaging is mediated by the window manager. Messages can be sent to any window from any thread *running on the same desktop*—the window manager does not allow a program to send a window message to a window on a different desktop. Process Monitor's **/Terminate** and **/WaitForIdle** commands must be invoked from the same desktop on which the target Procmon instance is running, because they use window messaging to tell the existing instance to shut itself down and to determine that the target instance is ready to process commands in the form of window messages.

Window messages can be used to simulate mouse or keyboard activity. RegJump and the Jump To feature in Process Monitor and Autoruns do exactly this to navigate to a key in Regedit. Because of the levels of abstraction between a physical keypress and the resulting window messages received by a GUI program, it is effectively impossible for the target program to know with absolute certainty whether a key was pressed on a keyboard or another program simulated a keypress by sending it window messages. (This is true of all windowing systems, not just Windows.)

Except for the introduction of multithreading support in 32-bit versions of Windows, this window messaging architecture dates back to Windows 1.0, and it brings forward a lot of legacy. In particular, window objects do not have security descriptors or access control lists. This is why allowing services to display windows on the user's desktop was a bad idea—user programs could send malformed or specially crafted messages to windows owned by processes running as System and, if successfully exploited, control those processes. (This is commonly called a *shatter attack*.) If the user was not already an administrator, elevation of privilege became trivially easy. This is the main reason that interactive users no longer log on to session 0.

With "standard user," which is the default mode in Windows Vista and newer—and with UAC elevation popularizing the ability of applications to run with administrator rights in the same desktop with nonadministrative processes—some additional protection was needed to reduce the risk of shatter attacks against windows owned by elevated processes. The result is User Interface Privilege Isolation (UIPI).

Prior to Windows Vista, any process running as a particular user could take complete control over any other process running as the same user. With Mandatory Integrity Control (MIC), processes are assigned and run at an *integrity level* (IL), a numeric value that indicates the relative trustworthiness of the process. Elevated apps run at High, normal user apps run at Medium, and low-rights processes such as Protected Mode Internet Explorer run at Low. (Process Explorer, described in Chapter 3, can show each process' IL.)

With UIPI, when the window manager mediates a window message that can change the target's state (such as a button click message), the window manager compares the IL of the process sending the message to the IL of the process that owns the window receiving the message. If the sender's IL is lower than that of the receiver's, the message is blocked. This is the reason that RegJump and similar Jump To features must execute at an IL at least as high as that of Regedit.

For more information about MIC and UIPI, see the Windows Vista Integrity Mechanism Technical Reference at *http://msdn.microsoft.com/en-us/library/bb625964.aspx.*

Part II
Usage Guide

Chapter 3

Process Explorer

Processes are the heart of any Microsoft Windows system. Knowing what processes are running at any given time can help you understand how your CPU and other resources are being used, and it can assist you in diagnosing problems and identifying malware. As you'll see, there is a reason why Process Explorer is the most popular download from Sysinternals.

To help provide Windows users with insight into process activity on their systems, Windows has always included Task Manager, an easy-to-use application for viewing the processes (applications and services) that are running on your system. To avoid overwhelming users, Task Manager provides limited details. It allows users to see a high-level, flat list of processes, services and users, graphs of system performance and network usage, and an abstraction called "applications" (effectively a list of the visible windows in the current user's session). Task Manager is the application users typically turn to in order to find out why their system is slow and perhaps to kill errant processes. It often doesn't provide deep enough insight into what is causing a process to misbehave, nor does it show key data that can help a technical user to identify a process as malware.

Early on in the life of Sysinternals, Bryce Cogswell and I created multiple utilities to fill the gaps in Task Manager. These utilities, each with a different perspective, began tracking more detailed information on Windows processes and services. Three of the first ones we developed—PsList, DLLView, and HandleEx (now just named Handle)—were the start for Sysinternals' mission of exposing detailed process information. All of these utilities are still available today and are covered in other chapters. Each filled a specific niche, but it soon became apparent that something more comprehensive was needed—a single GUI to really drill in to what was happening on a Windows system from a process perspective.

Process Explorer (Procexp) was born.

Procexp Overview

Of all the Sysinternals utilities, Procexp is arguably the most feature-rich and touches more aspects of Windows internals than any other. (To get the most out of Procexp, you should review Chapter 2, "Windows Core Concepts.") Here are just some of the key features of Procexp:

- Tree view shows parent/child process relationships.
- Color coding identifies the process type, such as services, .NET processes, processes running as the same user as Procexp, processes that are part of a job, and packed images.

- Tooltips show command-line and other process information.

- Highlighting to call attention to new and recently exited processes.

- Fractional CPU so that processes consuming less than 1 percent of CPU time do not appear completely inactive.

- More accurate indication of CPU consumption based on CPU cycle counts or context switches.

- Task Manager replacement—you can have Process Explorer run whenever Task Manager is requested.

- Identify which process owns any visible window on your desktop.

- Identify a top-level window belonging to a given process, and bring it forward or close it.

- Identify all dynamic-link libraries (DLLs) and mapped files loaded by a process and all handles to kernel objects opened by a process.

- Find which processes have open handles to kernel objects such as files or folders.

- Find which processes have loaded a DLL, and identify its path and other attributes.

- Graphical representations of CPU activity, memory usage, and I/O activity, both systemwide and per-process.

- Detailed metrics of memory usage and I/O activity.

- Detailed information about a process security context.

- Detailed information about process TCP/IP endpoints.

- View process threads, including their start addresses and stacks.

- Create process dumps.

Procexp provides several views to display process information. The default Procexp window consists of a process list, with processes arranged in a tree view (as shown in Figure 3-1). This window is discussed in the "Main Window" section later in this chapter. Procexp can split the main window into an upper pane and lower pane, with the process list in the upper pane and either DLL view or Handle view in the lower pane. DLL view lets you drill down into the DLLs and mapped files loaded by the process selected in the upper pane. Handle view lets you inspect all the kernel objects currently opened by the selected process, including (but not limited to) files, folders, registry keys, window stations, desktops, network endpoints, and synchronization objects. DLL view and Handle view are described in the "DLLs and Handles" section. Finally, the process' Properties dialog box offers a tremendous amount of information about a particular process and is discussed in the "Process Details" section.

Procexp runs on x86, x64, and IA64 versions of Windows XP and newer, and Windows Server 2003 and newer.

FIGURE 3-1 The Procexp process list, with tree view.

Measuring CPU Consumption

Older versions of Windows were able to track only an approximation of actual CPU usage. At a clock-generated interrupt that on most systems has a period of 15.6 milliseconds (ms), Windows identifies the thread currently executing on each CPU. If the thread is executing in kernel mode, its kernel-mode time is incremented by 15.6 ms; otherwise, its user-mode time is incremented by that amount. The thread might have been executing for only a few CPU cycles when the interrupt fired, but the thread is charged for the entire 15.6-ms interval. Meanwhile, hundreds of other threads might have executed during that interval, but only the thread currently running at the clock tick gets charged. Windows Task Manager uses these approximations to report CPU usage even on newer versions of Windows that have more accurate metrics available. Task Manager further reduces its accuracy by rounding to the nearest integer percentage, so processes with executing threads that consume less than 1 percent of CPU time are indistinguishable from processes that do not execute at all. Finally, Task Manager does not account for CPU time spent servicing interrupts or deferred procedure calls (DPCs), incorrectly including that time with the System Idle Process.

Procexp represents CPU usage more accurately than does Task Manager. First, Procexp shows per-process CPU utilization percentages rounded to a resolution of two decimal places by default instead of to an integer. Second, Procexp tracks the time spent servicing interrupts and DPCs and displays them separately from the Idle process. Finally, Procexp uses additional system metrics so that processes consuming small amounts of CPU can be identified and, when possible, provide a more accurate account of actual CPU consumption. Different metrics are available on Windows XP, Windows Vista, and Windows 7 and their corresponding server versions. Procexp takes advantage of whatever is available to report the most accurate measures possible.

On all supported versions of Windows, each thread tracks its context switches—the number of times that a CPU's context was switched to begin executing the thread. If you display the Context Switch Delta column, Procexp monitors and reports changes in these numbers, so you can see processes that consume even small amounts of CPU. These often include processes that periodically wake to look for status changes rather than using system-synchronization mechanisms that would allow the process not to execute until an actual status change occurs. Such processes consume more power than needed and also require that their code and data be paged into the working set and therefore occupy RAM. With this column enabled on Windows XP or Windows Vista, Procexp reports "< 0.01" in the CPU column if the process had any context switches in the refresh interval but not enough CPU usage to report 0.01%.

A context switch indicates that a thread has executed, but not how long it executed. In addition to context switches, Windows Vista and newer measure the actual kernel-mode and user-mode CPU cycles consumed by each thread. If you enable the display of the CPU Cycles Delta column, Procexp monitors and reports those changes. With this column enabled on Windows Vista, Procexp can report "< 0.01" for processes consuming small amounts of CPU. As with Context Switch Delta, CPU Cycles Delta can help identify processes that are wasting resources.

On Windows Vista, Procexp can measure context switches for interrupts and DPCs, but not the corresponding CPU cycles. On Windows 7, Procexp can accurately attribute all CPU cycles, including those for interrupts and DPCs. So on Windows 7 instead of using Windows' inaccurate timer-based accounting, Procexp reports CPU usage percentages based on actual CPU cycles consumed. Processes consuming small amounts of CPU report "< 0.01" without you having to enable additional columns for display. Procexp's calculation of CPU usage is much more accurate than Task Manager's, with the perhaps-surprising effect that the CPU usage it reports is generally higher.

Administrative Rights

Procexp does not absolutely require administrative rights, but a great deal of system information is accessible only when running with elevated permissions, particularly for processes not running in the current user's logon session. Procexp depends on the Debug Programs privilege (which is granted to Administrators by default) to do this. Environments that adopt security policies that do not grant the Debug Programs privilege to Administrators will not be able to take full advantage of Procexp's capabilities. Procexp makes a best effort to display the information that it can, and it leaves fields blank or reports "access denied" when it can't.

> **Note** On Windows Vista and newer, even full administrative rights are not sufficient to read detailed information from protected processes. The Audiodg.exe and System processes are protected processes, which Procexp reports on the security page of the process' Properties dialog box.

To run Procexp with administrative rights on Windows XP and Server 2003 if you are not already logged on as an administrator, you must use RunAs to launch Procexp, or start Procexp from another program (such as Cmd.exe) that is already running as an administrator. On Windows Vista and newer, the Run As Administrator option can serve an equivalent purpose.

On Windows Vista and newer, Procexp offers two additional options. If Procexp is running nonelevated, choosing Show Details For All Processes from the File menu restarts Procexp with User Account Control (UAC) elevation. The second option is to start Procexp with the **/e** command-line option, which also requests UAC elevation. (Of course, you must be running in a context in which elevation is possible.)

See the "Administrative Rights" section in Chapter 2 for more information on RunAs and UAC elevation.

Main Window

The process list is a table in which each row represents a process on the system, and the columns represent continually updated attributes of those processes. You can change which attributes are displayed, resize and reorder the columns, and save column sets for later use. The Procexp toolbar includes buttons for performing common actions and graphs representing systemwide metrics. Finally, the status bar shows user-selectable system metrics. Each of these features will be described in turn.

Process List

Each row in the process list represents a running process on the local computer. Actually, that's not technically accurate. As my friend and *Windows Internals* co-author David Solomon likes to point out, processes do not run—only *threads* can run. Threads—not processes—are the entities that Windows schedules for execution and that consume CPU time. A process is simply the container for a set of resources, including one or more threads. It's also not accurate to refer to "active processes" or to "processes with running threads," because many processes spend most of their lifetimes with none of their threads running or scheduled for execution. So each row in the process list really represents a process object on the system that has its own virtual address space and one or more threads that conceivably could execute code at some point. And as we'll discuss later, the first three rows in the default (tree) view are exceptions. Going forward, I'll refer to them as *running processes*.

Process Highlighting

One of the first things that stands out in the process list is the use of color highlighting to distinguish different types of processes. Although you can configure which process types are highlighted and in what color, these are the defaults:

- **Light blue**   These processes ("own processes") are the processes that are running in the same user account as Procexp. Note that although they are running in the same user account, they might be in different Local Security Authority (LSA) logon sessions, integrity levels, or terminal sessions, and therefore are not all necessarily running in the same security context. Also note that if you started Procmon as a different user, other applications on the desktop will not be highlighted as "own processes."

- **Pink**   Designates services. These are processes containing one or more Windows services.

- **Violet**   Denotes "packed images." Procexp uses simple heuristics to identify program files that might contain executable code in compressed form, encrypted form, or both. Malware often uses this technique to evade anti-malware and then unpack itself in memory and execute. Note that sometimes the heuristics result in false positives, most commonly with debug builds of Microsoft Visual C++ applications.

- **Brown**   Indicates jobs. These are processes that have been associated with a job. A *job* is a Windows construct that allows one or more processes to be managed as a unit. Jobs can have constraints applied to them, such as memory and execution time limits. A process can be associated with at most one job. Jobs are not highlighted by default.

- **Yellow**   Indicates .NET processes. These are processes that use the Microsoft .NET Framework.

- **Dark gray**   Indicates suspended processes. These are processes in which all threads are suspended and cannot be scheduled for execution. Processes that have crashed might appear as suspended while Windows Error Reporting handles the crash. (Don't confuse this gray with the lighter gray color that, with default Windows color schemes, indicates the selected row when the Procexp window does not have focus.)

If a process belongs to more than one of these categories, the precedence order is Suspended, Packed, .NET, Jobs, Services, Own Process. For example, if a process hosts a service and uses the .NET Framework, Procexp applies the highlight color associated with

.NET processes because that has higher precedence than Services. Procexp requires administrative rights to recognize a packed image, a .NET process, or association with a job if the process is running at a higher integrity level or in a different user account from Procexp.

In addition to highlighting process types, Procexp highlights new processes and processes that have just exited. By default, when Procexp identifies a new process, it highlights its row in the process list with a green background for one second. When a process exits, Procexp keeps it in the list for one second, highlighted in red. Note that even though the process appears in the list, if it is highlighted in red, the process has already exited and no longer exists. You can configure how long the "difference highlight" lasts by choosing Difference Highlight Duration from the Options menu and entering a number from 0 to 9 in the dialog box. (See Figure 3-2.) Note that the actual duration also depends on the Procexp refresh interval. The difference highlighting changes only when the display is refreshed.

FIGURE 3-2 Difference Highlighting Duration dialog box.

To change whether a process type or difference is highlighted and in what color, choose Configure Highlighting from the Options menu. As indicated by Figure 3-3, you can enable or disable the highlighting of changes or process types by selecting the corresponding boxes. New Objects and Deleted Objects also refer to items appearing in the DLL view and Handle view. Relocated DLLs, which is not selected by default, applies only to DLL view. Click the Change button to display a color-picker dialog box to change the highlighting color for the corresponding highlight type. (The highlight color for suspended processes is not customizable.)

FIGURE 3-3 Configure Highlighting dialog box.

Updating the Display

By default, Procexp updates dynamic attributes in the display once per second. Dynamic attributes are those that are likely to change regularly, such as CPU time. You can pause the updating by pressing the space bar; pressing space again resumes the automatic refresh. You can trigger a one-time update of all the displayed data (dynamic *and* static attributes) by pressing F5 or clicking the Refresh icon in the toolbar. Finally, you can change the automatic refresh duration through the Update Speed submenu of the View menu. The available intervals range from 0.5 seconds to 10 seconds.

> **Tip** Manually updating the display combined with difference highlighting is a great way to see all new and deleted objects across a time span of your choosing. Pause the update, perform actions on the system, and then press F5 in Procexp.

Default Columns

Each column in the process list represents some static or dynamic attribute of the process. Dynamic attributes are updated at each automatic refresh interval. The default configuration of Procexp shows these columns:

- **Process**   This column shows the name of the executable, along with its icon if Procexp can identify the full path to the executable. The first three rows represent "pseudo-processes," which I will describe in the "What You Can Expect to See" section shortly.

- **PID**   The process ID.

- **CPU**   The percentage of CPU time, rounded to two decimal places, consumed by the process in the last refresh interval. (This column is fully described in the "Process Performance Tab" section later in this chapter. Also see the "Measuring CPU Consumption" section earlier in this chapter for more information.)

- **Private Bytes**   The number of bytes allocated and committed by the process for its own use, and that are not shareable with other processes. Per-process private bytes include heap and stack memory. Memory leaks are often exhibited by a continual rise in this value.

- **Working Set**   The amount of physical memory assigned to the process by the memory manager.

- **Description and Company Name**   Extracted from the version information resource of the executable image file. These columns are populated only if Procexp is able to identify the path to the file and can read from it. If Procexp is not running with administrative rights, it will not be able to read that information from nonservice processes running in a different security context.

There are many more attributes you can choose to display, which will be described in the "Customizing Column Selections" section later in this chapter.

You can resize columns by dragging the border lines in the column headers. You can autosize a column to its current content by double-clicking the border line to the right of the column title. And you can reorder columns—except for the Process column, which is always the left-most—by dragging the column headers. The Process column is also always kept in the view; if the other columns are wider than can fit in the window, they can be scrolled horizontally.

Clicking on a column header sorts the table by the data in that column in ascending order. Clicking the same column header again toggles between ascending and descending order. For example, clicking on the CPU column to get a descending sort shows the processes consuming the most CPU at the top of the list. The list automatically reorders at each refresh interval as different processes consume more or less CPU. Again here, there is an exception for the Process column.

One hidden trick in Procexp is that in both the main window and in the lower pane, pressing Ctrl+C copies the content of the selected row to the clipboard as tab-separated text.

Process Tree

As mentioned, the Process column is always the first one displayed. It has three sorting modes: ascending, descending, and Process Tree.

By default, Procexp displays processes in a tree view, which shows the processes' parent/child relationships. Whenever a process creates another process, Windows puts the process ID (PID) of the creating process (the *parent*) into the internal data structure of the new process (the *child*). Procexp uses this information to build its tree view. Unlike in UNIX, the process parent/child relationship is not used by Windows, so when a process exits, processes that it created are not updated to identify another ancestor. In the Procexp tree view, processes that have no existing parent are left-aligned in the column.

You can collapse or expand portions of the tree by clicking the plus (+) and minus (–) icons to the left of parent processes in the tree, or you can do it by selecting those nodes and pressing the left and right arrow keys. Nodes that you collapse remain collapsed if you switch to an ascending or descending sort on the Process column or any other column.

Clicking the Process column header cycles through an ascending sort by process name, a descending sort, and the tree view. You can also switch to the tree view at any time by pressing Ctrl+T or by clicking the Show Process Tree toolbar icon.

Tooltips

Hovering the mouse cursor over a column entry in which the text does not fit within the column's width displays a tooltip with the full text content of that entry. And yet again, the Process column is a special case.

By default, hovering over any process name displays its command line and the full path to its executable image, if Procexp can obtain that information. As mentioned earlier, obtaining that information can require administrative rights in some cases. The command line and image path are not shown in the tooltip if the corresponding columns are enabled for display. Likewise, if the Description or Company Name columns are not enabled, the tooltip will display that information.

In addition, when you hover over a service process, the tooltip also lists the display and internal names of all the services hosted within that process. Hovering over taskeng.exe on Windows Vista or taskhost.exe on Windows 7 displays the tasks running within it. And hovering over an Internet Explorer 8 or newer iexplore.exe hosting one or more tabs adds the tabs' text to the tooltip, so you can tell which process is hosting which Web page.

If the process has a user-defined comment associated with it and the Comment column is not selected for display, the comment also appears in the tooltip. (A user-defined comment can be entered in the Image tab of the process' Properties dialog box. See the "Process Details" section later in the chapter for more information.)

What You Can Expect to See

There are some patterns you can always expect to see in Procexp on a normal Windows system. Some processes and parent/child relationships will always appear, as well as some pseudo-processes that Procexp uses to distinguish categories of kernel-mode activity.

System processes   The first three rows in the Process Tree view are System Idle Process, System, and Interrupts. System Idle Process and Interrupts are not real operating system processes, and the System process does not run user-mode code.

The System Idle Process (called just "Idle" by some utilities) has one "thread" per CPU and is used to account for CPU idle time when Windows is not running any program code. Because it isn't a real process, it doesn't have a PID—there is no PID 0 in Windows. However, because Task Manager shows an artificial System Idle Process and displays 0 in its PID column, Procexp follows suit and assigns it PID 0.

The System process hosts only kernel-mode system threads, which only ever run (as you might expect) in kernel mode. These threads typically execute operating system code from Ntoskrnl.exe and device driver code.

The Interrupts pseudo-process represents kernel-mode time spent servicing interrupts and deferred procedure calls (DPCs). Procexp represents Interrupts as a child process of System because its time is spent entirely in kernel mode. Windows does not charge the time represented by this pseudo-process to the System process nor to any other process. Task Manager incorrectly includes interrupt and DPC time in its numbers for the System Idle Process. A system with heavy interrupt activity will therefore appear to be idle according to Task Manager. If you have a high interrupt or DPC load, you might want to investigate the reason by using Xperf to trace interrupts and DPCs or Kernrate to monitor kernel-mode CPU usage. For more information about interrupts and DPCs, see *Windows Internals*.

Startup and Logon Processes   From the time Windows starts until the first user logs on, there is a well-defined sequence of processes. By the time you log on and are able to see the process tree in Procexp, some of these processes have exited, so the user shell (typically Explorer.exe) appears on the left edge of the window with no parent process. For much more information on the startup and logon sequences, see *Windows Internals*.

The startup sequence changed between Windows XP and Windows Vista. On Windows XP, as shown in Figure 3-4, the System process starts Smss.exe (the Session Manager), which starts Csrss.exe (the Windows subsystem) and Winlogon.exe. Winlogon starts Services.exe (the Service Control Manager process), Lsass.exe (the Local Security Authority subsystem), and two processes not seen in the figure: LogonUI.exe, which displayed the logon screen on non-domain-joined systems, and Userinit.exe, which Windows started after the user logged on. Userinit.exe launched Explorer.exe (the user shell application) and then exited. Most user applications are direct or indirect descendants of Explorer.exe. Service processes are almost always descendants of Services.exe. Note that on Windows XP, Services.exe hosts some services itself and thus gets the pink highlight.

FIGURE 3-4 Process tree on Windows XP.

On Windows Vista and newer, because the interactive user no longer logs on in the same terminal services session that the services are running in (session 0), the startup and logon sequence was refactored, with visible differences in the Procexp process tree, shown in Figure 3-5.

Process	PID	CPU	Private Bytes	Working Set	Description	Company Name
System Idle Process	0	93.24	0 K	24 K		
System	4	0.47	116 K	3,948 K		
Interrupts	n/a	0.75	0 K	0 K	Hardware Interrupts and DPCs	
smss.exe	296		352 K	328 K	Windows Session Manager	Microsoft Corporation
csrss.exe	380		1,832 K	1,688 K	Client Server Runtime Process	Microsoft Corporation
wininit.exe	428		1,296 K	228 K	Windows Start-Up Application	Microsoft Corporation
services.exe	524	0.01	4,800 K	5,148 K	Services and Controller app	Microsoft Corporation
svchost.exe	648		3,684 K	4,184 K	Host Process for Windows S...	Microsoft Corporation
WmiPrvSE.exe	3136		2,116 K	5,448 K	WMI Provider Host	Microsoft Corporation
svchost.exe	720		3,608 K	4,060 K	Host Process for Windows S...	Microsoft Corporation
svchost.exe	756		17,064 K	11,988 K	Host Process for Windows S...	Microsoft Corporation
audiodg.exe	3324		12,340 K	13,040 K	Windows Audio Device Grap...	Microsoft Corporation
svchost.exe	856	< 0.01	58,144 K	55,728 K	Host Process for Windows S...	Microsoft Corporation
dwm.exe	1952		1,604 K	2,052 K	Desktop Window Manager	Microsoft Corporation
svchost.exe	900	0.02	21,488 K	23,208 K	Host Process for Windows S...	Microsoft Corporation
svchost.exe	1008	0.02	9,480 K	11,840 K	Host Process for Windows S...	Microsoft Corporation
svchost.exe	444	0.03	26,120 K	25,204 K	Host Process for Windows S...	Microsoft Corporation
rdpclip.exe	3004		1,796 K	2,648 K	RDP Clip Monitor	Microsoft Corporation
spoolsv.exe	1032		5,800 K	2,268 K	Spooler SubSystem App	Microsoft Corporation
svchost.exe	1068		12,220 K	9,192 K	Host Process for Windows S...	Microsoft Corporation
vmicsvc.exe	1152	0.02	2,500 K	492 K	Virtual Machine Integration C...	Microsoft Corporation
vmicsvc.exe	1172		5,016 K	1,480 K	Virtual Machine Integration C...	Microsoft Corporation
vmicsvc.exe	1204		1,300 K	304 K	Virtual Machine Integration C...	Microsoft Corporation
vmicsvc.exe	1240		1,344 K	744 K	Virtual Machine Integration Component Service	ration
vmicsvc.exe	1268		1,384 K	540 K	Virtual Machine Integration C...	Microsoft Corporation
svchost.exe	1320	0.06	8,289 K	10,724 K	Host Process for Windows S...	Microsoft Corporation
svchost.exe	2016		65,728 K	33,756 K	Host Process for Windows S...	Microsoft Corporation
SearchIndexer.exe	1408		34,328 K	18,632 K	Microsoft Windows Search I...	Microsoft Corporation
taskhost.exe	1480		8,032 K	4,996 K	Host Process for Windows T...	Microsoft Corporation
wmpnetwk.exe	2576		7,124 K	8,264 K	Windows Media Player Netw...	Microsoft Corporation
svchost.exe	3296		1,756 K	5,652 K	Host Process for Windows S...	Microsoft Corporation
lsass.exe	532		4,416 K	6,452 K	Local Security Authority Proc...	Microsoft Corporation
lsm.exe	540		2,944 K	2,568 K	Local Session Manager Serv...	Microsoft Corporation
csrss.exe	440	0.24	1,996 K	4,120 K	Client Server Runtime Process	Microsoft Corporation
conhost.exe	2436		2,072 K	5,736 K	Console Window Host	Microsoft Corporation
winlogon.exe	480		2,792 K	1,284 K	Windows Logon Application	Microsoft Corporation
explorer.exe	2084	0.50	75,428 K	57,184 K	Windows Explorer	Microsoft Corporation
powershell.exe	3812		40,268 K	48,764 K	Windows PowerShell	Microsoft Corporation
notepad.exe	1824		1,380 K	5,396 K	Notepad	Microsoft Corporation
mspaint.exe	1768		19,288 K	39,672 K	Paint	Microsoft Corporation
csrss.exe	2748	0.01	1,504 K	272 K	Client Server Runtime Process	Microsoft Corporation
winlogon.exe	2844		2,404 K	308 K	Windows Logon Application	Microsoft Corporation
LogonUI.exe	2860		9,620 K	732 K	Windows Logon User Interfa...	Microsoft Corporation
procexp64.exe	3212	4.62	10,496 K	19,404 K	Sysinternals Process Explorer	Sysinternals - www.sysinter...

CPU Usage: 6.76%   Commit Charge: 19.86%   Processes: 43   Physical Usage: 30.61%

FIGURE 3-5 Process tree on Windows 7.

The System process starts an instance of Smss.exe, which remains running until system shutdown. That Smss.exe launches two new instances of Smss.exe, one in session 0 and one in session 1, which create processes in their respective sessions. Both of these instances end up exiting before a user logs on, so the initial Smss.exe always appears not to have child processes. The instance of Smss.exe in session 0 starts an instance of Csrss.exe in session 0 and Wininit.exe. Wininit.exe starts Services.exe, Lsass.exe, and Lsm.exe (the Local Session Manager Service). In session 1, Smss.exe starts a new instance of Csrss.exe and Winlogon.exe. Winlogon starts LogonUI.exe to prompt the interactive user for credentials, and then Userinit. exe (which starts Explorer) after the user has authenticated. Both LogonUI and Userinit typically exit before the shell initializes and the user can start Procexp. As on Windows XP, most services are descendants of Services.exe; but unlike on Windows XP, Services.exe no longer hosts any services itself.

To view the complete startup process tree for yourself, refer to the "Boot Logging" section in Chapter 4, "Process Monitor."

User Processes   There are some typical patterns you might wonder about in the Procexp display. For example, you might see "own processes" that are children of service processes rather than descendants of Explorer. The most common examples are out-of-process DCOM components. An application invokes a component that COM determines needs to be hosted in a separate process. Even though the new process might run as the interactive user, the new process is launched by the process hosting the DcomLaunch service rather than directly by the client process. Similarly, on Windows Vista and newer, the Desktop Window Manager (Dwm.exe) is launched as the desktop user by the Desktop Window Manager Session Manager service (UxSms).

Another frequent pattern is the use of job objects. Some DCOM components, particularly Windows Management Instrumentation (WMI) hosting processes, run with restrictions on the amount of memory they can allocate, the number of child processes they can start (if any), or the maximum amount of CPU time they can charge. Anything launched through the Secondary Logon service (for example, with RunAs) is added to a job so that the process and any children it launches can be tracked as a unit and terminated if they are still running when the user logs off. Finally, the Program Compatibility Assistant (PCA) on Windows Vista and newer tracks legacy applications so that it can offer a compatibility fix to the user if the PCA detects a potential compatibility problem for which it might have a solution after the last process in the job has exited.

Process Actions

You can perform a number of actions on a process by right-clicking on it, or by selecting it and choosing any of the following options from the Process menu:

- **Window submenu**   If the process owns a visible window on the desktop, the window submenu lets you bring it to the foreground, or restore, minimize, maximize, or close it. The window submenu is disabled if the process owns no visible windows.

- **Set Affinity**   On multi-CPU systems, you can set processor affinity for a process so that its threads will run only on the CPU or CPUs you specify. (See Figure 3-6.) This can be useful if you have a runaway CPU-hogging process that must be allowed to keep running but throttled back so that you can troubleshoot it. You can use Set Affinity to restrict the process to a single core temporarily and free up other CPUs so that the system is still usable. (If a particular process should always be restricted to a single CPU and you can't modify its source code, use the SingleProcAffinity application compatibility shim, or as a last resort, modify the file's PE header to specify affinity.)

FIGURE 3-6 Dialog box for setting processor affinity on a two-processor system.

- **Set Priority**   View or set the base scheduling priority for the process.

- **Kill Process**   You can forcibly terminate a process by choosing Kill Process or by clicking the Kill Process button in the toolbar. By default, Procexp prompts you for confirmation before terminating the process. You can disable that prompt by clearing Confirm Kill in the Options menu.

> **Warning** Forcibly terminating a process does not give the process an opportunity to shut down cleanly and can cause data loss or system instability. In addition, Procexp does not provide extra warnings if you try to terminate a system-critical process such as Csrss.exe. Terminating a system-critical process results in an immediate Windows blue screen crash.

- **Kill Process Tree**   When Procexp is in the process-tree sorting mode, this menu item is available and allows you to forcibly terminate a process and all its descendants. If the Confirm Kill option is enabled, you will be prompted for confirmation first.

- **Restart**   When you select this item, Procexp terminates the highlighted process (after optional confirmation) and starts the same image using the same command-line arguments. Note that the new instance might fail to work correctly if the original process depended on other operating characteristics, such as the security context, environment variables, or inherited object handles.

- **Suspend**   If you want a process to become temporarily inactive so that a system resource—such as a network, CPU, or disk—becomes available for other processes, you can suspend the process' threads. To resume a suspended process, choose the Resume item from the process context menu.

> **Tip** Suspend can be useful when dealing with "buddy system" malware, in which two or more processes watch for each other's termination, with the nonterminated one restarting its buddy if it dies. To defeat such malware, suspend the processes first and then terminate them.

- **Launch Depends**   If the Dependency Walker (Depends.exe) utility is found, Procexp launches it with the path to the executable image of the selected process as a command-line argument. Depends.exe shows DLL dependencies. It used to ship with various Microsoft products, and it's now distributed through *www.DependencyWalker.com*.

- **Debug**   This menu item is available only if a debugger is registered in HKEY_LOCAL_ MACHINE\Software\Microsoft\Windows NT\CurrentVersion\AeDebug. Choosing Debug launches the registered debugger with –p followed by the selected process' PID as the command-line arguments. Note that closing the debugger without detaching first will terminate the debugee as well. If the debugger registration is changed while Procexp is running, Procexp needs to be restarted to pick up the change.

- **Create Dump submenu**   The options on this submenu let you capture a minidump or a full memory dump of the selected process to a file location of your choosing. Capturing a dump does not terminate the process.

- **Properties**   This menu item displays the Properties dialog box for the selected process, which displays a wealth of information about the process. It is described in detail in the "Process Details" section later in this chapter.

- **Search Online**   Procexp will launch a search for the selected executable name using your default browser and search engine. This option can be useful when researching malware or identifying the source of an unrecognized process.

Customizing Column Selections

You can change which columns are displayed by right-clicking the column header row and selecting Select Columns, or by choosing Select Columns from the View menu. Procexp offers over 100 process attributes that can be displayed in the main window, and over three dozen more that can be displayed in the DLL and Handle views and in the status bar. The Select Columns dialog box (shown in Figure 3-7) categorizes these into ten tabs: Process Image, Process Performance, Process Memory, .NET, Process I/O, Process Network, Process Disk, Handle, DLL, and Status Bar. Let's look at the attributes that can be displayed in the main window.

FIGURE 3-7 The Process Image tab of the Select Columns dialog box.

Process Image Tab

The Process Image tab (shown in Figure 3-7) contains process attributes that, for the most part, are established at process start and do not change over the life of a process. These include the Process Name and PID columns, which are always displayed and cannot be deselected. The other columns you can select from this tab are as follows:

- **User Name**   The user account in which the process is running, in DOMAIN\USER format.

- **Description**   Extracted from the version resource of the executable image. If this column is not enabled, the information appears in the process name tooltip.

- **Company Name**   Extracted from the version resource of the executable image. If this column is not enabled, the information appears in the process name tooltip.

- **Verified Signer**   Indicates whether the executable image has been verified as digitally signed by a certificate that chains to a root authority trusted by the computer. See the "Verifying Image Signatures" section later in this chapter for more information.

- **Version**   The file version extracted from the version resource of the executable image.

- **Image Path**   The path to the executable image. Note that when this column is enabled, the process name tooltip no longer shows the full path.

- **Image Type (64 vs 32-bit)**   On 64-bit versions of Windows, this field indicates whether the program is running native 64-bit code or 32-bit code running in WOW64 (Windows On Windows64). On 32-bit versions of Windows, this check box is disabled.

- **Window Title**   If the process owns any visible windows, shows the text of the title bar of a top-level window, similar to the Applications tab of Task Manager. This attribute is dynamic and changes when the application's window title changes.

- **Window Status**   If the process owns any visible windows, indicates whether it responds in a timely fashion to window messages (Running or Not Responding). This is similar to the Status column on the Task Manager Applications tab. This attribute is also dynamic.

- **Session**   Identifies the terminal services session in which the process is running. Services and most system code runs in session 0. User sessions on Windows XP and Windows Server 2003 can be in any session; user sessions on Windows Vista and newer are always in session 1 or higher.

- **Command Line**   The command line that was used to start the process.

- **Comment**   A user-defined comment that can be entered in the Image tab of the process' Properties dialog box. See the "Process Details" section for more information.

- **DEP Status**   Indicates whether Data Execution Prevention (DEP) is enabled for the process. DEP is a security feature that mitigates buffer overflow and other attacks by disallowing code execution from memory that has been marked "no-execute," such as the stack and heap. The column text can be blank (DEP not enabled), *DEP* (enabled), *DEP (permanent)* (DEP enabled within the executable and cannot be disabled), or *<n/a>* if Procexp cannot determine the DEP status of the process.

- **Integrity Level**   On Windows Vista and newer, indicates the integrity level (IL) of the process. Services run at System level, elevated processes at High, normal user processes at Medium, and low-rights processes such as Protected Mode Internet Explorer at Low.

- **Virtualized**   On Windows Vista and newer, indicates whether UAC file and registry virtualization is enabled. File and registry virtualization is an application=compatibility technology that intercepts attempts by legacy Medium IL processes to write to protected areas and transparently redirects them to areas owned by the user.

- **ASLR Enabled**   On Windows Vista and newer, indicates whether Address Space Layout Randomization (ASLR) is enabled for the process. ASLR is a defense-in-depth security feature that can mitigate remote attacks that assume that function entry points are at predictable memory addresses.

Procexp requires administrative rights to access most of the preceding information from non-service processes running in a different security context. The exceptions are window title and status for windows on the same desktop as Procexp and User Name when running on Windows XP. Because the display of the *Comment* attribute depends on the image path, what gets displayed can be affected by whether the comment was entered when Procexp was running with the same rights as current.

Process Performance Tab

The Process Performance tab (shown in Figure 3-8) contains attributes relating to CPU usage as well as the number of threads and open handles in the process. Some of the attributes report cumulative data, while others show the delta (the difference) since the previous update. Procexp does not require administrative rights to display any of the information on this tab. See the "Measuring CPU Consumption" section earlier in this chapter for more information about how Procexp reports these metrics.

FIGURE 3-8 The Process Performance tab of the Select Columns dialog box.

With the exception of the Start Time column, all of these are dynamic attributes that are updated with each refresh:

- **CPU Usage** The percentage of the overall CPU time, rounded to two decimal places, attributed to the process (or pseudo-process) since the previous update. On Windows 7, the column shows < 0.01 if the process consumed any CPU cycles during the interval but less than a hundredth of 1%, and it shows no number only if the process did not consume any CPU time at all during the interval. On Windows Vista and older, this column shows < 0.01 only if the CPU Cycles Delta or Context Switch Delta columns are enabled and reported a delta during the interval. Otherwise, no number means that the process did not execute or consumed less than 0.01% of CPU time. The number can be rounded to a whole number instead of to two decimal places by disabling the Show Fractional CPU option on the View menu. See the "Measuring CPU Consumption" section earlier in this chapter for more information.

- **Tree CPU Usage** The percentage of the CPU time attributed to the process and all its descendants. Note that the Tree CPU Usage column always uses timer-based CPU usage accounting. (See the "Measuring CPU Consumption" section earlier in this chapter for more information.)

- **CPU History**   A graphical representation of the recent CPU usage charged to each process. Kernel-mode time is shown in red and user-mode time in green.

- **CPU Time**   The total amount of kernel-mode and user-mode CPU time charged to the process (or pseudo-process), shown as hours:minutes:seconds.milliseconds.

- **Start Time**   The time and date that the process was started.

- **Base Priority**   The scheduling priority for the process. A value of 8 is normal priority; numbers above 8 indicate a higher priority, and those below 8 indicate a lower priority.

- **Threads**   The number of threads in the process.

- **Handle Count**   The number of handles to kernel objects currently opened by the process.

- **CPU Cycles**   On Windows Vista and newer, the total number of kernel-mode and user-mode CPU cycles consumed by the process since it started. (On Windows Vista, this number is not tracked for the Interrupts pseudo-process.)

- **CPU Cycles Delta**   On Windows Vista and newer, the number of CPU cycles consumed by the process since the previous update. (On Windows Vista, this number is not tracked for the Interrupts pseudo-process.)

- **Context Switches**   The total number of times that the CPU context changed to begin executing a thread in the process. (For the Interrupts pseudo-process, this number represents the number of DPCs and interrupts.) Note that because Windows does not maintain a process-wide counter for context switches, this attribute shows the sum of switches for the existing threads. If a thread exits, its context switches will no longer be counted toward this number.

- **Context Switch Delta**   The number of times that the CPU context switched to begin executing a thread in the process since the last update. (For the Interrupts pseudo-process, this number represents the number of DPCs and interrupts since the last update.)

Process Memory Tab

The Process Memory tab (shown in Figure 3-9) contains attributes relating to memory usage, including virtual memory management metrics around working set and page faults, as well as counts of the windowing system's GDI and USER objects.

FIGURE 3-9 The Process Memory tab of the Select Columns dialog box.

These are obviously all dynamic properties and are updated with each refresh. Most of these metrics can be read for all processes on the system without administrative rights. Procexp requires administrative rights to read the following metrics for processes in other security contexts: minimum and maximum working set; working set (WS) shareable, shared, and private bytes; and GDI and USER object counts. In addition, GDI and USER counts can be obtained only for processes in the same terminal services session, regardless of privilege:

- **Page Faults**   The total number of times that the process accessed an invalid memory page, causing the memory manager fault handler to be invoked. Some reasons for pages being invalid are these: the page is on disk in a page file or a mapped file, first access requires copying or zeroing, and there was illegal access resulting in an access violation. Note that this total includes soft page faults (that is, faults resolved by referencing information not in the working set but already in physical memory).

- **Page Fault Delta**   The number of page faults that occurred since the previous display refresh. Note that the column header is labeled "PF Delta."

- **Private Bytes**   The number of bytes allocated and committed by the process for its own use and not shareable with other processes. Per-process private bytes include heap and stack memory. A continual rise in this value can indicate a memory leak.

- **Private Delta Bytes**   The amount of change—positive or negative—in the number of private bytes since the previous refresh.

- **Peak Private Bytes**   The largest number of private bytes the process had committed at any one time since the process started.

- **Private Bytes History**   A graphical representation of the process' private byte commit history. The wider you make this column, the longer the timeframe it shows. Note that the graph scale is the same for all processes and is based on the maximum number of private bytes currently committed by any process.

- **Virtual Size**   The amount of the process' virtual memory that has been reserved or committed.

- **Memory Priority**   In Windows Vista and newer, the default memory priority that is assigned to physical memory pages used by the process. Pages that are cached in RAM and not part of any working set get repurposed starting with the lowest priority.

- **Minimum Working Set**   The amount of physical memory reserved for the process; the operating system guarantees that the process' working set can always be assigned at least this amount. The process can also lock pages in the working set up to that amount minus eight pages. This minimum does not guarantee that the process' working set will always be at least that large, unless a hard limit has been set by a resource management application.

- **Maximum Working Set**   Indicates the maximum amount of working set assigned to the process. However, this number is ignored by Windows unless a hard limit has been configured for the process by a resource management application.

- **Working Set Size**   The amount of physical memory assigned to the process by the memory manager.

- **Peak Working Set Size**   The largest working set size the process has had since its start.

- **WS Shareable Bytes**   The portion of the process' working set that contains memory that can be shared with other processes, such as mapped executable images.

- **WS Shared Bytes**   The portion of the process' working set that contains memory that is currently shared with other processes.

- **WS Private Bytes**   The portion of the process' working set that contains private bytes that cannot be shared with other processes.

- **GDI Objects**   The number of Graphics Device Interface (GDI) objects—such as brushes, fonts, and bitmaps—owned by the process.

- **USER Objects**   The number of USER objects—such as windows and menus—owned by the process.

Note that GDI and USER objects are created by the windowing subsystem in the process' terminal server session. They are not kernel objects and do not have security descriptors associated with them.

.NET Tab

The .NET tab (shown in Figure 3-10) contains performance counters that measure behaviors of processes that use the .NET framework version 1.1 or higher.

FIGURE 3-10 The .NET tab of the Select Columns dialog box.

These numbers are all dynamic. Administrative rights are required to observe them in a process running in a different security context:

- **Methods Jitted**   Displays the total number of methods just-in-time (JIT) compiled since the application started.

- **% Time in JIT**   Displays the percentage of elapsed time spent in JIT compilation since the last JIT compilation phase.

- **AppDomains**   Displays the current number of application domains loaded in this application.

- **Total AppDomains**   Displays the peak number of application domains loaded since the application started.

- **Classes Loaded**   Displays the current number of classes loaded in all assemblies.

- **Total Classes Loaded**   Displays the cumulative number of classes loaded in all assemblies since the application started.

- **Assemblies**   Displays the current number of assemblies loaded across all application domains in the currently running application. If this keeps increasing, it could indicate an assembly leak.

- **Total Assemblies**   Displays the total number of assemblies loaded since the application started.

- **Gen 0, 1, 2 Collections**   Displays the number of times that generation 0, 1, or 2 objects have been garbage collected since the application began. Generation 0 objects are the newest, most recently allocated objects, while Gen 2 collections are also called *full garbage collections*. Higher generation garbage collections include all lower generation collections.

- **% Time in GC**   Displays the percentage of elapsed time that was spent performing a garbage collection since the last garbage collection cycle.

- **Allocated Bytes/s**   Displays the number of bytes per second allocated on the garbage collection heap.

- **Heap Bytes**   Displays the number of bytes allocated in all heaps in the process.

- **Runtime Checks**   Displays the total number of runtime code access security checks performed since the application started.

- **Contentions**   Displays the total number of times that threads in the runtime have attempted to acquire a managed lock unsuccessfully.

Process I/O Tab

The Process I/O tab (shown in Figure 3-11) contains attributes relating to file and device I/O, including file I/O through the LANMan and WebDAV redirectors. When you enable these columns, Procexp measures the numbers of NtReadFile, NtWriteFile, and NtDeviceIoControlFile system calls representing I/O reads, writes and "other" (respectively), and the numbers of bytes associated with those calls. The I/O counts shown by Procexp are for "private I/O"—that is, I/O operations that can be unequivocally attributed to a process. Note that memory-mapped file I/O is not necessarily attributable to a particular process.

FIGURE 3-11 The Process I/O tab of the Select Columns dialog box.

These are all dynamic properties, updated with each refresh. All require administrative rights in order to read these metrics for processes running under a different user account. However, they do not require administrative rights to read them for processes running under the same account even at a higher integrity level.

By default, Procexp reports exact numbers for byte counts. If you enable the Format I/O Bytes Columns option on the View menu, Procexp reports approximations as KB, MB, or GB as appropriate. Note that the attributes' display names in the column headers have "I/O" prepended. For example, if you enable the "Read Bytes" column on this tab, its column header will show "I/O Read Bytes".

- **I/O operations**   There are four metrics each for I/O Read, Write, and Other operations: the total number of operations performed by the process since it started (Reads), the total number of bytes involved in those operations (Read Bytes), the number of operations performed since the last update (Delta Reads), and the number of bytes since the last update (Delta Read Bytes).

- **Delta Total Bytes**   Represents the number of bytes involved in I/O operations since the previous update.

- **I/O History**   A graphical representation of the process' recent I/O throughput. The blue line represents the total throughput, while the pink line shows write traffic.

- **I/O Priority**   On Windows Vista and newer, shows the I/O priority for the process. I/O prioritization allows the I/O subsystem to distinguish between foreground processes and lower-priority background processes. Most processes have a priority of Normal, while others can be Low or Very Low. Only the memory manager has Critical I/O priority. A fifth level, High, is not used in current versions of Windows.

Process Network Tab

The Process Network tab (shown in Figure 3-12) lets you configure Procexp to show the numbers of TCP connect, send, receive, and disconnect operations; the number of bytes in those operations; and the deltas since the previous refresh. Note that these figures do not include file I/O through the LANMan redirector (as mentioned in the "Process I/O Tab" section), but they do include file I/O through the WebDAV redirector.

Also note that the display of any of the attributes on this tab requires administrative rights. The Select Columns dialog box does not display the Process Network tab when Procexp is not running with administrative rights. Procexp displays a warning if you enable any of these columns and later run Procexp without administrative rights.

FIGURE 3-12 The Process Network tab of the Select Columns dialog box.

As with the metrics on the Process I/O tab, the Network I/O metrics include total numbers of operations (Receives, Sends, and Other) since the process started and since the previous refresh, and the number of bytes since the process started and since the previous refresh.

The cumulative counts that Procexp displays when you enable these columns reflect only the numbers of operations and corresponding bytes since Procexp started. Windows does not track these metrics on a per-process basis, so Procexp has no way to show historical information from before it started.

By default, Procexp reports exact numbers for byte counts. If you enable the Format I/O Bytes Columns option on the View menu, Procexp reports approximations as KB, MB, or GB as appropriate.

Process Disk Tab

Enabling column displays of the attributes on the Process Disk tab (shown in Figure 3-13) shows I/O to local disks (not including CD/DVD drives). Unlike the attributes on the Process I/O tab, this includes all disk I/O, including that initiated from the kernel and file system drivers. It does not include file I/O resolved by network redirectors or by in-memory caches.

Note that display of any of the attributes on this tab requires administrative rights. The Select Columns dialog box does not display the Process Disk tab when Procexp is not running with administrative rights. Procexp displays a warning if you enable any of these columns and later run Procexp without administrative rights.

FIGURE 3-13 The Process Disk tab of the Select Columns dialog box.

As with the metrics on the Process I/O and Process Network tabs, the Disk I/O metrics include total numbers of operations (Reads, Writes, and Other) since the process started and since the previous refresh, and the number of bytes since the process started and since the previous refresh. And as with the Network I/O metrics, the cumulative counts that Procexp displays when you enable Process Disk columns reflect only the numbers of operations and corresponding bytes since Procexp started. Procexp has no visibility into a process' disk I/O prior to Procexp starting.

By default, Procexp reports exact numbers for byte counts. If you enable the Format I/O Bytes Columns option on the View menu, Procexp reports approximations as KB, MB, or GB as appropriate.

Column Sets

You can save a column configuration and its associated sort settings by choosing Save Column Set from the View menu. Procexp will prompt you to name the column set. (See Figure 3-14.) To modify an existing column set, save the updated configuration to the same name as the set you want to modify by choosing it from the drop-down combo box.

FIGURE 3-14 The Save Column Set dialog box.

You can load a saved column set by selecting it in the Load Column Set submenu on the View menu or by entering the accelerator keys that Procexp assigns to it and that appear on the submenu. To rename, reorder, or delete existing column sets, choose Organize Column Sets from the View menu. Reordering the column sets changes the order in which they appear in the Load Column Set submenu and the accelerator keys assigned to them.

> **Note** The saved column set accelerator keys assigned by Procexp conflict with the default hotkeys used by ZoomIt, described in Chapter 10, "Desktop Utilities."

Saving Displayed Data

Click the Save icon on the toolbar to save a snapshot of current process activity to a text file. Procexp saves the data from all the columns that are selected for display in the main window, and in the lower pane if it is open, to a tab-delimited text file. If a file has not already been selected, Procexp prompts for a file location. To change the file location, choose Save As from the File menu.

Toolbar Reference

The Procexp toolbar includes buttons for quick access to frequently used features, and four or six continually updated graphs displaying the recent history of systemwide metrics.

FIGURE 3-15 The Procexp menu and toolbar.

Graphs

The minigraphs in the Procexp toolbar can be resized or moved to separate rows by dragging their left-edge handles. Procexp displays graphs representing CPU usage, commit charge, physical memory usage, and file and device I/O. If Procexp is running with administrative rights, it adds graphs for network and disk I/O.

The CPU graph shows recent history for systemwide CPU usage, with red showing kernel usage and green showing the sum of kernel-mode and user-mode usage. The systemwide commit charge is shown in the yellow graph and physical memory usage in the orange graph. Recent systemwide I/O throughput is graphed with violet for writes and light blue for all I/O. Moving the mouse over the graphs displays a tooltip with numeric details and the time of day for that part of the graph, and for the CPU and I/O graphs it displays the process responsible for the largest proportion of the CPU or I/O at that moment. The wider you resize a graph, the longer the timeframe it displays. Clicking on any of the graphs displays the corresponding graph in the System Information dialog box. (See the "System Information" section later in this chapter for more complete descriptions of the meanings of these graphs.)

You can display tiny versions of each of these graphs (and their tooltips) in the notification area of the taskbar (commonly but mistakenly referred to as "the tray") by selecting options from the Tray Icons submenu of the Options menu. By default, only the CPU Usage icon is displayed, showing recent CPU utilization history with kernel usage in red and total usage in green. Clicking on any of the Procexp notification area icons toggles the display of the Procexp main window.

Right-clicking a Procexp notification area icon displays a context menu allowing you to display the System Information dialog box or the Procexp main window, or exit Procexp. Its Shutdown submenu lets you log off, shut down, or restart Windows, or lock the workstation.

Toolbar Buttons

This section identifies the Procexp toolbar icons and the sections of this chapter that describe what they do.

FIGURE 3-16 The Procexp toolbar buttons.

Referring to the Figure 3-16, the toolbar icons are, in order:

- **Save**   See the "Saving Displayed Data" section.
- **Refresh Now**   See the "Updating the Display" section.
- **System Information**   See the "System Information" section.
- **Show Process Tree**   See the "Process Tree" section.
- **Show/Hide Lower Pane (toggle)**   See the "DLLs and Handles" section.
- **View DLLs / View Handles (toggle)**   See the "DLL View" and "Handle View" sections.
- **Properties**   Displays the Properties dialog box for the selected process, handle, or DLL.
- **Kill Process/Close Handle**   If a process is selected, terminates the process; if a handle is selected in Handle view, closes the handle. (As discussed elsewhere in this chapter, these operations can be risky, especially closing a handle in use by a process.)
- **Find Handle or DLL**   See the "Finding DLLs or Handles" section.
- **Find Window's Process**   See the "Identifying the Process That Owns a Window" section.

Identifying the Process That Owns a Window

You can quickly identify the process that owns any visible window on your desktop. Click and hold the crosshairs icon in the toolbar, and then drag it over the window you are interested in. Procexp moves itself behind all other windows during this operation and draws a frame around the window the cursor is over. Release the mouse button, and Procexp will reappear with the process that owns the window selected in the main window. This is particularly valuable when trying to ascertain the source of an unexpected error message.

Status Bar

The status bar shows key systemwide metrics in numeric form, such as CPU usage, number of processes, and memory use. If Procexp's automatic refresh is disabled, the word "Paused" appears in the status bar.

By right-clicking on the status bar and choosing Select Status Bar Columns, you can select different metrics to display, as shown in Figure 3-17. The options include a number of system-wide metrics and corresponding metrics relating only to processes running under the same account as Procexp. Selecting Refresh Time displays the time of day when the display was last updated.

FIGURE 3-17 The Status Bar tab of the Select Columns dialog box.

DLLs and Handles

Procexp's lower pane lets you peer inside and list the contents of the process selected in the upper pane. DLL view lists all the dynamic-link libraries and other files mapped into the process' address space, while Handle view lists all the kernel objects opened by the process. Pressing Ctrl+D opens DLL view (shown in Figure 3-18), Ctrl+H opens Handle view, and Ctrl+L toggles the lower pane open or closed. Drag the pane separator to change the relative sizes of the panes.

FIGURE 3-18 Procexp's lower pane displaying DLL View.

The DLL View and Handle View lists are updated at the automatic refresh interval. Similarly to the process list, newly loaded DLLs and newly acquired handles are highlighted in green for the configured difference highlight duration, and newly unloaded DLLs and newly closed handles are highlighted in red. (See the "Process Highlighting" section earlier in this chapter.)

As with the main window, columns in DLL view and Handle view can be reordered, resized, and sorted, and the column selection can be customized. Configuration selections made in the DLL and Handle views are included when you save a column set.

Finding DLLs or Handles

One of Procexp's most powerful features is its ability to quickly identify the process or processes that have a DLL loaded or an object open. For example, suppose you're trying to delete a folder called ProjectX, but Windows won't let you because "it is open in another program"—but Windows won't tell you which program.

Press Ctrl+F to open the Search dialog box (shown in Figure 3-19), type the name or partial name of the DLL or object you're trying to find, and then click the Search button. Procexp matches the name you entered against every DLL path, handle type, and handle name that it can access, and it lists all the matches along with the processes that own them. Click on a match to select it in the lower pane and its owning process in the upper pane. Double-clicking selects them and closes the Search dialog box.

FIGURE 3-19 The Process Explorer Search dialog box.

If the Search returns many results, click on a column header to sort by that column to make it easier to find items of interest. The Type column identifies whether the matched item is a DLL (more accurately, a mapped file) or an object handle. The Handle or DLL column contains the handle name or the path to the DLL. A handle name might be blank if Show Unnamed Handles And Mappings is selected in the View menu and the name you entered matches the handle type.

DLL View

As you would expect, DLL view displays all the DLLs loaded by the selected process. It also displays other memory-mapped files, including the data files and the image file (EXE) being run. For the System process, DLL view lists the image files mapped into kernel memory, including ntoskrnl.exe and all the loaded device drivers. DLL view is empty for the System Idle Process and Interrupts pseudo-processes.

Procexp requires administrative rights to list DLLs loaded in processes running as a different user, but not to list the images loaded in the System process.

Customizing DLL View

With DLL view open, right-click on the column header in the lower pane and choose Select Columns to display the DLL tab of the Select Columns dialog box, as shown in Figure 3-20. The DLL tab lists attributes of DLLs and mapped files that can be selected to appear when Procexp's DLL view is open.

FIGURE 3-20 The DLL tab of the Select Columns dialog box.

The following describes the columns that can be displayed in DLL view:

- **Description**   Extracted from the file's version resource, if present.

- **Version**   The file version extracted from the file's version resource, if present.

- **Time Stamp**   The last modification time of the file, as reported by the file system.

- **Name**   The file name of the DLL or mapped file, or <Pagefile Backed> for an unnamed file mapping. Hover the mouse pointer over the name to display its full path in a tooltip.

- **Path**   The full path to the DLL or mapped file, or <Pagefile Backed> for an unnamed file mapping.

- **Company Name**   Extracted from the file's version resource, if present.

- **Verified Signer**   Indicates whether the file has been verified as digitally signed by a certificate that chains to a root authority trusted by the computer. See the "Verifying Image Signatures" section later in this chapter for more information.

- **Image Base Address**   For files loaded as executable images, the virtual memory address from the executable image header that indicates where the image should be loaded. If any of the necessary memory range is already in use, the image will need to be relocated to another address.

- **Base Address**   The virtual memory address where the file is actually loaded.

- **Mapped Size**   The number of contiguous bytes, starting from the base address, consumed by the file mapping.

- **Mapping Type**   The Mapping Type column displays "Image" for executable image files or "Data" for data files, including DLLs loaded for resources only (such as icons or localized text) and unnamed file mappings.

- **WS Total Bytes**   The total amount of working set (physical memory) currently consumed by the file mapping.

- **WS Private Bytes**   The amount of physical memory consumed by the file mapping that belongs solely to this process and cannot be shared with other processes.

- **WS Shareable Bytes**   The amount of physical memory consumed by the file mapping that can be shared with other processes.

- **WS Shared Bytes**   The amount of physical memory consumed by the file mapping that is also mapped into the address space of one or more other processes.

- **Image Type (64 vs 32-bit)**   (64-bit versions of Windows only) For executable image files, indicates whether the file's header specifies 64-bit or 32-bit code.

- **ASLR Enabled**   (Windows Vista and newer) For executable image files, displays ASLR if the file's header indicates support for Address Space Layout Randomization. The column is blank if the image does not support ASLR and n/a for data files.

Although they are not enabled by default, you can highlight DLLs that are not loaded at their programmed base address by selecting Relocated DLLs in the Configure Highlighting dialog box. (See the "Process Highlighting" section earlier in this chapter.) DLLs that cannot load at their base address because other files are already mapped there are relocated by the loader, which consumes CPU and makes the parts of the DLL that are modified as part of the relocation not shareable, which can reduce the efficiency of Windows memory management.

If Show Unnamed Handles And Mappings is selected in the View menu, DLL view also lists unnamed file mappings in the process' address space, labeled as <Pagefile Backed> in the Name and Path columns, if displayed. For unnamed mappings, many of the attribute columns contain no useful information, including those that are displayed by default. The columns that might be of interest for unnamed mappings are the base address, mapped size, and working set metrics.

When DLL view is open, the DLL menu offers the following options for named files:

- **Properties**   Displays a Properties dialog box for the selected file. See the "Peering Deeper into DLLs" section for more information.

- **Search Online**   Procexp will launch a search for the selected file name using your default browser and search engine. This option can be useful when researching malware or identifying the source of an unrecognized DLL.

- **Launch Depends**   If the Dependency Walker (Depends.exe) utility is found, Procexp launches it with the path to the selected file as a command-line argument. Depends. exe shows DLL dependencies. It used to ship with various Microsoft products and is now distributed through *www.DependencyWalker.com*.

Peering Deeper into DLLs

Double-click on a named item in DLL view to display its Properties dialog box, as shown in Figure 3-21. The Image tab displays information about the mapped file such as Description, Company, Version, Path, base address and size in the process' memory, and (on x64) whether it is 32-bit or 64-bit. Several of these fields can be selected and copied to the clipboard.

FIGURE 3-21 The Image tab of the DLL Properties dialog box.

The Company field is also used to indicate whether the executable file has been verified as digitally signed by a trusted publisher. (See the "Verifying Image Signatures" section later in this chapter for more information.) If the mapped file is an executable file type with a Company Name version resource and signature verification has not already been attempted, click the Verify button to perform validation. This feature can be useful to verify that a file that claims to be from a particular source is actually from that publisher and has not been modified. If the signature on the image has been verified, the Company field displays (Verified) and the subject name on the signing certificate. If verification has not been attempted, the field displays (Not verified) with the company name from the image's version resource. If the image is not signed or a signature check has failed, the column shows (Unable to verify) with the company name.

The Strings tab of the Properties dialog box (shown in Figure 3-22) shows all sequences of three or more printable characters found in the mapped file. If the Image radio button is selected, strings are read from the image file on disk. If the Memory radio button is selected, strings are read from the memory range in which the file is mapped. Image and memory strings might be different when an image is decompressed, or they might be decrypted when loaded into memory. Memory strings might also include dynamically constructed data areas of the image's memory range.

> **Note** In computer programming, the term "string" refers to a data structure consisting of a sequence of characters, usually representing human-readable text.

FIGURE 3-22 The Strings tab of the DLL Properties dialog box.

Click the Save button to save the displayed strings to a text file. To compare image and memory strings, save the image and memory strings to separate files and then identify the differences with a text-comparison utility.

To search for specific text in the strings list, click the Find button to display the standard Find dialog box. To search for additional occurrences of the same text, simply press F3 or click Find and Find Next again—the search continues from the currently selected row.

Handle View

Procexp's Handle view lists the object handles belonging to the process selected in the upper pane, as shown in Figure 3-23. Object handles are what programs use to manipulate system objects managed by kernel-mode code, such as files, registry keys, synchronization objects, memory sections, window stations, and desktops. Even though disparate types of resources are involved, all kernel object types use this consistent mechanism for managing access.

FIGURE 3-23 Handle view displayed in Procexp's lower pane.

When a process tries to create or open an object, it also requests specific access rights for the operations it intends to perform, such as read or write. If the create or open action is successful, the process acquires a handle to the object that includes the access rights that were granted. That handle can then be used for subsequent operations on the object, but only for the access rights that were granted. Even if the user could have been granted Full Control access to the object, if only Read access were requested, the handle could only be used for Read operations.

Although programs treat handles as opaque, at the program's level a handle is simply an integer. That integer serves as a byte offset into the process' handle table, which is managed in kernel memory. Information in the handle table includes the object's type, the access granted, and a pointer to the data structure representing the actual object.

> **Note** Windows programmers might be familiar with "handle" types to manipulate window manager objects, such as HWND for windows, HBRUSH for brushes, HDC for device contexts, and so on. These objects are managed through mechanisms that are completely distinct from and unrelated to what is described here, and they do not appear in the process handle table.

Note that loading a DLL or mapping another file type into a process' address space normally does not also add a handle to the process' handle table. Such files can therefore be in use and not be able to be deleted, even though a handle search might come up empty. This is why Procexp's Find feature searches both DLLs and handles.

Procexp must run with administrative rights to view handles owned by a process running in a different security context from Procexp.

By default, Handle view shows the type and name for all named objects opened by the process selected in the upper pane. You can choose to show additional information about each handle, as well as to show information about unnamed objects.

Customizing Handle View

To change the column selection that appears in Handle view, press Ctrl+H to open Handle view, and then right-click on the column header in the lower pane and choose Select Columns. This displays the Handle tab of the Select Columns dialog box, as shown in Figure 3-24.

FIGURE 3-24 The Handle tab of the Select Columns dialog box.

These attributes remain constant for as long as the handle is open:

- **Type**   The type of securable object that the handle grants access to, such as Desktop, Directory, File, Key, and Thread.

- **Name**   The name associated with the object. For most object types, the name is an object namespace name, such as \Device\Afd. For file system and registry objects, drive letters and friendly root keys replace internal names like \Device\HarddiskVolume1 (C:) and \REGISTRY\MACHINE\Software\Classes (HKCR). For process handles, the process name and PID is used; thread handles append the thread ID (TID) to that. Token handles use the principal and the logon session ID. Unnamed handles are not shown by default.

- **Handle Value**   The handle value in hexadecimal that the process passes to APIs to access the underlying object. This value is the byte offset into the process' handle table.

- **Access Mask**   The bitmask in hexadecimal that identifies what permissions the process is granted through the handle. Each bit that is set grants a permission specific to the object type. For example, "read" permission for a registry key is 0x00020019; for a file, it is usually 0x00120089. Full control permission for a registry key is 0x000F003F, while for a file it is usually 0x001F01FF. (For more information, search MSDN for the "Access Rights and Access Masks" topic.)

- **File Share Flags**   For file objects, the sharing mode that was set when the handle was opened. Flags can include R, W, or D, indicating that other callers (including other threads within the same process) can open the same file for reading, writing, or deleting, respectively. If no flags are set, the file system object is opened for exclusive use through this handle.

- **Object Address**   The memory address in kernel memory of the data structure representing the object. This information can be used with a kernel debugger to display more information about the object.

If Show Unnamed Handles And Mappings is selected in the View menu, Handle view also lists objects that do not have a name associated with them. (Note that some types of objects are always unnamed, and others are sometimes but not always unnamed.) Unnamed objects are typically created by the process for its own use. They can also be inherited and used by child processes, as long as the child process has a way to identify which inherited handle value it should use. Handles can also be duplicated from one process to another, provided that the process performing the handle duplication has the necessary access to the target process.

> **Note** Procexp consumes significantly more CPU resource when the Show Unnamed Handles And Mappings option is selected.

When Handle view is open, the Handle menu appears on the menu bar, offering the Properties and Close Handle options. Close Handle forces a handle to be closed. This is typically risky. Because the process that owns the handle is not aware that its handle has been closed, using this feature can lead to data corruption or crash the application; closing a handle in the System process or a critical user-mode process such as Csrss can lead to a system crash.

Double-clicking a handle or choosing Properties from the Handle menu displays the Properties dialog box for the selected handle. The caption of the Details tab, shown in Figure 3-25, displays the internal name of the object, while the Name field in the dialog box shows the more user-friendly equivalent. In the figure, \Device\HarddiskVolume2\Windows\System32 and C:\Windows\System32 are equivalent. The dialog box also includes a more detailed description of the one-word object type. The References group box indicates how many open handles and references still exist for the object. Because each handle includes a reference to the object, the reference count is never smaller than the handle count. The difference between the two figures is the number of direct references to the object structure from within kernel mode rather than indirectly through a handle. An object can be closed only when its reference count drops to zero—that is, when it has been closed as many times as it has been opened. The quota charges show how much paged and nonpaged pool is charged to the process' quota when it creates the object.

FIGURE 3-25 The Handle Properties dialog box.

The Security tab of the Handle Properties dialog box shows a standard security editor dialog box displaying the security descriptor of the underlying object referenced by the handle. Note that in some cases, particularly with unnamed objects, the dialog box will warn of a potential security risk because permissions had not been assigned for the object. For un-named objects, this generally isn't important because the lack of a name means that the only way for another process to gain access to the object is through an existing handle.

Process Details

With its customizable column sets, the Procexp main window process list can show a tremendous amount of information about all processes on the system. To view even more detailed information about a specific process, double-click it in the Procexp main window to display its Properties dialog box. Procexp categorizes the data into a number of tabs: Image, Performance, Performance Graph, Threads, TCP/IP, Security, Environment, and Strings. It adds a Disk And Network tab if running with administrative rights. Extra tabs are added for processes that are services, are associated with a job, or use the .NET Framework.

The Properties dialog box is modeless, meaning that you do not need to close it to interact with the main window; in fact, you can have multiple Properties dialog boxes open simultaneously. The dialog boxes can also be resized or maximized.

Most of the information shown in the Process Properties dialog box requires either full access to the process or the ability to identify the full path to the executable image file. If run without administrative rights, Procexp will be able to show detailed information only for processes running under the same account as Procexp. Other than the Disk And Network tab, which always requires administrative rights, the few exceptions will not be called out in this section.

Image Tab

The Image tab, shown in Figure 3-26, displays information about the process that mostly remains static for the lifetime of the process, including information collected from the executable image file's icon and version resources, the full path to the image file, the command line that was used to start the process, the user account under which the process is running, when it started, whether DEP is enabled, whether ASLR is enabled (Windows Vista and newer), and on x64 versions of Windows, whether the process is running 32-bit or 64-bit code. Two fields that can change if you open a new Properties dialog box for the process are the current directory and the parent process. If the parent process was still running when Procexp started, the field reports the image name and the PID; if it had exited, the field reports <Non-existent Process> and the PID.

FIGURE 3-26 The Image tab of the process' Properties dialog box.

The second field in the Image tab serves as a Verified Signer field, showing the company name from the version resource or the subject name from the verified signing certificate. If signature verification has not been attempted, you can click the Verify button to perform that verification. See the "Verifying Image Signature" section in this chapter for more information.

If the process owns a visible window on the current desktop, clicking the Bring To Front button brings it to the foreground. If the process owns more than one top-level window, Bring To Front brings the one closest to the top of the z-order to the foreground.

Clicking the Kill Process button forcibly terminates the process. By default, Procexp will prompt you for confirmation before terminating the process. You can disable that prompt by clearing the Confirm Kill check box in the Options menu.

> **Warning** Forcibly terminating a process does not give the process an opportunity to shut down cleanly and can cause data loss or system instability. In addition, Procexp does not provide extra warnings if you try to terminate a system-critical process such as Csrss.exe. Terminating a system-critical process results in an immediate Windows blue screen crash.

You can add a comment for a process in the Comment field. Comments are visible in the process list if you display the Comment column or, if you do not have the Comment column selected, in the tooltip for the process. Comments apply to all processes with the same path and are remembered for future executions of Procexp. Note that administrative rights are required to identify the executable image path for processes running in other accounts. If the image path cannot be identified, the process name is used instead. That means, for example, that a comment entered for a svchost.exe process while running Procexp with administrative rights might be associated with "C:\Windows\System32\svchost.exe", while a comment entered for the same process when running without administrative rights will be associated with "svchost.exe", and the comment associated with the full path will not be displayed. Procexp saves comments under the same registry key as its other configuration settings (HKCU\Software\Sysinternals\Process Explorer).

Performance Tab

The Performance tab, shown in Figure 3-27, reports metrics for CPU usage, virtual memory, physical memory (working set), I/O, kernel object handle count, and window manager handle counts. All the data on the tab is updated at the Procexp refresh interval.

FIGURE 3-27 The Performance tab of the process' Properties dialog box.

The Performance tab provides a convenient way for you to see a large number of process metrics in one place. Most of the fields on the Performance tab can also be viewed in the process list as described in the "Customizing Column Selections" section earlier in this chapter. The fields that appear in the Performance tab are specifically described in the sub-sections for the Process Performance, Process Memory, and Process I/O tabs of the Select Columns dialog box. The two additional pieces of information that are displayed only in the Performance tab are how much of the CPU utilization charged to the process is kernel time vs. user time and peak handle count.

Performance Graph Tab

The Performance Graph tab displays Task Manager–like graphs for a single process. (See Figure 3-28.) The top graph displays recent CPU usage history, with the red area indicating kernel-mode usage charged to the process and the green area above it indicating user-mode usage. Moving the mouse over this graph displays a tooltip with the percentage of the total CPU time consumed by the process at that time, along with the time of day that part of the graph represents. Note that this graph does not distinguish between CPUs. If the process consumed 100 percent of one CPU's time on a dual-core system and none of the second CPU's time, the graph would indicate 50 percent usage.

FIGURE 3-28 The Performance Graph tab of the process' Properties dialog box.

The second graph shows the recent history of the amount of the process' committed private bytes. It is scaled against the peak private bytes for the process; if the peak grows, the graph is rescaled against the new peak. Moving the mouse over this graph displays the private byte count and time of day for that part of the graph. Continual growth in this graph might indicate a memory leak.

The third graph represents the process' file and device I/O throughput history, with the light blue line indicating total I/O traffic between refreshes and the pink line indicating write traffic. The I/O graph is scaled against the peak I/O traffic the process has generated since the start of monitoring. Moving the mouse over this graph displays a tooltip showing the number of bytes for read, write, and other operations and the time of day for that part of the graph.

As mentioned, the dialog box can be resized or maximized. The wider you make the dialog box, the longer the historical timeframe displayed in the graphs.

Threads Tab

The Threads tab of the process' Properties dialog box shows detailed information, including current call stacks, for each of the threads in the selected process, and it lets you kill or suspend individual threads within the process. It will be described in the "Thread Details" section later in this chapter.

TCP/IP Tab

Any active TCP, TCPV6, UDP, or UDPV6 endpoints owned by the process are shown in a list on the TCP/IP tab. (See Figure 3-29.) The tab lists the protocol, state, and local and remote addresses and port numbers for each connection. For service processes on Windows Vista and newer, the tab adds a Service column showing the service that owns the endpoint. Select the Resolve Addresses check box to resolve endpoint addresses to their DNS names; clearing the check box displays the actual IPv4 or IPv6 addresses.

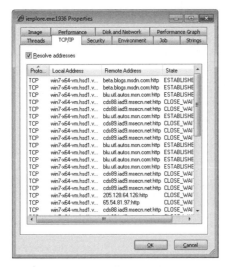

FIGURE 3-29 The TCP/IP tab of the process' Properties dialog box.

On Windows XP, this page includes a Stack button that opens a dialog box that shows the stack of the thread that opened the selected endpoint at the time of the open. (See Figure 3-30.) This can be useful for identifying the purpose of endpoints in the System process and in Svchost processes because the stack will include the name of the driver or service that is responsible for the endpoint.

FIGURE 3-30 The TCP/IP tab on Windows XP and the Thread Stack dialog box.

Security Tab

The process token defines the security context for the process: the user principal the process is running as, the groups that the user is a member of, and systemwide privileges that the account has. The Security tab (shown in Figure 3-31) displays these details, as well as whether User Account Control file and registry virtualization is enabled for the process, and the ID of the terminal services session in which the process is running. Selecting a group in the Group list displays its Security Identifier (SID) below the list box.

FIGURE 3-31 The Security tab of the process' Properties dialog box.

In most circumstances, particularly with desktop applications, access checks are performed with the process token, or in some cases with a thread token derived from the process token and that can never have more rights than the process token. The information on the Security tab can help explain the success or failure of operations.

Services and server applications can impersonate the security context of a different user when performing actions on behalf of that user. Impersonation is implemented by associating a copy of the other user's token with a thread within the process. During impersonation, access checks are performed with the thread token, so in these cases the process token might not be applicable. The dialog box does not show thread tokens.

I won't go into a detailed description of token contents here, but I would like to point out a few helpful tips and clear up some common misunderstandings:

- In practice, a group that has the Deny flag set can be considered effectively equivalent to not being present in the token at all. With User Account Control, powerful groups such as Administrators are marked Deny-Only except in elevated processes. The Deny flag indicates that if an object has an access-allowed access control entry (ACE) for Administrators in its permissions, that entry is ignored, but if it has an access-denied ACE for Administrators (not common), the access is denied.

- A privilege that is marked Disabled is not at all the same as the privilege not being present. If a privilege is in the token, the program can enable the privilege and then use it. If the privilege is not present, the process cannot acquire it. It's also important to note that several privileges are considered administrator-equivalent in Windows Vista and newer. Windows never allows these privileges to appear in a standard user token.

- If a domain-joined computer cannot contact a domain controller and has not cached the results of previous SID-to-name lookups, it cannot translate the SIDs for token groups into the group names. In this case, Procexp will display the SIDs.

- The group called Logon SID is based on a random number generated at the time the user logged on. One of its uses is to grant access to terminal server session-specific resources. Logon SIDs always begin with S-1-5-5-.

The Permissions button displays the security descriptor for the process object itself—that is, who can perform which actions on the process.

Environment Tab

The Environment tab lists the process' environment variables and their corresponding values. Processes usually inherit their environment variables from their parent process, and very often, the environment blocks of all processes will be substantially equivalent. However, there can be exceptions:

- A parent process can specify a different set of environment variables for a child process.

- Each process can add, delete, or modify its own environment variables.

- When a message is broadcast alerting running processes that the environment variable configuration for the system has changed, not all processes receive the notification (particularly console programs), and not all processes will update their own environment block with the new settings.

Strings Tab

The Strings tab of the process' Properties dialog box (shown in Figure 3-32) shows all sequences of three or more printable characters found in the image file of the process. If the Image radio button is selected, strings are read from the image file on disk. If the Memory radio button is selected, strings are read from the memory range in which the executable file is mapped. Note that it does not inspect all committed memory in the process' virtual address space—only the region where the executable is mapped. Image and memory strings can be different when an image is decompressed, or they can decrypted when loaded into memory. Memory strings can also include dynamically constructed data areas of the image's memory range.

> **Note** In computer programming, the term "string" refers to a data structure consisting of a sequence of characters, usually representing human-readable text.

FIGURE 3-32 The Strings tab of the process' Properties dialog box.

Click the Save button to save the displayed strings to a text file. To compare image and memory strings, save the image and memory strings to separate files and then identify the differences with a text-comparison utility.

To search for specific text in the strings list, click the Find button to display the standard Find dialog box. To search for additional occurrences of the same text, simply press F3 or click Find and Find Next again—the search continues from the currently selected row.

Services Tab

Windows services run in (usually noninteractive) processes that can be configured to start independently of any user logging on and that are controlled through a standard interface with the Service Control Manager. Multiple services can be configured to share a single process. A common example of this can be seen in Svchost.exe, which is specifically designed to host multiple services implemented in separate DLLs.

If the selected process hosts one or more services, the process' Properties dialog box adds a Services tab, as shown in Figure 3-33. Its list box lists the internal and display names for each service, and for services hosted within a Svchost.exe process, the path to the DLL that implements the service. Selecting a service in the list displays its description below the list box.

FIGURE 3-33 The Services tab of the process' Properties dialog box.

Individual services can be configured to allow or not allow stop or pause/resume operations. Procexp enables Stop, Pause, and Resume buttons if the selected service allows those operations.

The Permissions button displays the security editor dialog box for the service, and it lets you view or permanently change the permissions on the service. Specific rights for services include Start, Stop, Pause/Resume, Query Status, Query Config, Change Config, Interrogate, Enumerate Dependents, User-Defined Control, and the standard Read Permissions, Change Permissions, and Change Owner.

> **Warning** Granting any non-administrator Write permission or the Change Config, Change Permissions, or Change Owner specific rights for any service makes it very easy for that user to take full administrative control over the computer.

.NET Tabs

If the selected process uses the .NET Framework, Procexp adds up to two .NET tabs to the process' Properties dialog box. The .NET Performance tab (shown in Figure 3-34) lists the AppDomains in the process and displays data from nine sets of .NET performance counters. Select a performance object from the drop-down list (for example, .NET CLR Data, Exceptions, Interop, Memory, and Security), and the current counters for that object are displayed in the list below.

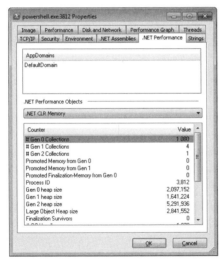

FIGURE 3-34 The .NET Performance tab of the process' Properties dialog box.

When Procexp runs with administrative rights on Windows Vista and newer, the .NET Assemblies tab (shown in Figure 3-35) displays all the AppDomains in the process, with the names of the assemblies loaded in each listed in a tree view. To the right of each assembly name, Procexp shows the flags and the full path to the assembly's executable image. Procexp uses undocumented .NET ETW events to obtain this information.

FIGURE 3-35 The .NET Assemblies tab of the process' Properties dialog box.

Job Tab

If the selected process is associated with a job, Procexp adds a Job tab to the process' Properties dialog box. The tab displays the name of the job if it has one, lists the processes associated with the job, and lists any limits that the job enforces. In Figure 3-36, a WMI host provider process is associated with a job that also includes another WMI host process. The job limits each process to 512 MB of committed memory, limits the entire job to a maximum of 1 GB of committed memory, and limits the job to a maximum of 32 active processes at a time.

FIGURE 3-36 The Job tab of the process' Properties dialog box.

Thread Details

As mentioned earlier, a process doesn't actually run code itself, but is a container for a set of resources, including a virtual address space, one or more mapped file images containing code to execute, and one or more threads of execution. A thread is the entity that actually runs code: its resources include a call stack and an instruction pointer that identifies the next executable instruction. (For more information, see the "Call Stacks and Symbols" section in Chapter 2.)

The Threads tab of the process' Properties dialog box (shown in Figure 3-37) displays detailed information about each thread in the current process, with the following information appearing in the list box in the top area of the dialog box:

- **TID**   The system-assigned, unique thread identifier. While a thread identifier can be reused at some point after the thread has exited, a TID is only ever associated with one thread on the system at a time.

- **CPU**   The percentage of total CPU time that the thread was executing during the previous refresh cycle. Note that because a thread can consume at most 100 percent of a single logical CPU, this number cannot exceed 50 percent on a two-CPU system, 25 percent on a four-CPU system, and so on.

- **Cycles Delta or CSwitch Delta**   If on Windows Vista or newer and Procexp is running in a context that gives it full control over the process, this column displays CPU Cycles Delta; otherwise, it displays the Context Switch Delta, even for protected processes. Cycles Delta is the number of processor cycles consumed by the thread since the previous update; Context Switch Delta is the number of times that the thread has been given control and has begun executing since the previous update.

- **Service**   This column appears on Windows Vista and newer for processes hosting one or more services, showing which service is associated with each thread. Windows tags the threads of service processes to associate threads and TCP/IP endpoints with their owning service.

- **Start Address**   The symbolic name associated with the program-specified location in the process' virtual memory where the thread began executing. The name is reported in module!function format. (Refer to the "Call Stacks and Symbols" section of Chapter 2 for information about how to configure and interpret symbols.) If Procexp is configured to use a symbol server, displaying this tab might introduce a lag as required symbols are downloaded. An indicator appears above the list box when this is happening.

FIGURE 3-37 The Threads tab of the Properties dialog box.

By default, the list is sorted by CPU time in descending order. Click on any column header to change the sort order. Columns can be resized but cannot be reordered.

Selecting a row in the list box displays more detail about that thread in the lower area of the Threads tab: when the thread started; how much CPU time it has consumed in kernel mode and in user mode; how many context switches and CPU cycles it has consumed; its base priority and dynamic priority; and on Windows Vista and newer, its I/O priority, memory priority, and ideal processor. Clicking the Permissions button displays the security descriptor for the thread—that is, who can perform which actions on the thread. Although this interface allows you to modify permissions on the thread, actually making changes is not advised and will usually lead to unpredictable results.

For the System Idle Process, the list box enumerates processors rather than threads. The processor number is shown instead of the Thread ID, and the CPU time represents the percentage of time the CPU spent idle during the refresh interval. When you select one of the processors in the list, the Kernel Time shown below the list box reports the total amount of idle time for that CPU.

Clicking the Module button displays a standard file properties dialog box for the EXE or DLL name in the selected row.

The Stack button displays the call stack for the selected thread, as shown in Figure 3-38. The start address is the bottom-most item in the stack, and the current location of the thread is at the top. The Copy button in the Stack dialog box copies the currently selected symbolic name in the stack to the clipboard. You can select multiple rows in the standard ways, such as holding Shift and pressing the down arrow key. (For more information, see the "Call Stacks and Symbols" section of Chapter 2,.)

FIGURE 3-38 Call stack for a thread.

Finally, the Kill and Suspend buttons allow you to terminate or suspend the selected thread. Unless you are intimately familiar with what the threads are running (for example, you wrote the program), it is almost always a bad idea to terminate or suspend a single thread within a process.

Verifying Image Signatures

The version resource can include the Company Name, Description, and Copyright fields, and other publisher information. However, by itself it provides no assurance of authenticity. Anyone can create a program and put "Microsoft" in the Company Name field. A digital signature associated with the file can help assure that the file came from the publisher and has not been modified since.

Procexp can verify whether executable files and DLLs in the processes it inspects have valid digital signatures. By default, verification is performed only on demand. The Image tab of both the process' Properties and DLL Properties dialog boxes include a Verify button that attempts to verify the authenticity and integrity of the executable image or DLL file. You can also opt to verify the signatures for all files automatically by selecting Verify Image Signatures on the Options menu. In addition to being displayed on those Properties dialog boxes, image verification status can also be seen by selecting the Verified Signer column for display in the main process list and in DLL view.

If the signature on the selected file has been verified, the verification status displays (Verified) and the subject name on the signing certificate. If signature verification has not been attempted (or if the selected file is not an executable file type), the field is blank or displays (Not verified) with the company name from the file's version resource. If the file is not signed or a signature check has failed, the status shows (Unable to verify) with the company name.

Note that the name on the signing certificate and the Company Name version resource might not be identical. For example, most executable files that ship as part of Windows have "Microsoft Corporation" as the company name but are signed with a "Microsoft Windows" certificate.

Some reasons that signature verification can fail include

- The file has not been signed.

- The file has been modified since its signing.

- The signing certificate does not derive from a root certificate authority that is trusted on the computer. (This can be a frequent occurrence if Automatic Root Certificates Update is disabled through group policy.)

- The signing certificate has been revoked.

System Information

Procexp's System Information dialog box, shown in Figure 3-39, is like Task Manager's Performance tab, but with much more information. To display it, press Ctrl+I or click any of the minigraphs in the main window toolbar.

FIGURE 3-39 The Summary tab of the System Information dialog box.

The Summary tab of the dialog box features several pairs of graphs representing system-wide metrics that are shown in more detail on the CPU, Memory, and I/O tabs (shown in Figures 3-40, 3-41, and 3-42, respectively). The left of each pair shows the current level in graphical and numeric form. The wider graph to its right shows recent history; the wider the dialog box is, the more history it can display. Moving the mouse over the history graphs displays a tooltip containing the time of day represented at that point in the graph, along with the metrics at that point in text format. For the CPU Usage and I/O graphs, the tooltip also indicates which process was consuming the most of that resource at that point in time. Clicking on any of the graphs freezes the tooltip at that point; even though the graphs might continue to update, the content in the tooltip doesn't change until you move the mouse.

In the CPU Usage graphs, the red area displays the percentage of time spent executing in kernel mode; the area under the green line represents total CPU utilization as a percentage. If the computer has multiple logical CPUs, selecting the Show One Graph Per CPU check box in the lower left of the CPU tab splits the CPU Usage History graph on that tab into separate per-CPU graphs. The CPU graphs are always scaled against a 100 percent peak. Note that if there are multiple graphs for CPUs, the CPU Usage tooltip will show the process with the highest *systemwide* CPU utilization at that moment; Procexp does not track which process consumed the most processor time on a particular CPU. Note also that when showing per-CPU graphs, Procexp must use timer-based usage metrics because per-CPU, cycle-based data is not tracked by Windows. This can result in the per-CPU graph showing different usage than the single-graph view and what the main Procexp window shows.

The lower area of the CPU tab shows the systemwide total numbers of open object handles, threads, and processes, and the number of CPU context switches, interrupts, and DPCs since the previous data refresh.

FIGURE 3-40 The CPU tab of the System Information dialog box.

The Memory tab shows the Commit and Physical Memory graphs. In the Commit graphs, the area under the yellow line indicates the commit charge—the total amount of private bytes committed across all processes, plus paged pool. The graph is scaled against the commit limit—the maximum amount of private bytes that can be committed without increasing pagefile size. The graph shows a series of snapshots captured at each update, and it does not show what happens between updates. For example, if the commit charge is 1.0 GB when Procexp performs an update and a process then allocates and commits 1.5 GB of memory and then releases it before Procexp updates again, the graph will show a steady 1.0 GB with no spike. The Physical Memory graphs show the amount of physical RAM that is in use by the system. It is scaled to the amount of physical memory installed on the computer and

available to Windows. Similarly to commit charge, the physical memory graph shows a sequence of snapshots and does not report transient changes that occur between updates.

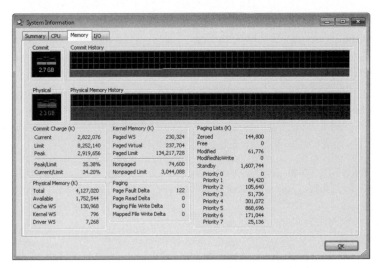

FIGURE 3-41 The Memory tab of the System Information dialog box.

The lower part of the Memory tab shows a number of memory-related metrics:

- **Commit Charge (K)**   The current commit charge, the limit at which no more private
  bytes can be allocated without increasing pagefile size, and the peak commit charge
  incurred on the system since its last boot. This group also shows the percentage of
  peak commit vs. the limit and the current charge vs. the limit.

- **Physical Memory (K)**   Total physical memory available to Windows in KB, available
  RAM that is not in use, and the sizes of the cache, kernel, and driver working sets.

- **Kernel Memory (K)**   Paged WS is the amount of paged pool in KB that is present in
  RAM. Paged Virtual is the total amount of allocated paged pool, including bytes that
  have been swapped out to the pagefile. Paged Limit is the maximum amount of paged
  pool that the system will allow to be allocated. Nonpaged is the amount of allocated
  nonpaged pool, in KB; Nonpaged Limit is the maximum amount of nonpaged pool that
  can be allocated. Procexp requires administrative rights and symbols to be correctly
  configured in order to display Paged Limit and Nonpaged Limit.

- **Paging**   The number of page faults since the previous data refresh, the number of
  paging I/O reads to a mapped file or the paging file, the number of writes to the
  paging file, and the number of writes to mapped files.

- **Paging Lists (K)**   This column of items appears only on Windows Vista and newer.
  It shows the amount of memory in KB in the various page lists maintained by the
  memory manager.

The I/O tab shows I/O Bytes and, if Procexp is running with administrative rights, Network Bytes and Disk Bytes. I/O Bytes represents the amount of file and device I/O throughput, Network Bytes represents network I/O, and Disk Bytes represents I/O throughput to local disks. All three are scaled against their peak levels since Procexp started monitoring them. The pink areas represent write traffic, while the light blue indicates total I/O bytes since the previous update. In contrast to the commit charge graph, at each update the I/O graphs show the number of bytes since the previous update. If you pause updating for a while, the next update will include all the I/O traffic that occurred while Procexp was paused. This will likely appear as spikes and possibly change the measured peaks, and thus the graph scales.

FIGURE 3-42 The I/O tab of the System Information dialog box.

The lower part of the I/O tab shows the number of I/O and Disk Read, Write, and Other operations and Network Receive, Send, and Other operations since the previous data refresh, and the number of bytes involved in those operations.

Display Options

In addition to extensive customizing of displayed content, Procexp provides a handful of display options not already described in this chapter:

- **Hide When Minimized**   When this option is selected from the Options menu, Procexp displays only a notification area icon when minimized and does not display a taskbar icon. Also, clicking its standard Close icon in the upper right corner of the title bar minimizes rather than exits Procexp. (Task Manager used to behave this way.)

- **Allow Only One Instance**   When Procexp starts after this option has been selected from the Options menu, Procexp checks whether another instance of Procexp is already running on the same desktop. If so, the new instance exits after trying to bring the previous instance to the foreground.

- **Always On Top**   When this option is selected from the Options menu, Procexp remains above all other windows on the desktop (with the possible exception of other windows marked "always on top").

- **Font**   This item on the Options menu lets you select a different font for the main window and the lower pane, and many dialog box elements of Procexp.

- **Opacity**   The Opacity submenu on the View menu lets you set the transparency level of Procexp's main window.

- **Scroll To New Processes**   When this option is selected from the View menu, Procexp scrolls the process list when a new process starts to bring the new process into view.

- **Show Processes From All Users**   This option appears in the View menu and is selected by default. When this option is selected, the process list includes all processes running on the computer. When this check box is cleared, the process list shows only processes running under the same account as Procexp. The highlight color for "own processes" is not used in that case. Task Manager has a similar but not identical feature. The distinction that Task Manager's Show Processes From All Users option makes is between processes running in the same terminal session vs. all sessions. Task Manager's option also requires administrative rights.

Procexp as a Task Manager Replacement

Because Procexp provides so much more useful information than Task Manager, you might well find yourself using Procexp exclusively and never using Task Manager again. In fact, Procexp provides an option to do just that. After you select Replace Task Manager in the Options menu, Windows will start Procexp whenever TaskMgr.exe is launched—no matter how it is launched. If you right-click on the taskbar and choose Start Task Manager, Procexp will start instead. If you press Ctrl+Shift+Esc, Procexp will start.

A few things to note about the Replace Task Manager option:

- This is a global setting that affects all users on the computer. If you have Procexp.exe in a location where another user has no access, that user will not be able to run Procexp or Task Manager.

- Selecting this option requires administrative rights.

- This option does not modify or delete Taskmgr.exe in the System32 folder. Instead, it uses Image File Execution Options to point to Procexp.exe when Taskmgr.exe is started.

- To restore the ability to run Task Manager, select Restore Task Manager in the Options menu. (Restore Task Manager appears in the menu when Task Manager has been replaced.)

Task Manager includes a few other capabilities that have also been added to Procexp, and of course Procexp builds on those as well.

Creating Processes from Procexp

Task Manager offers File, Run to start a new process. Procexp also offers File, Run, as well as the following other choices on the File menu to start the new process with elevated or diminished rights:

- On Windows Vista or newer, if Procexp is not running elevated, Run As Administrator requests elevation to start the new process.

- On Windows XP, Runas lets you start the new process with any other user account for which you have credentials.

- Run As Limited User starts the new process with reduced rights. On Windows Vista and newer, this starts the process at Low integrity level. On Windows XP and Windows Server 2003, the new process runs with a token with most privileges removed and powerful groups marked Deny-Only. If Procexp has administrative rights, the new process is approximately equivalent to the same user account running as a standard user. If Procexp is running as a standard user, the new process runs in an even more constrained context.

Other User Sessions

Task Manager's Users tab lets you see whether other users have interactive sessions on the same computer. With administrative rights, you can send a message that appears on that user's desktop, disconnect that user's session, or log the user off. Procexp offers those options on its Users menu, and it adds a Properties dialog box that shows the session ID, state of the session, and if it is active, the name and IP address of the remote connection's source, and the display resolution that the remote desktop is displaying.

Miscellaneous Features

Here are a few topics that don't seem to fit anywhere else.

Shutdown Options

The File, Shutdown submenu lets you log off, shut down, lock, or restart the computer. Hibernate and Stand By are also offered if the system supports those options.

Command-Line Switches

Table 3-1 describes Procexp's command-line options.

TABLE 3-1 Command-Line Options

Option	Description
/e	On Vista or newer, requests UAC elevation when Procexp is started.
/t	Start Procexp minimized and visible only in the notification area (the "tray").
/p:r /p:h /p:n /p:l	Sets the initial process priority for Procexp: Realtime, High, Normal, or Low. Procexp's default level is High if no priority is specified.
/s:*PID*	Selects the process identified by process identifier PID, which must be specified in decimal. For example: **Procexp.exe /s:520**

Restoring Procexp Defaults

Procexp stores all its configuration settings in the registry in "HKEY_CURRENT_USER\ Software\Sysinternals\Process Explorer". The simplest way to restore all Procexp configuration settings to their defaults is to close Procexp, delete the registry key, and then start Procexp again.

Keyboard Shortcut Reference

Keyboard shortcuts used by Procexp are shown in Table 3-2.

TABLE 3-2 Procexp Keyboard Shortcuts

Key Combination	Description
Ctrl+A	Save displayed data to a new file (File, Save As).
Ctrl+C	Copy the current row from the main window or lower pane.
Ctrl+D	Display DLL view.
Ctrl+F	Find the handle or DLL.
Ctrl+H	Display Handle view.
Ctrl+I	Display the System Information dialog box.
Ctrl+L	Display/hide the lower pane
Ctrl+M	Search online.

Key Combination	Description
Ctrl+R	Start a new process (File, Run).
Ctrl+S	Save the displayed data to a file (File, Save).
Ctrl+T	Show the process list in tree view (View, Show Process Tree).
Ctrl+1, Ctrl+2, and so on	Load the first column set, second column set, and so on.
Space	Pause/resume automatic updating.
Del	Kill the selected process.
Shift+Del	Kill the process tree—Selected process and its descendants.
F1	Display Help.
F5	Refresh now—Update displayed data.

Chapter 4
Process Monitor

David Solomon, my *Windows Internals* co-author, was hired to deliver a Microsoft Windows internals class for kernel-support engineers at a major Windows original equipment manufacturer (OEM). A couple of months before the class, the company asked if he would integrate one of its internal kernel-analysis tools into the training. Dave thought that whatever tool they had should be easy enough to learn and he charges a lot of money, so he agreed.

Of course, Dave waited until the flight the night before to even bother looking at the tool. After watching a few episodes of *Star Trek* on his laptop, he decided to take a break and launched the tool, only to be greeted with an error message: "This utility requires *[major Windows OEM]* hardware." He was using a different vendor's laptop, so his heart stopped. How was he going to show up in the morning and admit that he discovered just a few hours earlier that he couldn't run the tool?

He started to panic, breaking out into a sweat and calling the flight attendant to bring him a stiff drink (actually, refill it since he had enjoyed a few while watching *Star Trek*). She came back to his seat a few minutes later, saw that he was clearly flustered and in distress, and asked whether there was anything she could do to help. Dave, despondent and not expecting her to understand anything he was saying, pointed at the screen and explained his predicament. She paused for a second thinking about it and then asked, "Have you tried running Process Monitor?"

As this apocryphal story suggests, Process Monitor (Procmon) is the first utility that many people turn to when diagnosing computer problems. It is also often the last utility they use, as Procmon frequently pinpoints the source of their troubles. The majority of the "Case Of" troubleshooting stories I receive from users can be summarized as, "We had a mysterious problem; we ran Procmon; we found the cause of the problem."

Process Explorer, described in Chapter 3, is a great tool for observing the processes on a system: how much CPU and memory they are consuming, what DLLs they have loaded, what system objects they are using, the security context each is running under, and so forth. Procmon shows you a different view of system activity. Where Procexp is essentially a moving snapshot of the system, Procmon is an advanced logging tool that captures detailed information about registry, file, process/thread, and network activity. While Procexp can tell you that a process has an open handle to a particular file, Procmon can tell you what low-level operations the process is performing on that file, when they occurred, how long they took, whether they succeeded or why they failed, what the full call stack is (the trail of code leading to the operation), and more.

Because millions of operations can occur in a short amount of time, Procmon provides powerful and flexible filtering and highlighting capabilities so that you can find the events of interest to you quickly. Procmon can be scripted from batch files with command-line parameters, and its data can be saved to a file that can be viewed and analyzed on another system at a later time. In other words, it isn't terribly hard to get a novice user at a remote location to capture a Procmon trace and send it to you so that you can solve his or her problem.

Procmon was first released in 2006 and replaces Filemon and Regmon, two of the original Sysinternals tools. Filemon captured information about file system activity; Regmon did the same for the registry. Both tools suffered from diminishing performance as they collected more data, and their filtering capabilities were limited. In addition, a filter in effect during data collection caused filtered data never to be captured; a filter applied to collected data permanently deleted those records. Procmon was written from the ground up and provides a unified view of all file, registry, and process/thread activity (and more), capturing far more detail and scaling much better than Filemon and Regmon did, with much lower performance impact. Procmon also offers boot-time logging, nondestructive filtering, a log file format that retains all captured data, an API for injecting debug output into the capture, and much more. If you are still using Filemon and Regmon out of habit, stop! Filemon and Regmon remained on the Sysinternals site to support legacy systems that did not meet the minimum requirements for Procmon, but as those versions of Windows have long been out of support, Filemon and Regmon have been retired and are no longer available.

Procmon runs on x86 and x64 versions of Windows XP and newer, and Windows Server 2003 and newer.

Getting Started with Procmon

Because it loads a kernel driver, Procmon requires administrative rights to capture events, including the Load and Unload Device Drivers privilege. On Windows Vista and newer, Windows automatically prompts for User Account Control (UAC) elevation if you start Procmon from a nonelevated process such as Explorer. On Windows XP or Windows Server 2003, you need to be logged in as an administrator or use RunAs with an administrator account. See the "Administrative Rights" section in Chapter 2, "Windows Core Concepts," for more information.

 Note Procmon does not require administrative rights to open an existing log file with the **/OpenLog** command-line option.

The easiest way to get started with Procmon is just to run it. The Process Monitor window shown in Figure 4-1 will appear and immediately begin filling up with data. Each row in the table represents one low-level event that has occurred on your system. Although you can customize which columns appear in the table and in what order, the default column set includes the time of day, the process name and ID, the operation (with an icon identifying the type of operation, such as file system, registry, and so forth), the path of the object operated on (if applicable), the result of the operation, and additional details.

FIGURE 4-1 Process Monitor.

Among other things, the status bar shows how many events have been captured. This number will rapidly increase until you stop capturing events. To toggle the capture on and off, press Ctrl+E or click the Capture icon in the toolbar.

To clear the display of all captured events, press Ctrl+X or click the Clear icon in the toolbar.

Events are added to the end of the list as they occur. Procmon's Autoscroll feature (off by default) scrolls the display as new events are added so that the most recent addition is visible. To toggle Autoscroll on and off, press Ctrl+A or click the Autoscroll icon in the toolbar.

Display Options

You can keep Procmon visible when it doesn't have focus by checking Always On Top in the Options menu.

Choose Font on the Options menu to change the font that Procmon uses in the main window and in other tables such as the filter and highlight dialog boxes, event properties Stack tab, and the Trace Summary dialog boxes.

Events

Table 4-1 describes the types of events Procmon captures.

TABLE 4-1 Event Types

Icon	Event	Description
	Registry	Registry operations, such as creating, enumerating, querying, and deleting keys and values.
	File System	Operations on local storage and remote file systems, including file systems or devices added while Procmon was running.
	Network	UDP and TCP- network activity, including source and destination addresses (but not the actual data that was transmitted or received). Procmon can be configured to resolve network addresses to network names, or just show the IP addresses. The option to Show Resolved Network Addresses is on the Options menu. You can also toggle it by pressing Ctrl+N.
	Process	Process and thread events such as process creation by a parent process, process start, thread create, thread exit, process exit, and the loading of executable images and data files into the process' address space. (Note that Procmon does not log the unloading of these images.)
	Profiling	Generates and logs an event for every process and thread on the system, capturing the kernel and user time charged, memory use, and context switches since the previous profiling event. Process profiling events are always captured. By default, thread profiling events are not captured. Debug output profiling, described later, also falls under this event type.

You can toggle the displaying of each of these event types with the five buttons on the right side of the Procmon toolbar. These buttons are described in the "Filtering and Highlighting" section later in this chapter.

> **Tip** The Load Image event can help troubleshoot program start failures. If a program fails to start, identifying the last DLLs that loaded often provides clues to the root cause. For example, there might be a bug in the DLL that triggers an access violation; it might be triggering a loader lock issue or hanging the process at that point, or it might have an unresolved dependency on another DLL. In the last case, the Load Image event will typically be followed by File System events searching for the missing DLL.

Understanding the Column Display Defaults

Procmon displays event data in columns that you can customize. The default set of columns includes

- **Time of Day**   The time of day when the event occurred. The time shows fractional seconds out to seven decimal places, but the actual resolution depends on the processor's high-resolution timer, the precision of which is system dependent.

Procmon captures UTC time, but displays it in the time zone of the computer on which it is rendered. For example, if a log is captured at 9:00 A.M. Eastern Time (UTC5), the time will appear as 6:00 A.M. when the log is viewed on a system configured for the Pacific time zone.

- **Process Name**   The name of the process performing the operation, along with an icon from the process' executable file.

- **PID**   The process ID of the process.

- **Operation**   The name of the low-level operation being logged, along with an icon representing the event type (registry, file system, network, process, or profiling).

- **Path**   If applicable, the path of the object being operated on. Examples of paths include: a registry path beginning with the well-known hive name, a file system path beginning with a drive letter or UNC path, or source and destination network addresses and ports. Note that at the Win32 level, HKEY_CLASSES_ROOT is a merged view of HKLM\Software\Classes and HKCU\Software\Classes. For registry paths, the display of "HKCR" is a synonym for HKLM\Software\Classes; when the per-user portion of HKCR is accessed, the full HKCU or HKU path will be shown. Also, HKCU is a synonym for the HKEY_USERS hive of the account running Procmon. If Procmon is running under a different account from a process of interest, that process accessing its HKCU will appear in the display as HKU*{user SID}*.

- **Result**   The result of the operation. Common result codes include SUCCESS, ACCESS DENIED, NAME NOT FOUND, END OF FILE, and the frequently misunderstood BUFFER OVERFLOW. See the "Result = BUFFER OVERFLOW" sidebar for an explanation of that benign but scary-sounding result code and Table 4-2 for descriptions of other common result codes.

- **Detail**   Additional operation-specific information about the event, such as desired access when first opening an object; data size, type, and content when reading a registry value; or data length of a network send or receive. Some file system operations include the file attribute codes that are listed in Table 4-3.

Result = BUFFER OVERFLOW

With the rise of Internet-based attacks, the term "buffer overflow" became synonymous with malicious software taking unauthorized control over a remote computer. In that context, a buffer overflow occurs when a program copies more data into a memory buffer than the program was designed to accommodate, leading to the overwriting of program logic and the execution of code of the attacker's choosing. It is therefore not surprising that new Procmon users become alarmed when they see BUFFER OVERFLOW in the Result column. There's no need for concern, though.

As an NTSTATUS result code, STATUS_BUFFER_OVERFLOW occurs when a program requests variable-length information, such as data from a registry value, but doesn't provide a large enough buffer to receive the information because it doesn't know the actual data size in advance. The system will tell the program how large a buffer is required and might copy as much data as it can into the buffer, but it will not actually overflow the buffer. One typical coding pattern is that after a BUFFER OVERLOW result is received, the program then allocates a large enough buffer and requests the same data again—this time resulting in SUCCESS.

TABLE 4-2 Common Result Codes and Their Meanings

Result Code	Description
SUCCESS	The operation succeeded.
ACCESS DENIED	The operation failed because the security descriptor on the object does not grant the rights to the caller that the caller requested. The failure might also be the result of a file being marked as read-only. This result code is frequently a red flag when troubleshooting.
SHARING VIOLATION	The operation failed because the object is already opened and does not allow the sharing mode that the caller requested.
NAME COLLISION	The caller tried to create an object that already exists.
NAME NOT FOUND PATH NOT FOUND NO SUCH FILE	The caller tried to open an object that doesn't exist. One scenario in which these result codes can arise is when a DLL load routine looks in various directories as part of the DLL search process.
NAME INVALID	The caller requested an object with an invalid name—for example, C:\Windows\"regedit.exe".
NO MORE ENTRIES NO MORE FILES	The caller has finished enumerating the contents of a folder or registry key.
END OF FILE	The caller has read to the end of a file.
BUFFER TOO SMALL	Essentially the same as BUFFER OVERFLOW. It's rarely significant when troubleshooting.
REPARSE	The caller has requested an object that links to another object. For example, HKLM\System\CurrentControlSet might redirect to HKLM\System\ControlSet001.
NOT REPARSE POINT	The requested object does not link to another object.
FAST IO DISALLOWED	Indicates that a low-level optimized mechanism is not available for the requested file system object. It's rarely significant in troubleshooting.
FILE LOCKED WITH ONLY READERS	Indicates that a file or file mapping was locked and that all users of the file can only read from it.
FILE LOCKED WITH WRITERS	Indicates that a file or file mapping was locked and that at least one user of the file can write to it.
IS DIRECTORY	The requested object is a file system folder.

Result Code	Description
INVALID DEVICE REQUEST	The specified request is not a valid operation for the target device.
INVALID PARAMETER	An invalid parameter was passed to a service or function.
NOT GRANTED	A requested file lock cannot be granted because of other existing locks.
CANCELLED	An I/O request was canceled—for example, the monitoring of a file system folder for changes.
BAD NETWORK PATH	The network path cannot be located.
BAD NETWORK NAME	The specified share name cannot be found on the remote server.
MEDIA WRITE PROTECTED	The disk cannot be written to because it is write-protected.
KEY DELETED	Illegal operation attempted on a registry key that has been marked for deletion.
NOT IMPLEMENTED	The requested operation is not implemented.

Customizing the Column Display

Often the information in a column is too long to display within the column. In this case, you can move the mouse pointer over the entry and the full text content of that column appears in a tooltip. You can resize columns by dragging the border lines in the column headers. You can autosize a column to its content by double-clicking the border line to the right of the column title. And you can reorder columns by dragging the column headers.

You can change which columns are displayed by right-clicking the column header row and selecting Select Columns, or by choosing Select Columns from the Options menu. As shown in Figure 4-2, available columns are grouped as Application Details, Event Details, and Process Management.

FIGURE 4-2 Process Monitor Column Selection dialog box.

Application details include static information that is determined at process startup and never change for the life of the process, such as the image path, command line, and architecture.

Event details include information that is specific to an event. In addition to the columns that appear by default, here are some other event details:

- **Sequence Number**   The zero-based row number within the current display.

- **Event Class**   **This can be** Registry, File System, Network, Process, or Profiling.

- **Category**   Where applicable, operation categories are Read, Write, Read Metadata, or Write Metadata.

- **Relative Time**   The time of the operation relative to Procmon's start time or the last time that the Procmon display was cleared.

- **Duration**   How long the operation took, in seconds. For Thread Profiling events, this is the sum of kernel and user time charged to the thread since the previous Thread Profiling event; for Process Profiling events, this value is set to zero. See the "Displaying Profiling Events" section later in this chapter for more information.

Process Management columns include runtime information about the process, such as the following:

- **User Name**   The security principal under which the process is executing.

- **Session ID**   The terminal services session in which the process is running. Services always run in session 0. (See the "Sessions, Window Stations, Desktops, and Window Messages" section of Chapter 2 for more information.)

- **Integrity**   The integrity level of the process performing the operation (Windows Vista and newer).

- **Thread ID**   The ID of the thread performing the operation; also known as the TID, which is how it appears in the column header.

- **Virtualized**   Indicates whether UAC virtualization is enabled for the process performing the operation (Windows Vista and newer). Note that this is unrelated to application virtualization or machine virtualization.

Event Properties Dialog Box

To find more details about an event, double-click the event row to open the Event Properties dialog box. Pressing Ctrl+K opens the Event Properties dialog box with the Stack tab displayed. The Event Properties dialog box is modeless; not only can you continue to work with the main Procmon window, you can have multiple Event Properties dialog boxes open simultaneously. The dialog boxes are also resizable and can even be maximized.

Up and Down arrow buttons, shown in Figure 4-3, allow you to look at the properties of the immediately preceding or next event in the display. If you select the Next Highlighted check box, clicking the arrow buttons shows the properties of the preceding or next item that is highlighted. (Highlighting is described in the "Filtering and Highlighting" section later in this chapter.)

FIGURE 4-3 Navigation buttons in the Event Properties dialog box.

The Copy All button copies the content of the current tab to the clipboard as tab-separated plain text.

Event Tab

The Event tab of the Event Properties dialog box, shown in Figure 4-4, shows the following information for every event: Date and time, TID, event class, operation, result, path, and duration. Below the horizontal line is the operation-specific information that also appears in the Detail column, but it appears here in a more readable form.

TABLE 4-3 File Attribute Codes Used in the Detail Column

File Attribute Code	Meaning
A	A file or directory that is an archive file or directory. Applications typically use this attribute to mark files for backup or removal.
C	A file or directory that is compressed. For a file, all the data in the file is compressed. For a directory, compression is the default for newly created files and subdirectories.
D	The object is a directory, or the object is a device.
E	A file or directory that is encrypted. For a file, all data streams in the file are encrypted. For a directory, encryption is the default for newly created files and subdirectories.
H	The file or directory is hidden. It is not included in an ordinary directory listing.
N	A file that does not have other attributes set. This attribute is valid only when used alone.
NCI	The file or directory is not to be indexed by the content indexing service.
O	The data of a file is not available immediately. This attribute indicates that the file data is physically moved to offline storage. This attribute is used by Remote Storage, which is the hierarchical storage management software.
R	A file that is read-only. Applications can read the file but cannot write to it or delete it. This attribute is not honored on directories.

File Attribute Code	Meaning
RP	A file or directory that has an associated reparse point, or a file that is a symbolic link.
S	A file or directory that the operating system uses a part of, or uses exclusively.
SF	A file that is a sparse file.
T	A file that is being used for temporary storage. File systems avoid writing data back to mass storage if sufficient cache memory is available, because typically, an application deletes a temporary file after the handle is closed. In that scenario, the system can entirely avoid writing the data. Otherwise, the data is written after the handle is closed.

In the Figure 4-4, the operation was an attempted CreateFile operation on a file in the root folder of the C drive that resulted in Access Denied. The details include the desired access. The Disposition line indicates that an existing object would have been opened if the operation had been successful, rather than a new object being created. The ShareMode line indicates that it's not exclusive access and that other processes can open the object for read, write, or delete operations. These details are obviously specific to a CreateFile operation and would not appear for a Load Image operation, for example. (If the text is too wide to fit in the display, that situation can be remedied by resizing or maximizing the dialog box. You can also click Copy All—or right-click within the Details box—click Select All and Copy, and then paste the text elsewhere.)

FIGURE 4-4 The Event tab of the Event Properties dialog box.

Process Tab

The Process tab of the Event Properties dialog box, shown in Figure 4-5, displays detailed information about the process behind the selected event at the time the event occurred.

FIGURE 4-5 The Process tab of the Event Properties dialog box.

The information displayed on the Process tab includes

- Application icon extracted from the process image (or a default icon if the image has none).

- Description, company name, and file version extracted from the version information resource of the image.

- Process name.

- File path to the executable image.

- Command line that was used to start this process.

- Process ID for this process and for the parent process that started this one.

- Terminal services session ID in which this process is running.

- User account under which the process is running.

- Authentication ID (Auth ID) for the process token. The Authentication ID is a locally unique ID (LUID) that identifies the Local Security Authority (LSA) logon session that created the access token that this process is using. (An LUID is a system-generated, 64-bit value guaranteed to be unique during a single boot session on the system on which it was generated.) LogonSessions lists active LSA logon sessions and is described in Chapter 8, "Security Utilities."

- When the process started, and when it ended (if it has).

- Architecture (32-bit or 64-bit executable code).

- Whether UAC file and registry virtualization is enabled for this process (Windows Vista and newer only).

- The integrity level of the process (Windows Vista and newer only).

- The list of modules (executable images) loaded into the process' address space at the time this event occurred. A newly launched process will have an empty list until after some Load Image events load the exe, Ntdll.dll, and other modules.

Stack Tab

The Stack tab of the Event Properties dialog box, shown in Figure 4-6, displays the thread call stack when the event was recorded. The stack can be useful for determining the reason an event took place and the component responsible for the event. See the "Call Stacks and Symbols" section in Chapter 2 to understand what a call stack is and how to configure Procmon to maximize the information you can get from one.

Each row represents one stack frame, with five columns of data:

- **Frame**   Displays the frame number, and a K for a kernel-mode frame or a U for a user-mode frame. (User-mode stack frames are not captured on x64 versions of Windows prior to Windows Vista SP1 and Windows Server 2008.)

- **Module**   The name of the file containing the code being executed in this frame.

- **Location**   The specific location within the module where the code is executing. If symbols are available, the location is expressed as a function name and an offset from the beginning of that function; if source file information is also available, the location will include the path to and the line number within the source file. If symbols are not available and the module has an export table, the location is given as the nearest preceding exported name and an offset from that location. If no symbols or exports are available, the location is expressed as an offset from the base address of the module in memory. See the "Call Stacks and Symbols" section in Chapter 2 for more information.

- **Address**   The address of the code instruction in the virtual address space of the executing process.

- **Path**   The full path of the file identified in the Module column. With the default size of the dialog box, you need to scroll or resize the dialog box to see this column. This can help you verify which version of a DLL is executing.

FIGURE 4-6 The Stack tab of the Event Properties dialog box.

On the Stack tab, you can do the following:

- Click Save to save the stack trace as a comma-separated values (CSV) file.

- Double-click a row in the stack trace to open the Module Properties dialog box. This dialog box displays the name and path of the module in the stack trace, along with the description, file version, and company name extracted from the module's version information resource.

- Select a row and click Search to search online for more information about a symbol or module name in the Location column. Procmon will initiate a search using your default browser and search engine.

- Click the Source button, which is enabled if the symbol information for the selected stack frame includes source file information. The source file (if found at the expected location) is displayed in a new window, with the identified line of source code selected.

Note Symbols need to be configured for Procmon to enable some of these features. You configure them from the Procmon window (shown in Figure 4-1) by choosing Configure Symbols from the Options menu. Refer to the "Configuring Symbols" section in Chapter 2 for details.

Displaying Profiling Events

The four classes of events that Procmon displays by default—registry, file system, network, and process activity—represent operations initiated by processes on the computer. The fifth event class, profiling events, includes artificial events periodically generated by Procmon itself (except for Debug Output Profiling events, described in the "Injecting Debug Output into Procmon Traces" section later in this chapter). Profiling events are not displayed by default, but they can be displayed by toggling the Show Profiling Events icon on the toolbar.

Process Profiling events are generated for every process on the computer once per second. Each event captures the user-mode and kernel-mode CPU time charged to the process since it started, the private bytes currently allocated by the process, and the working set consumed by the process. The Duration attribute for Process Profiling events is fixed at 0.

Unlike with Process Profiling events, the data captured by *Thread Profiling* events is not cumulative. When enabled, Thread Profiling events capture the amount of user-mode and kernel-mode CPU time and the number of context switches since the thread's previous profiling event. The Duration attribute reports the sum of the user-mode and kernel-mode CPU time, and it can be used in a filter rule to help identify CPU spikes. Thread Profiling events are created only for threads that had at least one context switch during the polling interval, not for threads in the Idle process.

Process Profiling events are always generated once per second. Thread Profiling events are not generated by default, but they can be enabled with the Thread Profiling Options dialog box (shown in Figure 4-7), which you access by choosing Profiling Events from the Options menu. When Generate Thread Profiling Events is selected, Procmon generates Thread Profiling events either once per second or ten times per second, according to the period chosen in the Options dialog box.

Important   Enabling Thread Profiling capture is a potentially expensive option that should be used only when necessary.

FIGURE 4-7 The Thread Profiling Options dialog box.

Finding an Event

To find an event in the main Procmon window based on text in the event, open the Procmon Find dialog box by pressing Ctrl+F or clicking the binoculars icon in the toolbar. Enter the text you are looking for, and click Find Next. Procmon will select the next event that contains the search text in any of the displayed columns. Press F3 to repeat the search to find the next matching event. The Find feature can be useful for quickly locating an event while still seeing the context of preceding and following events that could be hidden if you had used a filter. (Filters are discussed in the "Filtering and Highlighting" section.)

Copying Event Data

Press Ctrl+C to copy the selected event data to the clipboard as tab-separated text. Note that you can use standard Windows techniques for selecting multiple items in the list, including Shift+arrow or Shift+click to extend a selection and Ctrl+click to select noncontiguous items. Procmon will dutifully copy text from whichever columns are displayed for the items that are selected.

You can copy the text from a single field by right-clicking the field and selecting Copy "*field-text*" from the context menu. In the example shown in Figure 4-8, choosing the eighth item in the context menu copies the text "HKCR\.exe\OpenWithProgids" to the clipboard.

FIGURE 4-8 Context menu from right-clicking on an event's Path field.

Jumping to a Registry or File Location

To jump to a registry or file location, select a registry or file system event that has a path that exists, and press Ctrl+J. Procmon will launch Regedit (for a registry path) or a new Explorer window (for a file system path) and navigate to the selected path. "Jump to" can also be invoked by clicking the Jump To Object toolbar icon, or choosing Jump To from the event's context menu as shown in Figure 4-8.

Searching Online

You can search online for the process name of an event by selecting the event and choosing Search Online from the Event menu, or by right-clicking the event and choosing Search Online from the context menu as shown in Figure 4-8. Procmon will launch a search using your default browser and search engine. This option can be useful when researching malware or identifying the source of an unrecognized process.

Filtering and Highlighting

Procmon can easily log millions of events in a short amount of time, initiated from dozens of different processes. To help you isolate the events of interest to you, Procmon provides powerful and flexible filtering options to limit what appears in the display, and it provides similar options for highlighting particular events. In the example in Figure 4-9, Procmon is displaying only Access Denied results from Cinmania.exe and highlighting those events in which the Path begins with "C:\Windows\Fonts". The status bar shows that although the log contains 355,859 events, only 63 of those events meet the filter criteria and are displayed. Over 99.9 percent of the captured events are removed from the display.

FIGURE 4-9 Procmon filtering and highlighting example.

Regmon and Filemon had limited filtering capabilities. One of their biggest limitations was that when a filter was applied that removed entries from the display, they were permanently removed and could not be recovered. With Procmon, filtered entries are removed only from the display, not from the underlying data. They can be displayed again simply by changing or removing the filter.

Configuring Filters

You can configure filters based on any event attributes, whether the data appears in a displayed column or not. You can look for an exact match to a value you specify; partial matches including "begins with", "ends with", or "contains"; or "less than" or "more than" comparisons. (See the "Understanding the Column Display Defaults" section earlier in this chapter for descriptions of the attributes you can use in a filter.)

The simplest filters to apply are the Event Class filters exposed in the five buttons on the right side of the toolbar (shown in Figure 4-10), which toggle the display of registry, file system, network, process/thread, and profiling events. When an event class is toggled off, an Exclude filter is added for that event class, hiding all events of that type.

FIGURE 4-10 Event Class toggles in the Procmon toolbar.

Another easy way to modify the filter is with Include Process From Window. This feature lets you set a filter on the PID of the process that owns a particular window. Click and hold the Crosshairs icon in the toolbar, and then drag it over the window you are interested in. Procmon hides itself during this operation and draws a frame around the window the cursor is over. Release the mouse button, and Procmon reappears with the PID of the process that owns the window added to the filter.

The full range of filtering options can be seen in the Process Monitor Filter dialog box (shown in Figure 4-11) by pressing Ctrl+L or clicking the Filter icon in the toolbar. You'll notice that the default filter already has a number of Exclude rules. These will be discussed later in the "Advanced Output" section.

To add a filter rule, choose an attribute from the first drop-down list, the type of test to perform in the second drop-down list, and the value to compare against in the third drop-down combo box. All text comparisons are case-insensitive. When you select an attribute in the first list, the third drop-down combo box will be pre-populated with all the values seen in the current data set. For example, when you choose Process Name, the third drop-down combo box will be pre-populated with all the process names that generated events. (Procmon does not do this for attributes such as Path that can have a very large number of distinct values.) You can also edit the value in this drop-down combo box directly. Choose whether to include matching events or exclude them from the display with the fourth drop-down list in the top row. Click the Add button to add the new filter criteria to the existing filter. When you are done modifying the filter list, click OK or Apply.

To edit or remove a rule from the filter, double-click it or select it and click the Remove button. It will be removed from the list and copied into the rule-editing drop-down menus so that you can easily edit it and re-add it to the list. You can disable an individual rule without permanently removing it by clearing its check box. To enable the rule again, simply select its check box again and click OK or Apply.

To reset the filter to default settings, click the Reset button in the Filter dialog box. You can reset the filter from the Procmon main window by pressing Ctrl+R.

FIGURE 4-11 Process Monitor Filter dialog box.

Procmon ORs together all the filter rules for a particular attribute and ANDs filters for different attributes. For example, if you specify Process Name "include" filters for Notepad.exe and Cmd.exe, and a Path "include" filter for C:\Windows, Procmon displays only events involving C:\Windows that originated from Notepad or Command Prompt. It doesn't show any other events involving other paths or other processes.

Another powerful way to add filter criteria is by right-clicking an event and selecting criteria from the context menu. Figure 4-12 shows just the context menu from Figure 4-8 and illustrates the available choices.

First, the context menu offers quick-filter entries for the value on which you click. For example, the fourth and fifth items in Figure 4-12 show Include and Exclude quick filters for registry path "HKCR\.exe\OpenWithProgids". The Exclude Events Before option hides all events preceding the selected one by adding a rule based on the event's Date & Time attribute; similarly, Exclude Events After hides all events following the selected one. Finally, the Include and Exclude submenus (the second and third items from the bottom) list most available filter attributes. Pick an attribute name from one of these submenus and the corresponding value from the selected event will be added to the filter. You can also add a filter based on the collection of values from multiple events simultaneously: select the events, right-click, and select an attribute name from the Include or Exclude submenu. Doing this configures a filter for all the unique values contained in the selected events.

FIGURE 4-12 Context menu detail from Figure 4-8.

These different methods for configuring a filter can be combined. Let's say you see processes accessing registry keys at and under HKCR\CLSID\{DFEAF541-F3E1-4C24-ACAC-99C30715084A} and you want to filter on that activity. That calls for a Begins With filter on that path. One way to get there without a lot of typing or copy and pasting is to find an event with that key, right-click, and choose Include 'HKCR\CLSID\{DFEAF541-F3E1-4C24-ACAC-99C30715084A}'. That sets a Path Is filter. Press Ctrl+L to open the Filter dialog box, double-click on the new criteria to move it from the list to the rule-editing drop-down menus, change "is" to "begins with," edit the path if needed, click Add, and then click OK.

The Process Tree and Summary dialog boxes, discussed later in this chapter, also offer mechanisms for modifying the current filter.

Procmon remembers the most recent filter you set. The next time you start Procmon after you have set a filter, Procmon will display the Filter dialog box before beginning event capture. This gives you an opportunity to keep, edit, or reset the filter before capturing data. You can bypass this step by running Procmon with the **/Quiet** command-line option. You can automatically clear the filter at startup with the **/NoFilter** command-line option. See the "Automating Procmon: Command-Line Options" section later in this chapter for more information.

Configuring Highlighting

While filtering removes events from the displayed list, highlighting makes selected events visually distinctive. By default, highlighted events appear with a bright blue background. You can change the highlight foreground and background colors by choosing Highlight Colors from the Options menu.

Configuring highlighting is almost identical to configuring filters. The Process Monitor Highlighting dialog box can be displayed by pressing Ctrl+H or by clicking the Highlight icon on the toolbar. The Highlight dialog box works exactly the same way the Filter dialog box does, and the right-click context menu on selected events offers the same options for highlighting as it does for applying filters.

The Event Properties dialog box discussed earlier in this chapter lets you look at the next or previous item in the event list. By selecting the Next Highlighted check box, you can navigate to the next or previous highlighted item instead.

Advanced Output

By default, Procmon hides events that are usually not relevant for application troubleshooting:

- Events originating from Procmon's own activity.
- Events originating from within the System process.
- Profiling events, including the Process Profiling events, which are generated every second.
- Low-level operations whose names begin with IRP_MJ_ (I/O Request Packets, used by Windows drivers for file or device I/O, PnP, power, and other I/O-related functions).
- Low-level operations whose names begin with FASTIO_. These are like an I/O request packet (IRP) except they are used by the I/O system and use the file system driver or cache manager to complete the I/O request.
- Results beginning with "FAST IO," such as "FAST IO DISALLOWED."
- Activity involving the system pagefile.
- NTFS and MFT (Master File Table) internal management

Selecting Advanced Output on the Filter menu removes all these exclusions (except for Profiling events) and displays driver-level names for file system operations. For example, the CreateFile operation in Basic mode appears as IRP_MJ_CREATE when in Advanced mode. Clearing Enable Advanced Output reapplies the exclusions just described and restores Basic-mode operation naming.

When Advanced Output is selected, Reset Filter removes all filter rules except for excluding Profiling events.

You can see all system activity but retain the friendly event names by removing default filters while keeping Advanced Output turned off.

Saving Filters for Later Use

After you configure a filter, you can save it for later use. This lets you reload and apply complex filters quickly or easily switch between different filter sets. You can also export your saved filters and import them onto another system or for another user account.

To save a filter, choose Save Filter from the Filter menu and type a name for it as shown in Figure 4-13. Procmon offers Filter 0, Filter 1, and so on, as defaults. You might want to choose a more descriptive name, like "IE Write operations."

FIGURE 4-13 The Save Filter dialog box.

To load and apply a saved filter, choose it from the Load Filter submenu on the Filter menu. Filters are listed in the menu in alphabetical order. (See Figure 4-14.)

FIGURE 4-14 The Procmon Load Filter menu.

You can rename or delete filters with the Organize Filters dialog box, as shown in Figure 4-15. Choose Organize Filters from the Filter menu. To export a filter, select it in the list, click the Export button, and choose a file location. Procmon uses the *.PMF extension to identify Procmon filter files. To import a filter, click Import and select the exported Procmon filter.

Note that saved and exported filters capture only filter rules. Highlight rules can be saved only by exporting the Procmon configuration (which also includes filter rules). See the "Importing and Exporting Configuration Settings" section later in this chapter for more information, and the "Automating Procmon: Command-Line Options" section for information about loading saved configurations from the command line.

FIGURE 4-15 The Procmon Organize Filters dialog box.

Process Tree

Pressing Ctrl+T or clicking the Process Tree toolbar button displays the Process Tree dialog box shown in Figure 4-16. The Process Tree dialog box displays all the processes that are referenced in the loaded trace in a hierarchy that reflects their parent-child relationships, similar to Procexp's tree view. You can collapse or expand portions of the tree by clicking the plus (+) and minus (–) icons to the left of parent processes in the tree, or selecting those nodes and pressing the left and right arrow keys. Processes that are aligned along the left side of the window have parent processes that have not generated any events in the trace.

FIGURE 4-16 The Process Tree dialog box.

Each process name appears next to its corresponding application icon. The icon is dimmed if the process exited during the trace. To show only processes that were still running at the end of the current trace, set the corresponding check box at the top of the dialog box.

Select a row to display information about the process in the bottom of the dialog box. Information includes the PID, description, image path, command line, start time, stop time (if applicable), company name, and user account under which the process runs. That information is also shown in the table itself, along with a graphical representation of the process' timeline.

The Life Time column shows the timeline of the process relative to the trace or to the boot session, depending on whether the Timelines Cover Displayed Events Only option is selected. With the option selected, a green bar going from edge to edge indicates that the process was running at the time the trace started and was still running when the trace ended. A green bar that begins further to the right (for example, the tree's last visible item in Figure 4-16) indicates the process' relative start time after the trace had begun. A darker green bar indicates a process that exited during the trace, with its extent indicating when during the trace it exited. If the Timelines Cover Displayed Events Only option is not selected, the graphs indicate the process' lifetimes relative to the boot session: a green bar closer to the left edge of the column indicates a process that has been running since system startup or that began shortly after.

In addition to graphically showing the parent-child relationship of processes, including those that have since exited, the Process Tree can help identify unusual conditions, such as short-lived processes being created over and over.

Selecting a process in the tree and clicking the Include Process button adds a PID Is rule to the filter with the selected process' PID. Clicking Include Subtree adds a PID Is rule for the selected process and all its descendants in the tree.

To find an event in the trace associated with a process, select the process in the tree and click Go To Event. Procmon locates and selects the first visible event in the trace in the main Procmon window. Note that filters can prevent a process from having any visible events. For example, a process might not have executed any code during the trace but still appear in the tree because of Process Profiling events, which are normally filtered out of the display.

Saving and Opening Procmon Traces

"Please send me a Procmon log" might be one of the most commonly used phrases by support technicians. The ability to see a detailed log of system activity on a remote computer enables troubleshooting to be performed across firewalls and time zones that would otherwise be much more difficult. And when this capability is combined with the command-line options described later in this chapter, the user receiving the assistance can just run a batch command and doesn't need to be told how to save the log or otherwise interact with Procmon.

Saving Procmon Traces

To save a Procmon trace, press Ctrl+S or click the Save icon on the toolbar to open the Save To File dialog box. (See Figure 4-17.)

FIGURE 4-17 Save To File dialog box.

You can opt to save all events whether they are displayed or not, save only events that are displayed by the current filter (with or without profiling events), or just save events that are selected by the current highlighting rules.

Procmon can save traces to one of three file formats. PML is Procmon's native file format, which preserves all captured data with full fidelity, including stack and module information, so that it can be loaded into Procmon on the same system or a different system. When later viewed on a system properly configured with the Debugging Tools for Windows, the module information saved in the PML file enables the correct symbol and binary files to be downloaded from symbol servers. (Binaries are downloaded in addition to symbols if the computer name from the trace is not the same as that of the current computer.) See the "Configuring Symbols" section of Chapter 2 for more information.

Note that the internal PML file format is different for traces on x86 and x64 versions of Windows. Although x86 captures can be viewed on x86 or x64 systems, logs captured on x64 editions of Windows can be viewed only on an x64 system. The "Opening Saved Procmon Traces" section provides the details.

Another option is to save captured data to a CSV file. CSV files are useful for importing into Microsoft Excel or other data analysis applications, or for performing comparisons using text-file-comparison utilities such as WinDiff or fc.exe. With CSV files, Procmon saves only the text data from the columns selected for display. The first line of the CSV contains the column names. To compare two captures saved as CSV files, make sure to remove columns, such as Time Of Day, that will always be different.

Procmon can also save its data to XML for processing by tools that can parse XML. For example, the following lines of Windows PowerShell script parses a Procmon XML file and outputs a sorted list of all unique module paths loaded from outside of the C:\Windows folder hierarchy:

```
$x = [xml]$(gc logfile.xml)
$x.SelectNodes("//module") |
   ?{ !$_.Path.ToLower().StartsWith("c:\windows\") } |
   %{ $_.Path } |
   sort -Unique
```

Here's the result of that script extracted from a 5-MB XML log file captured on a Virtual PC virtual machine:

```
C:\PROGRA~1\WI4EB4~1\wmpband.dll
C:\Program Files\Common Files\microsoft shared\ink\tiptsf.dll
C:\Program Files\Debugging Tools for Windows\DbgHelp.dll
c:\Program Files\Sysinternals\Procmon.exe
C:\Program Files\Virtual Machine Additions\mrxvpcnp.dll
C:\Program Files\Virtual Machine Additions\VMBACKUP.DLL
C:\Program Files\Virtual Machine Additions\vmsrvc.exe
C:\Program Files\Virtual Machine Additions\vmusrvc.exe
C:\Program Files\Virtual Machine Additions\vpcmap.exe
C:\Program Files\Virtual Machine Additions\VPCShExG.dll
c:\program files\windows defender\MpClient.dll
C:\Program Files\Windows Defender\MpRtMon.DLL
c:\program files\windows defender\mprtplug.dll
c:\program files\windows defender\mpsvc.dll
C:\Program Files\Windows Defender\MSASCui.exe
C:\Program Files\Windows Defender\MsMpRes.dll
C:\Program Files\Windows Media Player\wmpnetwk.exe
C:\Program Files\Windows Media Player\WMPNSCFG.exe
C:\Program Files\Windows Media Player\wmpnssci.dll
C:\Program Files\Windows Sidebar\sidebar.exe
C:\ProgramData\Microsoft\Windows Defender\Definition Updates\{02030721-61CF-400A-86EE-
1A0594D4B35E}\mpengine.dll
```

When saving to XML, you can optionally include stack traces and resolve stack symbols at the time of the save. Note that these options will increase the size of the saved file and the time required to save it. Note also that trying to render large XML files without schemas in Internet Explorer will bring IE to its knees.

Opening Saved Procmon Traces

Procmon running on an x86 system can open only traces captured on an x86 system. Procmon running on an x64 system can open x86 or x64 traces, but it must be in the correct mode for the architecture. To open an x86 trace on x64, Procmon must be started with the **/Run32** command-line option to run the 32-bit version of Procmon. Note that when running in 32-bit mode on x64, Procmon cannot capture events.

If Procmon is already running, open the File Open dialog box by clicking the Open toolbar icon. You can open a Procmon log file from the command line with the **/OpenLog** command line option as follows:

- For opening x86 traces on x64:

  ```
  procmon.exe /run32 /openlog logfile.pml
  ```

- Everyplace else:

  ```
  procmon.exe /openlog logfile.pml
  ```

Each time you run Procmon, it registers a per-user file association for .PML to the current Procmon path with the **/OpenLog** option. So after you have run Procmon one time, you can open a Procmon log file simply by double-clicking it in Explorer. If you run Procmon with the **/Run32** option, that option will also be added to the file association. So if you're analyzing a set of 32-bit logs, you can do so from Explorer. The **/Run32** option will be removed from the association if you later run Procmon without that option.

Procmon does not require administrative rights to open an existing log file, and it won't prompt for elevation on Windows Vista and newer versions when started with the **/OpenLog** option. However, if you later want to capture events, you'll need to restart Procmon with administrative rights.

The log file includes information about the system on which the data was collected, including the computer name, operating system version and whether it is 32-bit or 64-bit, system root path, number of CPUs, and amount of RAM. You can see this in the System Details dialog box (shown in Figure 4-18) on the Tools menu.

FIGURE 4-18 System Details dialog box.

To view symbols in stack traces, the system on which the trace was captured does not need to have debugging tools installed nor symbols configured, but the system on which the trace is viewed must have both. In addition, it must have access to symbol files and binaries for the trace system. For Windows files, the Microsoft public symbol server will usually provide these.

Logging Boot, Post-Logoff, and Shutdown Activity

Up to this point in the chapter, everything that has been described about Procmon assumes you're logged on at an interactive desktop. Procmon also provides ways to monitor system activity when no one has logged on and after users have logged off.

Boot Logging

You can configure Procmon to begin logging system activity from a point very early in the boot process. This is the feature you need if you're diagnosing issues that occur before, during, or in the absence of user logon, such as those involving boot-start device drivers, autostart services, the logon sequence itself, or shell initialization. Boot logging also enables you to diagnose issues that occur during user logoff and system shutdown.

Boot logging is the only Procmon mode that is tolerant of hard resets. Because of this, it can help diagnose system hangs and crashes, including those occurring during startup or shutdown.

When you Enable Boot Logging from the Options menu, Procmon configures its driver to run as a boot start driver that loads very early in the boot sequence at the next system startup, before most other drivers. Procmon's driver will log activity into %windir%\Procmon.PMB and it will continue logging through shutdown or until you run Procmon again. Thus, if you don't run Procmon during a boot session, you'll capture a trace of the entire boot-to-shutdown cycle. As a boot start driver, it remains loaded very late into the shutdown sequence.

After the boot-start driver loads, it changes its startup configuration to be a demand-start driver for subsequent boots. Consequently, when you enable boot logging, it is only for the next boot. To enable boot logging for subsequent boots, you must explicitly enable it again each time.

When you run Procmon, it looks to see whether an unsaved boot log has been generated, either from the current session or from a previous boot session. If Procmon finds one, it asks you whether and where you want to place the processed boot log output file. (See Figure 4-19.) Procmon then opens and displays the saved log. If you do not save the boot log to another location, it will be overwritten the next time you capture a boot-time log.

FIGURE 4-19 Procmon prompts whether and where to save a boot log.

When looking at boot-time activity, remember that the System process is the only process early in a boot and that activity originating from the System process is filtered by default. Choose Advanced Output on the Filter menu to see System process activity.

Note that tracing of network events depends on Event Tracing for Windows (ETW) and is not available in boot logs. Also, Process and Thread Profiling events are not captured during boot logs either. Finally, note that Procmon does not configure its boot logging to run during Safe Mode.

If you configure boot logging and the system crashes early in the boot, you can deactivate the boot logging by choosing the Last Known Good option from the Windows boot menu. Press F8 during Windows startup to access this option.

Keeping Procmon Running After Logoff

Boot logging is the only option Procmon offers to capture events very late in the shutdown sequence. If you need to capture events that occur during or after user logoff but don't need a complete trace of the shutdown, boot logging always remains an option. However, in addition to the post-logoff data you want to capture, you'll end up with a log of the entire boot session from system startup on, which might be far more data than you want. Another option, then, is to start Procmon in a way that survives user logoff.

One way to monitor a user's logoff is to leverage terminal services, using either Fast User Switching or Remote Desktop. With the target user already logged on, start a new session as a different user and start Procmon. Switch back to the original user's session and log off. Return to the second session, and stop capturing events. Set a filter on the Session attribute to see only the events that occurred within the original user's terminal services session.

Another effective way to capture post-logoff activity is to use PsExec with the –s option to run Procmon as System in the same environment in which noninteractive System services run. There are some tricks to this, though, because you won't be able to interact with this instance of Procmon:

- You need to specify a backing file on the command line with **/BackingFile**. Remember that this setting sticks. So if you run Procmon and capture data again as System without specifying a different backing file, you'll overwrite your previous trace.

- You must specify **/AcceptEula** and **/Quiet** on the command line to ensure that Procmon doesn't try to display dialog boxes that cannot be dismissed.

- Procmon must be shut down cleanly. To do this without shutting the system down, you must run **Procmon /Terminate** in the exact same manner as the original command.

See the "Backing Files" and "Automating Procmon: Command-Line Options" sections in this chapter for more information about these options. See "Sessions, Window Stations, Desktops, and Window Messages" in Chapter 2 to better understand the underlying concepts covered here. And see Chapter 6, "PsTools," for more information about PsExec.

Here is an example command line to start a Procmon trace that survives logoff:

```
PsExec -s -d Procmon.exe /AcceptEula /Quiet /BackingFile C:\Procmon.pml
```

And the following command line will stop that trace:

```
PsExec -s -d Procmon.exe /AcceptEula /Terminate
```

The **PsExec -d** option allows PsExec to exit without waiting for the target process to exit.

If a PsExec-launched instance of Procmon is running as System during a clean system shutdown, Procmon will stop logging when CSRSS tears down user-mode processes. To capture events beyond this point, boot logging is the only option.

Long-Running Traces and Controlling Log Sizes

Procmon trace files can become very large, particularly with boot logging or other long-running traces. Therefore, Procmon provides several ways to control log file size.

Drop Filtered Events

Ordinarily, Procmon will log all system activity, including events that are normally never displayed because of the active filters. That way, you always have the option to set a filter, explore the resulting output, and then change the filter to see a different set of output. However, if you know in advance of a long-running trace that you'll never need to see events for, you can keep them from taking space in the log by choosing the Drop Filtered Events option in the Filter menu.

When Drop Filtered Events is chosen, events that don't meet the filter criteria are never added to the log, reducing the impact on log size. Obviously, that event data cannot be recovered later. This option affects only newly collected events. Any events that were already in the log are not removed.

Note that filtering is not applied while a boot log is being collected, so Drop Filtered Events will not reduce disk usage impact during a boot log trace. But also note that the filters—and the Drop Filtered Events setting—are applied when the boot log is processed. So if you elect to drop events and need to see System process activity or other low-level events, make sure to choose Enable Advanced Output (Filter menu) before rebooting.

History Depth

Process Monitor watches committed memory usage and stops capturing events when system virtual memory runs low. By opening the History Depth dialog box (shown in Figure 4-20) from the Options menu, you can limit the number of entries kept so that you can leave Process Monitor running for long periods and ensure that it always keeps the most recent events. The range goes from a minimum of 1 million to 199 million events. The default is 199 million.

FIGURE 4-20 History Depth dialog box.

Backing Files

By default, Procmon uses virtual memory to store captured data. If virtual memory runs low, Procmon automatically stops logging and displays an error message. If your logging needs exceed the capacity of virtual memory, you can configure Procmon to store captured data to a named file on disk. The capacity limit when using a named file is the amount of free space on the hard drive.

You can configure and see information about backing files by choosing Backing Files from the File menu. The Process Monitor Backing Files dialog box shown in Figure 4-21 opens. Backing file configuration changes take effect the next time you begin capturing a new log or clear the current log.

FIGURE 4-21 Process Monitor Backing Files dialog box.

Note that if you choose a named file, Procmon might create additional files to keep individual file sizes manageable. Files will have the same base name, with an incrementing number appended, as shown in Figure 4-22. As long as the files are kept in the same folder and with the same base name, Procmon will treat the file set as a single log.

The Backing Files dialog box also displays diagnostic information, including the number of events captured and the number of processes observed.

FIGURE 4-22 Process Monitor Backing Files dialog box with named files.

Importing and Exporting Configuration Settings

From the File menu, you can export Procmon's entire configuration to a single Procmon Configuration (*.PMC) file, including settings for filters, highlight rules, column selection, column order and size, backing file settings, symbols, Advanced Output, and Drop Filtered Events. An exported configuration can be imported on another system or used in a scripted fashion with the **/LoadConfig** command-line option (described in the next section). You can also create multiple shortcuts to Procmon with different **/LoadConfig** configuration files specified for different tasks.

Filter rule sets can also be imported and exported individually. See the "Saving Filters for Later Use" section for details.

Note Procmon stores all its configuration settings in the registry in HKEY_CURRENT_USER\Software\Sysinternals\Process Monitor. The simplest way to restore all Procmon configuration settings to their defaults is to close all instances of Procmon, delete the registry key, and then start Procmon again. When viewing x86 Procmon logs on x64 versions of Windows, the 32-bit version of Procmon saves its configuration settings to HKCU\Software\Sysinternals\Process Monitor32.

Automating Procmon: Command-Line Options

Procmon offers a number of command-line options, which helps enable scripted execution. Say, for example, you need a novice user to run Procmon with a particular configuration and to send you the results. Instead of asking the user to follow detailed instructions for configuring and running Procmon, you can simply give that person a batch file to run.

Procmon's Help menu includes a quick summary of Procmon's command-line options. Table 4-4 describes them in more detail.

TABLE 4-4 Command-Line Options

Option	Description
/OpenLog *pml-file*	Opens a previously saved Procmon log file. Note that a log file must be opened by an instance of Procmon running in the same processor architecture as that which recorded it.
/BackingFile *pml-file*	Saves events in the specified backing file. Using a named backing file enables a log file capacity limited by free disk space. Note that this option is sticky—the file you specify becomes the Procmon log not just for the instance you're launching; it becomes a permanent setting change. (See the "Backing Files" section for more information.)
/PagingFile	Saves events in virtual memory, backed by the system page file. This option is used to revert the /BackingFile setting.
/NoConnect	Starts Procmon but does not automatically begin capturing data. By default, Procmon begins event capture on start.
/NoFilter	Clears the filter at startup. This removes all filter rules except the exclusion of Profiling events.
/AcceptEula	Doesn't display the End User License Agreement (EULA) dialog box on first use. Use of this option implies acceptance of the EULA.
/LoadConfig *config-file*	Loads a previously saved configuration file. (See the section on Configuration Files for more information.)
/Profiling	Enables the Thread Profiling feature.
/Minimized	Starts Procmon minimized.
/WaitForIdle	Waits for up to 10 seconds for another instance of Procmon on the same Win32 Desktop to become ready to accept commands. See below for an example of how to use this option.
/Terminate	Terminates any instance of Procmon running on the same Win32 Desktop and then exits. This option uses window messages to send the command to the target Procmon instance. (See "Sessions, Window Stations, Desktops, and Window Messages" in Chapter 2.)
/Quiet	Doesn't confirm filter settings during start up. By default, if filter rules have been configured, Procmon displays the filter dialog box to allow you to modify them before capturing data.
/Run32	Run the 32-bit version to load 32-bit log files (x64 only).

Option	Description
/HookRegistry	This switch, which is available only on 32-bit Windows Vista and newer, has Procmon use system-call hooking instead of the Registry callback mechanism to monitor registry activity, which enables it to see Microsoft Application Virtualization (App-V, formerly Softgrid) virtual registry operations. This option must be used the first time that Process Monitor is run in a boot session and should be used only to troubleshoot App-V sequenced applications.
/SaveAs *path*	When used with the /OpenLog option, exports the captured log to an XML, CSV, or PML file. The output format is determined by the path's file extension, which must be .xml, .csv, or .pml.
/SaveAs1 *path*	When used with the /OpenLog option, exports to XML and includes stack traces. See the "Saving and Opening Procmon Traces" section for more information.
/SaveAs2 *path*	When used with the /OpenLog option, exports to XML and includes stack traces and symbols. See the "Saving and Opening Procmon Traces" section for more information.

Here are some examples of putting these options to use:

- Opening a 32-bit log file on an x64 version of Windows:

```
Procmon.exe /Run32 /OpenLog c:\pmlLogs\logfile.pml
```

- Here's a more elaborate one. This batch captures "write" operations from an instance of Notepad.exe into C:\notepad.pml:

```
set PMExe="C:\Program Files\Sysinternals\Procmon.exe"
set PMHide= /AcceptEula /Quiet /Minimized
set PMCfg=  /LoadConfig C:\TEMP\PmCfg.pmc
set PMFile= /BackingFile C:\notepad.pml

start "" %PMExe% %PMHide% %PMCfg% %PMFile%
%PMExe% /WaitForIdle
notepad.exe
%PMExe% /Terminate
start "" %PMExe% /PagingFile /NoConnect /Minimized /Quiet
%PMExe% /WaitForIdle
%PMExe% /Terminate
```

Let's look at this last example line by line:

- Line 1 (*set PMExe*) identifies the path to Procmon so that it doesn't need to be repeated in the subsequent commands.

- Line 2 (*set PMHide*) specifies command-line options to make Procmon's running as unobtrusive to the user as possible.

- Line 3 (*set PMCfg*) specifies a previously saved configuration file that filters on write events for Notepad.exe and drops filtered events.

- Line 4 (*set PMFile*) configures the desired backing file.

- Line 5 uses the Command Prompt's **start** command to launch an instance of Procmon and return control to the batch file immediately.

- Line 6 invokes a second instance of Procmon that waits for the first instance to be up and running and actively capturing events (*/WaitForIdle*), and then it returns control to the batch file. Notepad is then started on line 7. When the user finishes using Notepad and closes it, control returns to the batch file.

- Line 8 terminates the instance of Procmon that was capturing events.

- To restore the pagefile as the backing store, Line 9 starts an instance of Procmon that sets the paging file as the backing store (*/PagingFile*) but doesn't log any events.

- When that instance is ready to accept commands (line 10), it can be terminated (line 11).

Analysis Tools

Procmon offers a number of ways to visualize captured data and allow you to perform simple data mining on the events collected in a trace. These can be found on the Tools menu:

- Process Activity Summary
- File Summary
- Registry Summary
- Stack Summary
- Network Summary
- Cross Reference Summary
- Count Occurrences

The Summary dialog boxes are all modeless, so you can open several at once and continue to interact with the main window.

Process Activity Summary

The Process Activity Summary dialog box (shown in Figure 4-23) displays a table listing every process for which data was captured with the current filter applied. Each row in the table shows the process name and PID, a CPU usage graph, the numbers of file, registry and network events, the commit peak and the working set peak, and graphs showing these and other numbers changing over the timeline of the process. You can save all the text information to a CSV file by clicking the Save button.

FIGURE 4-23 Process Activity Summary dialog box.

Selecting a row displays more information about the process at the bottom of the dialog box—the command line, start and stop time, and total user and kernel CPU time. Double-clicking a row or selecting it and clicking the Detail button displays the Process Timeline dialog box for that process (shown in Figure 4-24). Columns can be resized or reordered by dragging the appropriate parts of the column headers.

The Process Timeline (shown in Figure 4-24) displays the process' graphs from the Process Activity Summary dialog box stacked above each other in a resizable dialog box. Clicking on a point in a graph selects the nearest corresponding event for that process in the main window. So, for example, say that at about 40 percent through the graphs, you see a sudden spike in file I/O operations, private memory bytes, and working set. Click on that point in any of the graphs and the nearest corresponding event for that process is selected in the Procmon main window.

FIGURE 4-24 Process Timeline dialog box.

File Summary

The File Summary dialog box shown in Figure 4-25 aggregates information about every file and folder operation displayed by the current filter, and it groups the results on separate tabs by path, by folder, and by file extension. For each unique file system path, the dialog box displays how much total time was spent performing I/O to the file; the number of opens, closes, reads, writes, Get ACL, Set ACL and other operations; the total number of operations performed; and the number of bytes read from and written to the file.

FIGURE 4-25 By Path tab of the File Summary dialog box.

The By Path tab displays a simple list in which each unique path appears as a separate row.

The By Folder tab (shown in Figure 4-26) displays an expandable tree view based on the folder hierarchy. Expandable folder nodes represent the sum of the data from operations performed within that folder hierarchy. Nonexpandable nodes show data for operations performed on that object. For example, there might be two Program Files nodes: the nonexpandable one indicates operations performed on the folder itself, while the expandable one displays the sums of all operations performed on its files and subfolders.

FIGURE 4-26 By Folder tab of the File Summary dialog box.

The By Extension tab (shown in Figure 4-27) displays a one-level tree for each file extension: expanding a node for a file extension lists all files with that extension as immediate child nodes. The row containing the extension name contains the sum of all the data for files of that extension.

FIGURE 4-27 By Extension tab of the File Summary dialog box.

Clicking a column header sorts the table on the current tab by that column. On the By Folder and By Extension tabs, the groupings are maintained and rows are sorted within their groups. Sorting columns lets you quickly identify usage patterns. For example, column-sorting on the By Folder tab identifies which folder hierarchies have the largest number of operations, bytes read or written, or file I/O time. Column-sorting on the By Extension tab shows which file types are getting accessed the most. You can also reorder columns by dragging the column headers. (On the By Folder and By Extension tabs, the leftmost columns cannot be moved.)

Double-clicking a row sets a Path rule for the file path in that row to the current filter. Clicking the Filter button displays the Filter dialog box so that you can further refine the filter.

The Save button on each tab saves the current table view as a CSV file.

Registry Summary

Much like the File Summary dialog box, the Registry Summary dialog box (shown in Figure 4-28) lists every registry path referenced by registry operations in a table, along with how much total time was spent performing I/O to the key; the number of opens, closes, reads, writes, and other operations; and the sum total of these. Clicking on a column header sorts by the data in that column, and columns can be reordered by dragging the column headers. Double-clicking a row adds a Path rule for the registry path in that row to the current filter. The Filter dialog box can be displayed by clicking the Filter button, and you can save the data to a CSV file.

FIGURE 4-28 Registry Summary dialog box.

Stack Summary

The Stack Summary dialog box (Figure 4-29) takes all the stack traces for each Procmon-traceable event, identifies the commonalities and divergences in them, and renders them as expandable trees. For each frame within a call stack, you can see how many times its execution resulted in a Procmon-traceable event, the cumulative amount of time spent in the Procmon-captured operations, the name and path of the module, and the absolute offset within it. The Stack Summary also shows function names and the path to and line number within source files for each stack frame if symbolic information is available. (See "Call Stacks and Symbols" in Chapter 2 for more information.)

Note Stack Summary is not a comprehensive code coverage and profiling tool. The counts it reports reflect only the number of times that a Procmon-traceable event occurred, the times it reports indicate the amount of CPU time spent performing those operations, and the percentages are relative to those accumulated figures.

FIGURE 4-29 Stack Summary dialog box.

Figure 4-29 shows a stack summary for a program for which full symbolic information is available. The top two frames represented in the dialog box show that the C runtime library's startup function, *__tmainCRTStartup* called the standard *wmain* entry point, and that the functions they called resulted in 55,117 separate Procmon-tracked events with the current filter. By expanding child nodes that have the largest counts or times associated with them, you can quickly determine where the bulk of the activity occurred. Over 72 percent of the events displayed with the current filter were invoked from *InternalWorkItem+0x81*, and it invoked *RegSetValueExW* 39,806 times.

Selecting a stack frame and clicking the Go To Event button selects the first event in the trace with a corresponding call stack. The Source button is enabled if full symbolic information is available for the selected item. If the source file is available, clicking the Source button displays the file in the Procmon source file viewer, with the indicated line of source code selected.

As with the other summary dialog boxes, columns can be sorted by clicking on the headers, and all but the leftmost column can be reordered by dragging the headers.

Note that building the stack summary can be time consuming, especially when symbols are being resolved.

Network Summary

The Network Summary dialog box (shown in Figure 4-30) lists every TCP and UDP endpoint and port present in the filtered trace, along with the corresponding number of connects, disconnects, sends, and receives; the total number of these events; and the numbers of bytes sent and received. Clicking a column header sorts by the data in that column, and columns can be reordered by dragging the column headers. Double-clicking a row sets a Path rule in the filter for that endpoint and port. The Filter dialog box can be displayed by clicking the Filter button, and you can save the data to a CSV file.

FIGURE 4-30 Network Summary dialog box.

Cross Reference Summary

The Cross Reference Summary dialog box (shown in Figure 4-31) lists all paths displayed by the current filter that have been accessed by more than one process. Each row shows the path, the processes that have written to it, and the processes that have read from it. The columns can be sorted or reordered, and you can save the data to a CSV file. Double-clicking a row, or selecting the row and clicking the Filter On Row button, adds the selected path to the filter.

FIGURE 4-31 Cross Reference Summary dialog box.

Count Occurrences

Choose a column name in the Count Values Occurrences dialog box (shown in Figure 4-32), and click the Count button. Procmon displays all the distinct values for the selected attribute and the number of events that include that value with the current display filter applied. The columns can be sorted or reordered, and you can save the data to a CSV file. Double-clicking on an item sets a rule for that column/value to the filter.

FIGURE 4-32 Count Values Occurrences dialog box.

Injecting Debug Output into Procmon Traces

Procmon provides an application programming interface (API) allowing developers to create debug output events that appear in the Procmon event stream with custom text. For example, you can inject custom debug output in the trace upon entering or exiting a function to correlate those activities with file, registry, or other events. By applying the Exclude Events Before and Exclude Events After filters on these debug events, you can easily focus on the areas of interest in your program. Unlike standard Windows debug output that is captured by DebugView (described in Chapter 7, "Process and Diagnostic Utilities") or other debuggers, this interface specifically targets Procmon.

These events appear as Debug Output Profiling operations and are part of the Profiling events class, along with Process Profiling and Thread Profiling events. Note that by default all Profiling events are filtered out. To see your debug output events, enable the Show Profiling Events toggle button on the toolbar. After doing so, you might also want to highlight Debug Output Profiling operations and exclude the display of Process Profiling operations. Figure 4-33 shows debug output highlighted and interspersed with registry operations.

FIGURE 4-33 Debug Output Profiling events.

Any process, including one running at Low integrity, can use this interface, which accepts wide character (Unicode) text strings of up to 2048 characters in length. The following code sample demonstrates how to use the interface:

```
#include <stdio.h>
#include <windows.h>

const ULONG FILE_DEVICE_PROCMON_LOG = 0x00009535;
const ULONG IOCTL_EXTERNAL_LOG_DEBUGOUT =
    (ULONG) CTL_CODE( FILE_DEVICE_PROCMON_LOG, 0x81, METHOD_BUFFERED, FILE_WRITE_ACCESS );
```

```
BOOL WriteProcmonDebugOutput(const wchar_t * szDebugOutput)
{
    if (!szDebugOutput)
        return FALSE;
    HANDLE hDevice = CreateFileW( L"\\\\.\\Global\\ProcmonDebugLogger",
        GENERIC_READ | GENERIC_WRITE,
        FILE_SHARE_READ | FILE_SHARE_WRITE | FILE_SHARE_DELETE,
        NULL,
        OPEN_EXISTING,
        FILE_ATTRIBUTE_NORMAL,
        NULL );
    if ( hDevice == INVALID_HANDLE_VALUE )
        return FALSE;
    DWORD buflen = wcslen(szDebugOutput) * sizeof(wchar_t);
    DWORD unused = 0;
    BOOL ret = DeviceIoControl( hDevice, IOCTL_EXTERNAL_LOG_DEBUGOUT,
        (LPVOID)szDebugOutput, buflen, NULL, 0, &unused, NULL );
    CloseHandle(hDevice);
    return ret;
}
```

Debugging guru John Robbins has created helper classes that you can easily incorporate into your native or managed applications. Download them from the following URL:

http://www.wintellect.com/downloads/ProcMonDebugOutput.zip

Toolbar Reference

This section identifies the Procmon toolbar icons and the sections of this chapter that describe what they do. Figure 4-34 shows the toolbar.

FIGURE 4-34 The Procmon toolbar.

Referring to the Procmon toolbar shown in Figure 4-34, from left to right, the icons are

- **Open Log**   See the "Opening Saved Procmon Traces" section.
- **Save Log**   See the "Saving Procmon Traces" section.
- **Capture Events (toggle)**   See the "Getting Started with Procmon" section.
- **Autoscroll (toggle)**   See the "Getting Started with Procmon" section.
- **Clear Display**   See the "Getting Started with Procmon" section.
- **Filter dialog box**   See the "Filtering and Highlighting" section.
- **Highlight dialog box**   See the "Highlighting" section.

- **Include Process From Window**   See the "Basics of Filtering" section.

- **Show Process Tree**   See the "Process Tree" section.

- **Find**   See the "Finding an Event" section.

- **Jump To Object**   See the "Jumping to a Registry or File Location" section.

- **Show/Hide Registry Activity (toggle)**   See the "Basics of Filtering" section.

- **Show/Hide File System Activity (toggle)**   See the "Basics of Filtering" section.

- **Show/Hide Network Activity (toggle)**   See the "Basics of Filtering" section.

- **Show/Hide Process and Thread Activity (toggle)**   See the "Basics of Filtering" section.

- **Show/Hide Profiling Events (toggle)**   See the "Displaying Profiling Events" section.

Chapter 5
Autoruns

A question I often hear is, "Why is all this *stuff* running on my computer?" That's often followed with, "How do I get rid of it?" The Microsoft Windows operating system is a highly extensible platform. Not only can programmers write applications that users can choose to run, those programmers can "add value" by having their software run automatically without troubling the user to start it, by adding visible or nonvisible features to Windows Explorer and Internet Explorer or by supplying device drivers that can interact with custom hardware or change the way existing hardware works. Sometimes the "value" to the user is doubtful at best; sometimes the value is for someone else entirely and the software acts to the detriment of the user (which is when the software is called *malware*).

Autostarts is the term I use to refer to software that runs automatically without being intentionally started by a user. These include drivers and services that start when the computer is booted; applications, utilities, and shell extensions that start when a user logs on; and browser extensions that load when Internet Explorer is started. There are over 100 locations in the file system and registry that allow autostarts to be configured on x86 versions of Windows, and many more on x64. These locations are often referred to as *Autostart Extensibility Points*, or ASEPs.

ASEPs have legitimate and valuable purposes. For example, if you want your instant messaging contacts to know when you are online, having the messaging client start when you log on is a great help. Users enjoy search toolbars and PDF readers that become part of Internet Explorer. And much of Windows itself is implemented through ASEPs in the form of drivers, services, and Explorer extensions.

On the other hand, consider the plethora of "free" trial versions of programs that computer manufacturers install on new computers and that fill up the taskbar notification area. Consider also the semi-hidden processes that legitimate vendors run all the time so that their applications can appear to start more quickly. Do you really need all these processes constantly consuming resources? On top of that, malware almost always hooks one or more ASEPs, and virtually every ASEP in Windows has been used by malware at one point or another.

Although Windows offers the System Configuration Utility (msconfig.exe, shown in Figure 5-1) to let you see some of these autostarts, it shows only a small subset and is of limited usability. Msconfig also requires administrative rights, even just to view settings. That means it cannot identify or disable *per-user* autostarts belonging to nonadministrator users.

FIGURE 5-1 The MSConfig utility included in Windows exposes a very limited set of autostarts.

Bryce and I created the Autoruns utility to expose as many autostarts as we could identify, and to make it easy to disable or remove those autostarts. The information that Autoruns exposes can be discovered manually if you know where to look in the registry and file system. Autoruns automates that task, scanning a large number of ASEPs in a few seconds, verifying entries, and making it easier to identify entries with suspicious characteristics such as the lack of a digital signature. We also created a command-line version, AutorunsC, to make it possible to capture the same information in a scripted fashion.

Using either Autoruns or AutorunsC, you can easily capture a baseline of the ASEPs on a system. That baseline can be compared against results captured at a later time so that changes can be identified for troubleshooting purposes. Many organizations use Autoruns as part of a robust change management system, capturing a new baseline whenever the desktop image is updated.

Autoruns Fundamentals

Launch Autoruns and it immediately begins filling its display with entries collected from known ASEPs. As shown in Figure 5-2, each shaded row represents an ASEP location, with a Regedit icon if it is a registry location or a folder icon if it is stored in the file system.[1] The rows underneath a shaded row indicate entries configured in that ASEP. Each row includes the name of the autostart entry, the description and publisher of the item, and the path to the file to run and an icon for that file. Each row also has a check box to temporarily disable the entry. A panel at the bottom of the window displays details about the selected entry, including its full command line. The Everything tab, which is displayed when Autoruns starts, displays all ASEP entries on the system; the 17 other tabs let you view just specific categories of autostarts. Each of these categories will be described later in this chapter.

---

[1] Scheduled Tasks appear with a folder icon, because configuration settings for tasks were stored in %windir%\Tasks prior to Windows Vista. As part of the re-architecting of Task Scheduler, configuration settings are now in the registry under HKLM\SOFTWARE\Microsoft\Windows NT\CurrentVersion\Schedule\TaskCache.

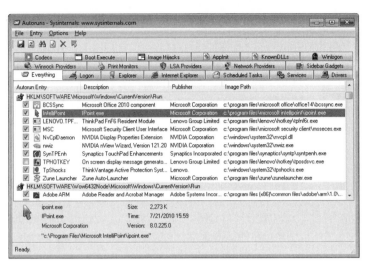

FIGURE 5-2 Autoruns main window.

The Image Path column shows the full path to the target file identified by the autostart entry. In some cases, this will be the first name in the autostart's command line. For autostarts that use a hosting process—such as Cmd.exe, Wscript.exe, Rundll32.exe, Regsvr32.exe, or Svchost.exe—the image path identifies the target script or DLL on the command line instead of the main executable. The Image Path column will include the text "File not found" if the target file cannot be found in the expected location.

The Description and Publisher columns in the display are taken from the Description and Company Name version resources, respectively, for files that contain version resources, such as EXE and DLL files. If the file's digital signature has been verified, the Publisher column displays the subject name from the corresponding code-signing certificate. (See the "Verifying Code Signatures" section later in this chapter for more information.)

The Description and Publisher columns are left blank if the target file cannot be found, has no Description and Company Name in its version resources, or has no version resource (which is always true of script files).

You can quickly search for an item by pressing Ctrl+F and entering text to search for. Autoruns will select the next row that contains the search text. Pressing F3 repeats the search from the current location. Pressing Ctrl+C copies the text of the selected row to the clipboard as tab-delimited text.

The Options menu is disabled while Autoruns is scanning the system. To cancel the scan so that you can change options (which are described later in this chapter), press the Esc key. Changing any of the selections in the Options menu (other than Font) takes effect during the next scan. After selecting the options you want, press F5 or click the Refresh button on the toolbar to run a new scan.

Disabling or Deleting Autostart Entries

Autoruns allows you to disable or delete autostart entries. Deleting an entry permanently removes it, and it's what you should do only if you're certain that you never want the software to autostart again. Select the entry in the list and press the Del key. Because there is no Undo, Autoruns prompts for confirmation before deleting the autostart entry.

By contrast, when you disable an entry by clearing its check box, Autoruns leaves a marker behind that Autoruns recognizes and with which it can reconstitute and re-enable the entry. For example, for most registry ASEPs, Autoruns creates an AutorunsDisabled subkey in the ASEP location and copies the registry value being disabled into that subkey before deleting the original value. Windows will not process anything in that subkey, so the items in it will not run, but Autoruns displays them as disabled autostarts. Checking the entry again puts the entry back into the actual ASEP location. For ASEPs in the file system such as in the Start menu, Autoruns creates a hidden folder named AutorunsDisabled and moves disabled entries into that folder.

Note that disabling or deleting an autostart entry prevents it from being automatically started in the future. It does not stop any existing processes.

Also note that if you disable autostarts that are critical for system boot, initialization, or correct operation, you can put the system into a state in which recovery is not possible without booting into an alternate operating system or recovery environment.

Autoruns and Administrative Permissions

The vast majority of ASEPs are in locations that grant Read permission to standard users. On some versions of Windows, the registry keys containing configuration information for some services are locked down, and many scheduled tasks are not user readable. But for the most part, Autoruns works perfectly fine without administrative rights for the purposes of viewing autostart entries. Administrative rights are required to view all autostarts, and they are required if you need to change the state of entries in systemwide locations, such as HKLM or the all users' Startup folder in the Start menu. If you select or clear a check box, or try to delete one of these entries without administrative rights, Autoruns will report Access Denied.

On Windows Vista and newer, the error message dialog box includes a Run As Administrator button that lets you restart Autoruns elevated. (See Figure 5-3.) When Autoruns has administrative rights, configuration changes should succeed. You can also restart Autoruns with User Account Control (UAC) elevation by choosing Run As Administrator from the File menu.

FIGURE 5-3 Access Denied and the option to restart Autoruns with UAC elevation.

To ensure that Autoruns has elevated rights when it launches, start Autoruns with the –**e** command-line option. On Windows Vista and newer, this will request UAC elevation if the invoker is not already running elevated. On Windows XP and Windows Server 2003, the Run As dialog box will appear. Select "The following user" and enter credentials for an account that has administrative rights.

See the "Administrative Rights" section in Chapter 2, "Windows Core Concepts," for more information on RunAs and UAC elevation.

Verifying Code Signatures

Anyone can create a program and stick the name "Microsoft Corporation" in it. Therefore, seeing that text in the Publisher column gives only a low degree of assurance that the file in question was created by Microsoft and has not been modified since. Verifying a digital signature associated with that file gives a much higher degree of assurance of the file's authenticity and integrity. The file format for some types of files allows for a digital signature to be embedded within the file. Files can also be "catalog-signed," meaning that the information needed to validate a file's content is in a separate file. Catalog signing means that even plain text files can be verified.

You can verify an entry's digital signature by selecting the entry and pressing Ctrl+V. If the file has been signed with a valid code-signing certificate that derived from a root certificate authority that is trusted on the computer, the text in the Publisher column changes to "(Verified)" followed by the subject name in the code-signing certificate. If the file has not been signed or the verification fails for any other reason, the text changes to "(Not verified)" followed by the company name from the file's version resource, if present.

Instead of verifying entries one at a time, you can enable Verify Code Signatures in the Options menu and rescan by pressing F5. Autoruns will then attempt to verify the signatures for all image paths as it scans autostarts. Note that the scan might take longer because it also verifies whether each signing certificate has been revoked by its issuer, which requires Internet connectivity to work reliably.

Files for which signature checks fail might be considered suspicious. A common malware technique is to install files that on casual inspection appear to be legitimate Windows files.

The Sysinternals Sigcheck utility, described in Chapter 8, "Security Utilities," provides deeper detail for file signatures, including whether the file is catalog-signed and the location of the catalog.

Hiding Microsoft Entries

The default list of ASEP entries is always large because, as mentioned earlier, Windows itself makes extensive use of ASEPs. Typically, these autostart entries are not of interest when troubleshooting. Likewise, autostart entries from other Microsoft-published software such as Microsoft Office are usually not the droids you're looking for[2]. You can choose to hide these autostart entries from the display by enabling the Hide Windows Entries or Hide Microsoft And Windows Entries from the Options menu and refreshing the display by pressing F5. The Hide Windows Entries option is enabled by default.

The behavior of these options depends on whether Verify Code Signatures is also enabled. If signature verification is not enabled, Hide Windows Entries omits from the display all entries for which the target image file has the word "Microsoft" in the version resource's Company Name field, and for which the image file resides in or below the %windir% folder. Hide Microsoft And Windows Entries checks only for "Microsoft" in the Company Name field and omits those entries. As mentioned earlier, it is easy for anyone to create a program that gets past this check, so the Verify Code Signatures option is recommended.

If signature verification is enabled, Hide Windows Entries omits entries that are signed with the Microsoft Windows code-signing certificate. (Windows components are signed with a different certificate from other Microsoft products.) Hide Microsoft And Windows Entries omits entries that are signed with any Microsoft code-signing certificate that chains to a trusted root certificate authority on the computer.

> **Note** Some files that ship with Windows, particularly drivers, are provided by third parties and have a third-party name in the Company Name field of the file's version resource, but they are catalog signed with the Windows code-signing certificate. Consequently, these entries can be hidden when signature verification is enabled but displayed when verification is not enabled.

The Verify and Hide options are saved in the registry, and they'll remain in effect the next time the same user starts Autoruns.

---

2   Cultural reference: "These aren't the droids you're looking for" is a quote from the film, *Star Wars IV: A New Hope*.

Getting More Information About an Entry

Right-clicking an entry displays the Entry submenu as a popup context menu. Four of the options use other programs to display more information about the selected entry than is displayed in Autoruns:

- **Properties**   Displays the Windows Explorer file Properties dialog box for the target image path.

- **Jump To**   Opens the location where the autostart entry is configured. For ASEPs configured in the registry, Jump To starts the registry editor (Regedit.exe) and sends it simulated keystrokes to navigate to the autostart entry. (If Regedit does not navigate to the correct location the first time, try the Jump To command again.) For ASEPs configured in the file system, Jump To opens a new Windows Explorer folder window in that location. For Scheduled Tasks, Jump To opens the Task Scheduler user interface. Note that on Windows Vista and newer, Autoruns' driving of the navigation of Regedit requires that Autoruns not be running at a lower integrity level than Regedit.

- **Search Online**   Initiates an online search for the file name using your default browser and search engine.

- **Process Explorer**   If the image path is an executable (as opposed to a script or DLL file) and a process with that name is still running, Autoruns tries to get Process Explorer (Procexp) to display its Process Properties dialog box for the process. For this option to work, Procexp needs to be in the same folder with Autoruns, found in the path, or already be running. If Procexp is already running, it cannot be at a higher integrity level than Autoruns. For example, if Autoruns is not elevated and Procexp is, this option will not work.

Viewing the Autostarts of Other Users

If Autoruns is running with administrative rights, the User menu will appear, listing the account names that have logged on to the computer and have an accessible user profile. Selecting a user account from that menu rescans the system, searching that user's ASEPs, including the Run keys under that user's HKCU and the Startup folder in that user's profile.

One example of when this option is useful is if a standard user has installed some harmful software. With only standard user privileges, only the user's per-user ASEPs could have been modified. Software that has only standard user privileges cannot modify systemwide settings nor touch the accounts of other users on the system. Rather than logging on and allowing that malware to run—and possibly interfering with an Autoruns scan—you can log on to the system with an administrative account, start Autoruns, select the potentially compromised account from the User menu, inspect the user's ASEPs, and perform a cleanup if problems are identified.

Viewing ASEPs of an Offline System

Autoruns allows you to view the ASEPs of an offline instance of Windows from a different, known-good instance of Windows. This can be helpful in several scenarios:

- If Windows will not start, offline analysis can identify and remove faulty or misconfigured ASEPs.

- Malware, and rootkits in particular, can prevent Autoruns from accurately identifying ASEPs. For example, a rootkit that intercepts and modifies registry reads can hide the content of selected keys from Autoruns. By taking the system offline and viewing its ASEPs from an instance of Windows in which that malware is not running, those entries will not be hidden.

- Malicious files on your system might appear to be signed by a trusted publisher, when in fact the root certificate might also have come from the attacker. A known-good system in which the bogus certificate is not installed will fail the signature verification for those files.

To perform offline analysis, Autoruns must run with administrative rights and must have access to the offline instance's file system. Choose Analyze Offline System from the File menu, and then identify the target's Windows (System Root) directory and a user's profile directory, as shown in Figure 5-4. Autoruns then scans that instance's directories and registry hives for its ASEPs. Note that the registry hives cannot be on read-only media.

FIGURE 5-4 Picking system and user profile directories of an offline system.

Listing Unused ASEPs

By default, Autoruns displays a shaded row only for ASEPs that have entries configured within them. If Include Empty Locations is enabled on the Options menu, Autoruns displays a shaded row for every ASEP that it scans, whether it has entries or not. Autoruns scans a tremendous number of ASEPs, so this increases the amount of output dramatically. Enabling this option can be useful to verify whether particular ASEPs are scanned, or to satisfy curiosity.

As with the "Hide" and "Verify" options, enabling the Include Empty Locations takes effect on the next scan.

Changing the Font

Choose Font from the Options menu to change the font Autoruns uses to display its results. Changing the font updates the display immediately.

Autostart Categories

When you launch Autoruns for the first time, all autostart entries on the system are displayed in one long list on the Everything tab. As Figure 5-5 shows, the display includes up to 17 other tabs that break down the complete list into categories.

FIGURE 5-5 Autostart categories are displayed on up to 18 different tabs.

Logon

This tab lists the "standard" autostart entries that are processed when Windows starts up and a user logs on, and it includes the ASEPs that are probably the most commonly used by applications. They include the various Run and RunOnce keys in the registry, the Startup folders in the Start menu, computer startup and shutdown scripts, and logon and logoff scripts. It also lists the initial user session processes, such as the Userinit process and the desktop shell. These ASEPs include both per-user and systemwide locations, and entries designed for control through Group Policy. Finally, it lists the Active Setup\Installed Components keys, which although never publicly documented or supported for third-party use have been reverse-engineered and repurposed both for good and for ill.

The following lists the Logon ASEP locations that Autoruns inspects on a particular instance of an x64 version of Windows 7.

The Startup Folder in the "All Users" Start Menu

%ALLUSERSPROFILE%\Microsoft\Windows\Start Menu\Programs\Startup

The Startup Folder in the User's Start Menu

%APPDATA%\Microsoft\Windows\Start Menu\Programs\Startup

Per-User ASEPs Under HKCU\Software

HKCU\Software\Microsoft\Windows\CurrentVersion\Run

HKCU\Software\Microsoft\Windows\CurrentVersion\RunOnce

HKCU\Software\Microsoft\Windows NT\CurrentVersion\Terminal Server\Install\Software\Microsoft\ Windows\CurrentVersion\Run

HKCU\Software\Microsoft\Windows NT\CurrentVersion\Terminal Server\Install\Software\Microsoft\ Windows\CurrentVersion\Runonce

HKCU\Software\Microsoft\Windows NT\CurrentVersion\Terminal Server\Install\Software\Microsoft\ Windows\CurrentVersion\RunonceEx

HKCU\Software\Microsoft\Windows NT\CurrentVersion\Windows\Load

HKCU\Software\Microsoft\Windows NT\CurrentVersion\Windows\Run

HKCU\Software\Microsoft\Windows NT\CurrentVersion\Winlogon\Shell

Per-User ASEPs Under HKCU\Software Intended to be Controlled Through Group Policy

HKCU\Software\Microsoft\Windows\CurrentVersion\Policies\Explorer\Run

HKCU\Software\Microsoft\Windows\CurrentVersion\Policies\System\Shell

HKCU\Software\Policies\Microsoft\Windows\System\Scripts\Logon

HKCU\Software\Policies\Microsoft\Windows\System\Scripts\Logoff

Systemwide ASEPs in the Registry

HKLM\Software\Microsoft\Windows\CurrentVersion\Run

HKLM\Software\Microsoft\Windows\CurrentVersion\RunOnce

HKLM\Software\Microsoft\Windows\CurrentVersion\RunOnceEx

HKLM\SOFTWARE\Microsoft\Active Setup\Installed Components

HKLM\Software\Microsoft\Windows NT\CurrentVersion\Terminal Server\Install\Software\ Microsoft\ Windows\CurrentVersion\Run

HKLM\Software\Microsoft\Windows NT\CurrentVersion\Terminal Server\Install\Software\ Microsoft\ Windows\CurrentVersion\Runonce

HKLM\Software\Microsoft\Windows NT\CurrentVersion\Terminal Server\Install\Software\ Microsoft\ Windows\CurrentVersion\RunonceEx

HKLM\Software\Microsoft\Windows NT\CurrentVersion\Winlogon\AppSetup

HKLM\Software\Microsoft\Windows NT\CurrentVersion\Winlogon\Shell

HKLM\Software\Microsoft\Windows NT\CurrentVersion\Winlogon\Taskman

HKLM\Software\Microsoft\Windows NT\CurrentVersion\Winlogon\Userinit

HKLM\SYSTEM\CurrentControlSet\Control\SafeBoot\AlternateShell

HKLM\System\CurrentControlSet\Control\Terminal Server\Wds\rdpwd\StartupPrograms

Systemwide ASEPs in the Registry, Intended to be Controlled Through Group Policy

HKLM\Software\Microsoft\Windows\CurrentVersion\Policies\Explorer\Run

HKLM\Software\Microsoft\Windows\CurrentVersion\Policies\System\Shell

HKLM\Software\Policies\Microsoft\Windows\System\Scripts\Logon

HKLM\Software\Policies\Microsoft\Windows\System\Scripts\Logoff

HKLM\Software\Policies\Microsoft\Windows\System\Scripts\Startup

HKLM\Software\Policies\Microsoft\Windows\System\Scripts\Shutdown

HKLM\Software\Microsoft\Windows\CurrentVersion\Group Policy\Scripts\Startup

HKLM\Software\Microsoft\Windows\CurrentVersion\Group Policy\Scripts\Shutdown

Systemwide ASEPs in the Registry—64-Bit Only

HKLM\Software\Wow6432Node\Microsoft\Windows\CurrentVersion\Run

HKLM\Software\Wow6432Node\Microsoft\Windows\CurrentVersion\RunOnce

HKLM\Software\Wow6432Node\Microsoft\Windows\CurrentVersion\RunOnceEx

HKLM\SOFTWARE\Wow6432Node\Microsoft\Active Setup\Installed Components

Systemwide ActiveSync ASEPs in the Registry

HKLM\SOFTWARE\Microsoft\Windows CE Services\AutoStartOnConnect

HKLM\SOFTWARE\Microsoft\Windows CE Services\AutoStartOnDisconnect

Systemwide ActiveSync ASEPs in the Registry—64-Bit Only

HKLM\SOFTWARE\Wow6432Node\Microsoft\Windows CE Services\AutoStartOnConnect

HKLM\SOFTWARE\Wow6432Node\Microsoft\Windows CE Services\AutoStartOnDisconnect

Explorer

The Explorer tab lists common autostart entries that hook directly into Windows Explorer and usually run in-process with Explorer.exe. Again, although most entries are systemwide, there are a number of per-user entries. Key entries on the Explorer tab include the following:

- Shell extensions that add context menu items, modify property pages, and control column displays in folder windows

- Namespace extensions such as the Desktop, Control Panel, and Recycle Bin, as well as third-party namespace extensions

- Pluggable namespace handlers, which handle standard protocols such as http, ftp, and mailto, as well as Microsoft or third-party extensions such as about, mk, and res

- Pluggable MIME filters

On 64-bit versions of Windows, in-process components such as DLLs can be loaded only into processes built for the same CPU architecture. For example, shell extensions implemented as 32-bit DLLs can be loaded only into the 32-bit version of Windows Explorer—and 64-bit Windows uses the 64-bit Explorer by default. Therefore, these extensions might not appear to work at all on 64-bit Windows.

The following lists the Explorer ASEP locations that Autoruns inspects on a particular instance of an x64 version of Windows 7.

Per-User ASEPs Under HKCU\Software

HKCU\Software\Classes*\ShellEx\ContextMenuHandlers

HKCU\Software\Classes*\ShellEx\PropertySheetHandlers

HKCU\Software\Classes\AllFileSystemObjects\ShellEx\ContextMenuHandlers

HKCU\Software\Classes\AllFileSystemObjects\ShellEx\DragDropHandlers

HKCU\Software\Classes\AllFileSystemObjects\ShellEx\PropertySheetHandlers

HKCU\Software\Classes\Directory\Background\ShellEx\ContextMenuHandlers

HKCU\Software\Classes\Directory\ShellEx\ContextMenuHandlers

HKCU\Software\Classes\Directory\Shellex\CopyHookHandlers

HKCU\Software\Classes\Directory\Shellex\DragDropHandlers

HKCU\Software\Classes\Directory\Shellex\PropertySheetHandlers

HKCU\Software\Classes\Folder\Shellex\ColumnHandlers

HKCU\Software\Classes\Folder\ShellEx\ContextMenuHandlers

HKCU\Software\Classes\Folder\ShellEx\DragDropHandlers

HKCU\Software\Classes\Folder\ShellEx\ExtShellFolderViews

HKCU\Software\Classes\Folder\ShellEx\PropertySheetHandlers

HKCU\SOFTWARE\Classes\Protocols\Filter

HKCU\SOFTWARE\Classes\Protocols\Handler

HKCU\Software\Microsoft\Ctf\LangBarAddin

HKCU\SOFTWARE\Microsoft\Internet Explorer\Desktop\Components

HKCU\Software\Microsoft\Windows\CurrentVersion\Explorer\ShellIconOverlayIdentifiers

HKCU\SOFTWARE\Microsoft\Windows\CurrentVersion\ShellServiceObjectDelayLoad

Systemwide ASEPs in the Registry

HKLM\Software\Classes*\ShellEx\ContextMenuHandlers

HKLM\Software\Classes*\ShellEx\PropertySheetHandlers

HKLM\Software\Classes\AllFileSystemObjects\ShellEx\ContextMenuHandlers

HKLM\Software\Classes\AllFileSystemObjects\ShellEx\DragDropHandlers

HKLM\Software\Classes\AllFileSystemObjects\ShellEx\PropertySheetHandlers

HKLM\Software\Classes\Directory\Background\ShellEx\ContextMenuHandlers

HKLM\Software\Classes\Directory\ShellEx\ContextMenuHandlers

HKLM\Software\Classes\Directory\Shellex\CopyHookHandlers

HKLM\Software\Classes\Directory\Shellex\DragDropHandlers

HKLM\Software\Classes\Directory\Shellex\PropertySheetHandlers

HKLM\Software\Classes\Folder\Shellex\ColumnHandlers

HKLM\Software\Classes\Folder\ShellEx\ContextMenuHandlers

HKLM\Software\Classes\Folder\ShellEx\DragDropHandlers

HKLM\Software\Classes\Folder\ShellEx\ExtShellFolderViews

HKLM\Software\Classes\Folder\ShellEx\PropertySheetHandlers

HKLM\SOFTWARE\Classes\Protocols\Filter

HKLM\SOFTWARE\Classes\Protocols\Handler

HKLM\Software\Microsoft\Ctf\LangBarAddin
HKLM\SOFTWARE\Microsoft\Windows\CurrentVersion\Explorer\SharedTaskScheduler
HKLM\Software\Microsoft\Windows\CurrentVersion\Explorer\ShellExecuteHooks
HKLM\Software\Microsoft\Windows\CurrentVersion\Explorer\ShellIconOverlayIdentifiers
HKLM\SOFTWARE\Microsoft\Windows\CurrentVersion\ShellServiceObjectDelayLoad

Systemwide ASEPs in the Registry—64-Bit Only

HKLM\Software\Wow6432Node\Classes\Directory\Shellex\CopyHookHandlers
HKLM\Software\Wow6432Node\Classes\Directory\Shellex\DragDropHandlers
HKLM\Software\Wow6432Node\Classes\Directory\Shellex\PropertySheetHandlers
HKLM\Software\Wow6432Node\Classes\Folder\Shellex\ColumnHandlers
HKLM\Software\Wow6432Node\Microsoft\Windows\CurrentVersion\Explorer\SharedTaskScheduler
HKLM\Software\Wow6432Node\Microsoft\Windows\CurrentVersion\Explorer\ShellExecuteHooks
HKLM\Software\Wow6432Node\Microsoft\Windows\CurrentVersion\Explorer\
    ShellIconOverlayIdentifiers
HKLM\Software\Wow6432Node\Microsoft\Windows\CurrentVersion\ShellServiceObjectDelayLoad

Internet Explorer

Internet Explorer is designed for extensibility, with interfaces specifically exposed to enable
Explorer bars such as the Favorites and History bars, toolbars, and custom menu items and
toolbar buttons. And Browser Helper Objects (BHOs) enable almost limitless possibilities for
extending the capabilities and user experiences for Internet Explorer.

However, because so much of users' computer time is spent in a browser, and because much
of the high-value information that users handle (such as passwords and credit card information) goes through the browser, it has become a primary target of attackers. The same programmatic interfaces that enable integration with third-party document readers and instant
messaging have also been used by spyware, adware, and other malicious endeavors.

The following lists the Internet Explorer ASEP locations that Autoruns inspects on a particular
instance of an x64 version of Windows 7.

Per-User ASEPs Under HKCU\Software

HKCU\Software\Microsoft\Internet Explorer\Explorer Bars
HKCU\Software\Microsoft\Internet Explorer\Extensions
HKCU\Software\Microsoft\Internet Explorer\UrlSearchHooks

Systemwide ASEPs in the Registry

HKLM\Software\Microsoft\Internet Explorer\Explorer Bars
HKLM\Software\Microsoft\Internet Explorer\Extensions
HKLM\Software\Microsoft\Internet Explorer\Toolbar
HKLM\Software\Microsoft\Windows\CurrentVersion\Explorer\Browser Helper Objects

Per-User and Systemwide ASEPs in the Registry—64-Bit Only
HKCU\Software\Wow6432Node\Microsoft\Internet Explorer\Explorer Bars
HKCU\Software\Wow6432Node\Microsoft\Internet Explorer\Extensions
HKLM\Software\Wow6432Node\Microsoft\Internet Explorer\Explorer Bars
HKLM\Software\Wow6432Node\Microsoft\Internet Explorer\Extensions
HKLM\Software\Wow6432Node\Microsoft\Internet Explorer\Toolbar
HKLM\Software\Wow6432Node\Microsoft\Windows\CurrentVersion\Explorer\Browser Helper Objects

Scheduled Tasks

The Scheduled Tasks tab displays entries that are configured to be launched by the Windows Task Scheduler. The Task Scheduler allows programs to be launched on a fixed schedule or upon triggering events, such as a user logging on or the computer being idle for a period of time. Commands scheduled with At.exe also appear in the list. The Task Scheduler was greatly enhanced in Windows Vista, so Windows now makes heavy use of it, and the list on the Scheduled Tasks tab will generally be long unless you hide verified Windows entries.

Because tasks can actually be disabled (unlike Start menu items), clearing the check box next to a scheduled task in Autoruns disables the task rather than copying it to a backup location.[3]

If you select Jump To from the Entry menu for a schedule task entry, Autoruns displays the Task Scheduler user interface, but it does not try to navigate to the selected entry.

Services

Windows services run in noninteractive, user-mode processes that can be configured to start independently of any user logging on, and that are controlled through a standard interface with the Service Control Manager. Multiple services can be configured to share a single process. A common example of this can be seen in Svchost.exe (Host Process for Windows Services), which is specifically designed to host multiple services implemented in separate DLLs.

Services are configured in the subkeys of HKLM\System\CurrentControlSet\Services. The Start value within each subkey determines whether and how the service starts.

Autoruns' Services tab lists services that are not disabled, unless they were disabled by Autoruns (indicated by an AutorunsDisabled value in the key). The content for the Description column comes from the text or the resource identified by the Description value in the configuration key. The image path column displays the path to the service executable;

---

[3] As of this writing, "At" jobs cannot be disabled on Windows Vista or newer, whether using Autoruns or the Windows Task Scheduler. "At" jobs can be deleted.

for Svchost services, Autoruns displays the path to the target DLL identified by the ServiceDll value in the service's key or its Parameters subkey. There are cases for some services in some versions of Windows where administrative rights are required to view the Parameters key; in these cases, Autoruns displays the path to Svchost.exe in the image path column.

Be certain you know what you are doing when disabling or deleting services. Missteps can leave your system with degraded performance, unstable, or unbootable. And again, note that disabling or deleting a service does not stop the service if it is already running.

One malware technique to watch for is a service that looks like it's supposed to be part of Windows but isn't, such as a file named *svchost.exe* in the Windows folder instead of in System32. Another technique is to make legitimate services dependent on a malware service; removing or disabling the service without fixing the dependency can result in an unbootable system. Autoruns' Jump To feature is handy for inspecting service dependencies in the registry before making changes.

Drivers

Drivers are also configured in the subkeys of HKLM\System\CurrentControlSet\Services, but they run in kernel mode, thus becoming part of the core of the operating system. Most are installed in System32\Drivers and have a .sys file extension. Drivers enable Windows to interact with various types of hardware, including displays, storage, smart card readers, and human input devices. They are also used to monitor network traffic and file I/O by antivirus software (and by Sysinternals utilities such as Procmon and Procexp!). And, of course, they are also used by malware, particularly rootkits.

As with services, the Drivers tab displays drivers that are not marked as disabled, except those disabled through Autoruns. The Description value comes from the version resource of the driver file, and the image path points to the location of the driver file.

Most blue-screen crashes are caused by an illegal operation performed in kernel mode, and most of those are caused by a bug in a third-party driver. (Less common reasons for blue screens are faulty hardware, the termination of a system-critical process such as Csrss.exe, or an intentional crash triggered through the keyboard driver's crash functionality, as described in Knowledge Base article 244139: *http://support.microsoft.com/kb/244139*.)

You can disable or delete a problematic driver with Autoruns. Doing so will usually take effect after a reboot. As with services, be absolutely certain you know what you are doing when disabling or deleting the configuration of drivers. Many are critical to the operating system, and any misconfiguration might prevent Windows from working at all.

Codecs

The Codecs category lists executable code that can be loaded by media playback applications. Buggy or misconfigured codecs have been known to cause system slowdowns and other problems, and these ASEPs have also been abused by malware. The following lists the keys that are shown on the Codecs tab.

Keys Inspected Under Both HKLM and HKCU
\Software\Classes\CLSID\{083863F1-70DE-11d0-BD40-00A0C911CE86}\Instance
\Software\Classes\CLSID\{7ED96837-96F0-4812-B211-F13C24117ED3}\Instance
\Software\Classes\CLSID\{ABE3B9A4-257D-4B97-BD1A-294AF496222E}\Instance
\Software\Classes\CLSID\{AC757296-3522-4E11-9862-C17BE5A1767E}\Instance
\Software\Classes\Filter
\Software\Microsoft\Windows NT\CurrentVersion\Drivers32

Keys Inspected Under Both HKLM and HKCU on 64-Bit Windows
\Software\Wow6432Node\Classes\CLSID\{083863F1-70DE-11d0-BD40-00A0C911CE86}\Instance
\Software\Wow6432Node\Classes\CLSID\{7ED96837-96F0-4812-B211-F13C24117ED3}\Instance
\Software\Wow6432Node\Classes\CLSID\{ABE3B9A4-257D-4B97-BD1A-294AF496222E}\Instance
\Software\Wow6432Node\Classes\CLSID\{AC757296-3522-4E11-9862-C17BE5A1767E}\Instance
\Software\Wow6432Node\Microsoft\Windows NT\CurrentVersion\Drivers32

Boot Execute

The Boot Execute tab shows you Windows native-mode executables that are started by the Session Manager (Smss.exe) during system boot. BootExecute typically includes tasks, such as hard-drive verification and repair (Autochk.exe), that cannot be performed while Windows is running. The Execute, S0InitialCommand, and SetupExecute entries should never be populated after Windows has been installed. The following lists the keys that are displayed on the Boot Execute tab.

Keys That Are Displayed on the Boot Execute Tab
HKLM\System\CurrentControlSet\Control\ServiceControlManagerExtension
HKLM\System\CurrentControlSet\Control\Session Manager\BootExecute
HKLM\System\CurrentControlSet\Control\Session Manager\Execute
HKLM\System\CurrentControlSet\Control\Session Manager\S0InitialCommand
HKLM\System\CurrentControlSet\Control\Session Manager\SetupExecute

Image Hijacks

Image Hijacks is the term I use for ASEPs that run a different program from the one you specify and expect to be running. The Image Hijacks tab displays three types of these redirections:

- **exefile**   Changes to the association of the .exe or .cmd file types with an executable command. The file association user interfaces in Windows have never exposed a way to change the association of the .exe or .cmd file types, but they can be changed in the registry. Note that there are and systemwide versions of these ASEPs.

- **Command Processor\Autorun**   A command line that is executed whenever a new Cmd.exe instance is launched. The command runs within the context of the new Cmd.exe instance. There is a per-user and systemwide variant, as well as a separate version for the 32-bit Cmd.exe on 64-bit Windows.

- **Image File Execution Options (IFEO)**   Subkeys of this registry location (and its echo in the 64-bit versions of Windows) are used for a number of internal and undocumented purposes. One purpose for IFEO subkeys that *has* been documented is the ability to specify an alternate program to start whenever a particular application is launched. By creating a subkey named for the file name of the original program and a "Debugger" value within that key that specifies an executable path to an alternate program, the alternate program is started instead and receives the original program path and command line on its command line. The original purpose of this mechanism was for the alternate program to be a debugger and for the new process to be started by that debugger, rather than having a debugger attach to the process later, after its startup code had already run. However, there is no requirement that the alternate program actually be a debugger, nor that it even look at the command line passed to it. In fact, this mechanism is how Process Explorer (described in Chapter 3, "Process Explorer") replaces Task Manager.

The following list shows the registry keys corresponding to these ASEPS that are shown on the Image Hijacks tab.

Keys Inspected for EXE File Hijacks

HKCU\SOFTWARE\Classes\Exefile\Shell\Open\Command\(Default)
HKCU\Software\Classes\.exe
HKCU\Software\Classes\.cmd
HKLM\SOFTWARE\Classes\Exefile\Shell\Open\Command\(Default)
HKLM\Software\Classes\.exe
HKLM\Software\Classes\.cmd

Command Processor Autorun Keys
HKCU\Software\Microsoft\Command Processor\Autorun
HKLM\Software\Microsoft\Command Processor\Autorun
HKLM\Software\Wow6432Node\Microsoft\Command Processor\Autorun

Keys Inspected for Image File Execution Options Hijacks
HKLM\Software\Microsoft\Windows NT\CurrentVersion\Image File Execution Options
HKLM\Software\Wow6432Node\Microsoft\Windows NT\CurrentVersion\Image File Execution Options

AppInit

The idea behind AppInit DLLs surely seemed like a good idea to the software engineers who incorporated it into Windows NT 3.1. Specify one or more DLLs in the Appinit_Dlls registry key, and those DLLs will be loaded into every process that loads User32.dll (that is, virtually all user-mode Windows processes). Well, what could go wrong with that?

- The AppInit DLLs are loaded into the process during User32's initialization—that is, while its *DllMain* function is executing. Developers are explicitly told not to load other DLLs within a *DllMain*. It can lead to deadlocks and out-of-order loads, which can lead to application crashes. And yet here, the AppInit DLL "feature" does exactly that. And yes, that has led to deadlock and application crashes.

- A DLL that automatically gets loaded into every process on the computer sounds like a winner if you are writing malware. Although AppInit has been used in legitimate (but misguided) software, it is frequently used by malware.

Because of these problems, AppInit DLLs are deprecated and disabled by default in Windows Vista and newer. For purposes of backward compatibility, it is possible to re-enable AppInit DLL functionality, but it is not recommended.

Keys Inspected for AppInit Entries
HKLM\Software\Microsoft\Windows NT\CurrentVersion\Windows\Appinit_Dlls
HKLM\Software\Wow6432Node\Microsoft\Windows NT\CurrentVersion\Windows\Appinit_Dlls

KnownDLLs

KnownDLLs helps improve system performance by ensuring that all Windows processes use the same version of certain DLLs, rather than choose their own from various file locations. During startup, the Session Manager maps the DLLs listed in HKLM\System\CurrentControlSet\Control\Session Manager\KnownDlls into memory as named section objects. When a new process is loaded and needs to map these DLLs, it uses the existing sections rather than searching the file system for another version of the DLL.

The Autoruns KnownDLLs tab should contain only verifiable Windows DLLs. On 64-bit versions of Windows, the KnownDLLs tab lists one ASEP, but file entries are duplicated for both 32-bit and 64-bit versions of the DLLs, in folders specified by the DllDirectory and DllDirectory32 values in the registry key.

To verify that malware hasn't deleted an entry from this key so that it can load its own version of a system DLL, save the autoruns results from the suspect system and compare it against the results from a known-good instance of the same operating system. See the "Saving and Comparing Results" section later in this chapter for more information.

Winlogon

The Winlogon tab displays entries that hook into Winlogon.exe, which manages the Windows logon user interface. On Windows XP and Windows Server 2003, these can include the GINA DLL interface and Winlogon notification packages. Those interfaces were removed in Windows Vista, which introduced the Credential Provider interface.

The Winlogon tab also includes the user's configured screen saver, which is started by Winlogon.exe after inactivity.

The following list specifies the registry keys that are shown on the Winlogon tab.

Per-User Specification of the Screen Saver

HKCU\Control Panel\Desktop\Scrnsave.exe

Per-User Specification of the Screen Saver, Controlled by Group Policy

HKCU\Software\Policies\Microsoft\Windows\Control Panel\Desktop\Scrnsave.exe

GINA, Notification Packages, and So Forth. (Windows XP and Windows Server 2003)

HKLM\Software\Microsoft\Windows NT\CurrentVersion\Winlogon\GinaDLL
HKLM\Software\Microsoft\Windows NT\CurrentVersion\Winlogon\Notify
HKLM\Software\Microsoft\Windows NT\CurrentVersion\Winlogon\SaveDumpStart
HKLM\Software\Microsoft\Windows NT\CurrentVersion\Winlogon\System
HKLM\Software\Microsoft\Windows NT\CurrentVersion\Winlogon\Taskman
HKLM\Software\Microsoft\Windows NT\CurrentVersion\Winlogon\UIHost

Credential Provider ASEPs (Windows Vista and newer)

HKLM\Software\Microsoft\Windows\CurrentVersion\Authentication\Credential Provider Filters
HKLM\Software\Microsoft\Windows\CurrentVersion\Authentication\Credential Providers
HKLM\Software\Microsoft\Windows\CurrentVersion\Authentication\PLAP Providers

Systemwide Identification of a Program to Verify Successful Boot

HKLM\System\CurrentControlSet\Control\BootVerificationProgram\ImagePath

Winsock Providers

Windows Sockets (Winsock) is an extensible API on Windows because third parties can add a *transport service provider* that interfaces Winsock with other protocols or layers on top of existing protocols to provide functionality such as proxying. Third parties can also add a *namespace service provider* to augment Winsock's name-resolution facilities. Service providers plug into Winsock by using the Winsock *service provider interface* (SPI). When a transport service provider is registered with Winsock, Winsock uses the transport service provider to implement socket functions, such as *connect* and *accept*, for the address types that the provider indicates it implements. There are no restrictions on how the transport service provider implements the functions, but the implementation usually involves communicating with a transport driver in kernel mode.

The Winsock tab lists the providers registered on the system, including those that are built into Windows. You can hide the latter group by enabling Hide Windows Entries and Verify Code Signatures to focus on the entries that are more likely to be causing problems.

Keys Inspected for Winsock Provider Entries
HKLM\System\CurrentControlSet\Services\WinSock2\Parameters\NameSpace_Catalog5\Catalog_ Entries
HKLM\System\CurrentControlSet\Services\WinSock2\Parameters\NameSpace_Catalog5\Catalog_ Entries64
HKLM\System\CurrentControlSet\Services\WinSock2\Parameters\Protocol_Catalog9\Catalog_Entries
HKLM\System\CurrentControlSet\Services\WinSock2\Parameters\Protocol_Catalog9\Catalog_ Entries64

Print Monitors

The entries listed on the Print Monitors tab are DLLs that are configured in the subkeys of HKLM\System\CurrentControlSet\Control\Print\Monitors. These DLLs are loaded into the Spooler service, which runs as Local System.

> **Note** One of the most common problems that affects the print spooler is misbehaving or poorly coded third-party port monitors. A good first step in troubleshooting print spooler issues is to disable third-party port monitors to see whether the problem persists.

LSA Providers

This category of autostarts comprises packages that define or extend user authentication for Windows, via the Local Security Authority (LSA). Unless you have installed third-party authentication packages, this list should contain only Windows verifiable entries. The DLLs listed in these entries are loaded by Lsass.exe or Winlogon.exe and run as Local System.

The SecurityProviders ASEP that is also shown on this tab lists registered cryptographic providers. DLLs listed in this ASEP get loaded into many privileged and standard user processes, so this ASEP has been targeted as a malware persistence vector. (This ASEP isn't truly related to the LSA, except that, like the LSA, it represents security-related functionality.)

Keys Inspected for Authentication Providers
HKLM\System\CurrentControlSet\Control\Lsa\Authentication Packages
HKLM\System\CurrentControlSet\Control\Lsa\Notification Packages
HKLM\System\CurrentControlSet\Control\Lsa\Security Packages
Keys Inspected for Registered Cryptographic Providers
HKLM\System\CurrentControlSet\Control\SecurityProviders\SecurityProviders

Network Providers

The Network Providers tab lists the installed providers handling network communication, which are configured in HKLM\System\CurrentControlSet\Control\NetworkProvider\Order. On a Windows desktop operating system, for example, this tab includes the default providers that provide access to SMB (file and print) servers, Microsoft RDP (Terminal Services/Remote Desktop) servers, and access to WebDAV servers. Additional providers are often visible in this list if you have a more heterogeneous network or additional types of servers that Windows needs to connect to. All entries in this list should be verifiable.

Sidebar Gadgets

On Windows Vista and newer, this tab lists the Sidebar Gadgets (now called Desktop Gadgets on Windows 7) that are configured to appear on the user's desktop. Although gadget software is often (but not always) installed in a systemwide location such as %ProgramFiles%, the configuration of which gadgets to run is in %LOCALAPPDATA%\Microsoft\Windows Sidebar\ Settings.ini, which is per-user and nonroaming. Disabling or deleting gadgets with Autoruns manipulates entries in the Settings.ini file.

The image path usually points to an XML file. The gadgets that ship with Windows are catalog signed and can be verified.

Saving and Comparing Results

Autoruns results can be saved to disk in two different file formats: tab-delimited text, or a binary format that preserves all the data captured. The binary format can be loaded into Autoruns for viewing at a later time or on a different system, and it can be compared against another set of Autoruns results.

In both cases, the results are read-only: they can't be used to roll back a system to an earlier state or configuration, and after they have been captured, you cannot add or remove options to modify the saved results.

Saving as Tab-Delimited Text

Click the Save button on the toolbar; in the Save dialog box change the Save As Type to Text (*.txt), and specify a file in which to save the current results. Data displayed on the Everything tab is written to the file in four-column, tab-delimited format. The output includes the ASEPs (the shaded rows) in the first column and three empty strings in the remaining columns. Entries that are enabled (the check boxes are selected) are written to the file prepended with a plus sign (+); those that are disabled are prepended with an X.

The text file can be imported into Microsoft Office Excel. You should specify the first column as Text instead of General so that the leading plus signs do not get interpreted as an instruction or other special character.

The tab-delimited format respects the selections on the Options menu. If Include Empty Locations is selected, the file will include all ASEPs, including those that have no entries. If Hide Microsoft and Windows Entries or Hide Windows Entries is selected, those entries will be omitted from the output. If Verify Code Signatures is selected, the Publisher column will include Verified or Not Verified, as appropriate.

Note that Autoruns results saved in text format cannot be read back in to Autoruns.

See the section on AutorunsC later in this chapter for a scriptable way to capture Autoruns data to other text file formats.

Saving in Binary (.arn) Format

The Autoruns binary file format with its default .arn file extension is the Autoruns "native" file format. Click the Save icon on the toolbar, and specify a file in which to save the results, leaving the Save As Type option as Autoruns Data (*.arn). All information shown on the Everything tab is preserved. If the Include Empty Locations option is selected, the data includes all empty ASEPs. If one of the Hide options is selected, the saved data does not include the omitted rows. And if any files had signature verification attempted, the saved file will retain the results of those verifications.

You can automate the capture of Autoruns data and saving it to a .arn file with the **–a** command-line option. The following command captures the state of autostart entries on the system to outputfile.arn, using default Autoruns options:

```
Autoruns -a outputfile.arn
```

To add signature verification, include the –v option. Make sure not to put it *between* the **–a** and the file name:

```
Autoruns -v -a outputfile.arn
```

Viewing and Comparing Saved Results

To view the .arn file on the same or another system, choose Open from the File menu and select the saved file.

To compare the results displayed in Autoruns—whether it's a fresh capture or from a saved file—choose Compare from the File menu and select the saved file to compare the displayed results against. Entries that have changed between the two sets are highlighted in green, as are any entries that were added in the first set and weren't found in the "compare" set. Note however, that items that were deleted aren't displayed. One workaround that will show these as well is to save the sets as FileOne.arn and FileTwo.arn, open FileOne.arn and compare FileTwo.arn, and then open FileTwo.arn and compare FileOne.arn.

AutorunsC

AutorunsC is a console-mode version of Autoruns that outputs results to its standard output. It is designed primarily for use in scripts. Its purpose is data collection only: it cannot disable or delete any autostart entries.

The command-line options are listed in Table 5-11. They let you capture all autostarts or just specific categories, verify digital signatures, omit Microsoft entries, specify a user account for which to capture autostarts, and output results as comma-separated values (CSV) or as XML. If you don't specify any options, AutorunsC outputs just the Logon entries without signature verification and in an indented list format designed for human reading.

Whether in the default list format, CSV, or XML, AutorunsC's output always includes the ASEP location, entry name, description, publisher, image path, and whether the entry is enabled. It also includes the MD5, SHA-1, and SHA-256 hashes of the image file.

The CSV format includes column headers, and it imports easily into Excel or relational databases. The XML format is easily consumed by Windows PowerShell or any other XML consumer. For example, the following lines of PowerShell run AutorunsC, read the XML, and then display disabled items:

```
$arcx = [xml]$( AutorunsC -a -x -accepteula)

$arcx.SelectNodes("/autoruns/item") | ?{ $_.enabled -ne "Enabled" }
```

TABLE 5-11 AutorunsC Command-Line Options

Options	
−c	Prints output as CSV
−x	Prints output as XML
−v	Verifies digital signatures
−m	Hides Microsoft entries
user	Specifies the name of the user account for which autostart entries will be shown
Autostart Types	
−a	Shows all entries
−b	Shows boot execute entries
−d	Shows Appinit DLLs
−e	Shows Explorer addons
−g	Shows Sidebar gadgets (Windows Vista and newer)
−h	Shows image hijacks
−i	Shows Internet Explorer addons
−k	Shows known DLLs
−l	Shows Logon autostart entries (the default)
−n	Shows Winsock protocol and network providers
−o	Shows codecs
−p	Shows print monitor DLLs
−r	Shows LSA security providers
−s	Shows services and drivers
−t	Shows scheduled tasks
−w	Shows Winlogon entries

Autoruns and Malware

One of the goals of most malware is to remain active on an infected system indefinitely. Malware has therefore always used ASEPs. Years ago, it usually just targeted simple locations such as the Run key under HKLM. As malware has become more sophisticated and difficult to identify, its use of ASEPs has become more sophisticated as well. Malware has been implemented as Winsock providers and as print monitors. Not only are such ASEP locations more obscure, but the malware doesn't show up in a process list because it loads as a DLL in an existing, legitimate process. Malware has also become more adept at infecting and running without requiring administrative privileges, because there are increasing numbers of users who only ever have standard user privileges.

In addition, malware often leverages rootkits, which subvert the integrity of the operating system. Rootkits intercept and modify system calls, lying to software that uses documented system interfaces about the state of the system. Rootkits can hide the presence of registry keys and values, files and folders, processes, sockets, user accounts, and more, or they can make software believe something exists when it doesn't. In short, a computer on which malware has run with administrative privileges cannot be trusted to report its own state accurately. Therefore, Autoruns cannot always be expected to identify malicious autostart entries on a system.

That said, not all malware is that sophisticated, and there are still some telltale signs that can point to malware:

- Entries with a well-known publisher such as Microsoft that fail signature verification. (Unfortunately, not all software published by Microsoft is signed.)

- Entries with an image path pointing to a DLL or EXE file that is missing Description or Publisher information (unless the target file is not found).

- A common Windows component that is launched from an unusual or nonstandard location—for example, svchost.exe launching from C:\Windows (instead of from System32) or from C:\System Volume Information.

- Entries for which the file date and time of the launched program correspond to when problems were first noticed or a breach is discovered to have occurred.

- Disabling or deleting an entry, pressing F5 to refresh the display, and finding the entry still present and enabled. Malware will often monitor its ASEPs and put them back if they get removed.

Malware and antimalware remains a moving target. Today's "best practices" will seem naïve and insufficient tomorrow.

There are some entries you might come across that seem suspicious but are innocuous:

- A default installation of Windows XP or Windows Server 2003 will show a number of "File not found" entries, particularly on the Drivers tab. These are legacy entries for which the files have been removed from the default installation but the registry entries were inadvertently retained.

- A default installation of Windows XP will show an entry on the Image Hijacks tab, under Image File Execution Options (IFEO). The entry name is "Your Image File Name Here without a path," and it points to Ntsd.exe in the System32 folder. The purpose of the entry is to serve as a sample for use of the IFEO key.

- A default installation of Windows Vista might have a small number of "File not found" entries on the Drivers tab for NetWare IPX drivers and for "IP in IP Tunnel Driver."

- A default installation of Windows 7 might have a small number of entries on the Scheduled Tasks tab under "\Microsoft\Windows" that show an entry name but no further information.

Chapter 6
PsTools

Sysinternals PsTools is a suite of 12 Microsoft Windows management utilities with common characteristics:

- They are all console utilities. That is, they are designed to run at a command prompt or from a batch file, and they write to the standard output and standard error streams (which can appear in the console window or be redirected to files).

- They can operate on the local computer or on a remote computer. Unlike most remote control programs, the PsTools utilities do not require preinstallation of client software on the remote systems. (And of course, like all other Sysinternals utilities, they require no installation on the local computer either.)

- They provide a standard syntax for specifying alternate credentials so that the utilities' tasks can be performed as another user.[1]

The utilities included in the PsTools suite are

- **PsExec**   Executes processes remotely and/or as Local System with redirected output

- **PsFile**   Lists or closes files opened remotely

- **PsGetSid**   Displays the Security Identifier (SID) of a computer, a user or a group

- **PsInfo**   Lists information about a system

- **PsKill**   Terminates processes by name or by process ID (PID)

- **PsList**   Lists information about processes

- **PsLoggedOn**   Lists accounts that are logged on locally and through remote connections

- **PsLogList**   Dumps event log records

- **PsPasswd**   Changes passwords for user accounts

- **PsService   Lists and** controls Windows services

- **PsShutdown**   Shuts down, logs off, or changes the power state of local and remote systems

- **PsSuspend**   Suspends and resumes processes

---

[1] Two exceptions are that PsLoggedOn does not accept alternate credentials, nor does PsPasswd when changing the password for a domain account.

Incidentally, the reason that the suite is named PsTools and that all the member utilities have *Ps* as a prefix to their names is that the first of these that I developed was PsList, which lists running processes. I named it after the *ps* utility that provides similar functionality on UNIX systems.

Before we get started on the utilities, an issue that still comes up is that occasionally antivirus products will flag some of the PsTools as Trojan-horse programs or other types of malware. Rest assured that *none* of the PsTools—or any Sysinternals utilities—are malware. However, miscreants have incorporated various PsTools, particularly PsExec, into malware payloads. Because my name and Web site are included in the PsTools, and the malware authors don't usually put their own contact information on the parts of the payload they write, I'm the one who gets the angry e-mails from Windows users berating me for writing viruses and infecting their systems. As I've had to explain many times, the PsTools serve legitimate purposes, and their misuse is not something that I have any control over. Furthermore, the utilities do not exploit vulnerabilities or gain unauthorized access. They either have to be already running with an account that has the necessary access, or be given the user name and password of an authorized account.

Common Features

All of the utilities in the PsTools suite work on all supported client and server versions of Windows. That includes x86 and x64 versions of Windows XP, Windows Vista, and Windows 7, and x86, x64, and IA-64 versions of Windows Server 2003, 2008, and 2008 R2. Support for 64-bit versions requires that WOW64, the components that support 32-bit applications on 64-bit Windows, be installed. (WOW64 can be uninstalled on Server Core.)

All of the PsTools utilities support remote operations using a syntax that is consistent across the entire suite. You can display the syntax for a utility by running it with **–?** on the command line. The command-line syntax for each of the PsTools utilities is listed in the "PsTools Command-Line Syntax" section near the end of this chapter.

Remote Operations

The PsTools utilities can perform operations on the local computer or on a remote computer. Each of the utilities accepts an optional **\\computer** command-line parameter: the backslash pair followed by a computer name or IP address directs the utility to perform actions on the specified computer. For example:

```
psinfo \\srv2008r2

psinfo \\192.168.0.10
```

Some of the utilities perform remote operations simply by using Windows APIs that allow specification of a remote computer on which to operate. Some of the utilities accomplish remote operations by extracting an EXE file embedded in its executable image, copying that file to the remote computer's Admin$ share, registering it as a service on that system and starting that service using the Windows Service Control Manager APIs, and then communicating with that service using named pipes. Creating a remote service requires that file sharing and the Admin$ share be enabled on the target computer. A table at the end of this chapter lists which of the PsTools utilities require these features for remote operation.

Remote Operations on Multiple Computers

Several of the utilities can operate on multiple remote computers with a single command. (The table at the end of this chapter lists which ones support this feature.) For these utilities, you can specify the remote computers directly on the command line or in an input file. The command-line syntax is a pair of backslashes, followed by the computer names or IP addresses separated with commas and with no spaces between them. For example:

```
psinfo \\server1,server2,192.168.0.3,server4
```

That command line lists system information from **server1**, then from **server2**, then from the computer at IP address **192.168.0.3**, and finally from **server4**.

Another way to specify the remote computers for utilities that can operate on multiple computers is by using a text file containing each computer name or IP address on a separate line, and naming the file on the command line prefixed with an @ symbol. The previous example can be accomplished with a file called *computers.txt* containing the following lines:

```
server1
server2
192.168.0.3
server4
```

And then running the following command line:

```
psinfo @computers.txt
```

Finally, for the utilities that can operate on multiple remote computers, passing ***** on the command line directs the utility to operate on all computers in the current domain or workgroup:

```
psinfo \\*
```

If none of these options are used, the utility operates on the local computer.

Alternate Credentials

When operating on remote computers, the PsTools utilities impersonate the account from which you run the utility on the local system. If it is running with a local account rather than with a domain account, the authentication can succeed only if the remote computer also has a local account with the same user name and password.

There are several reasons that you might want to run the utility with a different account on the remote system. First, most of the utilities require administrative privileges on the target system, so you need to use a different account if the one you are using doesn't have those privileges. Second, as I will discuss shortly in the "Troubleshooting Remote PsTools Connections" section, restrictions were introduced in Windows Vista on the use of local accounts for remote administration. Finally, there are several reasons that pertain only to PsExec; those are discussed in the "PsExec" section of this chapter.

To use a different user account, specify it with the **–u** command-line parameter, and optionally specify the account password with the **–p** parameter. For example:

```
psinfo \\server1 -u MYDOMAIN\AdminAccnt -p Pass@word123
```

If the user name or password contains spaces, enclose them in double quotes:

```
psinfo \\server1 -u "MYDOMAIN\Admin Account" -p "Password with spaces"
```

If you omit the **–p**, the utility will prompt you for the password. For security reasons, it will not echo the password characters to the screen as you type them. The utilities use the WNetAddConnection2 API, so passwords are not sent over the network in the clear to authenticate to remote systems. (However, in some cases PsExec needs to send the credentials after authenticating to create a new logon session; in this case, credentials are sent unencrypted.)

All of the PsTools support the **–u** and **–p** command-line parameters except for PsLoggedOn.

Troubleshooting Remote PsTools Connections

A number of dials and knobs need to be set just right for PsTools to work on remote systems. Obviously, they all require connectivity to the necessary network interfaces, which involves firewall settings and ensuring that services are running. Most of the utilities require administrative rights. And finally, User Account Control (UAC) applies restrictions to local accounts that must be taken into consideration.

Basic Connectivity

Unless you specify an IP address, name resolution needs to work. If DNS is not available, NetBIOS over TCP (NBT) might suffice, but it requires that 137 UDP, 137 TCP, 138 UDP, and 139 TCP be opened on the firewall of the target system.

Some of the utilities require that the administrative Admin$ share be available. This requires that file and print sharing be enabled (the Workstation service locally and the Server service on the target system), that the firewall not block the ports that are needed to support file and printer sharing, and also that "simple file sharing" be disabled.

Some of the utilities require that the Remote Registry service be running on the target system. (The table at the end of the chapter lists which ones require this feature.) Note that in the newer versions of Windows, this service is not configured for automatic start by default. It therefore needs to be manually started or configured for automatic start before some of these tools will work.

User Accounts

Most of the utilities require administrative rights. Before Windows Vista and User Account Control, administrative accounts were straightforward. If the account was a member of the Administrators group, everything run by that account also ran with full administrative rights. Successfully authenticating to the computer with an account in the Administrators group allowed full control over the computer.

Windows Vista introduced User Account Control, which (among other things) pioneered the concept of a user account that could be both an administrative account and a standard user account. This account type is sometimes called *Protected Administrator*. The idea is that programs started by the user will run with standard user privileges, and that for a program to run with full administrative rights, the user must explicitly approve the elevation. Programs running as the user should not be able to programmatically approve the elevation for the user or otherwise bypass the interaction. If they could, software developers would take those shortcuts and continue to write programs that required administrative rights rather than write software for standard users.

Network loopback is one of the automatic elevation paths that Windows Vista blocks. As described in Knowledge Base article 951016, if a network connection is established to a remote computer using a local account that is a member of the Administrators group, it connects only with standard user privileges. Because it is not an interactive logon, there is no opportunity to elevate to full administrator. Domain accounts are not subject to this restriction.

What this means is that although PsTools work perfectly well for remote administration using local accounts on Windows XP and Windows Server 2003, they do not work so well on Windows Vista and newer. If domain accounts are not an option, you can read KB 951016 to see how to set the LocalAccountTokenFilterPolicy setting to remove the restrictions on local accounts.

PsExec

PsExec lets you execute arbitrary processes on one or more remote computers. PsExec redirects the input and output streams of console applications so that they appear to be running locally, as though in a Telnet session. In this way, console utilities that normally operate only on the local computer can be remote-enabled. A particularly powerful use of this capability is to run a command prompt on a remote system and interact with it as though it were running on the local computer. Unlike most remote control utilities, PsExec does not require installation of agents or other client software on the target computer ahead of time. Of course, you do need an account that is authorized for remote administration of the computer.

PsExec also lets you execute programs locally or remotely in the System account, either interactively or noninteractively. For example, you can run Regedit and view registry key hierarchies that are accessible only to the System account, such as HKLM\SAM and HKLM\Security. And as described in Chapter 4, "Process Monitor," PsExec can launch a program in a noninteractive session that survives user logoff. PsExec offers many other options that control the way in which the local or remote target process should run, including user account, privilege level, priority level, and CPU assignment.

The command-line syntax to run a process on a remote computer is

```
psexec \\computer [options] program [arguments]
```

For example, to run **ipconfig /all** on a remote system and view its output locally, run the following:

```
psexec \\server1 ipconfig /all
```

To run a process on the local computer, simply omit the **\\computer** parameter:

```
psexec [options] program [arguments]
```

If the "program" part of the command line contains spaces, you must put quotation marks around the program path. If parts of the remote command line include special characters such as the pipe or redirection characters, use the command shell's escape character (^) to prevent their being treated as special characters by the local command shell. The following example runs **ipconfig /all** on server1 and redirects its standard output to **C:\ipconfig.out** on server1:

```
psexec \\server1 cmd.exe /c ipconfig /all ^> c:\ipconfig.out
```

Without the escape character (^), the standard output of the PsExec command (including the redirected console output of *ipconfig*) would be written to **c:\ipconfig.out** on the local computer. (PsExec's diagnostic output is written to its standard error stream rather than to its standard output so that local redirection captures only the output of the remote process.)

If the "program" part of the PsExec command line specifies only a file name, it must be found in the Path on the remote system. (Note that changes made to the global PATH environment variable are generally not seen by services until after a subsequent reboot.) If the "program" argument specifies an absolute path, realize that drive letters are relative to the global environment of the remote system. For example, *C:* will refer to the C: drive of the remote system, and network drive letter mappings on the local computer or those that are mapped during user logons will not be recognized. However, if the program is not already on the remote system, PsExec can copy a program file from the local computer to the remote system for you. (See the "Remote Connectivity Options" section later in this chapter.)

Remote Process Exit

By default, PsExec does not exit until the program it started has exited. When a process exits, it reports an exit code—a 32-bit integer—to the operating system, where it can be read by its parent process (or any other process that has an open handle to it). The exit code is often used to report whether the process succeeded at its task, with 0 (zero) typically indicating success. The exit code is what is tested by *Cmd*'s IF ERRORLEVEL command and its *&&* and || conditional operators. PsExec outputs the process' exit code to its console (for example, "Notepad.exe exited with error code 0"). PsExec then exits, using the target program's exit code as its own exit code so that a parent process or batch file can test it and perform conditional processing.

When PsExec's **–d** option is used, PsExec starts the remote process but does not wait for it to exit. On success, PsExec outputs the process ID of the new process to the *stderr* stream and exits, using the new PID as its own exit code. That PID can be captured in a batch file like this:

```
psexec \\server1 -d App.exe
SET NEWPID=%ERRORLEVEL%
ECHO The Process ID for App.exe is %NEWPID%
```

However, if PsExec cannot start the remote process, its exit code represents an error code. There isn't a reliable programmatic way to distinguish whether an exit code is a PID or an error code.

Redirected Console Output

To start a command prompt on a remote system and interact with it on the local computer, simply run

```
psexec \\server1 Cmd.exe
```

There are a few things to note about redirected console output:

- Operations that require knowledge of the containing console, such as cursor positioning or text coloring, do not work. These include the clear screen (**cls**) command, the **more** command, and tab completion for file and folder names.

- If you launch a program in a new window, such as with the **start** command or any GUI program, the program will run on the remote computer but you will not be able to interact with it.

- All Sysinternals utilities, including the console utilities, display a EULA dialog box that must be accepted the first time the utility runs under that account on that computer unless you add **/accepteula** to the command line. As mentioned in the previous bullet, you will not be able to dismiss that dialog box and the utility will hang until you terminate it by pressing Ctrl+C. Be sure to use the **/accepteula** flag when redirecting Sysinternals utility output.

> **Note** Some Sysinternals utilities have not yet been updated to support the **/accepteula** switch. For these utilities, you might need to manually set the flag indicating acceptance. You can do this with a command line like the following:
>
> ```
> psexec \\server1 reg add hkcu\software\sysinternals\pendmove /v eulaaccepted /t
> reg_dword /d 1 /f
> ```

- Windows PowerShell version 1 does not support having its console output redirected, but PowerShell version 2 does if started with the **−File −** command-line option. For example:

```
psexec \\server1 PowerShell.exe -file -
```

- Pressing Ctrl+C terminates the remote process, not just the current command. For example, if you are running a remote command shell and accidentally run **dir /s c:**, pressing Ctrl+C will terminate the command shell, not just the **dir** command.

Some common commands such as **dir** and **copy** are not separate executable programs, but are built in to *Cmd.exe*. To run a built-in command, use *Cmd*'s **/c** option to run the command within the context of a *Cmd.exe* process that exits after the command has finished. For example, the command

```
psexec \\server1 Cmd.exe /c ver
```

starts an instance of *Cmd.exe* on server1 that runs the built-in **ver** command and then exits. The output of **ver** from server1 appears in the local console window in which PsExec was launched. In this case, *Cmd.exe* is the "program" part of the PsExec command line and **/c ver** is the optional "arguments" part passed to the program when it starts.

PsExec Alternate Credentials

The "Alternate Credentials" section earlier in this chapter described the use of the **–u** and **–p** parameters to provide explicit credentials to PsTools utilities. If these options are not used, the logged-on user account that is running PsExec is used to authenticate to the remote system, and then that account is *impersonated* by the remote process started by PsExec. This raises several issues:

- To start a process on a remote system, PsExec must use an account that has administrative rights on the remote system.

- If the remote process accesses network resources, it will authenticate as *anonymous* unless Kerberos delegation has been enabled. This is the *one-hop* limitation of imper-sonation: the computer on which a logon session is established with explicit credentials can authenticate to a remote server that can impersonate that security context on that system, but the process on the remote computer cannot then use the security context to authenticate to a third system.

- The impersonated security context will not include any *logon SIDs* that would grant it access to any interactive user sessions.

You should provide explicit credentials if the account running PsExec does not have administrative access to the remote computer, if the remote process requires authenticated access to network resources, or if the remote process needs to run on an interactive user desktop. When explicit credentials are supplied, they are used to authenticate to the remote system, and then to create a new logon session that can run on a particular interactive desktop.

> **Important** The user name and password used to create the new logon session are transmitted to the remote system in the clear—that is, unencrypted. Anyone sniffing the network will be able to capture these credentials. Consider configuring your network to use IPsec with ESP (Encapsulating Security Payload) to encrypt all communications.

The **–u** and **–p** parameters can also be used when starting a process on the local computer, in a manner similar to RunAs.exe. And as with RunAs.exe, because of UAC the target process will not have full administrative rights on Windows Vista or newer, even if the user account is a member of the Administrators group (unless you specify **–h**, described later).

PsExec Command-Line Options

Let's take a look at PsExec's command-line options. They control aspects of process performance, remote connectivity, runtime environment, and whether PsExec should wait for the target process to exit. Table 6-1 summarizes these options, which are discussed in more detail after the table.

TABLE 6-1 **PsExec Command-Line Options**

Option	Description
–d	Doesn't wait for the process to terminate. (This is described earlier in the "Remote Process Exit" section.)
Process Performance Options	
–background –low –belownormal –abovenormal –high –realtime	Runs the process at a different priority.
–a n,n...	Specifies the CPUs on which the process can run.
Remote Connectivity Options	
–c [–f|–v]	Copies the specified program from the local system to the remote system. If you omit this option, the application must be in the system path on the remote system. Adding **–f** forces the copy to occur; **–v** performs a version or timestamp check and copies only if the source is newer.
–n *seconds*	Specifies timeout in seconds when connecting to remote computers.
Runtime environment options	
–s	Runs the process in the System account.
–i [*session*]	Runs the program on an interactive desktop.
–x	Runs the process on the Winlogon secure desktop.
–w *directory*	Sets the working directory of the process.
–e	Does not load the specified account's profile.
–h	Uses the account's elevated context, if available.
–l	Runs the process as a limited user.

Process Performance Options

By default, the target process runs with normal priority. You can set the process priority of the target process by specifying any of the following on the PsExec command line: **–background**, **–low**, **–belownormal**, **–abovenormal**, **–high**, and **–realtime**. The **–background** option is supported only on Windows Vista and newer; in addition to setting the process priority to Low, it sets the process' memory priority and I/O priority to Very Low.

If the target is a multiprocessor system, you can specify that the threads of the target process be scheduled only on specific CPUs. Add the **–a** option followed by the list of logical CPUs separated by commas (where *1* is the lowest-numbered CPU). For example, to run the process only on CPU 3, use the following:

```
psexec -a 3 app.exe
```

To run the target process on CPUs 2, 3 and 4, use this command line:

```
psexec -a 2,3,4 app.exe
```

Remote Connectivity Options

If the program you want to run on a remote system is not installed on that system, PsExec can copy it from the local file system to the remote computer's system32 folder, run it from that location, and then delete the program after it has finished execution. You can make the copy conditional on a newer version not already being present on the remote system. When you specify the **–c** option, the "program" on the PsExec command line specifies a file path relative to the local computer; that file is copied to the system32 folder of the remote system. Note, though, that this option copies only that one file; it does not copy any dependent DLLs or other files.

Using the **–c** option by itself, PsExec does not perform the file copy if the file already exists in the target location. Adding the **–f** option forces the file copy, even overwriting a file marked as read-only, hidden, or system. The **–v** option checks the file versions and time stamps, copying only if the local copy has a higher version and a newer time stamp, but starting the remote process in either case.

When trying to establish a connection with a remote system that is offline, is very busy, or has some other connectivity problems, PsExec uses the default system timeouts for each of the network operations required. To select a shorter timeout period, use the **–n** option followed by the maximum number of seconds that PsExec should allow for each remote connection. For example, to limit the amount of time spent trying to connect to a series of remote systems to 10 seconds each, use the following:

```
psexec @computers.txt -n 10 app.exe
```

Runtime Environment Options

PsExec offers several command-line options to control the runtime environment of the target process. These options include the ability to run the process in the System account or in a reduced-privileged mode, whether to run interactively and in which interactive session, whether to load the account's profile on the target system, and the ability to set the initial working directory of the target process.

The **–s** option runs the target application in the System account. If you don't also specify the **–i** "interactive" option (discussed shortly), the process will run in the same noninteractive environment in which other Windows services running as System execute (Session 0, window station Service-0x0-3e7$)[2], with console output redirected to the console in which PsExec is running. Review the "Redirected Console Output" section earlier in this chapter for issues to be aware of. One benefit of this mode of execution is that the process will continue to run even after interactive user logoff. The Process Monitor chapter includes an example of using PsExec in this way to monitor events during user logoff and system shutdown.

If the target system is the local computer, PsExec must already be running with full administrative permissions to use the **–s** option. For remote execution, PsExec already requires an administrative account on the remote system.

The **–i [*session*]** option is used to run the target process interactively on the target system—more specifically, on the default interactive desktop of a terminal services session. Without the **–i** switch, processes on remote computers will run in a noninteractive window station within session 0. The optional *session* parameter specifies the ID number of the terminal services session in which you want the process to run. If you use **–i** but omit the *session* parameter, PsExec runs the process in the current desktop session when run on the local computer, or in the current console session when run on a remote computer. The console session is the session currently associated with the keyboard and display attached to the computer (as opposed to a remote desktop session). Recall that explicit credentials are required to run an interactive process on a remote computer.

> **Tip** Enable the Session column in Process Explorer (which is discussed in Chapter 3, "Process Explorer") to see the session ID associated with processes.

The following command line runs Regedit as System and in the current interactive session so that you can view those portions of the registry that grant access only to System (such as HKLM\SAM and HKLM\Security):

```
psexec -s -i Regedit.exe
```

And this command line starts a command shell running as System on the current desktop:

```
psexec -s -i Cmd.exe
```

The **–x** option runs the target process on the secure Winlogon desktop. The Winlogon desktop is managed by the System account, and only processes running as System can access it. Generally, that means that **–x** needs to be used in conjunction with **–s**, and that PsExec must already be running with administrative permissions. In addition, the **–x** option can be

---

2 See "Sessions, Window Stations, Desktops, and Window Messages" in Chapter 2, "Windows Core Concepts," for more information.

used only on the local computer. By default, **–x** runs the target process on the Winlogon desktop of the console session. Use the **–i** option along with **–x** to run the target process on the Winlogon desktop of a different remote desktop session. The following command line runs a command prompt on the secure desktop of the console session:

```
psexec -x -s Cmd.exe
```

If you are logged on at the console, press Ctrl+Alt+Del to switch to the Winlogon desktop. If the version of Windows you are running displays a full-screen image on the secure desktop, press Alt+Tab to switch to the command prompt.

The **–w *directory*** option sets the initial directory for the target process. Note that the directory path you specify is relative to the target computer. For example, C:\Program Files refers to the C:\Program Files folder on the remote computer, not on the local computer. Note also that network drive letter mappings will usually not be recognized.

When you use the **–e** option, the user account's profile is not loaded. This feature can save a little execution time for short-lived processes where the user account's profile is not needed. However, it should not be used if any operations might depend on user-profile settings. The HKCU seen by the process refers to the System account's HKCU hive unless another logon session had already loaded the user's profile at the time the remote process was started. In that case, the process' HKCU refers to the user's normal HKCU hive. The %USERPROFILE% environment variable refers to the System account's profile directory regardless of whether the user's profile had been loaded. Because the System account's profile is always loaded, PsExec does not allow the use of the **–e** and **–s** options at the same time.

On Windows Vista and newer, a logon of "interactive" type (such as that which is invoked when you provide explicit credentials) is subject to token filtering—administrative groups are disabled and administrative privileges are removed. When providing explicit credentials, adding the **–h** option starts the target process on a remote system with the user account's full administrative token. If the target system is the local computer, **–h** can ensure that the target process runs with an elevated token only if PsExec is already running elevated.

The **–l** (lowercase *L*) option runs the target process with limited rights. If the Administrators group is present in the user's token, it is disabled; also, all privileges are removed except those that are granted to the Users group on the target computer. On Windows Vista and newer, the process runs at Low integrity, which prevents it from writing to most areas of the file system and registry. The following command line allows a Windows XP administrator to run Internet Explorer with reduced rights:

```
psexec -l -d "%ProgramFiles%\Internet Explorer\iexplore.exe"
```

Note The resulting "limited rights" process will not necessarily have the same characteristics as other "low rights" processes seen on Windows computers, such as Protected Mode Internet Explorer. PsExec does not disable powerful groups other than Administrators that UAC normally disables (such as Power Users and certain domain groups). Also, if executed from an elevated process, the new process token still derives from the user's "elevated" logon session, even though it is marked Low integrity. A command shell with this token will still say "Administrator" in its title bar, and child processes that require elevation will not be able to prompt for or gain elevation.

PsFile

The Windows "NET FILE" command shows you a list of the files that processes on other computers have opened on the system on which you execute the command. However, it truncates longer path names and doesn't let you see that information for remote systems. PsFile shows a list of files or named pipes on a system that are opened remotely via the Server service, and it also allows you to close remotely-opened files either by name or by an ID number.

The default behavior of PsFile is to list the files on the local system that are currently open from remote systems. To see files opened on a remote system, name the remote computer (providing alternate credentials if needed) using the syntax described in the "Common Features" section earlier in this chapter. Output looks similar to the following example:

```
Files opened remotely on win7_vm:
[332] C:\Users
    User:   ABBY
    Locks:  0
    Access: Read
[340] C:\Windows\TEMP\listing.txt
    User:   ABBY
    Locks:  0
    Access: Read Write
[352] \PIPE\srvsvc
    User:   ABBY
    Locks:  0
    Access: Read Write
```

The number in brackets is a system-provided identifier, followed by the path that is opened and the user account associated with the remote connection. When listing open files on a remote computer, you will always see the *srvsvc* named pipe open; this is because of the connection established by PsFile to the Server service.

You can filter the output by adding a resource's ID number or a matching path-name prefix to the command line. This shows only the information associated with the resource that was assigned ID number 340 on the computer named Win7_vm:

```
psfile \\Win7_vm 340
```

This shows information associated only with opened files under the C:\Users folder—that is, all resources with path names beginning with *C:\Users*:

```
psfile \\Win7_vm C:\Users
```

To close opened files, add **–c** to the command line after specifying an ID or path prefix. This command closes all remotely opened files under C:\Users on the local computer:

```
psfile C:\Users -c
```

You should close files using PsFile with caution because data cached on the client system does not get written to the file before it gets closed.

PsGetSid

In Windows, Security Identifiers (SIDs) uniquely identify users, groups, computers, and other entities. SIDs are what are stored in access tokens and in security descriptors, and they are what are used in access checks. The names that are associated with SIDs are only for user-interface purposes, and because of localization they can change from system to system. For example, all US English systems have an Administrators group with the SID S-1-5-32-544, but on German systems the same group is called Administratoren, on Italian systems it is Gruppo Administrators, and on Finnish systems, Järjestelmänvalvojat.

Each Windows computer has a local SID, also known as a *machine SID*, which is created during setup. Each local group and user account on the computer has a SID based on the machine SID with a relative ID (RID) appended to it. Likewise, each Active Directory domain has a SID, and entities within the domain (including domain groups, user accounts, and member computers) have SIDs based on that SID with a RID appended. In addition to these machine-specific and domain-specific SIDs, Windows defines a set of well-known SIDs in the NT AUTHORITY and BUILTIN domains.

PsGetSid makes it easy to translate SIDs to their corresponding names, to translate names to SIDs, and to get the SID for a computer or domain. As with all the PsTools, PsGetSid can perform the translations on remote systems and report the results locally.

To translate a name or a SID to its counterpart, run **PsGetSid** with the name or SID on the command line. Without parameters, PsGetSid displays the local computer's machine SID. For example:

```
C:\>psgetsid
SID for \\WIN_VM:
S-1-5-21-2292904206-3342264711-2075022165

C:\>psgetsid Administrator
SID for WIN_VM\Administrator:
S-1-5-21-2292904206-3342264711-2075022165-500
```

Use of fully qualified account names (DOMAIN\USERNAME) prevents ambiguity and improves performance. If only an account name is provided, PsGetSid checks well-known SIDs first, then built-in and administratively defined local accounts. If the name still hasn't been resolved, PsGetSid checks the primary domain, and finally trusted domains.

No translation is possible for Logon SIDs. Logon SIDs are randomly generated identifiers associated with nonpersistent objects and have the format S-1-5-5-*X-Y*.

The following line of PowerShell script lists the names associated with well-known SIDs in the range from S-1-5-32-544 to S-1-5-32-576, redirecting any error output to *nul*. The output from that command is shown in Figure 6-1.

```
0x220..0x240 | %{ psgetsid S-1-5-32-$_ 2> $nul }
```

FIGURE 6-1 PsGetSid enumerating a range of BUILTIN names.

And the next two lines of PowerShell script get the names of the first 10 local groups and users defined on the computer. The first command extracts the machine SID from PsGetSid output, and the second one appends 1000 through 1009 to that SID and passes each of those to PsGetSid:

```
$msid = $(psgetsid)[2] + "-"
1000..1009 | %{ psgetsid $msid$_ 2> $nul }
```

PsInfo

PsInfo gathers key information about systems, including the type of installation, kernel build number, system uptime, registered owner and organization, number of processors and their type, amount of memory, and Internet Explorer version. Command-line options also let you view disk volume information, installed hotfixes, and software applications. For example:

```
System information for \\WIN7-X86-VM:
Uptime:                      0 days 23 hours 58 minutes 9 seconds
Kernel version:              Windows 7 Ultimate, Multiprocessor Free
Product type:                Professional
Product version:             6.1
Service pack:                0
Kernel build number:         7600
Registered organization:     Microsoft
Registered owner:            Abby
IE version:                  8.0000
System root:                 C:\Windows
Processors:                  1
Processor speed:             2.3 GHz
Processor type:              Intel(R) Core(TM)2 Duo CPU     T7700  @
Physical memory:             2048 MB
Video driver:                Microsoft Virtual Machine Bus Video Device
```

The *Uptime* figure represents the accumulated amount of time that the computer has been running since the last boot. Time spent in sleep or hibernate mode does not count toward this figure, so *Uptime* does not necessarily indicate how much actual time has elapsed since the last system startup.

Note As of this writing, physical memory does not get reported for 64-bit versions of Windows.

To report only selected rows of this information, provide the full or partial name of the field or fields of interest on the command line. For example, if you run **psinfo register**, only the Registered Organization and Registered Owner fields will be reported.

By default, PsInfo captures information about the local computer, but by using the syntax described in the "Common Features" section of this chapter, it can report information for one or more remote computers. PsInfo does not require administrative rights locally, but it does need administrative rights on remote systems.

Adding **–d** to the PsInfo command line appends information about disk volumes to the report, similar to the following:

Volume	Type	Format	Label	Size	Free	Free
A:	Removable					0.0%
C:	Fixed	NTFS		126.99 GB	123.34 GB	97.1%
D:	CD-ROM	CDFS	VMGUEST	23.66 MB		0.0%
X:	Remote	NTFS		19.99 GB	13.35 GB	66.8%

In the preceding example, the user running PsInfo had X: mapped to a remote file share. When querying drive information from remote computers, PsInfo gathers information in the SYSTEM context, so only globally-visible volumes are reported. This will not include remote drive mappings unless the mappings are created in the SYSTEM context, which makes them visible to all processes on the computer.

> **Note** PsInfo does not distinguish SUBST associations. If a drive letter is associated with a local path, it will appear in the listing as another fixed drive with the exact same characteristics as the real volume on the system.

The **–h** option reports installed hotfixes on the target system. Hotfix information is gathered from several points in the registry that are known to contain information about Windows and Internet Explorer hotfixes.

The **–s** option reports installed software applications, according to uninstall information for the applications found in the registry.

To report the results as comma-separated values (CSVs), add the **–c** option to the command line. Results from each computer are reported on one line, which is helpful for generating a spreadsheet. To use a character other than a comma as the delimiter, add the **–t** option followed by the desired character. To use the tab character, use **\t** as in the following example:

```
psinfo -c -t \t
```

If PsInfo is reporting on the local computer or a single remote computer, PsInfo's exit code is the service pack number of that system. When reporting on multiple systems, PsInfo returns a conventional success or failure code.

PsKill

PsKill is a command-line utility to terminate processes by ID or by image name. It can also be used to terminate all the descendent processes of the target process. And as with all other PsTools, it can target processes and process trees on remote computers, using alternate credentials if needed.

> **Warning** **PsKill terminates processes immediately.** Forcibly terminating a process does not give it an opportunity to shut down cleanly and can cause data loss or system instability. In addition, PsKill does not provide extra warnings if you try to terminate a system-critical process such as Csrss.exe. Terminating a system-critical process results in an immediate Windows blue-screen crash.

Specify the process ID (PID) in decimal or the image name of the process to terminate on the PsKill command line. If the parameter can be interpreted as a decimal number, it is assumed to be a PID; otherwise, it is assumed to be an image name. The image name does not need to include ".exe", but otherwise must be an exact match—PsKill does not accept wildcards. If you specify an image name, PsKill will attempt to terminate all processes on the system that have that name.

If you have a case where the image name happens to be a decimal number, include the *.exe* part of the name so that the parameter will be treated as a name and not as a PID.

Add the **–t** option to the command line to terminate the process tree of the target process or processes. The *process tree* of a target process is that process and any descendant processes. The process tree can be visualized with Process Explorer (the topic of Chapter 3) or with the **–t** option of PsList, discussed next in this chapter.

PsKill does not require administrative rights to terminate processes running in the same security context as PsKill and on the same computer. Administrative rights are needed for all other cases.

> **Note** PsKill was originally developed when Windows came with relatively few command-line utilities. Windows XP and higher now includes both Taskkill.exe and Tskill.exe, which offer all the capabilities of PsKill and more.

PsList

PsList, the first of the PsTools utilities I wrote and which is based on the *ps* utility found on UNIX platforms, lists running processes and their runtime characteristics, such as memory and CPU usage. PsList can optionally show process parent-child relationships, list per-thread information, or continually self-update in task manager mode. PsList can report on local or remote processes.

PsList does not require administrative rights to list process information on the local computer. By default, listing process information on a remote Windows XP computer requires administrative rights on the target system. On Windows Vista and newer, members of the Administrators, Performance Monitor Users, or Performance Log Users groups can run PsList remotely. The Remote Registry service must be running on the target computer.

Without command-line arguments, PsList enumerates the processes running on the local computer in the order that they started, along with process ID (column header Pid), process priority (Pri), number of threads (Thd), number of handles to kernel objects (Hnd), private virtual memory in kilobytes (Priv), total amount of CPU time charged to the process, and the elapsed time since the process started.

Note PsList uses the name "Idle" to refer to the PID 0 pseudo-process that Process Explorer and other utilities call "System Idle Process." And like most other process-listing utilities, PsList does not separately identify the Interrupts pseudo-process that Process Explorer identifies, instead counting that CPU charge to the Idle process.

The **–t** option displays processes in a tree view, similar to that of Process Explorer, with child processes indented below their parent process. With tree view, the CPU Time and Elapsed Time columns do not appear; instead, PsList shows reserved virtual memory (VM) and working set (WS) in kilobytes.

The **–m** option displays memory-related information for each process rather than CPU information. The statistics shown include reserved virtual memory (VM), working set size (WS), private virtual memory (Priv), the peak private virtual memory in the process' lifetime (Priv Pk), page faults (Faults) including both hard and soft faults, and nonpaged and paged pool sizes (NonP and Page, respectively). All memory sizes are in kilobytes.

The **–d** option displays information about each thread on the system. Threads are grouped under the processes to which they belong and are sorted by start time. The information shown for each thread includes thread ID (Tid), thread priority (Pri), number of context switches or the number of times the thread has begun executing on a CPU (Cswtch), its current state (State), the amount of time it has executed in user mode (User Time) and in kernel mode (Kernel Time), and the Elapsed Time since the thread began execution.

The **–x** option displays CPU, memory, and thread information for each process. The **–m**, **–x**, and **–d** options can be combined, but they cannot be used with the **–t** option.

Instead of listing all processes, you can specify which processes to display by ID, by partial name, or by exact name. The following command line displays information about the process with PID 560 on the computer named Win7_vm:

```
pslist \\Win7_vm 560
```

The following command displays CPU, thread, and memory information about all processes with names beginning with **svc**:

```
pslist -x svc
```

Add **–e** to the command line to match the specified process name exactly. In the preceding example, only svc.exe processes would be listed; instances of svchost.exe would not be listed.

The **–s** option runs PsList in "task manager" mode, in which PsList periodically clears and refreshes the console screen with updated statistics. The list is sorted by the CPU column, which displays the percentage of CPU time charged to each process since the previous update. By default, PsList updates the display once per second until you press Escape. You can specify a number of seconds for PsList to run immediately following the **–s**, and you can set the refresh rate with the **–r** option. The following example runs PsList in task manager mode for 60 seconds (or until you press Escape), refreshing the display every five seconds:

```
pslist -s 60 -r 5
```

The **–s** option can be combined with the **–m** option to display continually updated memory statistics, and with processes sorted by private bytes rather than by CPU usage. It can also be combined with the **–t** option to continually display processes in a tree view as Process Explorer does. You can also specify a PID or a partial or exact process name with these options to limit which processes to display in task manager mode. If you specify a PID, you might want to specify it before the **–s** option so that it isn't interpreted as the number of seconds to run. The following command continually monitors the memory usage of **leakyapp.exe** on a remote computer:

```
pslist \\Win7_vm -s -m -e leakyapp
```

PsLoggedOn

PsLoggedOn tells you who is logged on to a particular computer, either locally or through resource shares. Alternately, PsLoggedOn can tell you which computers on your network a particular user is logged on to.

Without command-line parameters, PsLoggedOn reports which users are locally logged on to the current computer and when they logged on; it then reports users that are logged on through resource shares and at what time the session was started. (This latter information is similar to what the **net session** command reports.)

To view the same information for logons on a remote computer, add the computer name to the command line prefixed with a double backslash:

```
psloggedon \\Win7_vm
```

You need to run PsLoggedOn under an account that has administrative permissions on the remote computer. PsLoggedOn is the one PsTools utility that does not offer **–u** and **–p** options for specifying alternate credentials. Also, because PsLoggedOn uses the Remote Registry service to gather information from a remote computer, it will always show as a resource share connection on the computer from which you are retrieving information.

To show only local logons and not report resource share logons, add the **–l** (lower case L) command-line option. To show only account names without logon times, add the **–x** option.

If you specify a user name instead of a computer, PsLoggedOn searches all the computers in the current domain or workgroup and reports whether the user is locally logged on. Note that PsLoggedOn must be run with an account with administrative rights on all computers on the network, and that the search might be time-consuming on a large or bandwidth-constrained network.

PsLoggedOn's definition of a locally logged-on user is a user that has its profile loaded into the registry. When the user's profile is loaded, the user's security identifier (SID) appears as a subkey under HKEY_USERS. PsLoggedOn looks at the last-write time stamp under a subkey of that SID key as an approximation of the user's logon time. The logon time reported will be accurate in most cases but is not authoritative. For a more complete and accurate listing of logon sessions on a computer, see the LogonSessions utility, described in Chapter 8, "Security Utilities."

PsLogList

PsLogList displays records from the Windows event logs of the local computer or of remote computers. You can filter the output based on time stamp, source, ID, type, or other criteria. PsLogList also lets you export log records to a *.evt file, read from a saved *.evt file, or clear an event log.

Without parameters, PsLogList dumps all records from the System event log on the local computer. To view records from a different event log, just name it on the command line. For example, the following command lines dump records from the Application log and from the Windows PowerShell log, respectively:

```
psloglist application
```

```
psloglist "Windows Powershell"
```

To view records from one or more remote computers, specify computer names on the command line as described at the beginning of this chapter.

Every event log record includes an event source and an event ID. The event ID is used to look up and display localizable, human-readable text from a message resource DLL associated with the event source. That message text can contain placeholders for text that can vary per event (such as a file name or an IP address). That per-event text is associated with the event log record as zero or more *insertion strings*. Most event-viewing applications, including Event Viewer, display only the insertion strings (not the full text) when the referenced message resource DLLs are not present on the local system. This makes the text difficult to read. One of the features that distinguishes PsLogList when reading a remote event log is that it will get message text from the resource DLLs on those remote systems. However, this requires that the remote system's default administrative share (Admin$) be enabled and accessible, that the resource DLLs be located under that directory, and that the Remote Registry service is running on that system. Before using PsLogList to gather data from remote systems, be sure that this is the case on those systems; otherwise, PsLogList will not be able to display full event text.

PsLogList does not require administrative rights to display records from the local Application or System logs or from a saved *.evt file, or to export the Application or System logs to an *.evt file. Administrative rights might not be needed to view the Application log of a remote Windows XP computer, but event text will not be accessible. Administrative rights are required to clear event logs or to access the local Security log or any other remote event logs.

The rest of PsLogList's command-line options are summarized in Table 6-2 and are discussed in more detail in the rest of this section.

TABLE 6-2 PsLogList Command-Line Options

Option	Description
Output options	
−x	Displays extended data if that is present. (It's not applicable if **−s** used.)
−n #	Limits the number of records displayed to the specified number.
−r	Reverses the order—displays oldest to newest (with default being newest to oldest).
−s	Displays each record on one line with delimited fields.
−t *char*	Specifies the delimiter character to use with −s. Use **\t** to specify *Tab*.
−w	Waits for new events, displaying them as they are generated. PsLogList runs until you press Ctrl+C. (Local computer only.)
Timestamp options	
−a *mm/dd/yyyy*	Displays records time-stamped on or after the date *mm/dd/yyyy*.
−b *mm/dd/yyyy*	Displays records time-stamped before the date *mm/dd/yyyy*.
−d #	Displays only records from the previous # days.
−h #	Displays only records from the previous # hours.
−m #	Displays only records from the previous # minutes.
Event content filtering options	
−f *filter*	Filters event types, where each letter in *filter* represents an event type.
−i *ID[,ID,...]*	Shows only events with the specified ID or IDs (up to 10).
−e *ID[,ID,...]*	Shows events *excluding* those with the specified ID or IDs (up to 10).
−o *source[,source,...]*	Shows only events from the specified event source or sources. The * character can be appended for a substring match.
−q *source[,source,...]*	Shows events *excluding* the specified event source or sources. The * character can be appended for a substring match.
Log-management options	
−z	Lists event logs registered on the target system.
−c	Clears the event log after displaying records.
−g *filename*	Exports an event log to a *.evt file. (Local computer only.)
−l *filename*	Displays records from a saved *.evt file instead of from an active log.

By default, PsLogList displays the record number, source, type, computer, time stamp, event ID, and text description of each record. PsLogList loads message source modules on the system where the event log being viewed resides so that it correctly displays event log messages. For example:

```
[34769] Service Control Manager
    Type:     INFORMATION
    Computer: WIN7X86-VM
    Time:     12/22/2009 11:31:09   ID:       7036
The Application Experience service entered the stopped state.
```

The **–x** option displays any extended data in the event record in a hex dump format. With that option, the previous record would appear like this:

```
[34769] Service Control Manager
    Type:     INFORMATION
    Computer: WIN7X86-VM
    Time:     12/22/2009 11:31:09   ID:       7036
The Application Experience service entered the stopped state.
    Data:
    0000: 41 00 65 00 4C 00 6F 00 6F 00 6B 00 75 00 70 00 A.e.L.o.o.k.u.p.
    0010: 53 00 76 00 63 00 2F 00 31 00 00 00             S.v.c./.1...
```

The **–n** option limits the number of records displayed to the number you specify. The following command displays the 10 most recent records in the Application log:

```
psloglist –n 10 application
```

By default, PsLogList displays records from newest to oldest. The **–r** option reverses that order, displaying oldest records first. The following command combines **–r** with **–n** to display the 10 oldest records in the Application log:

```
psloglist –r –n 10 application
```

The **–s** option displays the content of each record on a single line with comma-delimited fields. This is convenient for text searches because you can search for any text in the record and see the entire record—for example, **psloglist –s | findstr /i luafv**. The **–t** option lets you specify a different delimiter character, which can help with importing into a spreadsheet. Note that PsLogList quotes only the text description field in **–s** mode, so choose a delimiter character that does not appear in any of the event text. You can use **\t** to specify the Tab character. Note also that **–x** extended data is not output when **–s** is used.

The **–w** option runs PsLogList in a continuous mode, waiting for and displaying new event records as they are added to the event log. Combined with other filtering options, PsLogList displays only new records that fit the criteria. PsLogList continues to run until you press Ctrl+C or Ctrl+Break. The **–w** option cannot be used when targeting a remote computer.

The **–a** and **–b** options filter records based on their time stamps. The **–a** option displays only records *on or after* the date specified; the **–b** option displays only records *before* the date specified. Note that dates must be in month/day/year format, regardless of the regional date-formatting option in effect. The following command displays all records from the System log from December 22, 2009:

```
psloglist -a 12/22/2009 -b 12/23/2009
```

Instead of using a specific date, you can get the most recent records from an event log going back a specific amount of time. The **–d**, **–h**, and **–m** options let you display the most recent records going back a specific number of days, hours, or minutes, respectively. The following command displays all records from the System log that occurred in the last three hours:

```
psloglist -h 3
```

The **–f *filter*** option filters the records to display based on the event type. For each event type to display, add its first letter to the filter. For example, **–f e** displays only error events, **–f ew** displays errors and warnings, and **–f f** displays failure audits. Use **i** for informational events and **s** for success audits.

To display only records with specific event IDs, use the **–i** option followed by a comma-separated list of up to 10 ID numbers. To exclude event IDs, use the **–e** option instead. Do not put any spaces within the list.

To display only records from specific event sources, use the **–o** option followed by a comma-separated list of source names. If any of the source names contains spaces, quote the entire set. Add a ***** character to match the text you specify anywhere in the source name. Do not put any spaces around the commas. To exclude rather than include records based on source name, use the **–q** option instead of **–o**. The following example displays all events in the System log from the Service Control Manager and any event source with *net* in its name, except for records with event IDs 1 or 7036:

```
psloglist -o "service control manager,net*" -e 1,7036
```

You can export an event log on the local computer to a *.evt file with the **–g** option. The following command exports the Application log to **app.evt** in the current directory:

```
psloglist -g .\app.evt Application
```

You can view records from a saved *.evt file instead of from an active event log with the **–l** (lowercase *L*) option. So that the event text is properly interpreted, specify the original name of the log as well. The following command displays the 10 most recent records in the saved app.evt file, using message files associated with the Application log:

```
psloglist -l .\app.evt -n 10 application
```

PsLogList supports viewing only from legacy-style event logs—specifically, those that have a named subkey under HKLM\System\CurrentControlSet\Services\EventLog. The **–z** option lists the event logs that are available for viewing on the target system. Note that the registered name for an event log might be different from the display name shown in Event Viewer.

Finally, you can clear an event log after displaying records with the **–c** option. To display no records, use a filter that excludes everything, such as **–f x** (no event types begin with "x"). The following command clears the security event log on a remote computer without displaying any records:

```
psloglist \\win7demo -c -f x security
```

PsPasswd

PsPasswd lets you set the password for domain or local user accounts. You can set the password for a named local account on a single computer, a specific set of computers, or all computers in your domain or workgroup. This can be useful particularly for setting passwords for service accounts or for local built-in Administrator accounts.

To set a domain password, simply specify the target account in domain\account format, followed by the new password. If the account name or password contains spaces, put quotes around it. The following example sets a highly complex yet easily memorized 28-character passphrase for the MYDOMAIN\Toby account:

```
pspasswd mydomain\toby "Passphrase++ 99.9% more good"
```

The password is optional. If you specify the user account but no new password, PsPasswd will apply a null password to the account, if the security policy allows it.

To set the password for an account on the local computer, specify just the account name and the new password. Again, the password is optional: omitting it from the command line blanks the password for the account, if security policy permits it.

> **Note** Resetting the password of a local user account can cause an irreversible loss of encrypted data belonging to that account, such as files protected with the Encrypting File System (EFS).

To set the password for a local account on one or more remote computers, use the remote-computers syntax described at the beginning of this chapter, along with alternate credentials if desired. Then specify the account name and the optional new password. The following example sets the password for the local Administrator account on all computers in the domain or workgroup to a random, 50-character password:

```
pspasswd \\* Administrator "^HVKh*iK:F`RvO[8<Zdp#|,I.:TI_K':W\xEwi9D3I,O}tQ>tK"
```

By default, only Domain Admins or Account Operators can set the password for a domain user account. Note that PsPasswd does not accept alternate credentials in the domain account case; you must run PsPasswd with sufficient privileges to change the target password. To set the password for a local user account, administrative rights are required on the target computer.

PsService

PsService lists or controls Windows services and drivers on a local or a remote system. It is similar in many respects to SC.EXE and to some features of NET.EXE, both of which come with Windows, but offers improvements in usability and flexibility. For instance, services can be specified using service names or display names and, in some cases, partial name matches. PsService also includes a unique service-search capability that lets you search for instances of a service on your network, as well as for services that are marked "interactive."

Without parameters, PsService lists status information for all Win32 (user-mode) services registered on the local computer. You can, of course, specify a computer name on the command line to perform commands on a remote system, and optionally supply a user name and password if your current credentials do not have administrative rights on the remote system.

PsService supports the following commands and options, which will be discussed in more detail in this section:

- **query [–g group] [–t {driver|service|interactive|all}] [–s {active|inactive|all}] [service]**
- **config [service]**
- **depend service**
- **security service**
- **find service [all]**
- **setconfig service {auto|demand|disabled}**
- **start service**
- **stop service**
- **restart service**
- **pause service**
- **cont service**

PsService /? lists these options. **PsService *command* /?** shows the syntax for the named command—for example, **psservice query /?**.

PsService does not explicitly require administrative permissions for operations on the local computer. Because permissions for each service can be set separately, the permissions required for any local operation can vary based on which service or services are involved. For example, although most don't, some services grant the interactive user permission to start and stop the service. As another example, **psservice depend server** is the command to list services that depend on the Server service. The list of services reported will differ for administrators and nonadministrators on Windows 7 because nonadmins aren't allowed to read status information for the HomeGroup Listener service, which depends on Server.

Query

The **query** command displays status information about services or drivers on the target system, using flexible criteria to determine which ones to include. For each matching service or driver, PsService displays the following:

- **Service name**   The internal name of the service or driver. This is the name that most **sc.exe** commands require.

- **Display name**   The display name, as shown in the Services MMC snap-in.

- **Description**   The descriptive text associated with the service or driver.

- **Group**   If specified, the load order group that the service belongs to.

- **Type**   User-mode services are either own-process or share-process, depending on whether the service's process can host other services. User-mode processes can also be marked "interactive" (although that's strongly discouraged). Drivers can be kernel drivers or file system drivers. (File system drivers must register with the I/O manager, and they interact more extensively with the memory manager.)

- **State**   Indicates whether the service is running, stopped, or paused, or in transition with a pending start, stop, pause, or continue. Below this line, PsService shows whether the service accepts stop or pause/continue commands, and whether it can process pre-shutdown and shutdown notifications.

- **Win32 exit code**   Zero indicates normal runtime operation or termination. A non-zero value indicates a standard error code reported by the service. The value 1066 indicates a service-specific error. The value 1077 indicates that the service has not been started since the last boot, which is normal for many services.

- **Service-specific exit code**   If the Win32 exit code is 1066 (0x42A), this value indicates a service-specific error code; otherwise, it has no meaning.

- **Checkpoint**   Normally zero, this value is incremented periodically to report service progress during lengthy start, stop, pause, or continue operations. It has no meaning when an operation is not pending.

- **Wait hint**   The amount of time, in milliseconds, that the service estimates is required for a pending start, stop, pause, or continue operation. If that amount of time passes without a change to the State or Checkpoint, it can be assumed that an error has occurred within the service.

By default, the PsService query command lists all Win32 services configured on the target system, whether they're running or not. (PsService without any command-line parameters is equivalent to **psservice query**.) To narrow down the list by service or driver name, specify the name at the end of the command line. PsService will report status information for all services and drivers with exact or partially matching service or display names. For example, **psservice query ras** will list all services and drivers that have service or display names beginning with **ras**. (The match is case insensitive.)

You can further filter the query results by type and by state. Add the **–t** option followed by **driver** to display only drivers, **service** to display only Win32 services, **interactive** to display only Win32 services that are marked **allow service to interact with desktop**, or **all** not to filter results based on type. To filter query results based on whether the service or driver is active, add **–s** to the command line followed by **active**, **inactive**, or **all**. If a service name is not added to the command line, PsService defaults to displaying only Win32 services and all states. If a service name is specified and **–t** is not specified, PsService displays matching services or drivers.

> **Note** It is strongly discouraged to mark services "interactive." Such services are often vulnerable to elevation-of-privilege attacks and often will not work on Windows Vista or newer, or on earlier versions of Windows with Fast User Switching or other terminal services. The **psservice query –t interactive** command is an easy way to identify these potentially problematic services.

To list only services or drivers that belong to a particular load order group, name the group after the **–g** option. Group name matching is case insensitive but must be an exact match, not a partial match.

All these options can be combined. The following command displays status information for kernel drivers on a remote computer that are in the PnP Filter group, that are not loaded, and that have service or display names beginning with *bth*:

```
psservice \\win7x86-vm query -g "pnp filter" -t driver -s inactive bth
```

Config

The **config** command displays configuration information about services or drivers. Used by itself, the PsService config command displays configuration information about all registered Win32 services on the target system. Add a name after the **config** command, and PsService will display configuration settings about all services and drivers with service or display names beginning with the name you specify. For example, **psservice config ras** displays configuration settings for all services and drivers with a service or display name beginning with "ras" (case insensitive).

The **config** command displays the following information:

- **Service name**   The internal name of the service or driver. This is the name that most **sc.exe** commands require.

- **Display name**   The display name, as shown in the Services MMC snap-in.

- **Description**   The descriptive text associated with the service or driver.

- **Type**   Indicates whether the item is configured as own-process or share-process service and whether it is marked "interactive"; configured as a kernel driver; or configured as a file system driver.

- **Start type**   Drivers that are loaded at startup can be marked boot-start or system-start; services that are loaded at startup are marked auto-start or auto-start (delayed). "Demand-start" (also known as "manual start") indicates services or drivers that can be started as needed. "Disabled" services and drivers cannot be loaded.

- **Error control**   Indicates what Windows should do if the service or driver fails to start during Windows startup. Ignore or Normal means that Windows will continue system startup, logging the error in the event log for the Normal case. If Severe or Critical, Windows restarts using the last-known-good configuration; if the failure occurs with the last-known-good, Severe continues booting while Critical fails the startup.

- **Binary path name**   Shows the path to the executable to be loaded, along with optional command-line parameters for an auto-start service.

- **Load order group**   The name of the load order group to which the service or driver belongs (blank if not part of a group).

- **Tag**   For boot-start and system-start drivers that are part of a load order group, the tag is a unique value within the group that can be used to specify load order within the group.

- **Dependencies**   Services or load order groups that must be loaded before this service or driver can start.

- **Service start name**   For services, the account name under which the service runs.

Depend

The **depend** command lists services and drivers that have direct or indirect dependencies on the named service. For example, **psservice depend tdx** lists services and drivers that cannot start unless the tdx driver (NetIO Legacy TDI Support Driver) is loaded.

The information displayed by the **depend** command is the same as that for the **query** command. The service name on the **psservice depend** command line must exactly match the service or display name of a registered service or driver; PsService will not perform partial name matching for the **depend** command.

To see which services a particular service depends upon, use the **psservice config** command.

Security

As you might guess, the **security** command displays security information about the named service or driver. Specifically, it displays its discretionary access control list (DACL) in a human-readable way. Instead of displaying arcane Security Descriptor Definition Language (SDDL) as **sc.exe sdshow** does, it lists the names of the accounts granted or denied access, and the specific permissions granted or denied. As you can see in Figure 6-2, PsService clearly shows that the Fax service can be started by any user. The equivalent but less-readable SDDL is shown by the **sc.exe** command in the same figure.

FIGURE 6-2 PsService Security command and equivalent SC.EXE output.

For Win32 services, PsService also displays the account name under which the service runs.

The name on the PsService Security command line must be an exact, case-insensitive match for either the service name or display name of the service or driver.

Find

One of PsService's unique capabilities is to search your network for instances of a service. The **find** command enumerates all the computers in your workgroup or domain and checks each for a running instance of the named service. You can search for a service using either its service name or display name. For example, the following command identifies all the Windows computers in your domain or workgroup that are running the DNS Server service:

```
psservice find "dns server"
```

To search for both running and inactive instances of the service, add the keyword **all** to the command line:

```
psservice find "dns server" all
```

The **find** command can also be used to search for loaded or inactive drivers on your network. For example, **psservice find vmbus** will search your network for Windows computers with the Virtual Machine Bus driver loaded.

SetConfig

The **setconfig** command lets you set the start type for a Win32 service. Follow the **setconfig** command with the service name or display name of the service, followed by the start type. The options are **auto** for an automatic-start service, **demand** for a manual-start service, or **disabled** to prevent the service from starting. For example, to disable the Fax service, use the following command line:

```
psservice setconfig fax disabled
```

Start, Stop, Restart, Pause, Continue

You can use PsService to start, stop, restart, or pause a service, or to resume (continue) a paused service. The syntax is simply to use the **start**, **stop**, **restart**, **pause**, or **cont** command, followed by the service name or display name of the service or driver. If the control command is successful, PsService displays "query" results showing the requested operation as pending or completed. Note that not all of these operations are valid for every service and driver. Note also that the **stop** and **restart** commands will not work if there are running services or loaded drivers that depend on the service or driver you are stopping.

PsShutdown

PsShutdown is similar to the Shutdown.exe console utility from older versions of the Windows Resource Kits and in current versions of Windows, providing a command-line mechanism to shutdown, reboot, or hibernate local and remote Windows systems. PsShutdown also pioneered the "shutdown reason" options that have since been added to the Windows Shutdown.exe.

Because PsShutdown was designed before the advent of Terminal Services and the prevalence of users running without administrative rights, its usefulness is limited primarily to Windows XP. PsShutdown requires administrative rights to create and start the custom service that ultimately performs most of its tasks, and user-specific operations such as "lock workstation" and "logoff" assume that services and the interactive user's desktop are in the same Terminal Services session ("session 0"). This assumption is never true on Windows Vista and newer, and it cannot be relied upon with Windows XP when Fast User Switching is in use or on Windows Server 2003 when using Remote Desktop. However, PsShutdown's **suspend** option to put the computer in sleep mode is a feature that is not available with Shutdown.exe.

PsShutdown's command-line options are described in Table 6-3. Note that to help prevent accidental use, PsShutdown requires you to specify a shutdown option on the command line.

TABLE 6-3   PsShutdown Command-Line Options

Option	Description
Shutdown commands (one required)	
–s	Shuts down. (Power remains on if BIOS does not support power-off.)
–k	Powers off the computer. (Reboots if BIOS does not support power-off.)
–r	Reboots the computer.
–h	Hibernates the computer.
–d	Suspends the computer (sleep mode).
–l	Locks the workstation (Windows XP/Windows 2003 only). It locks the workstation or disconnects a remote desktop user if the interactive user is logged in to terminal services session 0. Otherwise, it has no effect.
–o	Logs off (Windows XP/Windows 2003 only). It logs off an interactive user logged in to terminal services session 0. If **–f** is not also specified, logoff might be blocked by an application that refuses to exit. Otherwise, it has no effect.
–a	Aborts a PsShutdown-initiated shutdown operation (valid only when a countdown is in progress). This command does not require administrative rights when invoked on the current computer.

Option	Description
Display options	
–m *"message"*	For shutdown operations, displays a dialog box with the specified message to an interactive user. If this option is not specified, a default notification message will be displayed.
–c	For shutdown operations, adds a Cancel button to the notification dialog box, allowing an interactive user to cancel the operation.
–v *seconds*	Displays the notification dialog box only for the specified number of seconds before the shutdown. If this option is not set, the dialog box appears right away when the shutdown is scheduled. If this option is set to 0, no dialog box is displayed.
Other options	
–t [*seconds|hh:mm*]	Specifies when the shutdown operation should be performed, either in seconds or as time-of-day in 24-hour format. The default is 20 seconds. (It cannot be used with **–l**, **–o**, or **–a**.)
–f	Forces running applications to terminate. (Note that Shutdown.exe on Windows XP/Windows 2003 has a bug in which the logic for its **–f** option is unintentionally reversed.)
–e [u|p]:*xx:yy*	Specifies the shutdown reason code, with **u** for "unplanned" and **p** for "planned."
–n *seconds*	Specifies the timeout in seconds to connect to remote computers.

PsShutdown does not use the *InitiateSystemShutdown[Ex]* and *AbortSystemShutdown* APIs for remote shutdown or for cancellation by the interactive user. Instead, its service displays a custom interactive dialog box. Therefore, PsShutdown and other utilities cannot be intermixed to abort each other's shutdown operations.

The notification and cancellation dialog box is displayed by the PsShutdown service, which is remotely created and configured as an *interactive service*. Interactive services are a deprecated feature of Windows, so this feature works as intended only in certain scenarios:

- On Windows XP and Server 2003, the dialog box is displayed only to an interactive user that is logged on to terminal services session 0, and only if NoInteractiveServices has not been enabled. With Fast User Switching or Remote Desktop, users can be logged in to other sessions. The session 0 user can be disconnected or even logged out.

- On Windows Vista and newer, when the PsShutdown service displays the notification, an interactively logged-on user is notified by the Interactive Services Detection (UI0Detect) service. This service, if not disabled, allows the user to switch temporarily to session 0 to interact with the dialog box. If the service has been disabled, interactive users receive no notifications.

The reason you might want to use the **–n** option to control the remote connection timeout is that if you try to use PsShutdown to control a computer that is already off, the command might appear to hang for a minute before timing out. This delay, which is the standard

Windows timeout for computer connections, can severely lengthen shutdown operations that run against many computers. The **–n** option gives you the ability to shorten the length of time that PsShutdown will attempt to establish a connection before giving up.

The shutdown reason codes that can be used with the **–e** option are listed here:

```
Type   Major   Minor   Title
 U       0       0     Other (Unplanned)
 P       0       0     Other (Planned)
 U       1       1     Hardware: Maintenance (Unplanned)
 P       1       1     Hardware: Maintenance (Planned)
 U       1       2     Hardware: Installation (Unplanned)
 P       1       2     Hardware: Installation (Planned)
 U       2       2     Operating System: Recovery (Planned)
 P       2       2     Operating System: Recovery (Planned)
 P       2       3     Operating System: Upgrade (Planned)
 U       2       4     Operating System: Reconfiguration (Unplanned)
 P       2       4     Operating System: Reconfiguration (Planned)
 P       2      16     Operating System: Service pack (Planned)
 U       2      17     Operating System: Hot fix (Unplanned)
 P       2      17     Operating System: Hot fix (Planned)
 U       2      18     Operating System: Security fix (Unplanned)
 P       2      18     Operating System: Security fix (Planned)
 U       4       1     Application: Maintenance (Unplanned)
 P       4       1     Application: Maintenance (Planned)
 P       4       2     Application: Installation (Planned)
 U       4       5     Application: Unresponsive
 U       4       6     Application: Unstable
 U       5      19     Security issue
 P       5      19     Security issue
 U       5      20     Loss of network connectivity (Unplanned)
 P       7       0     Legacy API shutdown
```

The System event log might show errors relating to PsShutdown. Cancellation of a shutdown operation might be reported as an unexpected termination of the PsShutdown service; the log might also report an error because PsShutdown is configured as an interactive service. Both of these errors can be ignored.

PsSuspend

PsSuspend lets you suspend processes on the local system or a remote system. This can be useful if a process is consuming a resource (such as CPU) that you want to allow another process to use. Rather than kill the process that's consuming the resource, suspending it permits you to let it continue operation at some later point in time. It can also be useful when investigating or removing malware that involve multiple processes monitoring each other for termination.

To suspend a single process, specify its process ID (PID) on the PsSuspend command line. Specify a process name to suspend all processes that have that name. To resume a process, add **–r** to the command line.

Each thread in a process has a *suspend count* so that each call to the *SuspendThread* API for that thread must be matched by a *ResumeThread* call before the thread will resume execution. PsSuspend preserves the suspend counts of threads within a process so that threads that were already suspended when the process was suspended by PsSuspend will remain suspended when the process is resumed. If PsSuspend **–r** is invoked on a process that is not suspended but that has suspended threads, those threads will have their suspend counts decremented and will resume execution if decremented to zero. Programs that have suspended threads most likely have reasons for doing so, so you should be careful about "resuming" processes you did not suspend.

PsTools Command-Line Syntax

This section shows the command-line syntax for each of the PsTools utilities. Because the syntax for remote operations is consistent across the utilities, that syntax is shown here instead of within each utility. The RemoteComputers syntax applies to all of the utilities that can operate on multiple computers; the RemoteComputer syntax applies to those that can operate on only one remote computer.

```
RemoteComputers = \\computer[,computer2[,...]]|\\*|@file [-u username [-p password]]
RemoteComputer =  \\computer [-u username [-p password]]
```

PsExec

```
psexec [RemoteComputers] [-d] [-background|-low|-belownormal|-abovenormal|-high|-realtime]
       [-a n[,n[,...]]] [-c [-f|-v]] [-n seconds] [-s|-e] [-i [session]] [-x]
       [-w directory] [-h] [-l] [-u username [-p password]] command [arguments]
```

Unlike the other utilities, PsExec supports the use of the **–u** and **–p** options both for remote and local operations.

PsFile

```
psfile [RemoteComputer] [[Id | path] [-c]]
```

PsGetSid

```
psgetsid [RemoteComputers] [name | SID]
```

PsInfo

psinfo [RemoteComputers] [-h] [-s] [-d] [-c [-t *delimiter*]] [*field*]

PsKill

pskill [RemoteComputer] [-t] {*PID* | *name*}

PsList

pslist [RemoteComputer] [[-t] | [[-m] [-d] [-x]]] [-s [n] [-r n]] [*name* | *PID*]

PsLoggedOn

psloggedon [*computer*|*] [-l] [-x]

PsLogList

psloglist [RemoteComputers] [-s [-t *delimiter*] | -x] [-n #] [-r] [-w]
[-a *mm/dd/yyyy*] [-b *mm/dd/yyyy*] [-d #|-h #|-m #] [-f *filter*]
[-i *ID*[,*ID*[,...]] | -e *ID*[,*ID*[,...]]]
[-o *source*[,*source*[,...]] | -q *source*[,*source*[,...]]]
[-z] [-c] [-g *filename* | -l *filename*] [*eventlog*]

PsPasswd

For local accounts:

pspasswd [RemoteComputers] *LocalAccount* [*NewPassword*]

For domain accounts:

pspasswd *Domain\Account* [*NewPassword*]

PsService

psservice [RemoteComputer] [*command* [*options*]]

The supported commands and options for PsService are

query [-g *group*] [-t {driver|service|interactive|all}] [-s {active|inactive|all}] [*service*]

config [*service*]

```
depend service

security service

find service [all]

setconfig service {auto|demand|disabled}

start service

stop service

restart service

pause service

cont service
```

PsShutdown

```
psshutdown [RemoteComputers] {-s|-k|-r|-h|-d|-l|-o|-a} [-f] [-c] [-t [seconds|hh:mm]]
[-v seconds] [-e [u|p]:xx:yy] [-m "message"] [-n seconds]
```

PsSuspend

```
pssuspend [RemoteComputer] [-r] {PID|name}
```

PsTools System Requirements

Table 6-4 lists the requirements for local and remote operations for each of the PsTools utilities.

TABLE 6-4 **PsTools System Requirements**

Utility	Local	Remote		
	Requires administrative rights locally	Requires Admin$ share on remote	Requires RemoteRegistry service	Supports specification of multiple computer names
PsExec	Depends on command and options	Yes	No	Yes
PsFile	Yes	No	No	No
PsGetSid	No	Yes	No	Yes
PsInfo	No	Yes	Yes	Yes
PsKill	Depends on target process	Yes	No	No
PsList	No	Yes	Yes	No
PsLoggedOn	No	No	Yes	(Can scan network)
PsLogList	Depends on operation and target log	Yes	Yes	Yes
PsPasswd	Yes	No	No	Yes (for local accounts)
PsService	Depends on operation and specific services	No	No	No (but the **find** option can scan network)
PsShutdown	Yes	Yes	No	Yes
PsSuspend	Depends on target process	Yes	No	No

Chapter 7
Process and Diagnostic Utilities

Process Explorer and Process Monitor, discussed in Chapters 3 and 4, respectively, are the primary utilities for analyzing the runtime behavior and dynamic state of processes and of the system as a whole. This chapter describes six additional Sysinternals utilities for viewing details of process state:

- **VMMap** is a GUI utility that displays details of a process' virtual and physical memory usage.

- **ProcDump** is a console utility that can generate a memory dump for a process when it meets specifiable criteria, such as exhibiting a CPU spike or having an unresponsive window.

- **DebugView** is a GUI utility that lets you monitor user-mode and kernel-mode debug output generated from either the local computer or a remote computer.

- **LiveKd** lets you run a standard kernel debugger on a snapshot of the running local system without having to reboot into debug mode.

- **ListDLLs** is a console utility that displays information about DLLs loaded on the system.

- **Handle** is a console utility that displays information about object handles held by processes on the system.

VMMap

VMMap (shown in Figure 7-1) is a process virtual and physical memory analysis utility. It shows graphical and tabular summaries of the different types of memory allocated by a process, as well as detailed maps of the specific virtual memory allocations, showing characteristics such as backing files and types of protection. VMMap also shows summary and detailed information about the amount of physical memory (working set) assigned by the operating system for the different virtual memory blocks.

VMMap can capture multiple snapshots of the process' memory allocation state, graphically display allocations over time, and show exactly what changed between any two points in time. Combined with VMMap's filtering and refresh options, this allows you to identify the sources of process memory usage and the memory cost of application features.

VMMap can also instrument a process to track its individual memory allocations and show the code paths and call stacks where those allocations are made. With full symbolic information, VMMap can display the line of source code responsible for any memory allocation.

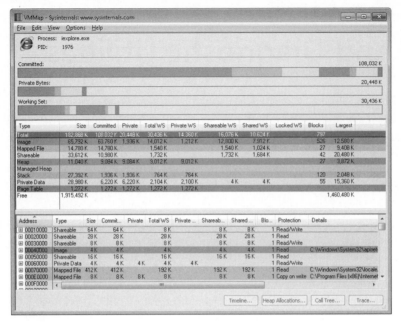

FIGURE 7-1 VMMap main window.

Besides flexible views for analyzing live processes, VMMap supports the export of data in multiple formats, including a native format that preserves detailed information so that you can load it back into VMMap at a later time. It also includes command-line options that enable scripting scenarios.

VMMap is the ideal tool for developers who want to understand and optimize their application's memory resource usage. (To see how Microsoft Windows allocates physical memory as a systemwide resource, see RAMMap, which is described in Chapter 14, "System Information Utilities.") VMMap runs on x86 and x64 versions of Windows XP and newer.

Starting VMMap and Choosing a Process

The first thing you must do when starting VMMap is to pick a process to analyze. If you don't specify a process or an input file on the VMMap command line (described later in this chapter), VMMap displays its Select or Launch Process dialog box. Its View A Running Process tab lets you pick a process that is already running, and the "Launch And Trace A New Process tab lets you start a new, instrumented process and track its memory allocations. You can display the Select or Launch Process dialog box at a later time by pressing Ctrl+P.

View a Running Process

Select a process from the View A Running Process tab (shown in Figure 7-2), and click OK. To quickly find a process by process ID (PID) or by memory usage, click on any column header to sort the rows by that column. The columns include User, Private Bytes, Working Set, and Architecture (that is, whether the process is 32-bit or 64-bit). Click Refresh to update the list.

FIGURE 7-2 VMMap Select or Launch Process dialog box lists running processes.

The View A Running Process tab lists only processes that VMMap can open. If VMMap is not running with administrative permissions (including the Debug privilege), the list includes only processes running as the same user as VMMap and at the same integrity level or a lower one. On Windows Vista and newer, you can restart VMMap with elevated rights by clicking the Show All Processes button in the dialog box, or by choosing File | Run As Administrator.

On x64 editions of Windows, VMMap can analyze 32-bit and 64-bit processes. VMMap launches a 32-bit version of itself to analyze 32-bit processes and a 64-bit version to analyze 64-bit processes. (See "Single Executable Image" in Chapter 1, "Getting Started with the Sysinternals Utilities," for more information.) With the **–64** command-line option, described later in this chapter, the 64-bit version is used to analyze all processes.

Launch and Trace a New Process

When you launch an application from VMMap, the application is instrumented to track all individual memory allocations along with the associated call stack. Enter the path to the application and optionally any command-line arguments and the start directory as shown in Figure 7-3, and then click OK.

FIGURE 7-3 Launch and trace a new process.

VMMap injects a DLL into the target process at startup and intercepts its virtual memory API calls. Along with the allocation type, size, and memory protection, VMMap captures the call stack at the point when the allocation is made. VMMap aggregates this information in various ways, which are described in the "Viewing Allocations from Instrumented Processes" section later in this chapter. (See "Call Stacks and Symbols" in Chapter 2, "Windows Core Components," for more information.)

On x64 editions of Windows, VMMap can instrument and trace x86 and x64 programs, launching a 32-bit or 64-bit version of itself accordingly. However, on x64 Windows VMMap cannot instrument and trace .NET programs built for "Any CPU.. It can instrument those programs on 32-bit versions of Windows, and you can analyze an "Any CPU" program on x64 without instrumentation by picking it from the View A Running Process tab of the Select or Launch Process dialog box.

Note "Any CPU" is the default target architecture for Microsoft C# and Visual Basic .NET applications built with Microsoft Visual Studio 2005 and newer.

The VMMap window

After you select or launch a process, VMMap analyzes the process, displaying graphical representations of virtual and physical memory, and tabular Summary and Details Views. Memory types are color coded in each of these components, with the Summary View also serving as a color key.

The first bar graph in the VMMap window (shown in Figure 7-1) is the *Committed* summary. Its differently-colored areas show the relative proportions of the different types of committed memory within the process' address space. It also serves as the basis against which the other two graphs are scaled. The total figure shown above the right edge of the graph is not *all* allocated memory, but the process' "accessible" memory. Regions that have only been reserved cannot yet be accessed and are not included in this graph. In other words, the memory included here is backed by RAM, a paging file, or a mapped file.

The second bar graph in the VMMap window is the *Private Bytes* summary. This is process memory not shareable with other processes and that's backed by physical RAM or by a paging file. It includes the stack, heaps, raw virtual memory, page tables, and read/write portions of image and file mappings. The label above the right side of the graph reports the total size of the process' private memory. The colored areas in the bar graph show the proportions of the various types of memory allocations contributing to the private byte usage. The extent of the colored areas toward the graph's right edge indicates its proportion to in-use virtual memory.

The third bar graph shows the *working set* for the process. The working set is the process' virtual memory that is resident in physical RAM. Like the Private Bytes graph, the colored areas show the relative proportions of different types of allocations in RAM, and their extent toward the right indicates the proportion of the process' committed virtual memory that is resident in RAM.

Note that these graphs show only the relative proportions of the different allocation types. They are not layout maps that show *where* in memory they are allocated. The Address Space Fragmentation dialog box, described later in this chapter, provides such a map for 32-bit processes.

Below the three graphs, the *Summary View* table lists the different types of memory allocations (described in the "Memory Types" section in this chapter), the total amount of each type of allocation, how much is committed, and how much is in physical RAM. Select a memory type in Summary View to filter what is shown in the Details View window. You can sort the Summary View table by the values in any column by clicking the corresponding column header. Clicking a column header again reverses the sort order for that column. The order of the colored areas in the VMMap bar graphs follows the sort order of the Summary View table. You can also change the column order for this table by dragging a column header to a new position, and resize column widths by dragging the borders between the column headers.

Below Summary View, *Details View* displays information about each memory region of the process' user-mode virtual address space. To show only one allocation type in Details View, select that type in the Summary View. To view all memory allocations, select the Total row in the Summary View. As with the Summary View, the columns in Details View allow sorting, resizing and reordering.

Allocations shown in Details View can expand to show sub-blocks within the original allocation. This can occur, for example, when a large block of memory is reserved, and then parts of it are committed. It also occurs when the image loader or an application creates a file mapping and then creates multiple mapped views of that file mapping; for example, to set protection differently on the different regions of the file mapping. You can expand or collapse individual groups of sub-allocations by clicking the plus (+) and minus (–) icons in Details View. You can also expand or collapse all of them by choosing Expand All or Collapse All from the Options menu. The top row of such a group shows the sums of the individual components within it. When a different sort order is selected for Details View, sub-blocks remain with their top-level rows and are sorted within that group.

If VMMap's default font is not to your liking, choose Options | Font to select a different font for Summary View, Details View, and some of VMMap's dialog boxes.

Memory Types

VMMap categorizes memory allocations into one of several types:

- **Image** The memory represents an executable file, such as an EXE or DLL, that has been loaded into a process by the image loader. Note that Image memory does not include executable files loaded as data files—these are included in the Mapped File memory type. Executable code regions are typically read/execute-only and shareable. Data regions, such as initialized data, are typically read/write or copy-on-write. When copy-on-write pages are modified, additional private memory is created in the process and is marked as read/write. This private memory is backed by RAM or a paging file and not by the image file. The Details column in Details View shows the file's path or section name.

- **Mapped File** The memory is shareable and represents a file on disk. Mapped files are often resource DLLs and typically contain application data. The Details column shows the file's path.

- **Shareable** Shareable memory is memory that can be shared with other processes and is backed by RAM or by the paging file (if present). Shareable memory typically contains data shared between processes through DLL shared sections or through pagefile-backed, file-mapping objects (also known as pagefile-backed sections).

- **Heap** A heap represents private memory allocated and managed by the user-mode heap manager and typically contains application data. Application memory allocations that use Heap memory include the C runtime malloc library, the C++ *new* operator, the Windows Heap APIs, and the legacy *GlobalAlloc* and *LocalAlloc APIs*.

- **Managed Heap** Managed Heap represents private memory that is allocated and managed by the .NET runtime and typically contains application data.

- **Stack**   Stack memory is allocated to each thread in a process to store function parameters, local variables, and invocation records. Typically, a fixed amount of Stack memory is allocated and reserved when a thread is created, but only a relatively small amount is committed. The amount of memory committed within that allocation will grow as needed, but it will not shrink. Stack memory is freed when its thread exits.

- **Private Data**   Private Data memory is memory that is allocated by *VirtualAlloc* and that is not further handled by the Heap Manager or the .NET runtime, or assigned to the Stack category. Private Data memory typically contains application data, as well as the Process and Thread Environment Blocks. Private Data memory cannot be shared with other processes.

> **Note** VMMap's definition of "Private Data" is more granular than that of Process Explorer's "private bytes." Procexp's "private bytes" includes *all* private committed memory belonging to the process.

- **Page Table**   Page Table memory is private kernel-mode memory associated with the process' page tables. Note that Page Table memory is never displayed in VMMap's Details View, which shows only user-mode memory.

- **Free**   Free memory regions are spaces in the process' virtual address space that are not allocated. To include free memory regions in Details View when inspecting a process' total memory map, choose Options | Show Free Regions.

Memory Information

Summary View and Details View show the following information for allocation types and individual allocations. To reduce noise in the output, VMMap does not show entries that have a value of 0.

- **Size**   The total size of the allocated type or region. This includes areas that have been reserved but not committed.

- **Committed**   The amount of the allocation that is committed—that is, backed by RAM, a paging file, or a mapped file.

- **Private**   The amount of the allocation that is private to the process.

- **Total WS**   The total amount of working set (physical memory) assigned to the type or region.

- **Private WS**   The amount of working set assigned to the type or region that cannot be shared with other processes.

- **Shareable WS**   The amount of working set assigned to the type or region that can be shared with other processes.

- **Shared WS**   The amount of Shareable WS that is currently shared with other processes.

- **Locked WS**   The amount of memory that has been guaranteed to remain in physical memory and not incur a page fault when accessed.

- **Blocks**   The number of individually allocated memory regions.

- **Largest**   In Summary View, the size of the largest contiguous memory block for that allocation type.

- **Address**   In Details View, the base address of the memory region in the process' virtual address space.

- **Protection**   In Details View, identifies the types of operations that can be performed on the memory. In the case of top-level allocations that show expandable sub-blocks, Protection identifies a summary of the types of protection in the sub-blocks. An access violation occurs on an attempt to execute code from a region not marked Execute (if DEP is enabled), to write to a region not marked Write or Copy-on-Write, or to access memory that is marked as no-access or is only reserved but not yet committed.

- **Details**   In Details View, additional information about the memory region, such as the path to its backing file, Heap ID (for Heap memory), Thread ID (for Stack memory), or .NET AppDomain and Garbage Collection generations.

Note The *VirtualProtect* API can change the protection of any page to something different from that set by the original memory allocation. This means that there can potentially be pages of memory private to the process in a shareable memory region, for instance, because the region was created as a pagefile-backed section, but then the application or some other software changed the protection to copy-on-write and modified the pages.

Timeline and Snapshots

VMMap retains a history of snapshots of the target process' memory allocation state. You can load any of these snapshots into the VMMap main view and compare any two snapshots to see what changed.

When tracing an instrumented process, VMMap captures snapshots automatically. You can set the automatic capture interval to 1, 2, 5, or 10 seconds from the Options | Trace Snapshot Interval submenu. You can pause and resume automatic snapshots by pressing Ctrl+Space, and manually capture a new snapshot at any time by pressing F5.

When you analyze a running process instead of launching an instrumented one, VMMap does not automatically capture snapshots. You must manually initiate each snapshot by pressing F5.

Click the Timeline button on the VMMap main view to display the Timeline dialog box (shown in Figure 7-4), which renders a graphical representation of the history of allocations in the process' working set. The Timeline lets you load a previous snapshot into the VMMap main view and compare any two snapshots. The graph's horizontal axis represents the number of seconds since the initial snapshot, and its vertical access to the process' working set. The colors in the graph correspond to the colors used to represent memory types in the VMMap main window.

FIGURE 7-4 VMMap Timeline dialog box.

When automatic capture is enabled for an instrumented trace, the Timeline dialog box automatically updates its content. You can click the Pause button to suspend automatic snapshot capture; click it again to resume automatic captures. When viewing a process without instrumented tracing, the Timeline dialog box must be closed and reopened to update its content.

Click on any point within the timeline to load the corresponding snapshot into the VMMap main view. To compare any two snapshots, click on a point near one of the snapshots and then drag the mouse to the other point. While you have the mouse button down, the timeline displays vertical lines indicating when snapshots were captured and shades the area between the two selected points, as shown in Figure 7-5. To increase the granularity of the timeline to make it easier to select snapshots, click the plus (+) and minus (−) zoom buttons and move the horizontal scroll.

FIGURE 7-5 VMMap Timeline dialog box while dragging between two snapshots.

When you compare two snapshots, the VMMap main view graphs and tables show the differences between the two snapshots. All displayed numbers show the positive or negative changes since the previous snapshot. Address ranges in Details View that are in the new snapshot but not in the previous one are highlighted in green; address ranges that were only in the previous screen shot are highlighted in red. You might need to expand sub-allocations to view these. Rows in Details View that retain their normal color indicate a change in the amount of assigned working set. To view changes only for a specific allocation type, select that type in Summary View.

If you choose Empty Working Set from the View menu, VMMap first releases all physical memory assigned to the process and then captures a new snapshot. This feature is useful for measuring the memory cost of an application feature: empty the working set, exercise the feature, and then refresh the display to look at how much physical memory the application referenced.

To switch from comparison view to single-snapshot view, open the Timeline dialog box and click on any snapshot.

Viewing Text Within Memory Regions

In some cases, the purpose of a memory region can be revealed by the string data stored within it. To view ASCII or Unicode strings of three or more characters in length, select a region in Details View and then choose View | Strings. VMMap displays a dialog box showing the virtual address range and the strings found within it, as shown in Figure 7-6. If the selected region has sub-blocks, the entire region is searched.

String data is not captured as part of a snapshot. The feature works only with a live process, and not with a saved VMMap (.mmp) file loaded from disk. Further, the strings are read directly from process memory when you invoke the Strings feature. That memory might have changed since the last snapshot was captured.

Note In computer programming, the term "string" refers to a data structure consisting of a sequence of characters, usually representing human-readable text.

FIGURE 7-6 The VMMap Strings dialog box.

Finding and Copying Text

To search for specific text within Details View, press Ctrl+F. The Find feature selects the next visible row in Details View that contains the text you specify in any column. Note that it will not search for text in unexpanded sub-blocks. To repeat the previous search, press F3.

VMMap offers two ways to copy text from the VMMap display to the clipboard:

- Ctrl+A copies all text from the VMMap display, including the process name and ID, and all text in Summary View and Details View, retaining the sort order. All sub-allocation data is copied even if it is not expanded in the view. If a specific allocation type is selected in Summary View, only that allocation type will be copied from Details View.

- Ctrl+C copies all text from the Summary View table if Summary View has focus. If Details View has focus, Ctrl+C copies the address field from the selected row, which can then be pasted into a debugger.

Viewing Allocations from Instrumented Processes

When VMMap starts an instrumented process, it intercepts the program's calls to virtual memory APIs and captures information about the calls. The captured information includes the following:

- The function name, which indicates the type of allocation. For example, *VirtualAlloc* and *VirtualAllocEx* allocate private memory; *RtlAllocateHeap* allocates heap memory.

- The operation, such as Reserve, Commit, Protect (change protection), and Free.

- The memory protection type, such as Execute/Read and Read/Write.

- The requested size, in bytes.

- The virtual memory address at which the allocated block was created.

- The call stack at the point when the API was invoked.

The call stack identifies the code path within the program that resulted in the allocation request. VMMap assigns a Call Site ID number to each unique call stack that is captured. The first call stack is assigned ID 1, the second unique stack is assigned ID 2, and so forth. If the same code path is executed multiple times, each instance will have the same call stack, and the data from those allocations are grouped together under a single Call Site ID.

> **Note** Symbols must be properly configured to obtain useful information from instrumented processes. See "Call Stacks and Symbols" in Chapter 2 for information on configuring symbols.

Refresh the VMMap main view, and then click the Trace button. The Trace dialog box (shown in Figure 7-7) lists all captured memory allocations grouped by Call Site ID. The Function column identifies the API that was called; the Calls column indicates how many times that code path was invoked; the Bytes column lists the total amount of memory allocated through that site. The values in the Operation and Protection columns are the values that were passed in the first time the call site was invoked.

FIGURE 7-7 VMMap Trace dialog box.

Click the plus sign to expand the call site and show the virtual memory addresses at which the requested memory was provided. The Bytes column shows the size of each allocation. Note that when memory is freed, a subsequent allocation request through the same call site might be satisfied at the same address. When this happens, VMMap does not display a separate entry. The Bytes column reports the size only of the first allocation granted at that address. However, the sum shown for the Call Site is accurate.

By default, the Trace dialog box shows only those operations for which "Bytes" is more than 0. Select the "Show all memory operations" check box to display operations that report no bytes. These include operations such as *RtlCreateHeap*, *RtlFreeHeap*, and *VirtualFree* (when releasing an entire allocation block).

In Figure 7-7, the call site assigned the ID 1136 was invoked eight times to allocate 26 MB of private memory. That node is expanded and shows the virtual memory addresses and the requested sizes. Because all of these requests went through a single code path, you can select any of them or the top node and click the Stack button to see that site's call stack, shown in Figure 7-8. If full symbolic information and source files are available, select a frame in the call stack and click the Source button to view the source file in the VMMap source file viewer with the indicated line of source selected.

FIGURE 7-8 Call stack for a call site accessed from the Trace dialog box.

Click the Call Tree button in the VMMap main window for another way to visualize where your program allocates memory. The Call Tree dialog box (shown in Figure 7-9) identifies the commonalities and divergences in all the collected call stacks and renders them as an expandable tree. The topmost nodes represent the outermost functions in the call stacks. Their child nodes represent functions that they called, and their child nodes represent the various functions they called on the way to a memory operation. Across each row, the Count and % Count columns indicate how many times in the collected set of call stacks that code path was traversed; the Bytes and % Bytes columns indicate how much memory was allocated through that path. You can use this to quickly drill down to the places where the most allocations were invoked or the most memory was allocated.

FIGURE 7-9 The VMMap Call Tree dialog box.

Finally, you can view the call stack for a specific heap allocation by selecting it in Details View and clicking the Heap Allocations button to display the Heap Allocations dialog box. (See Figure 7-10). Select the item in the dialog box, and click Stack to display the call stack that resulted in that allocation.

FIGURE 7-10 The Heap Allocations dialog box.

Address Space Fragmentation

Poor or unlucky memory management can result in a situation where there is plenty of free memory, but no individual free blocks large enough to satisfy a particular request. For 32-bit processes, the Address Space Fragmentation dialog box (shown in Figure 7-11) shows the layout of the different allocation types within the process' address space. This can help identify whether fragmentation is a problem and locate the problematic allocations.

FIGURE 7-11 Address Space Fragmentation (32-bit processes only).

When analyzing a 32-bit process, choose View | Fragmentation View to display Address Space Fragmentation. The graph indicates allocation types using the same colors as the VMMap main view, with lower virtual addresses at the top of the window. The addresses at the upper and lower left of the graph indicate the address range currently shown. If the entire address range cannot fit in the window, you move the vertical scroll bar to view other parts of the address range. The slider to the left of the graph changes the granularity of the graph. Moving the slider down increases the size of the blocks representing memory allocations in the graph. If you click on a region in the graph, the dialog box shows its address, size, and allocation type just below the graph, and it selects the corresponding allocation in Details View of the VMMap main view.

Saving and Loading Snapshot Results

The Save and Save As menu items in the File menu include several file formats to save output from a VMMap snapshot. The Save As Type drop-down list in the file-save dialog box includes the following:

- **.MMP**   This is the native VMMap file format. Use this format if you want to load the output back into the VMMap display on the same computer or a different computer. This format saves data from all snapshots, enabling you to view differences from the Timeline dialog box when you load the file back into VMMap.

- **.CSV**   This option saves data from the most recent snapshot as comma-separated values, which is ideal for generating output that you can easily import into Microsoft Excel. If a specific allocation type is selected in Summary View, details are saved only for that memory type.

- **.TXT**   This option saves data as formatted text, which is ideal for sharing the text results in a readable form using a monospace font. Like the .CSV format, if a specific allocation type is selected, details are saved only for that type.

To load a saved .MMP file into VMMap, press Ctrl+O, or pass the file name to VMMap on the command line with the **–o** option. Also, when a user runs VMMap, VMMap associates the .mmp file extension with the path to that instance of VMMap and the **–o** option so that users can open a saved .mmp file by double-clicking it in Windows Explorer.

VMMap Command-Line Options

VMMap supports the following command-line options:

```
vmmap [-64] [-p {PID | processname} [outputfile]] [-o inputfile]
```

–64

On x64 editions of Windows, VMMap will run a 32-bit version of itself when a 32-bit process is selected, and a 64-bit version when a 64-bit process is selected. With the **–64** option, the 64-bit version of VMMap is used to analyze all processes. For 32-bit processes, the 32-bit version of VMMap more accurately categorizes allocation types. The only advantages of the 64-bit version are that it can identify the thread ID associated with 64-bit stacks and more accurately report System memory statistics.

> **Note** The **–64** option applies only to opening running processes; it does not apply when instrumenting and tracing processes launched from VMMap.

–p {PID | processname} [outputfile]

Use this format to analyze the process specified by the PID or process name. If you specify a name, VMMap will match it against the first process that has a name that begins with the specified text.

If you specify an output file, VMMap will scan the target process, output results to the named file, and then terminate. If you don't include an extension, VMMap will add .MMP and save in its native format. Add a .CSV extension to the output file name to save as comma-separated values. Any other file extension will save the output using the .TXT format.

–o inputfile

When you use this command, VMMaps open the specified .MMP input file on startup.

Restoring VMMap defaults

VMMap stores all its configuration settings in the registry in "HKEY_CURRENT_USER\ Software\Sysinternals\VMMap." The simplest way to restore all VMMap configuration settings to their defaults is to close VMMap, delete the registry key, and then start VMMap again.

ProcDump

ProcDump lets you monitor a process and create a user-mode dump file when that process meets criteria that you specify, such as exceeding CPU or memory thresholds, hitting an exception or exiting unexpectedly, UI becoming nonresponsive, or exceeding performance counter thresholds. ProcDump can capture a dump for a single instance of criteria being met or continue capturing dumps each time the problem recurs. ProcDump can also generate an immediate dump or a periodic series of dumps.

A process dump file is a detailed snapshot of a process' internal state, and it can be used by an administrator or a developer to help determine the cause of an application problem. Dump files are analyzed with a debugger such as WinDbg, which ships with the Debugging Tools for Windows.

Because ProcDump has little impact on a system while monitoring a process, it is ideal for capturing data for problems that are difficult to isolate and reproduce, even if it takes weeks for a problem to repeat. ProcDump does not terminate the process being monitored, so you can acquire dump files from processes in production with little, if any, disruption in service.

ProcDump also introduces a new "Miniplus" dump type that is ideal for use with very large processes such as Microsoft Exchange Server and SQL Server. A Miniplus dump is the equivalent of a full memory dump but with large allocations (for example, cache) omitted, and it has been shown to reduce dump sizes of such processes by 50 to 90 percent without reducing the ability to do effective dump analysis. (See Figure 7-12.)

FIGURE 7-12 ProcDump launching a process and capturing a dump when it exceeds a CPU limit for three seconds.

Command-Line Syntax

The following code block shows the full command-line syntax for ProcDump, and Table 7-1 gives brief descriptions of each of the options. They are discussed in greater detail in the following sections.

```
procdump [-c percent [-u]] [-s n] [-n count] [-m commit] [-h] [-e [1] [-b]] [-t]
[-p counter threshold]
[-ma | -mp] [-r] [-o] [-64]
{ {processname | PID} [dumpfile] | -x {imagefile} {dumpfile} [arguments] }
```

TABLE 7-1 ProcDump Command-Line Options

Option	Description
Target Process and Dump File	
processname	Name of the target process. It must be a unique instance and already running.
PID	Process ID of the target process.
dumpfile	Name of dump file. This is optional if the process is already running; it's required if using **–x**.
–x	Starts the target process, using *imagefile* and command-line *arguments*.
imagefile	Name of executable file to launch.
arguments	Optional command-line arguments to pass to new process.
Dump Criteria	
–c *percent*	CPU usage above which to capture a dump.
–u	Used with **–c** to scale threshold against number of CPUs present.
–s *n*	Used with **–c**, sets duration of high CPU usage to trigger a dump.
	Used with **–p**, sets duration of a performance counter threshold exceeded to trigger a dump.
	Used with **–n** and no other dump criteria, dumps process every *n* seconds.
–n *count*	Used with **–c**, **–s**, or **–p**, specifies number of dumps to capture.
–m *commit*	Specifies commit charge limit in MB at which to capture a dump.
–h	Captures a dump when a hung window is detected.
–e	Captures a dump when an unhandled exception occurs. If followed with 1, it also captures a dump on a first-chance exception.
–b	Used with **–e**, treats breakpoints as exceptions. Otherwise, it ignores them.
–t	Captures a dump when the process terminates.
–p *counter threshold*	Captures a dump when the named performance counter exceeds the threshold.
Dump File Options	
–ma	Include all process memory in the dump.
–mp	"Miniplus"; creates the equivalent of a full dump but with large allocations omitted.

Option	Description
−r	Reflects (clones) the process for the dump to minimize the time the process is suspended. (This option requires Windows 7 or Windows Server 2008 R2 or higher.)
−o	Overwrites an existing dump file.
−64	Creates a 64-bit dump of the target process. (for x64 editions of Windows only).

Specifying Which Process to Monitor

You can launch the target process from the ProcDump command line or monitor an already-running process. To start the process with ProcDump, use the **–x** option, followed by the name of the executable to start, the name of the dump file to write to, and then any command-line arguments to pass to the program. Note that you must specify the actual executable to run—ProcDump will not launch an application via a file association. If you use this option, the **–x** and what follows it must be the last items on the ProcDump command line.

To monitor an already-running program, specify its image name or process ID (PID) on the command line. If you specify a name and there are multiple processes with that name, ProcDump will not pick one—you must specify a PID instead.

Administrative rights are not required to monitor a process running in the same security context as ProcDump. Administrative rights, including the Debug privilege, are required to monitor an application running as a different user or at a higher integrity level than ProcDump's.

Specifying the Dump File Path

The *dumpfile* command-line parameter specifies the path and base file name for the dump file. You are required to supply a *dumpfile* parameter when starting the target process with **–x**. The *dumpfile* parameter is optional when monitoring an already-running process; if you omit it, ProcDump creates the dump file in the current folder and uses the target process name as the base file name.

You can specify *dumpfile* as an absolute or relative path. If *dumpfile* names an existing folder, ProcDump creates the dump file in that folder, using the process name as the base name. Otherwise, the last part of the *dumpfile* parameter becomes the base file name for the dump file. For example, if you specify C:\dumps\sample as the *dumpfile* parameter and C:\dumps\ sample is an existing folder, ProcDump creates the dump file in that folder with the process name as the dump file's base name. If C:\dumps\sample does not exist, ProcDump creates the dump file in C:\dumps with "sample" as the base file name. The target folder must exist; otherwise, ProcDump reports an error and exits immediately.

To avoid an accidental overwrite of other dump files, ProcDump creates unique dump file names by incorporating the current date and time into the file name. The format for the file name is *basename_yyMMdd_HHmmss.dmp*. For example, the following command line creates an immediate dump file for Testapp.exe:

```
procdump testapp
```

If that dump were created at exactly 11:45:56 PM on December 28, 2010 its file name would be *Testapp_101228_234556.dmp*. This file naming ensures that an alphabetic sort of dump files associated with a particular executable will also be sorted chronologically (for files created from the years 2000 through 2099). Note that the format of the file name is fixed and is independent of regional settings. ProcDump also ensures that the dump file has a file extension of *.dmp*.

The one case where the date and time is not incorporated into the dump file name is if you capture an immediate dump of a running process *and* specify the dump file name. For example, the following command creates a dump file for Testapp.exe in c:\dumps\dumpfile. dmp (assuming that c:\dumps\dumpfile is not an existing folder):

```
procdump testapp c:\dumps\dumpfile
```

If c:\dumps\dumpfile.dmp already exists, ProcDump will not overwrite it unless you add the **–o** option to the command line.

Dumps that are created later as a result of satisfied dump criteria always have the date and time incorporated into the dump file name or names.

Specifying Criteria for a Dump

As mentioned, to capture an immediate dump of a running process, just specify it by name or PID with no other dump criteria, and an optional dump file name.

ProcDump can monitor a target process' CPU usage and create a dump file when it exceeds a threshold for a fixed period of time. In this example, if Testapp's CPU usage continually exceeds 90 percent for five seconds, ProcDump generates a dump file and then exits:

```
procdump -c 90 -s 5 testapp
```

If you omit the **–s** option, the default time period is 10 seconds. To capture multiple samples, in case the first was to the result of some transient condition not related to the problem you're tracking (that is, a false positive), use the **–n** option to specify how many dumps to capture before exiting. In the following example, ProcDump will continue monitoring Testapp and create a new dump file every time it sustains 95 percent CPU for two seconds, until it has captured 10 dumps:

```
procdump -c 95 -s 2 -n 10 testapp
```

On a multi-core system, a single thread cannot consume 100 percent of all the processors' time. On a dual core, the maximum one thread can consume is 50 percent; on a quad core, the maximum is 25 percent. To scale the **–c** threshold against the number of CPUs on the system, add **–u** to the command line. On a dual-core system, **procdump –c 90 –u testapp** creates a dump when Testapp exceeds 45 percent CPU for 10 seconds—the equivalent of 90 percent of one of the CPUs. On a 16-core system, the trigger threshold is 5.625 percent. Because **–c** requires an integer value, the **–u** option increases the granularity with which you can specify a threshold on multi-core systems. See "The Compound Case of the Outlook Hangs" in Chapter 17, "Hangs and Sluggish Performance", for an example of its use.

> **Note** A user-mode thread running a tight CPU-bound loop can, and often will, be scheduled to run on more than one CPU, unless its processor affinity has been set to tie it to one CPU. The **–u** option scales the threshold only against the number of cores; it doesn't mean, "Create a dump if the process exceeds the threshold on a single CPU." That wouldn't be possible anyway because Windows does not provide the tracking information to support such a query.

To capture a periodic series of dumps, use the **–s** and **–n** options together without any other dump criteria. The **–s** option specifies the number of seconds between the end of the previous capture and the beginning of the next capture. The **–n** option specifies how many dumps to capture. The following example captures a dump of Testapp immediately, another dump five seconds later, and again five seconds after that, for a total of three dumps:

```
procdump -s 5 -n 3 testapp
```

To capture a dump when the process hits an unhandled exception, use the **–e** option. Use **–e 1** to capture a dump on any exception, including a first-chance exception. Use **–t** to capture a dump when the process terminates. The **–t** option is useful to identify the cause of an unexpected process exit that is not caused by an unhandled exception. If you add **–b**, ProcDump treats debug breakpoints as exceptions; otherwise, it ignores them. For example, a program might contain code like the following:

```
if (IsDebuggerPresent())
    DebugBreak();
```

ProcDump attaches to the target program as a debugger, the *IsDebuggerPresent* API will return TRUE, and *DebugBreak* will be called. ProcDump will capture a dump when *DebugBreak* is called only if you specify **–b**.

ProcDump's **–h** option monitors the target process for a hung (nonresponsive) top-level window and captures a dump when detected. ProcDump uses the same definition of "not responding" that Windows and Task Manager use: if a window belonging to the process fails to respond to window messages for five seconds, it's considered hung. ProcDump must be running on the same desktop as the target process to use this option.

You can use a process' commit charge threshold to trigger a dump. Specify the memory threshold in MB with the **–m** option. The following example captures a dump when Testapp's commit charge exceeds 200 MB:

```
procdump -m 200 testapp
```

ProcDump checks the memory counters of the process once per second, and it captures a dump only if the amount of process memory charged against the system commit limit (the sum of the paging file sizes plus most of RAM) exceeds the threshold at the moment of the check. If the commit charge spikes only briefly, ProcDump might not detect it.

Finally, you can use any performance counter to trigger a dump. Specify the **–p** option, followed by the name of the counter and the threshold to exceed. Put the counter name in double quotes if it contains spaces. The following example captures a dump of Taskmgr.exe if the number of processes on the system exceeds 750 for three seconds or more:

```
procdump -p "\System\Processes" 750 -s 3 taskmgr.exe
```

One way to obtain valid counter names is to add them in Performance Monitor and then view the names on the Data tab of the Properties dialog box. However, Perfmon's default notation for distinguishing multiple instances of a process with a hash sign and a sequence number (for example, *cmd#2*) is neither predictable nor stable—the name associated with a specific process can change as other instances start or exit. Therefore, ProcDump does not support this notation, but instead supports the *process_PID* notation described in Microsoft Knowledge Base article 281884. For example, if you have two instances of Testapp with PIDs 1135 and 924, you can monitor attributes of the former by specifying it as **testapp_1135**. The following example captures a dump of that process if its handle count exceeds 200 for three seconds:

```
procdump -p "\Process(testapp_1135)\Handle Count" 200 -s 3 1135
```

The *process_PID* notation is not mandatory. You can specify just the process name, but results will be unpredictable if multiple instances of that process are running.

Options can be combined. The following command captures a dump if Testapp exceeds the CPU or the commit charge threshold, has a hung window or unhandled exception, or otherwise exits:

```
procdump -m 200 -c 90 -s 3 -u -h -t -e testapp
```

To stop monitoring at any time, just press Ctrl+C or Ctrl+Break.

Dump File Options

Different debug dump options are available depending on the version of dbghelp.dll that ProcDump uses. To get the latest and greatest features, install the latest version of

Debugging Tools for Windows, copy ProcDump.exe into the folder containing dbghelp.dll, and run it from there.

At a minimum, dumps created by ProcDump will contain basic information about the process and all its threads, including stack traces for all threads; data sections from all loaded modules, including global variables; and module signature information so that the corresponding symbol files can be downloaded from a symbol server, even if the dump is analyzed on a completely different platform.

> **Note** With Dbghelp.dll version 6.1 or higher, ProcDump adds thread CPU usage data so that the debugger's **!runaway** command can show the amount of time consumed by each thread. Version 6.1 is included with Windows 7 and Windows Server 2008 R2.

To include all the process' accessible memory in the dump, add the **–ma** option to the ProcDump command line. With newer versions of dbghelp.dll, this option also captures memory region information, including details about the allocations and protection settings. Note that the **–ma** option makes the dump file *much* larger and can be very time-consuming, potentially taking several minutes to write the memory of a large application to disk. (The Miniplus dump option, described in the next section, is as useful as a full dump but is up to 90 percent smaller.)

Ordinarily, ProcDump needs to suspend the target process while the dump is being captured. Windows 7 and Windows Server 2008 R2 introduced a *process reflection* feature, which allows the process to be "cloned" so that the process can continue to run while a memory snapshot is dumped. You can take advantage of this feature by using the **–r** option. ProcDump creates three files: *dumpfile*.dmp, which captures process and thread information; *dumpfile*-reflected. dmp, which captures the process' memory; and *dumpfile*.ini, which ties them together and is the file you should open with the debugger. Windbg treats *.ini as a valid dump file type, although the file-open dialog box doesn't indicate so.

On x64 editions of Windows, ProcDump creates a 32-bit dump file when the target process is a 32-bit process. To override this default and create a 64-bit dump file, add **–64** to the ProcDump command line.

Miniplus Dumps

The Miniplus (**–mp**) dump type was specifically designed to tackle the growing problem of capturing full dumps of large applications such as the Microsoft Exchange Information Store (store.exe) on large servers. For example, capturing a full dump of Exchange 2010 can take 30 minutes and result in a dump file of 48 GB. Compressing that file down to 8 GB can take another 60 minutes, and uploading the compressed file to Microsoft support can take another six hours. Capturing a Miniplus dump of the same Exchange server takes one minute, and results in a 1.5-GB dump file that takes two minutes to compress and about 15 minutes to upload.

Although originally designed for Exchange, the algorithm is generic and works as well on Microsoft SQL Server or any other native application that allocates large memory regions. This is because the algorithm uses heuristics to determine what data is to be included.

A Miniplus dump starts by creating a minidump and adds ("plus") memory deemed important. The first step is to consider only pages marked as read/write. This excludes the majority of the image pages but still retains the image pages associated with global variables. The next step is to find the largest read/write memory area larger than 512 MB. If found, the memory area is provisionally excluded. A memory area is the collection of same-sized memory allocations. For example, if there are twenty 64-MB regions (1280 MB total), and five 128-MB regions (640 MB total), the 64-MB regions will be excluded because they use more memory than the 128-MB regions even though the size of the allocations is not the largest. These excluded regions have a second chance to be included. They are divided into 4-MB chunks, and if referenced by any thread stack, the referenced 4-MB chunk is included.

Even if the process isn't overly large, Miniplus dumps are still considerably smaller than full dumps because they do not contain the process' executable image. For example, a full dump of Notepad is approximately 50 MB, but a Notepad Miniplus dump is only about 2 MB. And a full dump of Microsoft Word is typically around 280 MB, but a Miniplus dump of the same process is only about 36 MB. When the process isn't overly large, you can get an approximate size of the dump by viewing the Total/Private value in VMMap.

> **Note** When debugging Miniplus dumps, the debugger needs to substitute in the omitted image pages from a symbol store (.sympath) or executable store (.exepath). If you are capturing Miniplus dumps of your application, you need to maintain both a symbol and executable store that contains each build of your application.

An additional benefit of the Miniplus implementation is its ability to recover from memory read failures. A memory read failure is the reason why various dump utilities sometimes fail to capture a full dump. If you run across this issue when capturing a full dump, try using Miniplus instead to activate this recovery logic.

The Miniplus dump option can be combined with other ProcDump options as the following examples demonstrate. To capture a single Miniplus dump of store.exe, use the following command line:

```
procdump -mp store.exe
```

Use the following command to capture a single Miniplus dump when store.exe crashes:

```
procdump -mp -e store.exe
```

This command captures three Miniplus dumps of store.exe 15 seconds apart:

```
procdump -mp -n 3 -s 15 store.exe
```

To capture three Miniplus dumps when the RPC Averaged Latency performance counter is over 250 ms for 15 seconds, use this command:

```
procdump -mp -n 3 -s 15 -p "\MSExchangeIS\RPC Averaged Latency" 250 store.exe
```

> **Note** I don't recommend you capture a Miniplus dump of a managed (.NET) application, but that you capture a full dump (**–ma**) instead. The Miniplus algorithm tries to capture a full dump in this situation, but because it builds on top of a minidump, the resulting dump isn't as complete as a full dump. A full dump is needed because intact GC data structures and access to the NGEN image (which won't be on a symbol or executable store) are required by the debugger.

Running ProcDump Noninteractively

ProcDump does not need to be run in an interactive desktop session. Some reasons that you might want to run it noninteractively are that you have a long-running target process and don't want to remain logged in while monitoring it, or you're tracking a problem that happens when no one is logged on or during a logoff.

The following example shows how to use PsExec to run ProcDump as System in the same noninteractive session and desktop in which services running as System run. The example runs it within a Cmd.exe instance so that its console outputs can be redirected to files. Note the use of the escape (^) character with the output redirection character (>) so that it isn't treated as an output redirector on the PsExec command line but becomes part of the Cmd.exe command line. The following example should be typed as a single command line. (See Chapter 6, "PsTools," for more information about PsExec, and see Chapter 2 for more information about noninteractive sessions and desktops.)

```
psexec -s -d cmd.exe /c procdump.exe -e -t testapp c:\temp\testapp.dmp ^>
    c:\temp\procdump.out 2^> c:\temp\procdump.err
```

If the target application crashes during a logoff, this type of command will work better than if ProcDump were running in the same session, because ProcDump could end up exiting earlier than the target. However, if the logoff terminates the target application, ProcDump will not be able to capture a dump. ProcDump acts as a debugger for its target process, and logoff detaches any debuggers attached to processes that it terminates.

Note also that ProcDump cannot monitor for hung application windows when the target process is running on a different desktop from ProcDump.

Capturing All Application Crashes with ProcDump

You can use ProcDump to create a crash dump whenever any application crashes by configuring it as the postmortem debugger.[1] In the registry, go to HKLM\Software\Microsoft\ Windows NT\CurrentVersion\AeDebug. Set the "Debugger" REG_SZ value to the ProcDump command line to execute, using **%ld** as the placeholder for the PID of the crashing process. For example, the following command will create a full memory dump in C:\Dumps whenever any application crashes with the process name and time stamp in the file name:

```
"C:\Program Files\Sysinternals\procdump.exe" /accepteula -ma %ld C:\Dumps
```

It is important to specify the dump file path. Otherwise, ProcDump tries to create the dump file in the current directory, which is %SystemRoot%\System32 when started in this manner. Because the configured debugger is launched in the same security context as the crashing process, ProcDump cannot create the dump file there unless the crashing process had administrative rights. Also note that the target folder must exist before ProcDump launches, and it must be writable.

Viewing the Dump in the Debugger

For all dumps triggered by a condition, ProcDump records a comment in the dump that describes why the dump was captured. The comment can be seen in the initial text that WinDbg presents when you open the dump file. The first line of the comment shows the ProcDump command line that was used to create the dump. The second line of the comment describes what triggered the dump, along with other pertinent data if available. For example, if the memory threshold had been passed, the comment shows the memory commit limit and the process' commit usage:

```
*** Process exceeded 100 MB commit usage: 107 MB
```

If the CPU threshold has been passed, the comment shows the CPU threshold, the duration, and the thread identifier (TID) that consumed the largest amount of CPU cycles in the period:

```
*** Process exceeded 50% CPU for 3 seconds. Thread consuming CPU: 4484 (0x1184)
```

If the performance counter threshold had been exceeded, the comment reports the performance counter, threshold, duration, and TID that consumed the largest amount of CPU cycles in the period. (The following command should be typed on a single command line, with a space separating the period and "Thread".)

```
*** Counter "\Process(notepad_1376)\% Processor Time" exceeded 5 for 3 seconds.
    Thread consuming CPU: 1368 (0x558)
```

---

[1] Windows Error Reporting can capture crash dumps, but ProcDump can be easier to configure.

If a hung window triggered the dump, the comment includes the window handle in hexadecimal. If the dump was captured immediately, was timed, or was triggered by an exception or a normal termination, the comment reports only the cause with no additional data.

To avoid you having to change the thread context to the busy thread (the **~~[TID]s** command) when opening a dump that has been created because of a CPU or performance counter trigger, ProcDump inserts a fake exception to do it for you. This is very useful when you capture multiple dump files because you can open each dump file knowing that the default thread context is the thread of interest. The insertion of the fake exception into the dump results in the debugger reporting a false positive with text like the following:

```
This dump file has an exception of interest stored in it.
The stored exception information can be accessed via .ecxr.
(104c.14c0): Wake debugger - code 80000007 (first/second chance not available)
eax=000cfe00 ebx=00188768 ecx=00000001 edx=00000000 esi=00000000 edi=00000000
eip=01001dc7 esp=00feff70 ebp=00feff88 iopl=0         nv up ei pl zr na pe nc
cs=0023  ss=002b  ds=002b  es=002b  fs=0053  gs=002b            efl=00000246
```

Now that you know about that, you can safely ignore it.

DebugView

DebugView is an application that lets you monitor debug output generated from the local computer or from remote computers. Unlike most debuggers, DebugView can display user-mode debug output from all processes within a session, as well as kernel-mode debug output. It offers flexible logging and display options, and it works on all x86 and x64 versions of Windows XP and newer.

What Is Debug Output?

Windows provides APIs that programs can call to send text that can be captured and displayed by a debugger. If no debugger is active, the APIs do nothing. These interfaces make it easy for programs to produce diagnostic output that can be consumed by any standard debugger and that is discarded if no debugger is connected.

Debug output can be produced both by user-mode programs and by kernel-mode drivers. For user-mode programs, Windows provides the *OutputDebugString* Win32 API. 16-bit applications running on x86 editions of Windows can produce debug output by calling the Win16 *OutputDebugString* API, which is forwarded to the Win32 API. For managed applications, the Microsoft .NET Framework provides the *System.Diagnostics.Debug* and *Trace* classes with static methods that internally call *OutputDebugString*. Those methods can also be called from Windows PowerShell—for example:

```
[System.Diagnostics.Debug]::Print("Some debug output")
```

Kernel-mode drivers can produce diagnostic output by invoking the *DbgPrint* or *DbgPrintEx* routines, or several related functions. Programmers can also use the *KdPrint* or *KdPrintEx* macros, which produce debug output only in debug builds and do nothing in release builds.

Although Windows provides both an ANSI and a Unicode implementation of the *OutputDebugString* API, internally all debug output is processed as ANSI. The Unicode implementation of *OutputDebugString* converts the debug text based on the current system locale and passes that to the ANSI implementation. As a result, some Unicode characters might not be displayed correctly.

The DebugView Display

Simply execute the DebugView program file (Dbgview.exe). It will immediately start capturing and displaying Win32 debug output from all desktops in the current terminal server session.

> **Note** All interactive desktop sessions are internally implemented as terminal server sessions.

As you can see in Figure 7-13, the first column is a DebugView-assigned, zero-based sequence number. Gaps in the sequence numbers might appear when filter rules exclude lines of text or if DebugView's internal buffers are overflowed during extremely heavy activity. The sequence numbers are reset whenever the display is cleared. (DebugView filtering is described later in this chapter.)

FIGURE 7-13 DebugView.

The second column displays the time at which the item was captured, either in elapsed time or clock time. By default, DebugView shows the number of seconds since the first debug record in the display was captured, with the first item always being 0.00. This can be helpful when debugging timing-related problems. This timer is reset when the display is cleared. Choose Clock Time from the Options menu if you prefer that the local clock time be displayed instead. Additionally, choose Show Milliseconds from the Options menu if you want the time stamp to show that level of granularity. You can also configure the time display with command-line options: **/o** to display clock time, **/om** to display clock time with milliseconds, and **/on** to show elapsed time.

> **Tip** Changing the Show Milliseconds setting doesn't change the display of existing entries. You can refresh these entries by pressing Ctrl+T twice to toggle Clock Time off and back on. All entries will then reflect the new setting for Show Milliseconds.

The debug output is in the Debug Print column. For user-mode debug output, the process ID (PID) of the process that generated the output appears in square brackets, followed by the output itself. If you don't want the PID in the display, disable the Win32 PIDs option in the Options menu.

You can select one or more rows of debug output and copy them to the Windows clipboard by pressing Ctrl+C. DebugView supports standard Windows methods of selecting multiple rows such as holding down Shift while pressing the Up or Down arrow keys to select consecutive rows, or holding down Ctrl while clicking nonconsecutive rows.

By default, the Force Carriage Returns option is enabled, which displays every string passed to a debug output function on a separate line, whether or not that text is terminated with a carriage return. If you disable that option in the Options menu, DebugView buffers output text in memory and adds it to the display only when a carriage return is encountered or the memory buffer is filled (approximately 4192 characters). This allows applications and drivers to build output lines with multiple invocations of debug output functions. However, if output is being generated from more than one process, the output can be jumbled together, and the PID that appears on the line will be that of the process that output a carriage return or filled the buffer.

If the text of any column is too wide for that column, move the mouse over it and the full text will appear in a tooltip.

Debug output is added to the end of the list as it is produced. DebugView's Autoscroll feature (which is off by default) scrolls the display as new debug output is captured so that the most recent entry is visible. To toggle Autoscroll on and off, press Ctrl+A or click the Autoscroll icon in the toolbar.

You can annotate the output by choosing Append Comment from the Edit menu. The text you enter in the Append Comment dialog box is added to the debug output display and to the log file if logging is enabled. Note that filter rules apply to appended comments as well as to debug output.

You can increase the display space for debug output by selecting Hide Toolbar on the Options menu. You can also increase the number of visible rows of debug output by selecting a smaller font size. Choose Font from the Options menu to change the font.

To run DebugView in the background without taking up space in the taskbar, select Hide When Minimized from the Options menu. When you subsequently minimize the DebugView window, it will appear only as an icon in the notification area (also known as "the tray"). You can then right-click on the icon to display the Capture pop-up menu, where you can choose to enable or disable various Capture options. Double-click the icon to display the DebugView window again. You can enable the Hide When Minimized option on startup by adding **/t** to the DebugView command line.

Select Always On Top from the Options menu to keep DebugView as the topmost window on the desktop when it's not minimized.

Capturing User-Mode Debug Output

DebugView can capture debug output from multiple local sources: the current terminal services session, the global terminal services session ("session 0"), and kernel mode. Each of these can be selected from the Capture menu. All capturing can be toggled on or off by choosing Capture Events, pressing Ctrl+E, or clicking the Capture toolbar icon. When Capture Events is off, no debug output is captured; when it is on, debug output is captured from the selected sources.

By default, DebugView captures only debug output from the current terminal services session, called "Capture Win32" on the Capture menu. A terminal services session can be thought of as all user-mode activity associated with an interactive desktop logon. It includes all processes running in the window stations and (Win32) Desktops of that session.

On Windows XP and on Windows Server 2003, an interactive session can be in session 0, and it always is when Fast User Switching and Remote Desktop are not involved. Session 0 is the session in which all services also execute and in which *global* objects are defined. When DebugView is executing in session 0 and Capture Win32 is enabled, it will capture debug output from services as well as the interactive user's processes. Administrative rights are not required to capture debug output from the current session, even that from services. (See the "Sessions, Window Stations, Desktops, and Window Messages" section of Chapter 2 for more information.)

With Fast User Switching or Remote Desktop, Windows XP and Windows Server 2003 users often log in to sessions other than the global one. Also, beginning with Windows Vista, session 0 isolation ensures that users never log on to the session in which services run. When run in a session other than session 0, DebugView adds the Capture Global Win32 option to the Capture menu. When enabled, this option captures debug output from processes running in session 0. DebugView must run elevated on Windows Vista and newer to use this option. Administrative rights are not required to enable this option on Windows XP.

Capturing Kernel-Mode Debug Output

You can configure DebugView to capture kernel-mode debug output generated by device drivers or by the Windows kernel by enabling the Capture Kernel option on the Capture menu. Process IDs are not reported for kernel-mode output because such output is typically not related to a process context. Kernel-mode capture requires administrative rights, and in particular the Load Driver privilege.

Kernel-mode components can set the severity level of each debug message. On Windows Vista and newer, kernel-mode debug output can be filtered based on severity level. If you want to capture all kernel debug output, choose the Enable Verbose Kernel Output option on the Capture menu. If this option is not enabled, DebugView captures only debug output at the error severity level.

DebugView can be configured to pass kernel-mode debug output to a kernel-mode debugger or to swallow the output. You can toggle pass-through mode on the Capture menu or with the Pass-Through toolbar icon. The pass-through mode allows you to see kernel-mode debug output in the output buffers of a conventional kernel-mode debugger while at the same time viewing it in DebugView.

Because it is an interactive program, DebugView cannot be started until after you log on. Ordinarily, to view debug output generated prior to logon, you need to hook up a kernel debugger from a remote computer. DebugView's Log Boot feature offers an alternative, capturing kernel-mode debug output during system startup, holding that output in memory, and displaying it after you log in and start DebugView interactively. When you choose Log Boot from the Capture menu, DebugView configures its kernel driver to load very early in the next boot sequence. When it loads, it creates a 4-MB buffer and captures verbose kernel debug output in it until the buffer is full or DebugView connects to it. When you start DebugView with administrative rights and Capture Kernel enabled, DebugView checks for the existence of the memory buffer in kernel memory. If that is found, DebugView displays its contents. Configuring boot logging requires administrative permissions and applies only to the next boot.

If DebugView is capturing kernel debug output at the time of a bugcheck (also known as a blue-screen crash), DebugView can recover the output it had captured to that point from the crash dump file. This can be helpful if, for example, you are trying to diagnose a crash involving a kernel-mode driver you are developing. You can also instrument your driver to produce debug output so that users who experience a crash using your driver can send you a debug output file instead of an entire memory dump.

Choose Process Crash Dump from the File menu to select a crash dump file for DebugView to analyze. DebugView will search the file for its debug output buffers. If it finds them, DebugView will prompt you for the name of a log file in which to save the output. You can load saved output files into DebugView for viewing. Note that the system must be config-ured to create a kernel or full dump (not a minidump) for this feature to work. DebugView saves all capture configuration settings on exit and restores them the next time it runs. Note that if it had been running elevated and capturing kernel or global (session 0) debug output, DebugView displays error messages and disables those options if it doesn't have administrative rights the next time it runs under the same user account, because it will not be able to capture output from those sources. You can avoid these error messages by starting DebugView with the **/kn** option to disable kernel capture and **/gn** to disable global capture.

Searching, Filtering, and Highlighting Output

DebugView has several features that can help you focus on the debug output you are interested in. These capabilities include searching, filtering, highlighting, and limiting the number of debug output lines saved in the display.

Clearing the Display

To clear the display of all captured debug text, press Ctrl+X or click the Clear icon in the toolbar. You can also clear the DebugView output from a debug output source: when DebugView sees the special debug output string DBGVIEWCLEAR (all capitals) anywhere in an input line, DebugView clears the output. Clearing the output also resets the sequence number and elapsed timer to 0.

Searching

If you want to search for a line containing text of interest, press Ctrl+F to display the Find dialog box. If the text you specify matches text in the output window, DebugView selects the next matching line and turns off the Autoscroll feature to keep the line in the window. Press F3 to repeat a successful search. You can press Shift+F3 to reverse the search direction.

Filtering

Another way to isolate output you are interested in is to use DebugView's filtering capability. Click the Filter/Highlight button in the DebugView toolbar to display the Filter dialog box, shown in Figure 7-14. The Include and Exclude fields are used to set criteria for including or excluding incoming lines of debug text based on their content. The Highlight group box is used to color-code selected lines based on their content. Filter and Highlight rules can be saved to disk and then reloaded at a later time. (Highlighting is discussed in the next section of this chapter.)

FIGURE 7-14 The DebugView Filter dialog box.

Enter substring expressions in the Include field that match debug output lines that you want DebugView to display, and enter substring expressions in the Exclude field to specify debug output lines that you do not want DebugView to display. You can enter multiple expressions, separating each with a semicolon. Do not include spaces in the filter expression unless you want the spaces to be part of the filter. Note that the "*" character is interpreted as a wild-card, and that filters are interpreted in a case-insensitive manner and are also applied to the Process ID portion of the line if PIDs are included in the output. The default rules include everything ("*") and exclude nothing.

As shown in the example in Figure 7-14, say that you want DebugView to display debug output only if it contains the words "win," "desk," or "session," unless it also contains the word "error." Set the Include filter to "win;desk;session" (without the quotes) and the Exclude filter to "error." If you want DebugView to show only output that has "MyApp:" and the word "severe" following later in the output line, use a wildcard in the Include filter: "myapp:*severe".

Filtering is applied only to new lines of debug output as they are captured and to comments appended with the Append Comment feature. New text lines that match the rules that are in effect are displayed; those that don't match are dropped and cannot be "unhidden" by changing the filter rules after the fact. Also, changing the filter rules does not remove lines that are already displayed by DebugView.

If any filter rules are in effect when you exit DebugView, DebugView will display them in a dialog box the next time you start it. Simply click OK to continue using those rules, or change them first. You can edit them in place, click Load to use a previously saved filter, or click Reset to remove the filter. To bypass this dialog box and continue to use the rules that were in effect, add **/f** to the DebugView command line.

Highlighting

Highlighting lets you color-code selected lines based on the text content of those lines. DebugView supports up to 20 separate highlighting rules, each with its own foreground and background color. The highlight rule syntax is the same as that for the Include filter.

Use the Filter drop-down list in the Highlight group box to select which filter (numbered 1 through 20) you want to edit. By default, each filter is associated with a color combination but no highlight rule. To set a rule for that filter, type the text for the rule in the drop-down list showing the color combination. In Figure 7-14, Filter 1 highlights lines containing the word "Console."

Lower-numbered highlight filters take precedence over higher-numbered rules. If a line of text matches the rules for Filter 3 and Filter 5, the line will be displayed in the colors associated with Filter 3. Changing highlight rules updates all lines in the display to reflect the new highlight rules.

To change the colors associated with a highlight filter, select that filter in the drop-down list and click on the Colors button. To change the foreground color, select the FG radio button, choose a color, and click the Select button. Do the same using the BG radio button to change the background color, and then click OK.

Saving and Restoring Filter and Highlight Rules

Use the Load and Save buttons on the Filter dialog box to save and restore filter settings, including the Include, Exclude, and Highlight filter rules, as well as the Highlight color selections. DebugView uses the .INI file extension for its filter files, even though they are not formatted as initialization files.

Clicking the Reset button resets all Filter and Highlight rules to DebugView defaults. Note that Reset does not restore default Highlight colors.

History Depth

A final way to control DebugView output is to limit the number of lines that are retained in the display. Choose History Depth from the Edit menu to display the History Depth dialog box. Enter the number of output lines you want DebugView to retain, and it will keep only that number of the most recent debut output lines, discarding older ones. A history depth of 0 (zero) represents no limit on the number of output lines retained. You can specify the history depth on the command line with the **/h** switch, followed by the desired depth.

You do not need to use the History Depth feature to prevent all of a system's virtual memory from being consumed in long-running captures. DebugView monitors system memory usage, alerts the user, and suspends capture of debug output when it detects that memory is running low.

Saving, Logging, and Printing

DebugView lets you save captured debug output to file, either on demand or as it is being captured. Saved files can be opened and displayed by DebugView at a later time. DebugView also lets you print all or parts of the displayed output.

You can save the contents of the DebugView output window as a text file by choosing Save or Save As from the File menu. DebugView uses the .LOG extension by default. The file format is tab-delimited ANSI text. You can display the saved text in DebugView at a later time by choosing Open from the File menu, or by specifying the path to the file on the DebugView command line, as in the following example:

```
dbgview c:\temp\win7-x86-vm.log
```

Logging

To have DebugView log output to a file as it displays it, choose Log To File from the File menu. The first time you choose that menu item or click the Log To File button on the toolbar, DebugView displays the Log-To-File Settings dialog box shown in Figure 7-15, prompting you for a file location. From that point forward, the Log To File menu option and toolbar button toggle logging to that file on or off. To log to a different file or to change other log file settings, choose Log To File As from the File menu. (If log-to-file is currently enabled, choosing Log To File As has the same effect as toggling Log To File off.)

FIGURE 7-15 The DebugView Log-to-File Settings dialog box.

The other configuration options in the Log-To-File Settings dialog box are

- **Unlimited Log Size**   This selection allows the log file to grow without limit.

- **Create New Log Every Day**   When this option is selected, DebugView will not limit the size of the log file, but will create a new log file every day, with the current date appended to the base log file name. You can also select the option to clear the display when the new day's log file is created.

- **Limit Log Size**   When this option is selected, the log file will not grow past the size limit you specify. DebugView will stop logging to the file at that point, unless you also select the Wrap option. With Wrap enabled, DebugView will wrap around to the beginning of the file when the file's maximum size is reached.

If Append is not selected and the target log file already exists, DebugView truncates the existing file when logging begins. If Append is selected, DebugView appends to the existing log file, preserving its content.

If you are monitoring debug output from multiple remote computers and enable logging to a file, all output is logged to the one file you specify. Ranges of output from different computers are separated with a header that indicates the name of the computer from which the subsequent lines were recorded.

Logging options can also be controlled by using the command-line options listed in Table 7-2:

TABLE 7-2 Command-Line Options for Logging

Option	Description
−l *logfile*	Logs output to the specified logfile
−m *n*	Limits log file to *n* MB
−p	Appends to the file if it already exists; otherwise, overwrites it
−w	Used with **−m**, wrap to the beginning of the file when the maximum size is reached
−n	Creates a new log file every day, appending the date to the file name
−x	Used with **−n**, clears the display when a new log file is created

Printing

Choose Print or Print Range from the File menu to print the contents of the display to a printer. Choose Print Range if you want to print only a subset of the sequence numbers displayed, or choose Print if you want to print all the output records. Note that capture must be disabled prior to printing.

The Print Range dialog box also lets you specify whether or not sequence numbers and time stamps will be printed along with the debug output. Omitting these fields can save page space if they are not necessary. The settings you choose are used in all subsequent print operations.

To prevent wrap-around when output lines are wider than a page, consider using landscape mode instead of portrait when printing.

Remote Monitoring

DebugView has remote monitoring capabilities that allow you to view debug output generated on remote systems. DebugView can connect to and monitor multiple remote computers and the local computer simultaneously. You can switch the view to see output from a computer by selecting it from the Computer menu as shown in Figure 7-16, or you can cycle through them by pressing Ctrl+Tab. The active computer view is identified in the title bar and by an arrow icon in the Computer menu. Alternatively, you can open each computer in a separate window and view their debug outputs simultaneously.

FIGURE 7-16 DebugView monitoring two remote computers and the local computer.

To perform remote monitoring, DebugView runs in agent mode on the remote system, sending debug output it captures to a central DebugView viewer that displays the output. Typically, you will start DebugView in agent mode on the remote system manually. In some circumstances, the DebugView viewer can install and start the remote agent component automatically, but with host-based firewalls now on by default, this is usually impractical.

To begin remote monitoring, press Ctrl+R or choose Connect from the Computer menu to display a computer connection dialog box. Enter the name or IP address of the remote computer, or select a previously-connected computer from the drop-down list, and click OK. DebugView will try to install and start an agent on that computer; if it cannot, DebugView tries to find and connect to an already-running, manually-started agent on the computer. If its attempt is successful, DebugView begins displaying debug output received from that computer, adding the remote computer name to the title bar and to the Computer menu.

To begin monitoring the local computer, choose Connect Local from the Computer menu. Be careful not to connect multiple viewers to a single computer because the debug output will be split between those viewers.

To view debug output from two computers side by side, choose New Window from the File menu to open a new DebugView window before establishing the second connection. Make the connection from that new window.

To stop monitoring debug output from a computer, make it the active computer view by selecting it in the Computer menu, and then choose Disconnect from the Computer menu.

Running the DebugView Agent

To manually start DebugView in agent mode, specify **/a** as a command-line argument. DebugView displays the "Waiting for connection" dialog box shown in Figure 7-17 until a DebugView monitor connects to it. The dialog box then indicates "Connected." Note that in agent mode, DebugView does not capture or save any debug output when not connected to a DebugView monitor. When connected, the DebugView agent always captures Win32 debug output in the current terminal services session. To have the agent capture kernel debug output, add **/k** to the command line; to capture verbose kernel debug output, also add **/v** to the command line. To capture global (session 0) output, add **/g** to the command line.

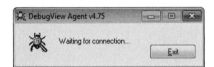

FIGURE 7-17 The DebugView Remote Agent window.

If the monitor disconnects or the connection is otherwise broken, the agent status window reverts to "Waiting for connection" and DebugView awaits another connection. By adding **/e** to the DebugView agent command line, you can opt to display an error message when this occurs and not accept a new connection until the error message is dismissed.

You can hide the agent status window and instead display an icon in the taskbar notification area by adding **/t** to the command line. The icon is gray when the agent is not connected to a monitor and colored when it is connected. You can open the status window by double-clicking on the icon and return it to an icon by minimizing the status window. You can hide the DebugView agent user interface completely by adding **/s** to the DebugView command line. In this mode, DebugView remains active until the user logs off, silently accepting connections from DebugView monitors. Note that **/s** overrides **/e**: if the viewer disconnects, DebugView will silently await and accept a new connection without displaying a notification.

The manually-started DebugView agent listens for connections on TCP port 2020. The Windows Firewall might display a warning the first time you run DebugView in agent mode. If you choose to allow the access indicated in the warning message, Windows will create a program exception for DebugView in the firewall. That or a port exception for TCP 2020 will enable the manually-started DebugView agent to work. Note that connections are anonymous and not authenticated.

The agent automatically installed and started on the remote computer by the viewer is implemented as a Windows service. Therefore, it runs in terminal services session 0, where it can monitor only kernel and global Win32 debug output; it cannot monitor debug output from interactive user sessions outside of session 0. Also, it listens for a connection on a random high port, which isn't practical when using a host-based firewall. In most cases, the manually started DebugView agent will generally be much more reliable and is the recommended way to monitor debug output remotely.

When using the agent automatically installed by the monitor, the state of global capture, Win32 debug capture, kernel capture, and pass-through for the newly established remote session are all adopted from the current settings of the DebugView viewer. Changes you make to these settings on the viewer take effect immediately on the monitored computer.

LiveKd

LiveKd allows you to use kernel debuggers to examine a snapshot of a live system without booting the system in debugging mode. This can be useful when kernel-level troubleshooting is required on a machine that wasn't booted in debugging mode. Certain issues might be hard to reproduce, so rebooting a system can be disruptive. On top of that, booting a computer in debug mode changes how some subsystems behave, which can further complicate analysis. In addition to not requiring booting with debug mode enabled, LiveKd allows the Microsoft kernel debuggers to perform some actions that are not normally possible with local kernel debugging, such as creating a full memory dump file.

In addition to examining the local system, LiveKd supports the debugging of Hyper-V guest virtual machines (VMs) externally from the Hyper-V host. In this mode, the debugger runs on the Hyper-V host and not on the guest VMs, so there is no need to copy any files to the target VM or configure the VM in any way.

LiveKd creates a snapshot dump file of kernel memory, without actually stopping the kernel while the snapshot is captured. LiveKd then presents this simulated dump file to the kernel debugger of your choosing. You can then use the debugger to perform any operations on this snapshot of live kernel memory that you could on any normal dump file.

Because LiveKd relies on physical memory to back the simulated dump, the kernel debugger might run into situations in which data structures are in the middle of being changed by the system and are inconsistent. Each time the debugger is launched, it starts with a fresh view of the system state. If you want to refresh the snapshot, quit the debugger (with the **q** command), and LiveKd will ask you whether you want to start it again. If the debugger enters a loop in printing output, press Ctrl+C to interrupt the output, quit, and rerun it. If it hangs, press Ctrl+Break, which will terminate the debugger process and ask you whether you want to run the debugger again.

LiveKd Requirements

LiveKd supports all x86 and x64 versions of Windows. It must be run with administrative rights, including the Debug privilege.

LiveKd depends on the Debugging Tools for Windows, which must be installed on the same machine before you run LiveKd. The URL for the Debugging Tools for Windows is *http://www.microsoft.com/whdc/devtools/debugging/default.mspx*. The Debugging Tools installer used to be a standalone download, but it is now incorporated into the Windows SDK. To get the Debugging Tools, you must run the SDK installer and select the Debugging Tools options you want. Among the options are the Debugging Tools redistributables, which are the standalone Debugging Tools installers, available for x86, x64, and IA64. These work well if you want to install the Debugging Tools on other machines without running the SDK installer.

LiveKd requires that kernel symbol files be available. These can be downloaded as needed from the Microsoft public symbol server. If the system to be analyzed does not have an Internet connection, see the "Online Kernel Memory Dump Using LiveKd" sidebar to learn how to acquire the necessary symbol files.

Running LiveKd

The LiveKd command-line syntax is

```
livekd [-w | -k debugger-path | -o dumpfile] [[-hvl] | [-hv VMName][-p]] [debugger options]
```

Table 7-3 summarizes the LiveKd command-line options, which are then discussed in more detail.

TABLE 7-3 LiveKd Command-Line Options

Option	Description
–w	Runs WinDbg.exe instead of Kd.exe
–k *debugger-path*	Runs the specified debugger instead of Kd.exe
–o *dumpfile*	Saves a kernel dump to the *dumpfile* instead of launching a debugger
–hvl	From Hyper-V host, lists the GUIDs and names of available guest VMs
–hv *VMName*	From Hyper-V host, debugs the VM identified by GUID or name
–p	From Hyper-V host, pauses the target VM while capturing the dump (recommended for use with **–o**)
debugger options	Additional command-line options to pass to the kernel debugger

By default, LiveKd takes a snapshot of the local computer and runs Kd.exe. The **–w** and **–k** options let you specify WinDbg.exe or any other debugger instead of Kd.exe. LiveKd passes any additional command-line options that you specify on to the debugger, followed by **–z** and the path to the simulated dump file.

To debug a Hyper-V virtual machine from the host, specify **–hv** and either the friendly name or the GUID of the VM. To list the names and GUIDs of the available VMs, run LiveKd with the **–hvl** option. Note that you can debug only one VM on a host at a time.

With the **–o** option, LiveKd just saves a kernel dump of the target system to the specified *dumpfile* and doesn't launch a debugger. This option is useful for capturing system dumps for offline analysis. If the target is a Hyper-V VM, you can also add **–p** to the command line to pause the VM while the snapshot is being captured in order to get a completely consistent snapshot.

If you are launching a debugger and don't specify **–k** and a path to a debugger, LiveKd will find Kd.exe or WinDbg.exe if it is in one of the following locations:

- The current directory when you start LiveKd

- The same directory as LiveKd

- The default installation path for the Debugging Tools ("%ProgramFiles%\Debugging Tools for Windows (x86)" on x86 or "%ProgramFiles%\Debugging Tools for Windows (x64)" on x64)

- A directory specified in the PATH variable

If the _NT_SYMBOL_PATH environment variable has not been configured, LiveKd will ask if you want it to configure the system to use Microsoft's symbol server, and then it will ask for the local folder in which to download symbol files (C:\Symbols by default).

Refer to the Debugging Tools documentation regarding how to use the kernel debuggers.

> **Note**   The debugger will complain that it can't find symbols for LiveKdD.SYS. This is expected because I have not made symbols for LiveKdD.SYS available. The lack of these symbols does not affect the behavior of the debugger.

LiveKd Examples

This command line debugs a snapshot of the local computer, passing parameters to WinDbg to write a log file and not to display the Save Workspace? dialog box:

```
livekd -w -Q -logo C:\dbg.txt
```

This command line captures a kernel dump of the local computer and does not launch a debugger:

```
livekd -o C:\snapshot.dmp
```

When run on a Hyper-V host, this command lists the virtual machines available for debugging; it then shows sample output:

```
C:\>livekd -hvl

Listing active Hyper-V partitions...

Hyper-V VM GUID                         Partition ID   VM Name
-----------------------------------     ------------   -------
3187CB6B-1C8B-4968-A501-C8C22468AB77              29   WinXP x86 (SP3)
9A489D58-E69A-48BF-8747-149344164B76              30   Win7 Ultimate x86
DFA26971-62D7-4190-9ED0-61D1B910466B              28   Win7 Ultimate x64
```

You can then use either a GUID or a VM name from the listing to specify the VM to debug. This command pauses the "Win7 Ultimate x64" VM from the example and captures a kernel dump of that system, resuming the VM after the dump has been captured:

```
livekd -p -o C:\snapshot.dmp -hv DFA26971-62D7-4190-9ED0-61D1B910466B
```

Finally, this command debugs a snapshot of the "WinXP x86 (SP3)" VM using Kd.exe:

```
livekd -hv "WinXP x86 (SP3)"
```

Online Kernel Memory Dump Using LiveKd

How many times have you had to acquire a kernel memory dump, but you or your customer (quite rightly) refused to have the target system attached to the Internet, preventing the downloading of required symbol files? I have had that dubious pleasure far too often, so I decided to write down the process for my future reference.

The key problem is that you need to get the correct symbol files for the kernel memory dump. At a minimum, you must have symbols for Ntoskrnl.exe. Just downloading the symbol file packages from WHDC or MSDN for your operating system and service pack version is not quite good enough, because files and corresponding symbols might have been changed by updates since the service pack was released.

Here is the process I follow:

- Copy Ntoskrnl.exe and any other files for which you want symbols from the System32 folder on the computer to be debugged to a folder (for example, C:\DebugFiles) on a computer with Internet access.

- Install the Debugging Tools for Windows on the Internet-facing system.

- From a command prompt on that system, run **Symchk** to download symbols for the files you selected into a new folder. The command might look like this:

  ```
  symchk /if C:\DebugFiles\*.* /s srv*C:\DebugSymbols*http://msdl.microsoft.
  com/download/symbols
  ```

- Copy the downloaded symbols (for example, the C:\DebugSymbols folder in the previous example) from the Internet-facing system to the original system.

- Install the Debugging Tools for Windows on the computer from which you require a kernel memory dump, and copy LiveKd.exe into the same folder with the debuggers. Add this folder to the PATH.

- With administrator privileges, open a command prompt and set the environment variable _NT_SYMBOL_PATH to the folder containing symbol files. For example:

  ```
  SET _NT_SYMBOL_PATH=C:\DebugSymbols
  ```

- At the command prompt, run **LiveKd -w -Q to start WinDbg**.

- When the WinDbg prompt appears, type the following command to create a full memory dump:

  ```
  .dump /f c:\memory.dmp
  ```

  You need to make sure there is enough space on this drive.

- Type **q** to quit WinDbg and then **n** to quit LiveKd.

You should find the full memory dump in C:\memory.dmp, which you can compress and deliver for analysis.

 Note This sidebar is adapted from a blog post by Carl Harrison. Carl's blog is at *http://blogs.technet.com/carlh*.

ListDLLs

ListDLLs is a console utility that displays information about DLLs loaded in processes on the local computer. It can show you all DLLs in use throughout the system or in specific processes, and it can let you search for processes that have a specific DLL loaded. It is also useful for verifying which version of a DLL a process has loaded and from what path. It can also flag DLLs that have been relocated from their preferred base address or that have been replaced after they have been loaded.

ListDLLs requires administrative rights, including the Debug privilege, only to list DLLs in processes running as a different user or at a higher integrity level. It does not require elevated permissions for processes running as the same user and at the same integrity level or a lower one.

The command-line syntax for ListDLLs is

```
listdlls [-r] [processname | PID | -d dllname]
```

Run ListDLLs without command-line parameters to list all processes and the DLLs loaded in them, as shown in Figure 7-18. For each process, ListDLLs outputs a dashed-line separator, followed by the process name and PID. If ListDLLs has the necessary permissions to open the process, it then displays the full command line that was used to start the process, followed by the DLLs loaded in the process. ListDLLs reports the base address, size, version, and path of the loaded DLLs in tabular form with column headers. The base address is the virtual memory address at which the module is loaded. The size is the number of contiguous bytes, starting from the base address, consumed by the DLL image. The version is extracted from the file's version resource, if present; otherwise, it is left blank. The path is the full path to the DLL.

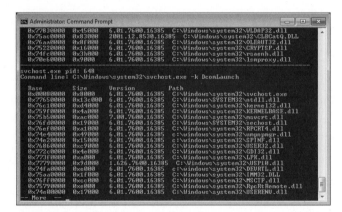

FIGURE 7-18 ListDLLs output.

ListDLLs compares the time stamp in the image's Portable Executable (PE) header in memory to that in the PE header of the image on disk. A difference indicates that the DLL file was replaced on disk after the process loaded it. ListDLLs flags these differences with output like the following:

```
*** Loaded C:\Program Files\Utils\PrivBar.dll differs from file image:
*** File timestamp:        Wed Feb 10 22:06:51 2010
*** Loaded image timestamp: Thu Apr 30 01:48:12 2009
*** 0x10000000  0x9c000    1.00.0004.0000  C:\Program Files\Utils\PrivBar.dll
```

ListDLLs reports only DLLs that are loaded as executable images. Unlike Process Explorer's DLL View (discussed in Chapter 3), it does not list DLLs or other files or file mappings loaded by the image loader as data, including DLLs that are loaded for resources only.

The **–r** option flags DLLs that have been relocated to a different virtual memory address from the base address specified in the image.[2] With **–r** specified, a DLL that has been relocated will be preceded in the output with a line reporting the relocation and the image base address. The following example output shows webcheck.dll with an image base address of 0x00400000 but loaded at 0x01a50000:

```
### Relocated from base of 0x00400000:
0x01a50000   0x3d000    8.00.6001.18702   C:\WINDOWS\system32\webcheck.dll
```

To limit which processes are listed in the output, specify a process name or PID on the command line. If you specify a process name, ListDLLs reports only on processes with an image name that matches or begins with the name you specify. For example, to list the DLLs loaded by all instances of Internet Explorer, run the following command:

```
listdlls iexplore.exe
```

ListDLLs will show each *iexplore.exe* process and the DLLs loaded in each. If you specify a PID, ListDLLs shows the DLLs in that one process.

To identify the processes that have a particular DLL loaded, add **–d** to the command line followed by the full or partial name of the DLL. ListDLLs searches all processes that it has permission to open and inspect the full path of each of its DLLs. If the name you specified appears anywhere in the path of a loaded DLL, ListDLLs outputs the information for the process and for the matching DLLs. For example, to search for all processes that have loaded Crypt32.dll, run the following command:

```
listdlls -d crypt32
```

You can use this option not only to search for DLLs by name, but for folder locations as well. To list all DLLs that have been loaded from the Program Files folder hierarchy, you can run this command:

```
listdlls -d "program files"
```

---

[2] With Address Space Layout Randomization (ASLR), introduced in Windows Vista, an ASLR-compatible DLL's base address is changed at first load after each boot. ListDLLs reports a DLL as relocated only if it is loaded in a process to a different address from its preferred ASLR address in that boot session because of a conflict with another module.

Handle

Handle is a console utility that displays information about object handles held by processes on the system. Handles represent open instances of basic operating system objects that applications interact with, such as files, registry keys, synchronization primitives, and shared memory. You can use the Handle utility to search for programs that have a file or folder open, preventing its access or deletion from another program. You can also use Handle to list the object types and names held by a particular program. For more information about object handles, see "Handles" in Chapter 2.

Because the primary purpose for Handle is to identify in-use files and folders, running Handle without any command-line parameters lists all the File and named Section handles owned by those processes. Handle's command-line parameters in various combinations allow you to list all object types, search for objects by name, limit which process or processes to include, display handle counts by object type, show details about pagefile-backed Section objects, display the user name with the handle information, or (although generally ill-advised) close open handles.

Note that loading a DLL or mapping another file type into a process' address space via the *LoadLibrary* API does not also add a handle to the process' handle table. Such files can therefore be in use and not be able to be deleted, even though a handle search might come up empty. ListDLLs, described earlier in this chapter, can identify DLLs loaded as executable images. More powerfully, Process Explorer's Find feature searches for both DLL and handle names in a single operation, and it includes DLLs mapped as data. Process Explorer is described in Chapter 3.

Handle List and Search

The command-line syntax to list object handles is

```
handle [-a [-l]] [-p process|PID] [[-u] objname]
```

If you specify no command-line parameters, Handle lists all processes and all the File and named Section handles owned by those processes, with dashed-line separators between the information for each process. For each process, Handle displays the process name, PID, and account name that the process is running under, followed by the handles belonging to that process. The handle value is displayed in hexadecimal, along with the object type and the object name (if it has one).

"File" handles can include folders, device drivers, and communication endpoints, in addition to normal files. File handle information also includes the sharing mode that was set when the handle was opened. The parenthesized sharing flags can include *R*, *W*, or *D*, indicating that other callers (including other threads within the same process) can open the same file for reading, writing, or deleting, respectively. A hyphen instead of a letter indicates that the sharing mode is not set. If no flags are set, the object is opened for exclusive use through this handle.

A named Section, also called a *file mapping object*, can be backed by a file on disk or by the pagefile. An open file-mapping handle to a file can prevent it from being deleted. Pagefile-backed named Sections are used to share memory between processes.

To search for handles to an object by name, add the object name to the command line. Handle will list all object handles where the object's name contains the name you specified. The search is case insensitive. When performing an object name search, you can also add the **–u** option to display the user account names of the processes that own the listed handles.

The object name search changes the format of the output. Instead of grouping handles by process with separators, each line lists a process name, PID, object type, handle value, handle name, and optionally a user name.

So if you are trying to find the process that is using a file called MyDataFile.txt in a folder called MyDataFolder, you can search for it with a command like this:

```
handle mydatafolder\mydatafile.txt
```

To view all handle types rather than just Files and named Sections, add **–a** to the Handle command line. Handle will list all handles of all object types, including unnamed objects. You can combine the **–a** parameter with **–l** (lower case L) to show all Section objects and the size of the pagefile allocation (if any) associated with each one. This can help identify leaks of system commit caused by mapped pagefile-backed sections.

To limit which processes are included in the output, add **–p** to the command line, followed by a partial or full process name or a process ID. If you specify a process name, Handle lists handles for those processes with an image name that matches or begins with the name you specify. If you specify a PID, Handle lists handles for that one process.

Let's look at some examples. This command line lists File and named Section object handles owned by processes where the process name begins with *explore*, including all running instances of Explorer.exe:

```
handle -p explore
```

Partial output from this command is shown in Figure 7-19.

FIGURE 7-19 Partial output from **handle –p explore**.

By contrast, the following command lists object handles of every type and in every process where the object name contains "explore":

```
handle -a explore
```

Partial output from this object name search includes processes that have file, registry key, process, and thread handles with "explore" in the names and is shown in Figure 7-20.

FIGURE 7-20 Partial output from **handle –a explore**.

The following contrived example demonstrates searching for an object name that contains a space and includes the user name in the output. It shows all object types that contain the search name, including registry keys, but it limits the search to processes that begin with *c*:

```
handle -a -p c -u "session manager"
```

The output from this command is shown in Figure 7-21.

Handle requires administrative privilege to run. Because some objects grant full access only to System but not to Administrators, you can generally get a more complete view by running Handle as System, using PsExec (discussed in Chapter 6). If Handle.exe and PsExec are both in the system Path, this can be accomplished with the following simple command:

```
psexec -s handle -accepteula -a
```

FIGURE 7-21 Output from **handle –a –p c –u "session manager"**.

Handle Counts

To see how many objects of each type are open, add **–s** to the **Handle** command line. Handle will list all object types for which there are any open handles systemwide, and the number of handles for each. At the end of the list, Handle shows the total number of handles.

To limit the handle count listing to handles held by specific processes, add **–p** followed by a full or partial process name, or a process ID:

```
handle -s [-p process|PID]
```

Using the same process name-matching algorithm described in the "Handle List and Search" section earlier, Handle shows the counts of the object handles held by the specified process or processes and by object type, followed by the total handle count. This command lists the handle counts for all Explorer processes on the system:

```
handle -s -p explorer
```

The output looks like the following:

```
Handle type summary:
  ALPC Port       : 44
  Desktop         : 5
  Directory       : 5
  EtwRegistration : 371
  Event           : 570
  File            : 213
  IoCompletion    : 4
  Key             : 217
  KeyedEvent      : 4
  Mutant          : 84
  Section         : 45
  Semaphore       : 173
  Thread          : 84
```

```
Timer            : 7
TpWorkerFactory : 8
UserApcReserve  : 1
WindowStation   : 4
WmiGuid         : 1
Total handles: 1840
```

Closing Handles

As described earlier, a process can release its handle to an object when it no longer needs that object, and its remaining handles are also closed when the process exits. You can use Handle to close handles held by a process without terminating the process. This is typically risky. Because the process that owns the handle is not aware that its handle has been closed, using this feature can lead to data corruption or can crash the application; closing a handle in the System process or a critical user-mode process such as Csrss can lead to a system crash. Also, a subsequent resource allocation by the same process could be assigned the old handle value because it is no longer in use. If the program tried to access the now-closed object, it could end up operating on the wrong object.

With those caveats in mind, the command-line syntax for closing a handle is

```
handle -c handleValue -p PID [-y]
```

The handle value is interpreted as a hexadecimal number, and the owning process must be specified by its PID. Before closing the handle, Handle displays information about the handle, including its type and name and ask for confirmation. You can bypass the confirmation by adding **–y** to the command line.

Note that Windows protects some object handles so that they cannot be closed except during process termination. Attempts to close these handles fail silently, so Handle will report that the handle was closed even though it was not.

Chapter 8
Security Utilities

This chapter describes a set of Sysinternals utilities focused on Microsoft Windows security management and operations:

- **SigCheck** is a console utility for verifying file digital signatures, listing file hashes, and viewing version information

- **AccessChk** is a console utility for searching for objects—such as files, registry keys, and services—that grant permissions to specific users or groups, as well as providing detailed information on permissions granted.

- **AccessEnum** is a GUI utility that searches a file or registry hierarchy and identifies where permissions might have been changed.

- **ShareEnum** is a GUI utility that enumerates file and printer shares on your network and who can access them.

- **ShellRunAs** is a shell extension that restores the ability to run a program under a different user account on Windows Vista.

- **Autologon** is a GUI utility that lets you configure a user account for automatic logon when the system boots.

- **LogonSessions** is a console utility that enumerates active Local Security Authority (LSA) logon sessions on the current computer.

- **SDelete** is a console utility for securely deleting files or folder structures and erasing data in unallocated areas of the hard drive.

SigCheck

SigCheck is a multipurpose console utility for performing security-related functions on one or more files or a folder hierarchy. Its primary purpose is to verify whether files are digitally signed with a trusted certificate. As Figure 8-1 shows, SigCheck can also report catalog and image signer information, calculate file hashes using several hash algorithms, and display extended version information. It can also display a file's embedded manifest, scan folders for unsigned files, and report results in comma-separated value (CSV) format.

```
C:\>sigcheck -a -i -h c:\windows\explorer.exe

Sigcheck v1.65 - File version and signature viewer
Copyright (C) 2004-2010 Mark Russinovich
Sysinternals - www.sysinternals.com
        Verified:       Signed
        Catalog:        C:\Windows\system32\CatRoot\{F750E6C3-38EE-11D1-85E5-00C
        Signers:
                Microsoft Windows
                Microsoft Windows Verification PCA
                Microsoft Root Certificate Authority
        Signing date:   2:00 PM 10/2/2009
        Publisher:      Microsoft Corporation
        Description:    Windows Explorer
        Product:        Microsoft« Windows« Operating System
        Version:        6.1.7600.16385
        File version:   6.1.7600.16385 (win7_rtm.090713-1255)
        Strong Name:    Unsigned
        Original Name:  EXPLORER.EXE.MUI
        Internal Name:  explorer
        Copyright:      « Microsoft Corporation. All rights reserved.
        Comments:       n/a
        MD5:            b95eeb0f4e5efbf1038a35b3351cf047
        SHA1:           131d489169c9af3660c79976fb57430a60945147
        SHA256:         5a13d3dc56a479dd514d8d1a32233d3b4ea13b6a6ac26d138a25696a5e4eec0c
C:\>
```

FIGURE 8-1 Output from **sigcheck –a –i –h c:\windows\explorer.exe**.

A digital signature associated with a file helps to ensure the file's authenticity and integrity. A verified signature demonstrates that the file came from the owner of the code-signing certificate and that the file has not been modified since its signing. The assurance provided by a code-signing certificate depends largely on the diligence of the certification authority (CA) that issued the certificate to authenticate the proposed owner, on the diligence of the certificate owner to protect the certificate's private key from disclosure, and on the verifying system not allowing the installation of rogue root CA certificates.

As part of the cost of doing business and providing assurance to customers, most legitimate software publishers will purchase a code-signing certificate from a legitimate CA, such as VeriSign or Thawte, and sign the files they distribute to customer computers. The lack of a valid signature on an executable file that purports to be from a legitimate publisher is reason for suspicion.

Note In the past, malware was rarely signed. As the sophistication of malware publishers has increased, however, even this is no longer a guarantee. Some malware publishers are now setting up front organizations and purchasing code-signing certificates from legitimate CAs. Others are stealing poorly-protected private keys from legitimate businesses and using those keys to sign malware.

SigCheck's command-line parameters provide numerous options for performing verifications, specifying the files to scan, and formatting output. The syntax is shown here, followed by Table 8-1, which provides a summary of the parameters:

```
sigcheck.exe [-e] [-s] [-i] [-r] [-u] [-c catalogFile] [-a] [-h] [-m] [-n] [-v] [-q] target
```

TABLE 8-1 **SigCheck Command-Line Parameters**

Parameter	Description
target	Specifies the file or directory to process. It can include wildcard characters.
Signature Verification	
−i	Shows the catalog name and image signers.
−r	Checks for certificate revocation.
−u	Reports unsigned files only, including files that have invalid signatures.
−c	Looks for a signature in the specified catalog file.
Which Files to Scan	
−e	Scans executable files only. (It looks at the file headers, not the extension, to determine whether a file is an executable.)
−s	Recurses subdirectories.
Additional File Information	
−a	Shows extended version information.
−h	Shows file hashes.
−m	Shows the manifest.
−n	Shows the file version number only.
Output Format	
−v	CSV output (not compatible with **–i** or **–m**).
−q	Quiet (suppresses the banner).

The **target** parameter is the only required one. It can specify a single file, such as explorer.exe; it can specify multiple files using a wildcard, such as *.dll; or it can specify a folder, using relative or absolute paths. If you specify a folder, SigCheck scans every file in the folder. The following command scans every file in the current folder:

```
sigcheck .
```

Signature Verification

Without further parameters, SigCheck reports the following for each file scanned:

- **Verified**   If the file has been signed with a code-signing certificate that derives from a root certification authority that is trusted on the current computer, and the file has not been modified since its signing, this field reports Signed. If it has not been signed, this field reports Unsigned. If it has been signed but there are problems with the signature, those problems are noted. Problems can include the following: the signing certificate was outside its validity period at the time of the signing; the root authority is not trusted (which can happen with a self-signed certificate, for example); the file has been modified since signing.

- **Signing date**   Shows the date on which the file was signed. This field shows *n/a* if the file has not been signed.

- **Publisher**   The Company Name field from the file's version resource, if found.

- **Description**   The Description field from the file's version resource, if found.

- **Product**   The Product Name field from the file's version resource, if found.

- **Version**   The Product Version field from the file's version resource, if found. Note that this is from the *string* portion of the version resource, not the binary value that is used for version comparison.

- **File version**   The File Version field from the file's version resource, if found. Note that this, too, is from the *string* portion of the version resource.

To show additional signature details, add **–i** to the command line. Using this parameter shows the following two additional fields if the file's signature is valid:

- **Catalog**   Reports the file in which the signature is stored. In many cases, the file indicated will be the same as the file that was signed. However, if the file was *catalog-signed*, the signature will be stored in a separate, signed catalog file. Many files that ship with Windows are catalog-signed. Catalog-signing can improve performance in some cases, but it's particularly useful for signing nonexecutable files that have a file format that does not support embedding signature information.

- **Signers**   Shows the Subject CN name from the code-signing certificate and from the CA certificates in its chain.

By default, SigCheck does not check whether the signing certificate has been revoked by its issuer. To verify that the signing certificate and the certificates in its chain have not been revoked, add **–r** to the command line. Note that revocation checking can add significant network latency to the signature check, because SigCheck has to query certificate revocation list (CRL) distribution points.

To focus your search only for unsigned files, add **–u** to the command line. SigCheck then scans all specified files, but it reports only those that are not signed or that have signatures that cannot be verified.

Windows maintains a database of signature catalogs to enable quick lookup of signature information based on a file hash. If you want to verify a file against a catalog file that is not registered in the database, specify the catalog file on the SigCheck command line with the **–c** option.

Which Files to Scan

Most nonexecutable files are not digitally signed with code-signing certificates. Some nonexecutable files that ship with Windows and that are never modified might be catalog-signed, but data files that can be updated—including initialization files, registry hive backing files, document files, and temporary files—are never code-signed. If you scan a folder that contains a large number of such files, you might have difficulty finding the unsigned executable files that are usually of greater interest. To filter out these *false positives*, you could search just for *.exe*, then *.dll*, then *.ocx*, then *.scr*, and so on. The problem with that approach isn't all the extra work or that you might miss an important extension. The problem is that an executable file with a .tmp extension, or any other extension, or *no* extension at all can still be launched! And malware authors often hide their files from inspection by masquerading under apparently innocuous file extensions.

So instead of filtering on file extensions, add **–e** to the SigCheck command line to scan only executable files. When you do, SigCheck will verify whether the file is an executable before verifying its signature and ignore the file if it's not. Specifically, SigCheck checks whether the first two bytes are *MZ*. All 16-bit, 32-bit, and 64-bit Windows executables—including applications, DLLs, and system drivers—begin with these bytes. SigCheck ignores the file extension, so executables masquerading under other file extensions still get scanned.

To search a folder hierarchy instead of a single folder, add **–s** to the SigCheck command line. SigCheck then scans files matching the *target* parameter in the folder specified by *target* parameter (or in the current folder if *target* doesn't specify a folder) and in all subfolders. The following command scans all *.dll files in and under the C:\Program Files folder:

```
sigcheck -s "c:\program files\*.dll"
```

Additional File Information

Add the **–a** option to extract additional information from every file scanned. Adding **–a** augments the SigCheck output with these fields:

- **Strong Name**   If the file is a .NET assembly and has a strong-name signature, this field reports Signed; otherwise, it shows Unsigned. (.NET's *strong-name signing* is independent of certificate-based code-signing and does not imply any level of trust.

- **Original Name**   The Original Name field from the file's version resource, if found.

- **Internal Name**   The Internal Name field from the file's version resource, if found.

- **Copyright**   The Copyright field from the file's version resource, if found.

- **Comments**   The Comments field from the file's version resource, if found.

A hash is a statistically unique value generated from a block of data using a cryptographic algorithm, such that a small change in the data results in a completely different hash. Because a good hash algorithm makes it computationally infeasible using today's technology to modify the data without modifying the hash, hashes can be used to detect changes to data from corruption or tampering. If you add the **–h** option, SigCheck calculates and displays hashes for the files it scans, using the MD5, SHA1 and SHA256 algorithms. These hashes can be compared to hashes calculated on a known-good system to verify file integrity. Hashes are useful for files that are unsigned, but that have known master versions. Also, some file-verification systems rely on hashes instead of signatures.

Application manifests are XML documents that can be embedded in application files. They were first introduced in Windows XP to enable the declaration of required side-by-side assemblies. Windows Vista and Windows 7 each extended the manifest file schema to enable an application to declare its compatibility with Windows versions and whether it requires administrative rights to run. The presence of a Windows Vista-compatible manifest also disables file and registry virtualization for the process. To dump a file's embedded manifest, add **–m** to the SigCheck command line. Here is the output from SigCheck reporting its own manifest:

```
c:\program files\sysinternals\sigcheck.exe:
        Verified:       Signed
        Signing date:   19:14 6/7/2010
        Publisher:      Sysinternals - www.sysinternals.com
        Description:    File version and signature viewer
        Product:        Sysinternals Sigcheck
        Version:        1.70
        File version:   1.70
        Manifest:
<assembly xmlns="urn:schemas-microsoft-com:asm.v1" manifestVersion="1.0">
  <trustInfo xmlns="urn:schemas-microsoft-com:asm.v3">
    <security>
      <requestedPrivileges>
        <requestedExecutionLevel level="asInvoker" uiAccess="false"></
requestedExecutionLevel>
      </requestedPrivileges>
    </security>
  </trustInfo>
</assembly>
```

To output *only* the file's version number, add **–n** to the SigCheck command line. SigCheck displays only the value of the File Version field in the file's version resource, if found, and it displays *n/a* otherwise. This option can be useful in batch files, and it's best used when specifying a single target file.

Command-line options, of course, can be combined. For example, the following command searches the system32 folder hierarchy for unsigned executable files, displaying hashes and detailed version information for those files:

```
sigcheck -u -s -e -a -h c:\windows\system32
```

Output Format

SigCheck normally displays its output as a formatted list, as shown in Figure 8-1. To report output as comma-separated values (CSVs) to enable import into a spreadsheet or database, add **–v** to the SigCheck command line. SigCheck outputs column headers according to the file information you requested through other command-line options, followed by a line of comma-separated values for each file scanned. Note that the **–v** option cannot be used with the **–i** or **–m** option.

You can suppress the display of the SigCheck banner with the **–q** option. Removing these lines can help with batch-file processing of SigCheck output as well as with CSV output.

AccessChk

AccessChk is a console utility that reports effective permissions on securable objects, account rights for a user or group, or token details for a process. It can search folder or registry hierarchies for objects with read or write permissions granted (or not granted) to a user or group, or it can display the raw access control list for securable objects.

What Are "Effective Permissions"?

Effective permissions are permissions that a user or group has on an object, taking into account group memberships, as well as permissions that might be specifically denied. For example, consider the C:\Documents and Settings folder on a Windows 7 computer, which is actually a junction that exists for application compatibility purposes. It grants full control to Administrators and to System, and Read permissions to Everyone. However, it also specifically denies List Folder permissions to Everyone. If MYDOMAIN\Abby is a member of Administrators, Abby's effective permissions include all permissions except for List Folder; if MYDOMAIN\Abby is a regular user, and thus an implicit member of Everyone, Abby's permissions include just the Read permissions except List Folder.

Windows includes the Effective Permissions Tool in the Advanced Security Settings dialog box that is displayed by clicking the Advanced button in the permissions editor for some object types. The Effective Permissions Tool calculates and displays the effective permissions for a specified user or group on the selected object. AccessChk uses the same APIs as Windows and can perform the same calculations, but for many more object types and in a scriptable utility. AccessChk can report permissions for files, folders, registry keys, processes, and any object type defined in the Windows object manager namespace, such as directories, sections and semaphores.

Note that the "effective permissions" determination in Windows is only an approximation of the actual permissions that a logged-on user would have. Actual permissions might be different because permissions can be granted or denied based on how a user logs on (for example, interactively or as a service); logon types are not included in the effective permissions calculation. Share permissions, and local group memberships and privileges are not taken into account when calculating permissions on remote objects. In addition, there can be anomalies with the inclusion or exclusion of built-in local groups (See Knowledge Base article 323309 at *http://support.microsoft.com/kb/323309*.) In particular, I recently came across an undocumented bug involving calculation of permissions for the Administrators group. And finally, effective permissions can depend on the ability of the user performing the calculations to read information about the target user from Active Directory. (See Knowledge Base article 331951 at *http://support.microsoft.com/kb/331951*.)

Using AccessChk

The basic syntax of AccessChk is

```
accesschk [options] [user-or-group] objectname
```

The **objectname** parameter is the securable object to analyze. If the object is a container, such as a file system folder or a registry key, AccessChk will report on each object in that container instead of on the object itself. If you specify the optional **user-or-group** parameter, AccessChk will report the effective permissions for that user or group; otherwise it will show the effective access for all accounts referenced in the object's access control list (ACL).

By default, the objectname parameter is interpreted as a file system object, and can include ? and * wildcards. If the object is a folder, AccessChk reports the effective permission for all files and subfolders within that folder. If the object is a file, AccessChk reports its effective permissions. For example, here are the effective permissions for c:\windows\explorer.exe on a Windows 7 computer:

```
c:\windows\explorer.exe
  RW NT SERVICE\TrustedInstaller
  R  BUILTIN\Administrators
  R  NT AUTHORITY\SYSTEM
  R  BUILTIN\Users
```

For each object reported, AccessChk summarizes permissions for each user and group referenced in the ACL, displaying R if the account has any Read permissions, W if the account has any Write permissions, and nothing if it has neither.

Named pipes are considered file system objects; use the "\pipe\" prefix to specify a named pipe path, or just "\pipe\" to specify the container in which all named pipes are defined: **accesschk \pipe** reports effective permissions for all named pipes on the computer; **accesschk \pipe\srvsvc** reports effective permissions for the srvsvc pipe, if it exists.

Note that wildcard searches such as **\pipe\s*** are not supported because of limitations in Windows' support for named-pipe directory listings.

Volumes are also considered file system objects. Use the syntax \\.\X: to specify a local volume, replacing X with the drive letter. For example, **accesschk \\.\C:** reports the permissions on the C volume. Note that permissions on a volume are not the same as permissions on its root directory. Volume permissions determine who can perform volume maintenance tasks using the disk utilities described in Chapter 12, for example.

The *options* let you specify different object types, which permission types are of interest, whether to recurse container hierarchies, how much detail to report, and whether to report effective permissions or the object's ACL. Options are summarized in Table 8-2, and then described in greater detail.

TABLE 8-2 AccessChk Command-Line Options

Parameter	Description
Object Type	
–d	Object name represents a container; reports permissions on that object rather than on its contents
–k	Object name represents a registry key
–c	Object name represents a Windows service
–p	Object name is the PID or (partial) name of a process
–f	Used with **–p**, shows full process token information for the specified process
–o	Object name represents an object in the Windows object manager namespace
–t	Used with **–o**, **–t** *type* specifies the object type
	Used with **–p**, reports permissions for the process' threads
–a	Object name represents an account right
Searching for Access Rights	
–s	Recurses container hierarchy
–n	Shows only objects that grant no access (usually used with **user-or-group**)
–w	Shows only objects that grant Write access
–r	Shows only objects that grant Read access
–e	Shows only objects that have explicitly set integrity levels (Windows Vista and newer)
Output	
–l	Shows ACL rather than effective permissions
–u	Suppresses errors
–v	Verbose
–q	Quiet (suppresses the banner)

Object Type

As mentioned, if the named object is a container—such as a file system folder, a registry key, or an object manager directory—AccessChk reports on the objects within that container rather than on the container itself. To have AccessChk report on the container object, add the **–d** option to the command line. For example, **accesschk c:\windows** reports effective permissions for every file and subfolder in the Windows folder; **accesschk -d c:\windows** reports the permissions on the Windows folder. Similarly, **accesschk .** reports permissions on everything in the current folder, while **accesschk -d .** reports permissions on the current folder only. As a final example, **accesschk *** reports permissions on all objects in the current folder, while **accesschk -d *** reports permissions only on subfolder objects in the current folder.

To inspect permissions on a registry key, add **–k** to the command line. You can specify the root key with short or full names (for example, HKLM or HKEY_LOCAL_MACHINE), and you can follow the root key with a colon (:), as Windows PowerShell does. (Wildcard characters are not supported.) All of the following equivalent commands report the permissions for the subkeys of HKLM\Software\Microsoft:

```
accesschk -k hklm\software\microsoft
```

```
accesschk -k hklm:\software\microsoft
```

```
accesschk -k hkey_local_machine\software\microsoft
```

Add **–d** to report permissions just for HKLM\Software\Microsoft but not for its subkeys.

To report the permissions for a Windows service, add **–c** to the command line. Specify ***** as the object name to show all services, or **scmanager** to check the permissions of the Service Control Manager. (Partial name or wildcard matches are not supported.) For example, **accesschk –c lanmanserver** reports permissions for the Server service on a Windows 7 computer, and this is its output:

```
lanmanserver
  RW NT AUTHORITY\SYSTEM
  RW BUILTIN\Administrators
  R  NT AUTHORITY\INTERACTIVE
  R  NT AUTHORITY\SERVICE
```

This command reports the permissions specifically granted by each service to the "Authenticated Users" group:

```
accesschk -c "authenticated users" *
```

In the context of services, **W** can refer to permissions such as Start, Stop, Pause/Continue, and Change Configuration, while **R** includes permissions such as Query Configuration and Query Status.

To view permissions on processes, add **–p** to the command line. The object name can be either a process ID (PID) or a process name, such as "explorer." AccessChk will match partial names: **accesschk –p exp** will report permissions for processes with names beginning with "exp", including all instances of Explorer. Specify * as the object name to show permissions for all processes. Note that administrative rights are required to view the permissions of processes running as another user or with elevated rights. The following output is what you can expect to see for an elevated instance of Cmd.exe on a Windows 7 computer, using **accesschk –p 3048**:

```
[3048] cmd.exe
  RW BUILTIN\Administrators
  RW NT AUTHORITY\SYSTEM
```

Combine **–p** with **–t** to view permissions for all the threads of the specified process. (Note that the **t** option must come after **p** in the command line.) Looking at the same elevated instance of Cmd.exe, **accesschk –pt 3048** reports:

```
[3048] cmd.exe
  RW BUILTIN\Administrators
  RW NT AUTHORITY\SYSTEM
  [3048:7148] Thread
  RW BUILTIN\Administrators
  RW NT AUTHORITY\SYSTEM
  R  Win7-x86-VM\S-1-5-5-0-248063-Abby
```

The process has a single thread with ID 7148, with permissions similar to that of the containing process.

Combine **–p** with **–f** to view full details of the process token. For each process listed, AccessChk will show the permissions on the process token, and then show the token user, groups, group flags, and privileges.

You can view permissions on objects in the object manager namespace—such as events, semaphores, sections and directories—with the **–o** command line switch. To limit output to a specific object type, add **–t** and the object type. For example, the following command reports effective permissions for all objects in the \BaseNamedObjects directory:

```
accesschk -o \BaseNamedObjects
```

The following command reports effective permissions only for Section objects in the \BaseNamedObjects directory:

```
accesschk -o -t section \BaseNamedObjects
```

If no object name is provided, the root of the namespace directory is assumed. WinObj, described in Chapter 14, "System Information Utilities," provides a graphical view of the object manager namespace.

Although they aren't securable objects per se, privileges and account rights can be reported by AccessChk with the **–a** option. Privileges grant an account a systemwide capability not associated with a specific object, such as **SeBackupPrivilege**, which allows the account to bypass access control to read an object. Account rights determine who can or cannot log on to a system and how. For example, **SeRemoteInteractiveLogonRight** must be granted to an account in order to log on via Remote Desktop. Privileges are listed in access tokens, while account rights are not.

I'll demonstrate usage of the **–a** option with examples. Note that AccessChk requires administrative rights to use the option. Use * as the object name to list all privileges and account rights and the accounts to which they are assigned:

```
accesschk -a *
```

An account name followed by * lists all the privileges and account rights assigned to that account. For example, the following command displays those assigned to the Power Users group (it is interesting to compare the results of this from a Windows XP system and a Windows 7 system):

```
accesschk -a "power users" *
```

Finally, specify the name of a privilege or account right to list all the accounts that have it. (Again, you can use **accesschk –a *** to list all privileges and account rights.) The following command lists all the accounts that are granted **SeDebugPrivilege**:

```
accesschk -a sedebugprivilege
```

Searching for Access Rights

One of AccessChk's most powerful features is its ability to search for objects that grant access to particular users or groups. For example, you can use AccessChk to verify whether anything in the Program Files folder hierarchy can be modified by Users, or whether any services grant Everyone any Write permissions.

The **–s** option instructs AccessChk to search recursively through container hierarchies, such as folders, registry keys, or object namespace directories. The **–n** option lists objects that grant no access to the specified account. The **–r** option lists objects that grant Read permissions, and **–w** lists objects that grant Write permissions. Finally, on Windows Vista and newer, **–e** shows objects that have an explicitly set integrity label, rather than the implicit default of Medium integrity and No-Write-Up.

Let's consider some examples:

- Search the Windows folder hierarchy for objects that can be modified by Users:

```
accesschk -ws Users %windir%
```

- Search for global objects that can be modified by Everyone:

```
accesschk -wo everyone \basenamedobjects
```

- Search for registry keys under HKEY_CURRENT_USER that have an explicit integrity label:

```
accesschk -kse hkcu
```

- Search for services that grant Authenticated Users any Write permissions:

```
accesschk -cw "Authenticated Users" *
```

- List all named pipes that grant anyone Write permissions:

```
accesschk -w \pipe\*
```

- List all object manager objects under the \sessions directory that do not grant any access to Administrators:

```
accesschk -nos Administrators \sessions
```

This last example points out another powerful feature of AccessChk. Clearly, to view the permissions of an object, you must be granted the Read Permissions permission for that object. And just as clearly, there are many objects throughout the system that do not grant any access to regular users; for example, each user's profile contents are hidden from other nonadministrative users. To report on these objects, AccessChk must be running with elevated/administrative rights. Yet there are some objects that do not grant any access to Administrators but only to System. So that it can report on these objects when an administrative token is insufficient, AccessChk duplicates a System token from the Smss.exe process and impersonates it to retry the access attempt. Without that feature, the previous example would not work.

Output Options

Instead of reporting just **R** or **W** to indicate permissions, you can view verbose permissions by adding **–v** to the AccessChk command line. Beneath each account name, AccessChk lists the specific permissions using the symbolic names from the Windows SDK. These are the effective permissions reported with the **–v** option for %SystemDrive%\ on a Windows 7 system:

```
C:\
  Medium Mandatory Level (Default) [No-Write-Up]
  RW BUILTIN\Administrators
        FILE_ALL_ACCESS
  RW NT AUTHORITY\SYSTEM
        FILE_ALL_ACCESS
  R  BUILTIN\Users
        FILE_LIST_DIRECTORY
        FILE_READ_ATTRIBUTES
        FILE_READ_EA
        FILE_TRAVERSE
        SYNCHRONIZE
        READ_CONTROL
  W NT AUTHORITY\Authenticated Users
        FILE_ADD_SUBDIRECTORY
```

The verbose output shows that Administrators and System have full control, Users have Read access, and Authenticated Users additionally have the ability to create subfolders within that folder.

Instead of showing effective permissions, you can display the object's actual access control list (ACL) with the **–l** (lower case L) option. Here is the ACL for the "C:\Documents and Settings" junction on Windows 7 that was described at the beginning of the AccessChk section. Each access control entry (ACE) is listed in order, identifying a user or group, whether access is allowed or denied, and which permissions are allowed or denied. If present, ACE flags are shown in square brackets, indicating inheritance settings. If [INHERITED_ACE] is not present, the ACE is an explicit ACE.

```
C:\Documents and Settings
  Medium Mandatory Level (Default) [No-Write-Up]
  [0] Everyone
        ACCESS_DENIED_ACE_TYPE
          FILE_LIST_DIRECTORY
  [1] Everyone
        ACCESS_ALLOWED_ACE_TYPE
          FILE_LIST_DIRECTORY
          FILE_READ_ATTRIBUTES
          FILE_READ_EA
          FILE_TRAVERSE
          SYNCHRONIZE
          READ_CONTROL
  [2] NT AUTHORITY\SYSTEM
        ACCESS_ALLOWED_ACE_TYPE
          FILE_ALL_ACCESS
  [3] BUILTIN\Administrators
        ACCESS_ALLOWED_ACE_TYPE
          FILE_ALL_ACCESS
```

AccessChk reports any errors that occur when enumerating objects or retrieving security information. Add **–u** to the command line to suppress these error messages. Objects that trigger errors will then go unreported. Finally, to omit the AccessChk banner text, add **–q** to the command line.

AccessEnum

AccessEnum is a GUI utility that makes it easy to identify files, folders, or registry keys that might have had their permissions misconfigured. Instead of listing the permissions on every object it scans, AccessEnum identifies the objects within a file or registry hierarchy that have permissions that differ from those of their parent containers. This lets you focus on the point at which the misconfiguration occurred, rather than on every object that inherited that setting.

For example, sometimes in an effort to get an application to work for a nonadministrative user, someone might grant Full Control to Everyone on the application's subfolder under Program Files, which should be read-only to nonadministrators. As shown in Figure 8-2, AccessEnum identifies that folder and shows which users or groups have been granted access that differs from that of Program Files. In the example, the first line shows the permissions on C:\Program Files; the second line shows a subfolder that grants Everyone at least some read and write permissions (possibly full control), while the last two items do not grant Administrators any Write access.

FIGURE 8-2 AccessEnum.

In the text box near the top of the AccessEnum window, enter the root path of the folder or registry subkey that you want to examine. Instead of typing a path, you can pick a folder by clicking the Directory button, or pick a registry key by clicking the Registry button. Click the Scan button to begin scanning.

AccessEnum abstracts Windows' access-control model to just Read, Write and Deny permissions. An object is shown as granting Write permission whether it grants just a single write permission (such as Write Owner) or the full suite of write permissions via Full Control. Read permissions are handled similarly. Names appear in the Deny column if a user or group is explicitly denied any access to the object. Note that the legacy folder junctions described in the AccessChk section deny Everyone the List Folder permission. AccessEnum reports Access Denied if it is unable to read an object's security descriptor.

When AccessEnum compares an object and its parent container to determine whether their permissions are equivalent, it looks only at whether the same set of accounts are granted Read, Write and Deny access, respectively. If a file grants just Write Owner access and its parent just Delete access, the two will still be considered equivalent because both allow some form of writing.

AccessEnum condenses the number of accounts displayed as having access to an object by hiding accounts with permissions that are duplicated by a group to which the account belongs. For example, if a file grants Read access to both user Bob and group Marketing, and Bob is a member of the Marketing group, then only Marketing will be shown in the list of accounts having Read access. Note that with UAC's Admin-Approval Mode on Windows Vista and newer, this can hide cases where non-elevated processes run by a member of the Administrators group have more access. For example, if Abby is a member of the Administrators group, AccessEnum will report objects that grant Full Control explicitly to Abby as well as to Administrators as granting access only to Administrators, even though Abby's non-elevated processes also have full control.

By default, AccessEnum shows only objects for which permissions are less restrictive than those of their parent containers. To list objects for which permissions are different from their parents' in any way, choose File Display Options from the Options menu and select Display Files With Permissions That Differ From Parent.

Because access granted to the System account and to other service accounts is not usually of interest when looking for incorrect permissions, AccessEnum ignores permissions involving those accounts. To consider those permissions as well, select Show Local System And Service Accounts from the Options menu.

Click a column header to sort the list by that column. For example, to simplify a search for rogue Write permissions, click on the Write column, and then look for entries that list the Everyone group or other nonadministrator users or groups. You can also reorder columns by dragging a column header to a new position.

When you find a potential problem, right-click the entry to display AccessEnum's context menu. If the entry represents a file or folder, clicking Properties displays Explorer's Properties dialog box for the item; click on the Security tab to examine or edit the object's permissions. Clicking Explore in the context menu opens a Windows Explorer window in that folder. If the entry represents a registry key, clicking Explore opens Regedit and navigates to the selected key, where you can inspect or edit its permissions. Note that on Windows Vista and newer, AccessEnum's driving of the navigation of Regedit requires that AccessEnum run at the same or a higher integrity level than Regedit.

You can hide one or more entries by right-clicking an entry and choosing Exclude. The selected entry and any others that begin with the same text will be hidden from the display. For example, if you exclude C:\Folder, then C:\Folder\Subfolder will also be hidden.

Click the Save button to save the list contents to a tab-delimited Unicode text file. Choose Compare To Saved from the File menu to display the differences in permissions between the current list against a previously saved file. You can use this feature to verify the configuration of one system against that of a baseline system.

ShareEnum

An aspect of Windows network security that is often overlooked is file shares. Lax security settings are an ongoing source of security issues because too many users are granted unnecessary access to files on other computers. If you didn't specify permissions when creating a file share in Windows, the default used to be to grant Everyone Full Control. That was later changed to grant Everyone just Read access, but even that might expose sensitive information to more people than those who should be authorized.

Windows provides no utilities to list all the shares on a network and their security settings. ShareEnum fills that void, giving you the ability to enumerate all the file and printer shares in a domain, an IP address range, or your entire network to quickly view the share permissions in a table view, and to change the permissions on those shares.

Because only a domain administrator has the ability to view all network resources, ShareEnum is most effective when you run it from a domain administrator account.

ShareEnum is a GUI utility and doesn't accept any command line parameters (other than **/accepteula**). From the drop-down list, select <All domains>, which scans your entire network, <IP address range>, which lets you select a range of addresses to scan, or the name of a domain. Click Refresh to scan the selected portion of your network. If you selected <IP address range>, you will be prompted to enter a range of IP addresses to scan.

ShareEnum displays share information in a list view, as shown in Figure 8-3.

FIGURE 8-3 ShareEnum.

Click on a column header to sort the list by that column's data, or drag the column headers to reorder them. ShareEnum displays the following information about each share:

- **Share Path**   The computer and share name

- **Local Path**   The location in the remote computer's file system that the share exposes

- **Domain**   The computer's domain

- **Type**   Whether the share is a file share (Disk), a printer share (Printer), or Unknown.

- **Everyone**   Permissions that the share grants to the Everyone group, categorized as Read, Write, Read/Write, or blank if no permissions are granted to the Everyone group

- **Other Read**   Entities other than the Everyone group that are granted Read permission to the share

- **Other Write**   Entities other than the Everyone group that are granted Change or Full Control permissions to the share

- **Deny**   Any entities that are explicitly denied access to the share

Click the Export button to save the list contents to a tab-delimited Unicode text file. Choose Compare To Saved from the File menu to display the differences in permissions between the current list and a previously exported file.

To change the permissions for a share, right-click it in the list and choose Properties. ShareEnum displays a permissions editor dialog box for the share. To open a file share in Windows Explorer, right-click the share in the list and choose Explore from the popup menu.

ShellRunAs

In Windows XP and Windows Server 2003, you could run a program as a different user by right-clicking the program in Windows Explorer, choosing Run As from the context menu, and entering alternate credentials in the Run As dialog box. This feature was often used to run a program with an administrative account on a regular user's desktop. Beginning with Windows Vista, the Run As menu option was replaced with Run As Administrator, which triggers UAC elevation. For those who had used the Run As dialog box to run a program under a different account without administrative rights, the only remaining option was the less-convenient Runas.exe console utility. To restore the capabilities of the graphical RunAs interface with added features, I co-wrote ShellRunAs with Jon Schwartz of the Windows team.

> **Note** Some features of ShellRunAs were restored in Windows 7. Holding down Shift while right-clicking a program or shortcut adds Run As A Different User to the context menu.

ShellRunAs lets you start a program with a different user account from a context menu entry, displaying a dialog box to collect a user name and password (shown in Figure 8-4) or a smartcard PIN on systems configured for smartcard logon. You can also use ShellRunAs similarly to Runas.exe but with a more convenient graphical interface. None of ShellRunAs' features require administrative rights, not even the registering of context menu entries. ShellRunAs can be used on Windows XP or newer.

FIGURE 8-4 ShellRunAs prompting for user credentials.

ShellRunAs also supports the Runas.exe *netonly* feature, which was never previously available through a Windows GUI. With the netonly option, the target program continues to use the launching user's security context for local access, but it uses the supplied alternate credentials for remote access. (See Figure 8-5.) Note that a console window might flash briefly when ShellRunAs starts a program with netonly.

FIGURE 8-5 "Run As Different User" options added to the Explorer context menu.

The valid command-line syntax options for ShellRunAs are listed next, followed by descriptions of the command-line switches:

```
ShellRunAs /reg [/quiet]

ShellRunAs /regnetonly [/quiet]

ShellRunAs /unreg [/quiet]
```

- **/reg**   Registers Run As Different User as an Explorer context menu option for the current user. (See Figure 8-5.)

- **/regnetonly**   Registers Run As Different User (Netonly) as an Explorer context menu option for the current user.

- **/unreg**   Unregisters any registered ShellRunAs context menu options for the current user.

- **/quiet**   Does not show a result dialog box for registration or unregistration.

```
ShellRunAs [/netonly] program [arguments]
```

This syntax allows the direct launching of a program from the ShellRunAs command line. With **/netonly**, you can specify that the credentials collected should be used only for remote access.

Autologon

The Autologon utility enables you to easily configure Windows' built-in autologon mechanism, which automatically logs on a user at the console when the computer starts up. To enable autologon, simply run Autologon, enter valid credentials in the dialog box, and click the Enable button. You can also pass the user name, domain, and password as command-line arguments, as shown in the following example:

```
autologon Abby MYDOMAIN Pass@word1
```

The password is encrypted in the registry as an LSA secret. The next time the system starts, Windows will try to use the entered credentials to log on the user at the console. Note that Autologon does not verify the submitted credentials, nor does it verify that the specified user account is allowed to log on to the computer. Also note that although LSA Secrets are encrypted in the registry, a user with administrative rights can easily retrieve and decrypt them.

To disable autologon, run Autologon and click the Disable button or press the Escape key. To disable autologon one time, hold down the Shift key during startup at the point where the logon would occur. Autologon can also be prevented via Group Policy.

Autologon is supported on Windows XP and newer, and requires administrative privileges.

LogonSessions

The LogonSessions utility enumerates active logon sessions created and managed by the Local Security Authority (LSA). A logon session is created when a user account or service account is authenticated to Windows. Authentication can occur in many ways. Here are some examples:

- Via an interactive user logon at a console or remote desktop dialog box
- Through network authentication to a file share or a Web application
- By the service control manager using saved credentials to start a service
- Via the Secondary Logon service using Runas.exe
- Simply "asserted" by the operating system, as is done with the System account and for NT AUTHORITY\ANONYMOUS LOGON, which is used when performing actions on behalf of an unauthenticated user or an "identify" level impersonation token.

An access token is created along with the logon session to represent the account's security context. The access token is duplicated for use by processes and threads that run under that security context, and it includes a reference back to its logon session. A logon session remains active as long as there is a duplicated token that references it.

Each logon session has a locally-unique identifier (LUID). A LUID is a system-generated 64-bit value guaranteed to be unique during a single boot session on the system on which it was generated. Some LUIDs are predefined. For example, the LUID for the System account's logon session is always 0x3e7 (999 decimal), the LUID for Network Service's session is 0x3e4 (996), and Local Service's is 0x3e5 (997). Most other LUIDs are randomly generated.

There are a few resources that belong to logon sessions. These include SMB sessions and network drive letter mappings (for example, NET USE), and Subst.exe associations. You can see these in the Windows object manager namespace using the Sysinternals WinObj utility (discussed in Chapter 14), under \Sessions\0\DosDevices*LUID*. Resources belonging to the System logon session are in the global namespace.

Note that these LSA logon sessions are orthogonal to terminal services (TS) sessions. TS sessions include interactive user sessions at the console and remote desktops, and "session 0", in which all service processes run. A process' access token identifies the LSA logon session from which it derived, and (separately) the TS session in which it is running. Although most processes running as System (logon session 0x3e7) are associated with session 0, there are two System processes running in every interactive TS session (an instance of Winlogon.exe and Csrss.exe). You can see these by selecting the Session column in Process Explorer.

LogonSessions is supported on Windows XP and newer, and it requires administrative privileges. Run LogonSessions at an elevated command prompt and it will list information about each active logon session, including the LUID that is its logon session ID, the user name and SID of the authenticated account, the authentication package that was used, the logon type (such as Service or Interactive), the ID of the terminal services session with which the logon session is primarily associated, when the logon occurred (local time), the name of the server that performed the authentication, the DNS domain name, and the User Principal Name (UPN) of the account. If you add **/p** to the command line, LogonSessions will list under each logon session all of the processes with a process token associated with that logon session. Here is sample output from LogonSessions:

```
[0] Logon session 00000000:000003e7:
    User name:    MYDOMAIN\WIN7-X64-VM$
    Auth package: Negotiate
    Logon type:   (none)
    Session:      0
    Sid:          S-1-5-18
    Logon time:   6/9/2010 23:02:35
    Logon server:
    DNS Domain:   mydomain.lab
    UPN:          WIN7-X64-VM$@mydomain.lab
```

```
[1] Logon session 00000000:0000af1c:
    User name:
    Auth package: NTLM
    Logon type:   (none)
    Session:      0
    Sid:          (none)
    Logon time:   6/9/2010 23:02:35
    Logon server:
    DNS Domain:
    UPN:

[2] Logon session 00000000:000003e4:
    User name:    MYDOMAIN\WIN7-X64-VM$
    Auth package: Negotiate
    Logon type:   Service
    Session:      0
    Sid:          S-1-5-20
    Logon time:   6/9/2010 23:02:38
    Logon server:
    DNS Domain:   mydomain.lab
    UPN:          WIN7-X64-VM$@mydomain.lab

[3] Logon session 00000000:000003e5:
    User name:    NT AUTHORITY\LOCAL SERVICE
    Auth package: Negotiate
    Logon type:   Service
    Session:      0
    Sid:          S-1-5-19
    Logon time:   6/9/2010 23:02:39
    Logon server:
    DNS Domain:
    UPN:

[4] Logon session 00000000:00030ee4:
    User name:    NT AUTHORITY\ANONYMOUS LOGON
    Auth package: NTLM
    Logon type:   Network
    Session:      0
    Sid:          S-1-5-7
    Logon time:   6/9/2010 23:03:32
    Logon server:
    DNS Domain:
    UPN:

[5] Logon session 00000000:0006c285:
    User name:    MYDOMAIN\Abby
    Auth package: Kerberos
    Logon type:   Interactive
    Session:      1
    Sid:          S-1-5-21-124525095-708259637-1543119021-20937
    Logon time:   6/9/2010 23:04:06
    Logon server:
    DNS Domain:   MYDOMAIN.LAB
    UPN:          abby@mydomain.lab
```

```
[6] Logon session 00000000:000709d3:
    User name:    MYDOMAIN\Abby
    Auth package: Kerberos
    Logon type:   Interactive
    Session:      1
    Sid:          S-1-5-21-124525095-708259637-1543119021-20937
    Logon time:   6/9/2010 23:04:06
    Logon server:
    DNS Domain:   MYDOMAIN.LAB
    UPN:          abby@MYDOMAIN.LAB
```

Because the System and Network Service accounts can authenticate with the credentials of the computer account, the names for these accounts appear as **domain\computer$** (or **workgroup\computer$** if they're not domain-joined). The logon server will be the computer name for local accounts and can be blank when logging on with cached credentials.

Also note that on Windows Vista and newer with User Account Control (UAC) enabled, two logon sessions are created when a user interactively logs on who is a member of the Administrators group,[1] as you can see with MYDOMAIN\Abby in entries [5] and [6] in the preceding sample. One logon session contains the token representing the user's full rights, and the other contains the *filtered* token with powerful groups disabled and powerful privileges removed. This is the reason that when an administrator elevates, the drive-letter mappings that are present for the non-elevated processes aren't defined for the elevated ones. You can see these and other per-session data by navigating to \Sessions\0\DosDevices\ *LUID* in WinObj, described in Chapter 14. (Also see Knowledge Base article 937624 (available at *http://support.microsoft.com/kb/937624*) for information about configuring **EnableLinkedConnections**.)

SDelete

Object reuse protection is a fundamental policy of the Windows security model. This means that when an application allocates file space or virtual memory it is unable to view data that was previously stored in that space. Windows zero-fills memory and zeroes the sectors on disk where a file is placed before it presents either type of resource to an application. Object reuse protection does not dictate that the space that a file occupies be zeroed when it is deleted, though. This is because Windows is designed with the assumption that the operating system alone controls access to system resources. However, when the operating system is not running it is possible to use raw disk editors and recovery tools to view and recover data that the operating system has deallocated. Even when you encrypt files with Windows' Encrypting File System (EFS), a file's original unencrypted file data might be left on the disk after a new encrypted version of the file is created. Space used for temporary file storage might also not be encrypted.

---

[1] More accurately, two logon sessions are created if the user is a member of a well-known "powerful" group or is granted administrator-equivalent privileges such as **SeDebugPrivilege**.

The only way to ensure that deleted files, as well as files that you encrypt with EFS, are safe from recovery is to use a secure delete application. Secure delete applications overwrite a deleted file's on-disk data using techniques that are shown to make disk data unrecoverable, even if someone is using recovery technology that can read patterns in magnetic media that reveal weakly deleted files. SDelete (Secure Delete) is such an application. You can use SDelete both to securely delete existing files, as well as to securely erase any file data that exists in the unallocated portions of a disk (including files you have already deleted or encrypted). SDelete implements the U.S. Department of Defense clearing and sanitizing standard DOD 5220.22-M, to give you confidence that after it is deleted with SDelete, your file data is gone forever. Note that SDelete securely deletes file data, but not file names located in free disk space.

Using SDelete

SDelete is a command-line utility. It works on Windows XP and newer and does not require administrative rights. It uses a different command-line syntax for secure file deletion and for erasing content in unallocated disk space. To securely delete one or more files or folder hierarchies, use this syntax:

```
sdelete [-p passes] [-a] [-s] [-q] file_spec
```

The *file_spec* can be a file or folder name, and it can contain wildcard characters. The **–p** option specifies the number of times to overwrite each file object. The default is one pass. The **–a** option is needed to delete read-only files. The **–s** option recurses subfolders to delete files matching the specification or to delete a folder hierarchy. The **–q** option (quiet) suppresses the listing of per-file results. Here are some examples:

```
REM  Securely deletes secret.txt in the current folder
sdelete secret.txt

REM  Securely deletes all *.docx files in the current folder and subfolders
sdelete -s *.docx

REM  Securely deletes the C:\Users\Bob folder hierarchy
sdelete -s C:\Users\Bob
```

To securely delete unallocated disk space on a volume, use this syntax:

```
sdelete [-p passes] [-z|-c] [d:]
```

There are two ways to overwrite unallocated space: the **–c** option overwrites it with random data, while the **–z** option overwrites it with zeros. The **–c** option supports DoD compliance; the **–z** option makes it easier to compress and optimize virtual hard disks. The **–p** option specifies the number of times to overwrite the disk areas. If the drive letter is not specified, the current volume's unallocated space is cleansed. Note that the colon must be included in the drive specification.

Note The Windows **Cipher /W** command is similar in purpose to **SDelete –c**, writing random data over all hard drive free space outside of the Master File Table (MFT).

Note that during free-space cleaning, Windows might display a warning that disk space is running low. This is normal, and the warning can be ignored. (The reason this happens will be explained in the next section.)

How SDelete Works

Securely deleting a file that has no special attributes is relatively straightforward: the secure delete program simply overwrites the file with the secure delete pattern. What is trickier is to securely delete compressed, encrypted, or sparse files, and securely cleansing disk free spaces.

Compressed, encrypted and sparse files are managed by NTFS in 16-cluster blocks. If a program writes to an existing portion of such a file, NTFS allocates new space on the disk to store the new data, and after the new data has been written NTFS deallocates the clusters previously occupied by the file. NTFS takes this conservative approach for reasons related to data integrity, and (for compressed and sparse files) in case a new allocation is larger than what exists (for example, the new compressed data is larger than the old compressed data). Thus, overwriting such a file will not succeed in deleting the file's contents from the disk.

To handle these types of files SDelete relies on the defragmentation API. Using the defragmentation API, SDelete can determine precisely which clusters on a disk are occupied by data belonging to compressed, sparse and encrypted files. When SDelete knows which clusters contain the file's data, it can open the disk for raw access and overwrite those clusters.

Cleaning free space presents another challenge. Because FAT and NTFS provide no means for an application to directly address free space, SDelete has one of two options. The first is that—like it does for compressed, sparse and encrypted files—it can open the disk for raw access and overwrite the free space. This approach suffers from a big problem: even if SDelete were coded to be fully capable of calculating the free space portions of NTFS and FAT drives (something that's not trivial), it would run the risk of collision with active file operations taking place on the system. For example, say SDelete determines that a cluster is free, and just at that moment the file system driver (FAT, NTFS) decides to allocate the cluster for a file that another application is modifying. The file system driver writes the new data to the cluster, and then SDelete comes along and overwrites the freshly written data: the file's new data is gone. The problem is even worse if the cluster is allocated for file system metadata because SDelete will corrupt the file system's on-disk structures.

The second approach, and the one SDelete takes, is to indirectly overwrite free space. First, SDelete allocates the largest file it can. SDelete does this using noncached file I/O so that the contents of the NT file system cache will not be thrown out and replaced with use-less data associated with SDelete's space-hogging file. Because noncached file I/O must be sector (512-byte) aligned, there might be some left over space that isn't allocated for the SDelete file even when SDelete cannot further grow the file. To grab any remaining space, SDelete next allocates the largest cached file it can. For both of these files, SDelete performs a secure overwrite, ensuring that all the disk space that was previously free becomes securely cleansed.

On NTFS drives, SDelete's job isn't necessarily through after it allocates and overwrites the two files. SDelete must also fill any existing free portions of the NTFS MFT (Master File Table) with files that fit within an MFT record. An MFT record is typically 1 KB in size, and every file or directory on a disk requires at least one MFT record. Small files are stored entirely within their MFT record, while files that don't fit within a record are allocated clusters outside the MFT. All SDelete has to do to take care of the free MFT space is allocate the largest file it can; when the file occupies all the available space in an MFT record, NTFS will prevent the file from getting larger, because there are no free clusters left on the disk (they are being held by the two files SDelete previously allocated). SDelete then repeats the process. When SDelete can no longer even create a new file, it knows that all the previously free records in the MFT have been completely filled with securely overwritten files.

To overwrite the file name of a file that you delete, SDelete renames the file 26 times, each time replacing each character of the file's name with a successive alphabetic character. For instance, the first rename of *sample.txt* would be to *AAAAAA.AAA*.

The reason that SDelete does not securely delete file names when cleaning disk free space is that deleting them would require direct manipulation of directory structures. Directory structures can have free space containing deleted file names, but the free directory space is not available for allocation to other files. Hence, SDelete has no way of allocating this free space so that it can securely overwrite it.

Chapter 9
Active Directory Utilities

Sysinternals publishes three utilities to help manage Active Directory, and to diagnose and troubleshoot issues involving Active Directory.

- **AdExplorer** is an advanced Active Directory viewer and editor.

- **AdInsight** is a real-time monitor that traces Lightweight Directory Access Protocol (LDAP) API calls.

- **AdRestore** enumerates tombstoned Active Directory objects and lets you restore those objects.

AdExplorer

Active Directory Explorer (AdExplorer) is an advanced, low-level Active Directory viewer and editor. AdExplorer provides much of the same functionality as Windows' ADSI Edit, but its many features and ease of use make AdExplorer more powerful and convenient. You can use AdExplorer to navigate an Active Directory database; quickly view object attributes without having to open dialog boxes; edit object properties, attributes, and permissions; navigate directly from an object to its schema; define favorite locations; execute sophisticated searches and save them for later re-use; and save snapshots of an Active Directory database for offline viewing and comparing. AdExplorer also opens all Active Directory naming contexts that it can find automatically, so you don't have to connect separately to Configuration, Schema, and so forth.

Connecting to a Domain

AdExplorer can display multiple domains and previously-saved snapshots simultaneously in its tree view. The Connect To Active Directory dialog box, shown in Figure 9-1, lets you connect to a live directory server or open a saved snapshot. You can display this dialog box with the Open toolbar icon or from the File menu. AdExplorer also displays this dialog box on startup unless you saved previous connections or added **–noconnectprompt** to the command line.

FIGURE 9-1 The AdExplorer Connect To Active Directory dialog box.

Directory services that AdExplorer works with include Active Directory, Active Directory Lightweight Directory Services (LDS), and Active Directory Application Mode (ADAM). To connect to a live directory server, type the Active Directory domain name or the name or IP address of the directory server and the user name and password of an authorized account. You can connect to the default Active Directory domain using the credentials of the account in which you are running by selecting the first radio button and leaving the text fields blank.

To open a previously-saved snapshot, select the second radio button in the dialog box and browse to the snapshot file. Note that snapshots are read-only; objects and their attributes and permissions cannot be modified or deleted. We'll discuss snapshots in more detail in a later section.

The Save This Connection check box saves the information for the connection or snapshot so that when you run AdExplorer again it reestablishes the connection to the domain or snapshot. Note that for security reasons, AdExplorer does not save your password when saving a connection to a domain, so you must re-enter it every time you reconnect. To delete a saved connection, select the connection in the tree and choose Remove from the File menu or the context menu.

To remove a directory from the AdExplorer display, right-click its root node and choose Remove from the context menu. You can also remove a connection by selecting any object in its tree and choosing Remove from the File menu.

The AdExplorer Display

AdExplorer displays information in two panes: the left pane shows the Active Directory object tree, and the right pane lists the attributes defined for the object selected in the left pane. As shown in Figure 9-2, each object in the tree is labeled with its name (for example, CN=Abby) and an icon provided by Active Directory. The object's distinguished name (DN) can be derived by walking up the tree from the object to the root, appending the names of the intervening objects; the DN is also shown in the Path text box immediately above the panes. You can copy the object's DN to the clipboard by selecting it and choosing Copy Object Name from the Edit menu, or by right-clicking and choosing that option from the context menu.

The selected object's attributes are listed in the right pane in a four-column table, sorted in alphabetical order by name. The Syntax column indicates the data type for the attribute. The Count column indicates how many values the attribute has (attributes can be multivalued). The Value(s) column shows the attribute's value or values.

FIGURE 9-2 The AdExplorer main window.

AdExplorer maintains a history as you navigate through objects. You can go forward and backward through the navigation history by using the Back and Forward entries in the History menu or the corresponding toolbar buttons. To view the full navigation history, click the History toolbar button or choose History | All. You can jump to a particular object in the history by choosing it from the displayed list.

To remember the currently-selected object in the Active Directory hierarchy, choose Add To Favorites from the Favorites menu and specify a name of your choosing. You can later return to this object by selecting it from the Favorites menu. To rename or remove an entry in the Favorites list, open the Favorites menu, right-click on the name, and then choose Rename or Delete from the popup menu.

Objects

You can view additional information about an object by right-clicking it and selecting Properties from the context menu. The content on the tabs of the Properties dialog box depends on whether it is a root node for a connection and, if so, whether it is an active connection or a snapshot.

The Properties dialog box for a root node includes tabs listing basic information about the connection and schema statistics such as the number of classes and properties. If the node is a RootDSE node (the root node of an active connection), the dialog box includes a RootDSE Attributes tab listing data about the directory server, such as *defaultNamingContext* and *configurationNamingContext*. The Properties dialog box for the root node of a saved snapshot includes the path to the snapshot file, when it was captured, and any description saved with the snapshot.

The Properties dialog box for non-root objects has three tabs: Object Properties, Security, and Attributes. The Object Properties tab displays the object's name, DN, object class, and schema. Click the Go To button next to the schema, and AdExplorer's main window will navigate to and select that schema object, where you can inspect or modify the schema definition for that object. The Security tab is a standard permissions editor that lets you view or modify the object's permissions. The Attributes tab lists the objects attributes, displaying the value or values in a separate list rather than in a single line as it does in the Attributes pane.

You can rename or delete an object by selecting the object, and then choosing Rename or Delete from the context menu or from the Edit menu. You can also rename it by clicking the object again after having selected it and then typing a new name.

To create a new object, right-click a parent container, choose New Object from the context menu, and then select an object class for the new object from the New Object dialog box's drop down list, shown in Figure 9-3.

FIGURE 9-3 Selection of object class for a new object.

AdExplorer then displays the New Object – Advanced dialog box, shown in Figure 9-4.

FIGURE 9-4 Creation of a new object: The New Object – Advanced dialog box.

In the New Object – Advanced dialog box, type a name in the Name text box. The name must begin with *CN=* and must be unique within the container. The Attributes list is prepopulated with attributes that are mandatory for the selected class. These need to be edited before you can create the object. To add other attributes to the object, select from the All Attributes drop-down list and click Add. You can remove a nonmandatory attribute that you have added by selecting it in the list and clicking Remove. To edit an attribute in the list, double-click it to display the Modify Attribute dialog box, which is described in the next section.

Attributes

AdExplorer lists an object's attributes in the main window's right pane when you select the object in the left pane. The object's attributes are also listed on the Attributes tab of the object's Properties dialog box. Right-click any attribute and choose Copy Attributes from the context menu to copy the content of the list to the clipboard as tab-delimited values. (You can also select any attribute and choose Copy Attributes from the Edit menu.) The Display Integers As option in the same menus offers the option to display all integer values as decimal, as hexadecimal, or as an AdExplorer-determined default.

You can open an attribute's Properties dialog box, shown in Figure 9-5, by double-clicking on the attribute or by selecting it and choosing Properties from the Edit menu. The Properties dialog box displays the attribute's name, the DN of the object to which it belongs, its syntax (the attribute type), its schema, and its values. The same dialog box is used to display single-value and multi-value attributes, so the values are shown in a list box with one value per row. Click the Go To button next to the attribute's schema, and AdExplorer will navigate to the directory location where that schema is defined.

FIGURE 9-5 The Attribute Properties dialog box.

The Attribute Properties dialog box is read only. To delete an attribute, right-click the attribute from the right pane and choose Delete from the context menu. To edit an attribute's value, right-click the attribute and choose Modify from the context menu. To define a new attribute for the object, right-click any existing attribute and choose New Attribute from the context menu. To add a new attribute or modify an existing attribute, use the Modify Attribute dialog box, described in the next paragraph. Note that the Delete, Modify, and New Attribute operations can also be found by selecting an attribute and then choosing the desired option from the Edit menu.

The Modify Attribute dialog box, shown in Figure 9-6, supports the creating and editing of single-value and multivalue attributes, and it treats them the same. To add an attribute to an object, select the attribute you want to define from the Property drop-down list. To edit an existing attribute, select it in the list. A new attribute has no initial value; click Add to enter a new value. Take care not to add multiple values for a single-value attribute. You can modify or remove an existing value by selecting it in the list and clicking Modify or Remove, respectively. Note that the Modify Attribute dialog box can create or modify only one attribute at a time. You must click OK after establishing the attribute's value or values to commit those changes. Choose New Attribute or Modify again to add or edit another attribute, respectively.

FIGURE 9-6 The Modify Attribute dialog box.

Searching

AdExplorer has rich search functionality that allows you to search a selected object container for objects that have attribute values matching flexible search criteria. Search definitions can be saved for later use.

To start a general search, choose Search Container from the Search menu to display the Search Container dialog box, shown in Figure 9-7. To search within a particular container object, right-click the container and choose Search Container from the context menu. This method initializes the search criteria with a *distinguishedName* restriction that limits results to the selected object and its subtree.

FIGURE 9-7 The AdExplorer Search Container dialog box.

The current search criteria are displayed in a list in the middle of the dialog box. To add a search criterion, specify the attribute for which you want to search in the Attribute combo box, specify a relational operation and a value, and then click Add. To remove a search criterion, select it in the list and click Remove.

The list of available attributes is extensive. To make it easier to find an attribute, select the class to which it belongs in the Class drop-down list. The attributes list is then limited only to attributes that are allowed by that class' schema. If any of the attributes have display names, those are shown first, with the remaining attributes listed under --Advanced--. Note that the class name is not used by the filter—it is used only to help find attributes more quickly in the drop-down list.

After specifying the search criteria, click the Search button. The results pane will populate with the paths to objects that match, and by double-clicking a result you can navigate to its object in the main window.

To save a search criteria, click the Save button. The name you assign the search will appear in the Search menu. You can rename or delete a saved search from the context menu that appears when you right-click on the saved search entry in the Search menu.

Snapshots

You can use AdExplorer to save a snapshot of an Active Directory database that you can open later in AdExplorer to perform off-line inspection and searches of Active Directory objects and attributes. You can also compare two snapshots to see what objects, attributes, or permissions are different. Note that AdExplorer snapshots only the default, configuration, and schema naming contexts.

To save a snapshot, click the Save toolbar button or choose Create Snapshot from the File menu. The Snapshot dialog box lets you add a comment to the snapshot, specify where to save the snapshot, and apply a throttle to slow the rate at which AdExplorer will scan the Active Directory object tree to reduce the impact to the target domain controller.

When you load a saved snapshot (using the Connect To Active Directory dialog box described earlier), you can browse and search it as you would a live database. Note that snapshots are read only; you cannot make any changes to a snapshot.

After you load a snapshot, you can compare it against another snapshot file. Select any object within a snapshot, and then choose Compare Snapshot from the Compare menu to display the Compare Snapshots criteria setup dialog box, shown in Figure 9-8. Select another snapshot to compare with the one loaded. You can limit which classes and attributes to compare by selecting them in the classes and attributes lists. If you want to remember the class and attribute selections for later comparisons, click the Save button and enter a name to remember it by; this name will then appear in the Compare menu. Click the Compare button to initiate the comparison.

FIGURE 9-8 The Compare Snapshots criteria setup dialog box.

Differences are listed when the comparison completes, as shown in Figure 9-9. Double-clicking on a difference causes AdExplorer to navigate within the loaded snapshot to the object. To modify the comparison, click the New Compare button to return to the criteria setup dialog box.

FIGURE 9-9 The Compare Snapshots results dialog box.

Choose Compare Snapshot Security from the Compare menu to compare the permissions settings of objects in a loaded snapshot against those of another snapshot on disk. After running the comparison, double-click on a difference to display the Effective Permissions Comparison dialog box, which shows which permissions are different, as well as the complete permissions for the object from Snapshot 1 and Snapshot 2.

You can script AdExplorer to create a snapshot by starting it with the **–snapshot** command-line option. The option requires two parameters: the connection string and the snapshot path. *Connection string* is just the server name, or you can use a pair of double quotes to specify the default directory server. It is not possible to specify alternate credentials for the connection. To snapshot the default domain using current credentials, use this command:

```
adexplorer -snapshot "" c:\snapshots\snapshot1.dat
```

AdExplorer Configuration

AdExplorer's configuration settings are stored in two separate registry keys. The *EulaAccepted* value is stored in HKCU\Software\Sysinternals\Active Directory Explorer. The rest of AdExplorer's settings—including Favorites, snapshot paths, and other dialog box settings—are stored in HKCU\Software\MSDART\Active Directory Explorer.

AdInsight

AdInsight is a real-time monitoring utility that tracks LDAP API calls. Because LDAP is the communication protocol used by Active Directory, AdInsight is ideal for troubleshooting Active Directory client applications.

AdInsight uses DLL injection techniques to intercept calls that applications make in the Wldap32.dll library, which is the standard Windows library that implements low-level LDAP functionality, and upon which higher-level libraries such as ADSI (Active Directory Service Interfaces) rely. Unlike network monitoring tools, AdInsight intercepts and interprets all client-side APIs, including those that do not result in transmission to a server.

AdInsight monitors any process into which it can load its tracing DLL. It works most reliably when it is executed in the same security context and on the same desktop as the application being monitored. If the client application does not have administrative rights, AdInsight should not either.

To monitor Windows services, AdInsight needs to execute in Terminal Services session 0. On Windows XP and Windows Server 2003, this is typically the case when the AdInsight user has logged on at the console. However, on Windows Vista and newer, the interactive user desktop is never in session 0. You can start AdInsight in session 0 by running the following PsExec command with administrative rights:

```
psexec -d -i 0 adinsight.exe
```

AdInsight will then be able to inject its tracing DLL into other processes in session 0, including Windows services.

Note that the DLL that AdInsight injects into other processes cannot unload without risking a process crash, so the DLL remains in a process until the process exits. Although the DLL shouldn't cause any problems for host processes, it is advisable to reboot after you are done using AdInsight.

AdInsight Data Capture

AdInsight starts with capture mode on, so it immediately begins tracing LDAP API calls in other processes and displaying information about them in its main window. As shown in Figure 9-10, AdInsight's upper pane—the Event Pane—consists of a table, with each row representing a separate LDAP event. The Details Pane below it contains detailed parameter information for the event selected in the Event Pane. Autoscroll is on by default, so the display is scrolled to show new events as they are captured. Autoscroll can be toggled from the View menu by pressing Ctrl+A or by clicking the Autoscroll toolbar button. Similarly, capture mode can be toggled on and off from the File menu by pressing Ctrl+E or by clicking the Capture toolbar button.

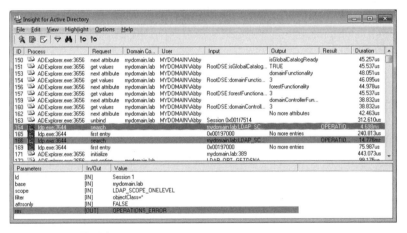

FIGURE 9-10 AdInsight.

Columns in both the Event Pane and Details Pane can be resized by dragging the right border of the column header, or they can be moved by dragging the column header to a new position. If data in a column is larger than the column can display, hover the cursor over the displayed portion and the full text will be displayed in a tooltip.

You can choose which columns appear in the display by choosing Select Columns from the Options menu or from the context menu that appears when you right-click on the table header in the top or bottom pane. Select the columns you want the Event Pane and Details Pane to show in the Select Columns dialog box (shown in Figure 9-11).

FIGURE 9-11 AdInsight's Select Columns dialog box.

The meaning of each column is described in the following list. These are the columns that can be displayed in the Event Pane:

- **ID** The unique sequence number assigned by AdInsight to the event. Gaps in sequence numbers might indicate dropped events resulting from heavy activity or from filtering that prevents some items from appearing in the display.

- **Time** The time that the event occurred. By default, the time is represented as the amount of time since AdInsight began monitoring. Other time-display options are described later in the chapter.

- **Process** The name and PID of the process making the LDAP call, and the icon from the process' image file.

- **Request** The name of the LDAP function call. By default, AdInsight displays a simple name representing the function, such as *open*, *search*, or *get values*. To display the actual LDAP function name, such as *ldap_open*, *ldap_search_s*, or *ldap_get_values*, deselect Show Simple Event Name in the Options menu.

- **Type** Indicates whether the request is synchronous or asynchronous.

- **Session** The LDAP session handle.

- **Event ID** The LDAP event handle.

- **Domain Controller** The name of the domain controller, if any, to which the request was directed. If a domain controller (DC) was not specified, the request was directed to all DCs within the site.

- **User** The user account used to access the LDAP server. This column is empty if the server was not contacted.

- **Input** Data passed from the process to the LDAP server as part of the request. If multiple pieces of data were passed to the server, AdInsight selects one to be displayed in this column. The Details Pane shows all input data sent to the server.

- **Output**   Data passed from the LDAP server to the process as a result of the request. If the operation returned multiple data items, AdInsight selects one to be displayed in this column. The Details Pane shows all output data returned from the server.

- **Result**   The result code returned by the request. To make it easier to see failure results, success results are not displayed by default. To display success results as well, deselect Suppress Success Status from the Options menu.

- **Duration**   The elapsed time from the start of the API call to its completion. See the upcoming section on time display options.

The Details Pane shows the input and output parameters for the event selected in the Event Pane. You can select any of the following columns to appear in the Details Pane:

- **Parameter**   The parameter names for the selected LDAP call

- **In/Out**   Whether the parameter is being sent to the LDAP server ("[IN]") or received by the application ("[OUT]")

- **Value**   The parameter value sent or received by the process

To view more information about a request, right-click the event and choose Event Information. A pop-up window appears, showing the LDAP function name, a one-sentence description of the function, and a hyperlink that opens your browser to search for more information about the function on the MSDN Library Web site.

To view more information about an Active Directory object, right-click an event associated with that object and choose Explore. AdInsight will launch AdExplorer and navigate to the object in the AdExplorer view.

To view more information about a process, right-click the event and choose Process Information. A dialog box like the one shown in Figure 9-12 displays process information including the path to the executable, the command line that launched it, the current directory, and the user account under which the process is running.

FIGURE 9-12 AdInsight Process Information dialog box.

To view information about all processes for which requests were captured, choose Processes from the View menu. The Processes dialog box lists the name, PID and image path for each process in the report. Double-click a process name to display the Process Information dialog box for that process.

To clear the Event Pane, click the Clear toolbar button or press Ctrl+X. Clearing events also resets the sequence number to 0. It also resets the values displayed in the Time column if relative time is selected.

By default, AdInsight retains the most recent 50,000 events and discards older lines. To change this history depth, choose History Depth on the View menu and specify a different number. If you specify 0, AdInsight will retain all event data and never discard older events. Note that turning off Autoscroll disables the History Depth limit so as to stop new items pushing the currently viewable items out of the list.

Display Options

In addition to changing the font AdInsight uses and making AdInsight appear Always On Top (both on the Options menu), you can decide whether AdInsight uses "friendly" or technical terms and customize their format.

Setting Time Display Options

By default, the Time column shows the amount of time since AdInsight began monitoring (which is reset when Clear Display is invoked). Select Clock Time from the Options menu if you prefer to show the actual local time when the event occurred. With Clock Time enabled, the Options menu also offers the choice whether to Show Milliseconds in that representation.

The Time column (when not showing Clock Time) and the Duration column show their values formatted as *simple time*. That is, they are represented as a number of seconds, milliseconds, or microseconds so that there are always one to three digits to the left of the decimal. If you deselect Show Simple Time on the Options menu, these values display as seconds, with eight digits to the right of the decimal point. For example, a Duration can be represented as "25.265ms" (simple time) or as "0.025265".

Display Names

By default, AdInsight displays a simple name representing the LDAP function, such as *open*, *search*, or *get values*. To display the actual LDAP function name, such as *ldap_open*, *ldap_search_s*, or *ldap_get_values*, deselect Show Simple Event Name on the Options menu.

AdInsight represents distinguished names in an easier-to-read format, such as *mydomain.lab\Users\Abby*. To view the actual distinguished names (for example, *CN=Abby,CN=Users,DC=mydomain,DC=lab*), select Show Distinguished Name Format from the Options menu.

When AdInsight shows LDAP filter strings in the Details Pane, it uses an easier-to-read infix notation, like the following:

```
(( NOT((showInAdvancedViewOnly=TRUE)) AND (samAccountType=805306368)) AND
    ((name=rchase-2k8*) OR (sAMAccountName=rchase-2k8*)))
```

If you prefer to view the standard (prefix) LDAP syntax, deselect Show Simple LDAP Filters in the Options menu. This is what the previous query filter looks like in standard syntax:

```
(&(&(!(showInAdvancedViewOnly=TRUE))(samAccountType=805306368)) (|(name=rchase-2k8*)
    (sAMAccountName=rchase-2k8*)))
```

Finding Information of Interest

AdInsight offers several ways to find information of interest. These include text search, visual highlighting, and navigation options.

Finding Text

To search for an occurrence of text in the Event Pane, press Ctrl+F or click the Find toolbar icon to open the Find dialog box, shown in Figure 9-13. In addition to providing the usual options to match whole words only, make the search case sensitive, and specify direction, the Find dialog box lets you specify in which of the visible columns to search for the text. If the text you entered is found in the Event Pane, the matching event will be selected and Auto Scroll will be turned off to keep the line in the window.

FIGURE 9-13 AdInsight Find dialog box.

The Find dialog box is modeless, meaning that you can switch back to the AdInsight main window without closing the Find dialog box. After performing a search and with focus on the

AdInsight main window, you can repeat the previous search down the event list by pressing F3; press Shift+F3 to repeat the previous search up the event list.

Highlighting Events

Highlighting calls attention to information of interest visually. By default, events with error results are highlighted in red, and events that took more than 50 ms to complete are highlighted in dark blue. To toggle all highlighting on or off, choose Enable Highlighting from the Highlight menu. To customize highlighting, choose Highlight Preferences from the Highlight menu; this displays the Highlight Preferences dialog box, shown in Figure 9-14.

FIGURE 9-14 AdInsight Highlight Preferences dialog box.

In the Event Item Highlighting group, Sessions and Related Items highlight items similar to the selected event. When you select an item in the Event Pane, the highlighting is updated to identify associated events. If Sessions is selected, all events with the same session handle as the selected event are highlighted with that option's color (black text on light blue by default). If Related Items is selected, all events with the same event handle are highlighted (black text on yellow, by default).

To highlight events belonging to particular processes by name, select Process and type a text expression matching the process name or names in the Process Name Filter list. Events with a process name that contains the specified text will be highlighted (by default, black text on green). Filter expression rules apply to text in the Process Name Filter list. For example, to highlight *ldp.exe* and *svchost.exe*, you can type a filter like this: **ldp;svchost**.

The Error Highlighting group identifies events that reported error results or that took longer than a specified amount of time to complete. You can enable these highlights independently, and specify the time threshold in seconds at which an event gets highlighted. Note that the feature that navigates to the next or previous error event requires that Error Result highlighting be enabled.

To change a highlight color, click the Color button corresponding to the highlight option. This opens the Highlight Color dialog box, which lets you set both foreground and background colors for that highlight.

Viewing Associated Events

AdInsight offers two options to open a new AdInsight window listing just events associated with the selected event. Select the event of interest in the main AdInsight window, and then choose View Related Events or View Session Events from the View menu or from the right-click context menu.

View Related Events opens the Related Transaction Events window. It lists all events from the main window with the same event handle as the selected event. View Session Events opens the Related Session Events window. This lists all events from the main window with the same LDAP session handle as the selected event.

The Related Events windows are very similar to the main AdInsight window. The window is divided into an Events Pane and a Details Pane. The column sets that appear in these panes are the same as those of the main window. These columns can be resized and reordered, but the column selection cannot be changed from here.

Finding Event Errors

Click the Goto Next Event Error toolbar button to find and select the next event in the Event Pane that returned an error result. To find and select the previous error, click the Goto Previous Event Error toolbar button. These features can also be found by right-clicking an event and choosing Next Event Error or Previous Event Error from the context menu.

Note that these toolbar buttons and context menu items are enabled only when highlighting is on and Error Result highlighting is selected.

Filtering Results

To reduce the amount of information to analyze, you can configure filters that apply while data is collected. Filtering allows you to display or hide events based on process name or on specific LDAP functions. Note that filters are applied only during data capture; changing a filter does not affect the list of events that have already been captured.

To configure the data capture filter, click the Filter toolbar button or choose Event Filter from the View menu. This opens the Event Filters dialog box, shown in Figure 9-15. The Process Filter group lets you specify filter match strings to include or exclude events based on process name. By default, all processes are included: the Include filter is set to the wildcard character (*), and the Exclude filter is empty. You can specify one or more matching strings in the Include or Exclude text box, separated by semicolons. If an event's process contains one or more of the text substrings in the Exclude filter, the event will not be displayed; otherwise, if the Include filter is *, the event will be displayed. If the Include filter is set to one or more other text substrings, the event will be displayed only if its process name includes one of the substrings. Text comparisons are case insensitive. Do not include spaces in the text filters unless you want the spaces to be part of the filter.

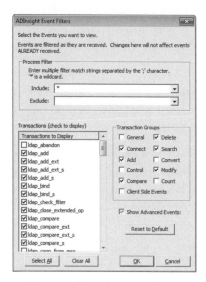

FIGURE 9-15 AdInsight Event Filters dialog box.

The Transactions list in the lower left of the Event Filters dialog box specifies which LDAP functions (transactions) will be displayed in the AdInsight Event Pane. Note that the default filter does not select all events. You can select or unselect individual low-level functions by name in this list. To select or clear the entire list, click the Select All or Clear All button. To select or unselect entire sets of related APIs at once, select or unselect the corresponding check boxes in the Transaction Groups group. For example, to view only functions involved with connecting, binding, or disconnecting from the server, click the Clear All button and then select the Connect check box. To display events not commonly used for troubleshooting and configuration, select Show Advanced Events.

To reset all filters to their default values, click the Reset To Default button. Note that when you start AdInsight with a process filter applied from a previous session, the Event Filters dialog box opens to confirm your filter settings. To start the console without opening the Filter dialog box, add the **–q** parameter to your startup command.

Saving and Exporting AdInsight Data

To save all data captured by AdInsight, choose Save or Save As from the File menu. The default extension for AdInsight's native file format is .wit; this file format preserves all the data that was captured with full fidelity so that it can be loaded into AdInsight on the same system or on a different one at a later time. To open a saved AdInsight file, press Ctrl+O or choose Open from the File menu.

To save AdInsight data as a text file, press Ctrl+Alt+S or choose Export To Text File from the File menu. AdInsight exports the data as a tab-delimited ANSI text file with column headers, with each row representing one event. AdInsight asks whether you want to export all column data or only data from the columns selected for display. If you select the Include Detailed Information option, data from the Details Pane is appended to the event as additional tab-delimited fields. Note that only the first of these additional columns will have a column header.

To copy a row of text from the Event Pane or the Details Pane to the Windows clipboard, select the row and press Ctrl+C. Data in the visible columns is copied to the clipboard as tab-delimited text.

Finally, you can use AdInsight to view HTML-formatted reports of the captured events in your Web browser. Choose HTML Reports in the View menu and then one of the following report types:

- **Events**   This report produces an HTML report containing data from the visible columns in the Event Pane, with one row per event. Data in the Request column is rendered as a hyperlink to documentation about the function on the MSDN Library Web site. Note that if you have a significant amount of data, this report can be quite large and can take a long time for a browser to render.

- **Events with Details**   This report shows the same information as the Events report, but it adds a table beneath each event row showing the content of the Details Pane for that event.

- **Event Time Results**   This report produces a *histogram* report of the LDAP calls in the Event Pane, the number of times each one was called, the total time for all the calls, the longest duration of any one of the calls, and the average time per call. To include all LDAP functions in the report, including those that were not called and captured by AdInsight, choose Preferences from the Options menu and deselect Suppress Uncalled Functions In Reports.

- **Highlighted Events**   This report is the same as the Events With Details report, but it includes only events that are currently highlighted.

AdInsight creates these reports in your TEMP folder. To save them to another location, you can use your browser's Save As function, or copy or move them directly from your TEMP folder. (The file location should be in your browser's address bar.)

Command-Line Options

You can use command-line parameters to set AdInsight startup options from a batch file or command window. The AdInsight command-line syntax is

```
adinsight [-fi IncludeFilter] [-fe ExcludeFilter] [-f SavedFile] [-q] [-o] [-t]
```

Here is an explanation of the items shown in the preceding command line:

- **–fi** *IncludeFilter*   Sets the text for an Include process name filter. See the "Filtering Results" section earlier in this chapter for more information.

- **–fe** *ExcludeFilter*   Sets the text for an Exclude process name filter. See the "Filtering Results" section earlier in this chapter for more information.

- **–f** *SavedFile*   Opens a saved AdInsight file for viewing.

- **–q**   Starts AdInsight without opening the Filter dialog box. By default, the Filter dialog box is displayed at startup if any process filters are applied.

- **–o**   Turns off event capture at startup.

- **–t**   Displays a notification icon on the Taskbar.

AdRestore

Windows Server 2003 Active Directory introduced the ability to restore deleted (*tombstoned*) objects. AdRestore is a simple command-line utility that enumerates deleted objects in a domain and gives you the option of restoring each one.

AdRestore's command-line syntax is

```
adrestore [-r] [searchfilter]
```

Without any command-line options, AdRestore enumerates the deleted objects in the current domain, showing the CN, DN, and last-known parent container for each object. With the **–r** option, AdRestore displays objects one at a time, prompting the user to enter **y** or **n** after each one to restore or not restore the object.

You can specify any text as the search filter to list an object only if its CN contains that text. Search-filter comparison is case insensitive and should be enclosed in quotes if it contains spaces. The following example looks for deleted objects with the name "Test User" in its CN and prompts the user to restore those objects:

```
adrestore -r "Test User"
```

By default, only domain administrators can enumerate or restore deleted objects, though this capability can be delegated to others. If you do not have permission to enumerate deleted objects, Active Directory (and therefore AdRestore) returns 0 entries rather than an error. In addition, the following limitations apply to restoring deleted objects:

- A tombstone retains only a subset of the original object's attributes, so AdRestore cannot fully restore a deleted object. A restored user object requires that its password be set again.

- An object cannot be restored when the tombstone lifetime for the object has expired because when the tombstone lifetime has expired, the object is permanently deleted.

- Objects that exist at the root of the naming context, such as a domain or application partition, cannot be restored.

- Schema objects cannot be restored. Schema objects should never be deleted because that can lead to invalid Active Directory objects.

- An object cannot be restored if its parent container has been deleted and not restored.

- It is possible to restore deleted containers, but the restoration of the deleted objects that were in the container before the deletion is difficult because the tree structure under the container must be manually reconstructed.

Chapter 10
Desktop Utilities

Unlike most of the Sysinternals utilities, the ones described in this chapter are not primarily for diagnostic or troubleshooting purposes. BgInfo displays computer configuration information as desktop wallpaper. Desktops lets you run applications on separate virtual desktops and to switch between those desktops. And ZoomIt is a screen magnification and annotation utility that I use in all my presentations.

BgInfo

How many times have you walked up to a system that you manage and needed to run several console commands or click through several diagnostic windows to identify important aspects of its configuration such as its name, IP address, or operating system version? Sysinternals BgInfo can automatically display this information and much more on the desktop wallpaper. By running BgInfo from your startup folder, you can always ensure that this information is immediately visible and up to date when you log on. (See Figure 10-1.) In addition to displaying a wealth of data, BgInfo offers many options for customizing its appearance. And because BgInfo creates the wallpaper image and then exits, you don't have to worry about it consuming system resources or interfering with other applications.

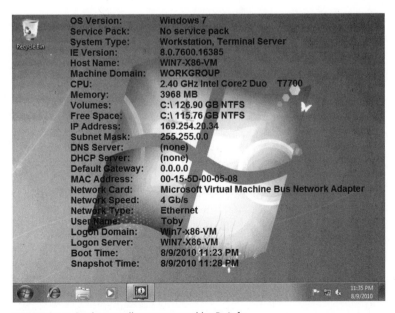

FIGURE 10-1 Desktop wallpaper created by BgInfo.

When you start BgInfo without command-line options, it displays its configuration editor with a 10-second Time Remaining indicator in the upper right portion of the dialog box, as shown in Figure 10-2. You can stop the timer by clicking on something within the window. If the timer expires, BgInfo sets the wallpaper according to the displayed configuration and then exits.

FIGURE 10-2 BgInfo editor window, with 10 seconds remaining until the displayed configuration is applied.

Configuring Data to Display

The BgInfo editor lets you position and shape the data to display in the wallpaper. You can combine text of your choosing with data fields referenced within angle brackets. BgInfo's default configuration lists labels and data fields for all its built-in fields in alphabetical order. For example, when the configuration shown in Figure 10-2 is used to generate a wallpaper image, the text "Boot Time:" will appear in the wallpaper, and to its right "<Boot Time>" will be replaced with the actual boot time of the computer.

To change which fields are displayed, simply change the text in the editor window. For example, to have the CPU information appear first in Figure 10-2, select the entire line containing "CPU" in the editor window, press Ctrl+X to cut it, move the insertion point to the top of the editor window, and press Ctrl+V to paste it as the top line. You can also insert a label and a corresponding angle-bracketed data field at the current insertion point in the editor window by selecting an entry in the Fields list and clicking the Add button, or simply by double-clicking the entry in the list.

The labels are optional. For example, to show the logged-on user in DOMAIN\USER format, specify two data fields separated by a backslash: **<Logon Domain>\<User Name>**.

Table 10-1 lists the data fields that BgInfo defines.

TABLE 10-1 BgInfo Data Fields

Name of Field	Description
Operating System Attributes	
OS Version	The name of the operating system, such as Windows 7. If BgInfo doesn't recognize the operating system, it displays the Windows version number instead.
Service Pack	The service pack number, such as Service Pack 1 or No Service Pack.
System Type	The type of system, such as Workstation or Domain Controller. On Microsoft Windows XP and newer, BgInfo also reports "Terminal Server" because terminal services are now a core feature of Windows.
IE Version	The Internet Explorer version, as reported by the Version value in the HKLM\Software\Microsoft\Internet Explorer registry key.
Host Name	The computer name.
Machine Domain	The domain or workgroup to which the computer belongs.
Hardware Attributes	
CPU	The CPU type—for example, Dual 2.50 GHz Intel Core2 Duo T9300.
Memory	The amount of physical RAM visible to Windows.
Volumes	Lists the fixed volumes by drive letter, showing the total space and file system on each.
Free Space	Lists the fixed volumes by drive letter, showing the free space and file system on each.
Network Attributes	
IP Address	Lists the IP address for each network interface on the computer.
Subnet Mask	Lists the subnet mask associated with the IP addresses listed in the preceding field.
DNS Server	Lists the DNS server (or servers) for each network interface on the computer.
DHCP Server	Lists the DHCP server for each network interface on the computer.
Default Gateway	Lists the default gateway for each network interface on the computer.
MAC Address	List the MAC address for each network interface on the computer.
Network Card	Identifies the network card name for each network interface on the computer.
Network Speed	Shows the network speed for each network card—for example, 100 Mb/s.
Network Type	Shows the network type for each network card—for example, Ethernet.
Logon Attributes	
User Name	The account name of the user running BgInfo.
Logon Domain	The account domain of the user running BgInfo.
Logon Server	The name of the server that authenticated the user running BgInfo.
Timestamps	
Boot Time	The date and time that the computer was last started.
Snapshot Time	The date and time that the BgInfo wallpaper was created.

In addition to using BgInfo's 24 built-in fields, you can add your own items to the Fields list and then insert them into a wallpaper configuration. BgInfo offers a variety of potential information sources, shown in Table 10-2.

TABLE 10-2 BgInfo Information Sources

Name of Field	Description
Custom (User-Defined) Fields	
Environment variable	The value of an environment variable
Registry value	The text value of any registry value
WMI query	The text output of any Windows Management Instrumentation (WMI) query
File version	The file version of a file
File timestamp	The date and time that a file was last modified
File content	The text content of a file
VBScript file	The text output from executing a VBScript file

To define and manage custom fields, click the Custom button to open the User Defined Fields dialog box. Figure 10-3 shows the dialog box with some examples of custom fields, including a field called Num CPUs that displays the value of the NUMBER_OF_PROCESSORS environment variable, a Legal Notice Text field that displays the same policy-mandated text in the registry that appears before a user logs on, and the BIOS version reported by a WMI query.

FIGURE 10-3 Management of user-defined fields.

Click the New button to define a new custom field. Select an existing custom field in the list, and click the Edit or Remove button to modify or remove that custom field. When you click OK, BgInfo updates the Fields list in its main window.

Figure 10-4 shows the Define New Field dialog box used to create or modify a custom field. BgInfo uses the identifier you enter as the default label to use when you add it to a wallpaper configuration, as well as the data field name to use between angle brackets. For example, the data field for a field named Num CPUs would be *<Num CPUs>*. Identifiers can contain only letters, numbers, spaces, and underscores.

FIGURE 10-4 Defining a new user-defined field.

Select one of the seven types of information sources, and then type the name of the source in the Path field. The Browse button displays a different dialog box based on the information type. If you select the Environment option, clicking Browse displays a list of environment variables from which to choose. For the WMI Query option, clicking Browse displays a dialog box that helps you build and evaluate a valid WMI query. For the four file-based source types, clicking Browse displays a standard file chooser. The Registry Value option is the one type for which the Browse button does not work; for this type, enter the full path to the registry value—for example:

```
HKLM\Software\Microsoft\Windows NT\CurrentVersion\CurrentBuildNumber
```

On a 64-bit system, selecting 64-Bit Registry View ensures that the specified registry path will not be redirected to the *Wow6432Node* subkey.

Appearance Options

The BgInfo wallpaper editor is a rich text editor with full undo/redo support. You can select part or all of the text and change its font face, size, style, alignment, and bulleting using the toolbar or the Format menu. Rich text pasted from the clipboard retains its formatting. Dragging the anchor in the horizontal ruler changes the first tab stop for the selected paragraphs so that text can be lined up in columns. You can also add a bitmap image inline with the text by choosing Insert Image from the Edit menu.

Click the Background button to select the wallpaper background. As shown in Figure 10-5, BgInfo can integrate its data display with the user's current wallpaper settings, or you can specify a background bitmap and position (center, tile or stretch), or select a solid background color. The NT 4.0, 2000, and XP buttons set the background color to the default wallpaper colors for those versions of Windows. With Make Wallpaper Visible Behind Text selected, BgInfo writes its text directly on the background bitmap. If you deselect that option, BgInfo puts the text inside a solid rectangle with the selected background color, and it places that rectangle over the background bitmap.

FIGURE 10-5 The BgInfo Background dialog box.

Click the Position button to specify where to place the text on the screen. Select one of the nine positions in the Locate On Screen group shown in the Set Position dialog box (shown in Figure 10-6) to position the text in that area of the display. If some items are very long (for example, some network card names), you can use the Limit Lines To option to line-wrap them. Selecting the Compensate For Taskbar Position option ensures that the text area will not be obscured by the taskbar. If you have a more than one monitor connected to your system, click the Multiple Monitor Configuration button to choose whether to display the text on all display monitors, only on the primary monitor, or on any single monitor.

FIGURE 10-6 The BgInfo Set Position dialog box.

You can set the color depth of the resulting wallpaper on the Bitmap menu. Select from 256 Colors (8-bit color), 16-bit color, 24-bit color, or Match Display, which sets the color depth according to the color quality of the current display.

Choose Location from the Bitmap menu to specify where the resulting wallpaper bitmap should be created. By default the bitmap will be created in the user's temporary files folder. Note that administrative rights are required to create the file in the Windows folder. You can incorporate environment variables in the path and specify the target file name if you select Other Directory.

To see what the BgInfo-generated background would look like without actually changing the wallpaper, click the Preview toggle button. While Preview is selected, BgInfo shows the background in a full-screen window on the primary display. You can continue changing the background's content and format and see the changes immediately in the preview. Choose Refresh from the File menu or press F5 to update the data in the preview.

Saving BgInfo Configuration for Later Use

Choose Save As from the File menu to save the current BgInfo configuration settings to a file. After you've created it, you can apply the configuration to other users' desktops or on other computers simply by specifying the file on the BgInfo command line. You can open the configuration file for further editing by choosing File, Open. You can also open it by double-clicking it in Explorer—when you run BgInfo for the first time, it creates a BgInfo file association for .bgi.

When you start BgInfo with an initial configuration file on the command line, the BgInfo editor appears with its 10-second Time Remaining indicator, applying the configuration only after the timer expires. Adding **/timer:0** to the command line makes BgInfo apply the configuration immediately and without displaying its window. For example, to display updated information on the desktop whenever any user logs on, you can create a shortcut with a command line like the following in the all-users Startup folder:

```
Bginfo.exe c:\programdata\bginfo.bgi /timer:0 /silent
```

The **/silent** option suppresses the display of any error messages.

In addition to a visual layout, the configuration file includes custom field definitions, which desktops to update, and alternate output options (which are described next). Choose Reset Default Settings from the File menu to remove all configuration information and to restore BgInfo to its initial state. BgInfo's current settings are stored in the registry in HKCU\Software\Winternals\BgInfo, except for the *EulaAccepted* value, which is stored in HKCU\Software\Sysinternals\BgInfo.

Other Output Options

Because BgInfo collects so much useful information, it seemed natural to us to add the capability to save that information to destinations other than bitmap files. BgInfo can write the data it collects to a variety of file formats or to a Microsoft SQL Server database. It can also display its information in a separate window that you can bring to the foreground. To use these options without also updating the wallpaper, click the Desktops button and select Do Not Alter This Wallpaper for all desktops.

To save data to a plain-text comma-separated values (CSV) file, a Microsoft Excel spreadsheet or Access database, choose Database from the File menu to display the Database Settings dialog box shown in Figure 10-7, and type the full path to a file with a **.txt**, **.xls**, or **.mdb** extension, respectively. BgInfo will create or update the target file according to the extension that you specify. The File button displays a file-picker dialog box that you can use to help set the path correctly. To append records to an existing file, choose Create A New Database Record For Every Run. To retain only a single record for the current computer, choose Record Only The Most Recent Run For Each Computer. You can save this configuration to a .bgi file and apply it at a later time, or just click OK or Apply in the BgInfo main window. Note that the output includes all default and custom fields, not just those that are selected for display.

FIGURE 10-7 BgInfo Database Settings dialog box.

To write the data to a SQL Server database, choose Database from the File menu, click the SQL button, select a SQL Server instance and then select Use Trusted Connection (to use your Windows logon) or type a value in the Logon ID and Password (for the legacy SQL Standard Authentication) text boxes. You need to pick an existing database in the Options portion of the SQL Server Login dialog box, as shown in Figure 10-8. The first time it logs information, BgInfo creates and configures a table in the database with the name you specify in the Application Name field. BgInfo configures a datetime column with the timestamp, and an nvarchar(255) column corresponding to each default and custom field. These one-time operations require that the first caller have the CREATE TABLE and ALTER permissions. After the table has been created, callers need CONNECT permission to the database, and SELECT, INSERT, and UPDATE permissions on the table.

FIGURE 10-8 BgInfo configuration to write to a SQL Server database table.

To write the data to a Rich Text File (.RTF) document, run BgInfo with **/rtf:**path on the command line, along with a BgInfo configuration file (.bgi). Note that this feature incorporates the formatting of the text, but not of the background. Therefore, you should change the text color from the default white. You will probably also want to include **/timer:0** on the command line to bypass the 10-second timer.

Finally, to display the BgInfo data in a popup window instead of as wallpaper, add **/popup** to the BgInfo command line. Add **/taskbar** to the command line to display a BgInfo icon in the taskbar notification area, which you can click to display the BgInfo popup window.

Updating Other Desktops

On Windows XP and Windows Server 2003, BgInfo can change the desktop wallpaper that appears prior to user logon. Click the Desktops button to display the Desktops dialog box, shown in Figure 10-9. You can individually select whether to update the wallpaper for the current user desktop, the logon desktop for console users, and the logon desktop for terminal services (remote desktop) users. You can also choose to set the wallpaper for any of those desktops to None. Note that changing the logon desktops requires administrative privileges and that the feature does not work on Windows Vista and newer. You can opt to have BgInfo display an error message if permissions problems prevent it from updating a logon desktop.

FIGURE 10-9 The Desktops dialog box.

On a computer with multiple interactive sessions, including disconnected remote desktop or Fast User Switching sessions, you can update the wallpaper of all interactive users' desktops with the **/all** command-line option. When you add **/all**, BgInfo starts a service that enumerates the current interactive sessions and launches an instance of BgInfo within each session, running as the user who owns the session. Because each instance of BgInfo launches in a different user context, you should specify the configuration file with an absolute path and in a location that all users can read. You should also add **/accepteula** and **/timer:0** to the command line.

Desktops

Sysinternals Desktops allows you to organize your applications on up to four virtual desktops. Read e-mail on one, browse the Web on the second, and do work in your productivity software on the third—without the clutter of the windows you're not using. After you configure hotkeys for switching desktops, you can create and switch desktops either by clicking on the notification area icon to open a desktop preview and switching window or by using the hotkeys.

Unlike other virtual desktop utilities that implement their virtual desktops by showing the windows that are active on a desktop and hiding the rest, Sysinternals Desktops uses a Windows desktop object for each desktop. Application windows are bound to a desktop object when they are created, so Windows maintains the connection between windows and desktops and knows which ones to show when you switch a desktop. That makes Sysinternals Desktops very lightweight and free from bugs that the other approach is prone to, where the utility's view of active windows becomes inconsistent with the visible windows. (See "Sessions, Window Stations, Desktops, and Window Messages" in Chapter 2, "Windows Core Concepts.")

When you run Desktops for the first time, it displays its configuration dialog box, shown in Figure 10-10. Use this dialog box to configure the hotkeys that will be used to switch between desktops and to specify whether Desktops should run automatically whenever you log on. You can display the configuration dialog box again by right-clicking on the Desktops notification area icon and choosing Options.

FIGURE 10-10 Desktops configuration dialog box.

To switch between desktops, click the Desktops notification area icon. Desktops will display the desktop switch window shown in Figure 10-11. The desktop switch window shows thumbnails of the four available desktops. When you first run Desktops, only Desktop 1 has been created. When you click one of the other three thumbnails, Desktops creates a new Windows desktop, starts Explorer on that desktop, and switches to that desktop. A quicker way to switch to another desktop is to press its hotkey (for example, Alt+3 for Desktop 3). After you have switched to a desktop, you can start applications on that desktop. Desktop's notification area icon highlights which desktop is the one you're currently viewing and displays its name in a tooltip. Note that themes or wallpaper set on any desktop apply to all four desktops.

FIGURE 10-11 The Desktops switch window, with applications running on three of the four desktops.

Desktops' reliance on Windows desktop objects means that it cannot provide some of the functionality of other virtual desktop utilities, however. For example, Windows doesn't provide a way to move a window from one desktop object to another, and because a separate Explorer process must run on each desktop to provide a taskbar and start menu, most notification area icons are visible only on the first desktop. Currently, Aero works only on the first desktop. Further, there is no way to delete a desktop object, so Desktops does not provide a way to close a desktop—doing so would result in orphaned windows and processes. The recommended way to exit Desktops, therefore, is to log off. Logging off from any desktop logs off all desktops.

Sysinternals Desktops is compatible with all supported versions of Windows and is fully compatible with remote desktop sessions.

ZoomIt

ZoomIt is a screen magnification and annotation utility. I originally wrote it to fit my specific needs in my presentations, both with my Microsoft PowerPoint slides and with application demonstrations. I also frequently use it outside of presentations to quickly magnify a portion of my screen and to capture magnified and annotated screen shots.

ZoomIt runs in the background and activates with customizable hotkeys to zoom in on an area of the screen and to draw and write text on the magnified image. It also includes a break timer that I use during longer training sessions to let attendees know when the session will resume.

ZoomIt has two zooming modes. The normal zoom mode takes a snapshot of the desktop when the zoom hotkey is pressed, and LiveZoom magnifies the desktop while programs continue to update the display in real time.

ZoomIt works on all supported versions of Windows, and you can use pen input for ZoomIt drawing on Tablet PCs.

Using ZoomIt

The first time you run ZoomIt, it presents a configuration dialog box. (See Figure 10-12.) The configuration dialog box describes how to use the features and lets you specify alternate hotkeys for its various actions. Whether you press OK to confirm any changes or Cancel, ZoomIt will continue to run in the background. To display the configuration dialog box again, click the ZoomIt icon in the notification area and choose Options from the menu. Another alternative, if you have opted not to show the notification area icon, is to start another instance of ZoomIt.

FIGURE 10-12 The Zoom tab of the ZoomIt configuration dialog box.

By default, Ctrl+1 zooms, Ctrl+2 starts drawing mode without zooming, Ctrl+3 starts the break timer, and Ctrl+4 starts LiveZoom. For the remainder of this discussion, I will assume that the defaults have been retained. On multimonitor systems, ZoomIt operates on the "current" display—that is, the one in which the mouse cursor points when the hotkey is pressed. Other monitors will continue to operate normally.

In all the ZoomIt modes except for LiveZoom, you can copy the current display content, including annotations, to the clipboard by pressing Ctrl+C. You can also save the display content to a Portable Network Graphic (PNG) file—press Ctrl+S and ZoomIt will prompt for a file location to save the image.

Zoom Mode

To use the normal zoom mode, press Ctrl+1. ZoomIt captures a screen shot of the desktop of the current monitor and doubles the screen magnification, zooming to the current location of the mouse cursor. You can increase or decrease the magnification level by pressing the Up or Down arrow keys or by scrolling the mouse wheel. You can move the zoom focus to another part of the screen by moving the mouse.

While in normal zoom mode, you can enter drawing mode by pressing the left mouse button, or enter typing mode by pressing the T key.

To exit the normal zoom mode, press the Escape key or the right mouse button.

Drawing Mode

Drawing mode lets you draw shapes, straight lines, or free form on the screen in various colors and various pen widths. (See Figure 10-13). You can also clear the screen to a white or black sketch pad.

FIGURE 10-13 ZoomIt drawing mode.

To draw free-form lines on the screen, move the mouse cursor to where you want to begin drawing, and then hold the left mouse button and move the cursor. Release the mouse button to stop drawing. ZoomIt will remain in drawing mode. To exit drawing mode, click the right mouse button.

To draw a straight line, move the cursor to where you want the line to begin. Press and hold the Shift button, and then hold the left mouse button and move the cursor to the line's endpoint. The proposed line displays on the screen as you move the cursor until you release the mouse button, at which point the line will remain drawn on the screen. If the line is close to horizontal (or vertical), ZoomIt automatically adjusts it to make it horizontal (or vertical). Similarly, to draw an arrow, move the cursor to where you want the head of the arrow to appear, hold down Shift+Ctrl, hold the left mouse button, and move the cursor to the arrow's starting point.

To draw a rectangle, move the cursor to where you want the upper left or lower right corner of the rectangle to begin. Press and hold the Ctrl key, and then hold the left mouse button and move the cursor. The proposed rectangle resizes as you move the cursor until you release the mouse button, at which point the rectangle will remain drawn on the screen. Similarly, to draw an ellipse, hold down the Tab key instead of the Ctrl key. The starting and ending points that you drag define the rectangle within which the ellipse will be drawn.

To undo the last drawing item, press Ctrl+Z. To erase all drawn or typed annotations, press e.

To clear the screen to a white sketch pad for drawing or typing, press w. To clear the screen to a black sketch pad, press k. To enter typing mode, press t.

While in drawing mode, you can change the color of the pen. Press r for red, g for green, b for blue, o for orange, y for yellow or p for pink. The pen color is also used for typing mode.

You can change the pen width by pressing the left Ctrl button with the Up and Down arrow keys or with the mouse wheel.

Typing Mode

While in zoom or drawing mode, press t to enter typing mode. The cursor changes to a vertical line indicating the size, position, and color of the text. Move the mouse cursor to change the position, and move the mouse wheel or press the Up and Down arrow keys to change the font size. The font face can be changed from the Type tab of the ZoomIt Options dialog box. To fix the starting location for the text, click the left mouse button or just begin typing. Typed text will appear in the current location, as shown in Figure 10-14. To exit typing mode, press Esc.

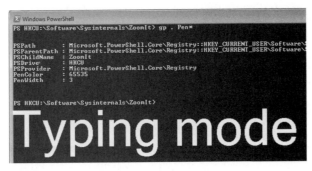

FIGURE 10-14 An example of ZoomIt's typing mode.

Break Timer

Start the Break Timer by pressing Ctrl+3. By default, the timer will count down 10 minutes. You can change the counter while the timer is running by pressing the Up and Down arrows, which adjust the minutes, or by pressing the Left and Right arrows, which increase or decrease by 10-second intervals. You can change the default timer start from the Break tab of the ZoomIt Options dialog box. The break timer font is the same as that for typing mode.

The Show Time Elapsed After Expiration option determines whether the counter stops when it reaches zero or continues to count negative time. The Advanced button lets you set advanced options, including playing a sound on timer expiration, changing the opacity and screen position of the timer, and indicating whether to show a background bitmap or the current desktop behind the timer instead of the default white background.

LiveZoom

Whereas normal zoom mode takes a snapshot of the current desktop and then lets you zoom in and out and annotate that screen shot, LiveZoom magnifies the live desktop, while applications continue to update the display in real time. LiveZoom mode is supported on Windows Vista and newer, and it works best when Aero is enabled.

Because your mouse and keyboard actions need to be able to interact with the live system rather than a snapshot, drawing and typing mode are not operational while in LiveZoom mode. And because you are likely to want to use arrow keys and the Esc key while interacting with applications, LiveZoom uses the Ctrl+Up Arrow and Ctrl+Down Arrow keys to change the zoom level, and it uses the LiveZoom hotkey to exit LiveZoom mode. Also, moving the mouse changes what portion of the zoomed screen is displayed only when the mouse is moved close to one of the edges of the display.

When in LiveZoom mode, you can quickly switch to drawing mode by pressing Ctrl+1. When you are done drawing, press Esc to return to LiveZoom mode. Again, this works best when Aero is enabled.

Chapter 11
File Utilities

This chapter describes a set of Sysinternals utilities focused on file management and manipulation. All of the utilities described in this chapter are console utilities:

- **Strings** searches files for embedded ASCII or Unicode text.

- **Streams** identifies file system objects that have alternate data streams and, optionally, deletes those streams.

- **Junction** and **FindLinks** report on and manipulate directory junctions and hard links, which are two types of NTFS links.

- **DU** reports the logical and on-disk sizes of a directory hierarchy.

- **PendMoves** and **MoveFile** report on and register file operations to take place during the next system boot.

Strings

In computer programming, the term "string" refers to a data structure consisting of a sequence of characters, usually representing human-readable text. There are numerous utilities that search files for embedded strings. However, many of them, such as Microsoft Windows' *findstr*, search only for ASCII text and ignore Unicode text, and others, like Windows' *find*, do not search binary files correctly. Sysinternals Strings does not have these limitations, which makes it useful for searching for specific files and looking inside unknown image files for strings that might reveal information about their origin and purpose.

Strings' command-line syntax is

```
strings [-a] [-b bytes] [-n length] [-o] [-q] [-s] [-u] file_or_directory
```

The ***file_or_directory*** parameter is mandatory and accepts wildcards (for example, *.dll). All matching files are searched, and by default all embedded ASCII or Unicode strings of more than three characters are written to Strings' standard output in the order in which they are found in the file. To search only for ASCII or only for Unicode strings, use the **–a** or **–u** option, respectively. The **–s** option searches directories recursively. To set a minimum string length other than the default of 3, specify it with the **–n** option. With the **–o** option, Strings also reports the offset within the file where the string begins. To search only the beginning of a file, use **–b** to limit the number of bytes that Strings will examine. Finally, the **–q** (quiet) option omits the Strings banner from the output; this is particularly useful when Strings' output will be processed by another utility, such as a sort.

The following command searches the first 850,000 bytes of explorer.exe for Unicode strings of at least 20 characters, omitting the Strings banner text. Those strings are then sorted alphabetically. Figure 11-1 shows partial results.

```
strings -b 850000 -u -n 20 -q explorer.exe | sort
```

FIGURE 11-1 Strings extracting text from explorer.exe.

Streams

Sysinternals Streams reports file system objects that have alternate data streams and, optionally, allows you to delete them. NTFS provides the ability for files and directories to have alternate data streams (ADSes). By default, a file has no ADSes and its content is stored in its main unnamed stream. But by using the syntax *filename:streamname*, you are able to read and write to alternate streams. Not all applications are designed to handle alternate streams, but you can easily demonstrate them. Open a command prompt, change to a writable directory on an NTFS volume, and then type this command:

```
echo hello > test.txt:altdata
```

You have just created a stream named *altdata* that is associated with the file *test.txt*. Note that when you look at the size of test.txt with the **DIR** command or in Explorer, the file size is reported as zero (assuming that test.txt didn't exist before you ran that command) and the file appears to be empty when opened in a text editor. (On Windows Vista and newer, **DIR /R** reports ADSes and their sizes.) To see the alternate stream content, type this command:

```
more < test.txt:altdata
```

The **type** and **more** commands do not accept stream syntax, but Cmd.exe and its redirection operators do.

The most apparent use of alternate data streams by Windows is with downloaded files. Windows' Attachment Execution Service adds a *Zone.Identifier* stream that specifies the security zone from which a file was downloaded so that Windows can continue to treat the file as from that zone. One way to remove that indicator from a file is to open its Properties dialog box in Explorer and click the Unblock button. However, that button and other user interfaces to remove security zone information are often hidden from users by Group Policy.

Sysinternals Streams examines files and directories you specify and reports the names and sizes of any alternate streams it encounters. You can search directory structures and list all the files and directories with ADSes. Optionally, you can also delete those streams—for example, to unblock downloaded content. Its command-line syntax is

```
streams [-s] [-d] file_or_directory
```

The ***file_or_directory*** parameter is mandatory and accepts wildcards. For example, the command **streams *.exe** examines all file system objects ending in ".exe" in the current directory and lists those that have ADSes with output like the following:

```
C:\Users\Abby\Downloads\msvbvm50.exe:
   :Zone.Identifier:$DATA      26
```

In this example, the file msvbvm50.exe has a 26-byte ADS called "Zone.Identifier". You can see that stream's content by running **more < msvbvm50.exe:Zone.Identifier** at a command prompt.

The **–s** option examines directories recursively, and the **–d** option deletes ADSes that it finds. For example, the command

```
streams -s -d C:\Users\Abby\Downloads
```

searches in and under Abby's Downloads folder, reporting on and deleting any ADSes it finds. Streams reports the names of alternate streams that it deletes.

Figure 11-2 shows Streams identifying the Zone.Identifier ADS on a downloaded SysinternalsSuite.zip, and then deleting that stream. Deleting the Zone.Identifier stream before extracting the utilities allows them to run without security warnings and allows the Compiled HTML (.chm) files to display help content.

FIGURE 11-2 Streams identifying and deleting alternate data streams.

NTFS Link Utilities

NTFS supports both hard links and soft links, also known as *symbolic links*. Hard links are supported only for files, while symbolic links can be used with files or directories.

A hard link allows multiple paths to refer to the same file on a single volume. For example, if you create a hard link named C:\Docs\Spec.docx that refers to the existing file C:\Users\Abby\Documents\Specifications.docx, the two paths link to the same on-disk content and you can make changes to either path. NTFS implements hard links by keeping a reference count on the file data on disk. Each time a hard link is created, NTFS adds a file name reference to the data. Because the file data is not deleted until the reference count is zero, you can delete the original file (C:\Users\Abby\Documents\Specifications.docx in our example) and continue to use other hard links (C:\Docs\Spec.docx). The file data shared by hard links includes not only the file's content and alternate stream data, but also the file's security descriptor, time stamps, and attributes such as whether the file is read-only, system, hidden, encrypted, or compressed.

By contrast, symbolic links are strings that are interpreted dynamically and can be relative or absolute paths that refer to file or directory locations on any storage device, including ones on a different local volume or even a share on a different system. This means that a symbolic link does not increase the reference count of the original file system object. Deleting the original object deletes the data and leaves the symbolic link pointing to a nonexistent object. File and directory symbolic links have their own permissions and other attributes, independent of the target file system object.

Junctions are very similar to directory symbolic links, except that they can only point to local volumes. Junctions are widely used by Windows Vista and newer for application compatibility. For example, on a default US English installation of Windows 7, the name "C:\Documents and Settings" is a junction to C:\Users. This allows many programs that have hard-coded legacy file paths to continue to work. The permissions on these application-compatibility junctions do not allow listing of the junction content, so that backup programs that are not junction-aware do not back up the same files multiple times. These junctions are also marked Hidden and System, so they do not normally appear in directory listings.

You can create hard links, symbolic links, and junctions in Windows Vista and newer with the **mklink** command built into Cmd.exe. Non-administrators can create hard links and junctions using **mklink**. Creation of file or directory symbolic links requires the Create Symbolic Links privilege, granted by default only to administrators. Note that **mklink** is not available in Windows XP or Windows Server 2003. Hard links can also be created using the **fsutil hardlink** command, and **fsutil reparsepoint** can display detailed information about or delete existing junctions and symbolic links. However, **fsutil** always requires administrative rights.

Sysinternals offers two utilities that fill in some of the gaps in link management left by Windows: Junction and FindLinks.

Junction

Junction lets you create, delete, search for, and display information about junctions. As long as you have the necessary rights in the directory where the junction is being created or deleted, Junction does not require administrative rights, and it works on all supported versions of Windows.

The syntax for creating a junction is

```
junction JunctionName JunctionTarget
```

where ***JunctionName*** is the path name of the new junction and ***JunctionTarget*** is the existing directory that the new junction points to.

The syntax for deleting a junction is

```
junction -d JunctionName
```

Note that you can also delete a junction with the **rd** command built into Cmd.exe. Deleting a junction with **rd** does not delete files or subdirectories in the target directory as long as you don't use the **/S** option.

To determine whether a directory is a junction and, if so, to display its target, use this syntax:

```
junction [-s] [-q] JunctionName
```

where ***JunctionName*** is a path specification, which can include wildcard characters. Junction reports "No reparse points found" if the name does not specify a junction. Use **–s** to recurse into subdirectories matching the specification. Use **–q** to specify not to report errors. For example, this command lists all junctions found on the C drive:

```
junction -s -q C:\
```

This command lists the junctions in the user's profile folder:

```
junction %USERPROFILE%\*
```

This command lists all junctions beginning with "My" that are found anywhere in the user's profile:

```
junction -s -q %USERPROFILE%\My*
```

In Figure 11-3, Junction lists all the application-compatibility junctions in the ProgramData folder.

FIGURE 11-3 Junction.

FindLinks

FindLinks lists other hard links pointing to a file's data. Simply run **findlinks *filename***; if the file you specify is referenced from other hard links, FindLinks will list them. For example, Windows 7 x64 has one copy of the 64-bit version of Notepad.exe, hard-linked from multiple locations. Figure 11-4 shows the output from **findlinks System32\Notepad.exe**, and then from **findlinks SysWOW64\notepad.exe**.

FIGURE 11-4 FindLinks.

As you can see, the four instances of Notepad.exe in the Windows and System32 directories and in two winsxs directories are in fact just one file. In addition, there is a 32-bit version in the SysWOW64 folder, linked to a copy in a winsxs folder. FindLinks also shows the file's index, a 64-bit identifier that NTFS assigns to each unique file and directory on the volume.

Beginning with Windows 7, you can find other hard links associated with a file using the **fsutil hardlink list *filename*** command, but again, **fsutil** always requires administrative rights.

DU (Disk Usage)

You might think that calculating the size of a directory would be as simple as enumerating its contents, recursing through subdirectories, and adding up file sizes. However, it is much more complex than that, because if you want to be accurate at all, you have to consider hard links, directory and file symbolic links, junctions, compressed and sparse files, alternate data streams, and unused cluster space.

DU reports the disk space usage for a directory hierarchy, taking those factors into account. By default, it recurses directories but does not traverse junctions or directory symbolic links, and it ignores file symbolic links. It includes the sizes of content found in alternate data streams, including ADSes associated with directory objects. Files that are referenced through multiple hard links are counted only once. Finally, DU reports both logical size and actual size on disk to account for compressed and sparse files and for unused cluster space. For example, if a directory contains just one 10-byte file, DU reports the size as 10 bytes, and "size on disk" as 4096 bytes to account for the entire cluster consumed by the file.

DU's command line syntax is

```
du [-n | -l levels | -v] [-q] directory
```

By default, DU recurses the entire target directory structure and displays summary results, including the numbers of files and directories processed, the total file sizes, and the amount of actual disk space consumed. Figure 11-5 shows the results from running **du –q "C:\Program Files"** on my computer. (The **–q** option omits the DU banner.)

FIGURE 11-5 Results of **du –q "C:\Program Files"**.

The **–n**, **–l**, and **–v** options are mutually exclusive. With the **–n** option, DU does not recurse into subdirectories and considers only the files and directories that reside in the target directory itself. With the **–v** option, DU shows the size in KB of intermediate directories as they are processed. Figure 11-6 shows partial results when I run the same DU command as shown previously, except with the **–v** option.

FIGURE 11-6 Running **du** with the **–v** option.

The **–l** option is just like the **–v** option and scans the entire directory hierarchy, but it reports the intermediate results only for the number of directory levels that you specify. Figure 11-7 shows partial results of the same DU example, but using **–l 1** instead of **–v**.

FIGURE 11-7 A **du** example showing intermediate results for one directory level.

Post-Reboot File Operation Utilities

Installation programs often find that they cannot replace, move, or delete files because those files are in use. Windows therefore provides a way for applications to register these operations to be performed by the Session Manager process (Smss.exe), the first user-mode process to start during the boot process, early in the next system boot before any applications or services start that might prevent a file from being modified. Specifically, applications running with administrative rights can invoke the *MoveFileEx* API with the MOVEFILE_DELAY_UNTIL_REBOOT flag, which appends the move or delete requests to the *PendingFileRenameOperations* and *PendingFileRenameOperations2* REG_MULTI_SZ values in the HKLM\System\CurrentControlSet\Control\Session Manager key.

PendMoves

PendMoves reads the *PendingFileRenameOperations* and *PendingFileRenameOperations2* values and lists any pending file rename or deletion operations that will take place on the next reboot. PendMoves also verifies the presence of the original file and displays an error if it is not accessible. Finally, PendMoves displays the date and time that content in the Session Manager key was last modified. This can provide a clue about when rename or delete operations were registered.

This sample PendMoves output shows a pending file deletion and two pending file moves, the source for one of which is not present:

```
Source: C:\Config.Msi\3ec7bbbf.rbf
Target: DELETE

Source: C:\Windows\system32\spool\DRIVERS\x64\3\New\mxdwdrv.dll
Target: C:\Windows\system32\spool\DRIVERS\x64\3\mxdwdrv.dll

Source: C:\Windows\system32\spool\DRIVERS\x64\3\New\XPSSVCS.DLL
   *** Source file lookup error: The system cannot find the file specified.
Target: C:\Windows\system32\spool\DRIVERS\x64\3\XPSSVCS.DLL

Time of last update to pending moves key: 8/29/2010 11:55 PM
```

MoveFile

MoveFile allows you to schedule file move, rename, or delete operations for the next reboot. Simply specify the name of the existing directory or file, followed by target name. Use two double-quotes as the target name to delete the file on reboot. You can use MoveFile to delete a directory only if it is empty. Move operations can be performed only on a single volume, and they require that the target directory already exists. Note that a rename is simply a move where the directory does not change.

MoveFile requires administrative rights. See Microsoft Knowledge Base article 948601 (*http://support.microsoft.com/kb/948601*)for information about limited cases where delayed file operations might not succeed.

The following example moves sample.txt from c:\original to c:\newdir after reboot, assuming that c:\newdir exists at that time:

```
movefile c:\original\sample.txt c:\newdir\sample.txt
```

This example both relocates and renames sample.txt:

```
movefile c:\original\sample.txt c:\newdir\renamed.txt
```

And this two-line example deletes c:\original\sample.txt and then the c:\original directory, assuming it is empty at that point.

```
movefile c:\original\sample.txt ""
movefile c:\original ""
```

Chapter 12
Disk Utilities

The utilities described in this chapter focus on disk and volume management:

- **Disk2Vhd** captures a VHD image of a physical disk.
- **Diskmon** is a real-time monitoring utility that logs sector-level hard disk activity.
- **Sync** flushes unwritten changes from disk caches to the physical disk.
- **DiskView** displays a cluster-by-cluster graphical map of a volume, letting you find what file is in particular clusters and which clusters are occupied by a given file.
- **Contig** lets you defragment specific files or see how fragmented a particular file is.
- **PageDefrag** defragments system files at boot time that cannot be defragmented while Microsoft Windows is running.
- **DiskExt** displays information about disk extents.
- **LDMDump** displays detailed information about dynamic disks from the Logical Disk Manager (LDM) database.
- **VolumeID** lets you change a volume's ID, also known as its *serial number*.

Disk2Vhd

Disk2Vhd captures an image of a physical disk as a virtual hard disk (VHD). VHD is the file format for representing a physical disk to virtual machines (VMs) running under Microsoft Hyper-V, Virtual PC, or Virtual Server. The difference between Disk2Vhd and other physical-to-virtual utilities is that Disk2Vhd can capture an image of a Windows system while it is running. Disk2Vhd uses Windows' Volume Snapshot capability, introduced in Windows XP, to create consistent point-in-time snapshots of the disks you want to include in a conversion. You can even have Disk2Vhd create the VHDs on local disks, even the ones being converted (although performance is better when the VHD is written to a disk other than the ones being converted).

Disk2Vhd runs on all supported versions of Windows and requires administrative rights.

The Disk2Vhd user interface lists the volumes present on the system, as shown in Figure 12-1, and how much space is required to convert each to a VHD. To create a VHD, simply select the volumes to capture, specify the VHD path and file name to write them to, and click Create.

FIGURE 12-1 Disk2Vhd.

Disk2Vhd creates one VHD for each disk on which selected volumes reside. It preserves the partitioning information of the disk, but copies the data contents only for volumes on the disk that are selected. This enables you to capture just system volumes and exclude data volumes, for example. To optimize VHD creation, Disk2Vhd does not copy paging or hiberna-tion files into the VHD.

To use VHDs produced by Disk2Vhd, create a virtual machine with the desired characteristics and add the VHDs to the VM's configuration as IDE disks. On first boot, a VM booting a captured copy of Windows will detect the VM's hardware and automatically install drivers, if any are present in the image. If the required drivers are not present, install them via the Virtual PC or Hyper-V integration components. You can also attach to VHDs using the Windows 7 or Windows Server 2008 R2 Disk Management or Diskpart utilities.

If you create a VHD from a Windows XP or Windows Server 2003 system and plan to boot the VHD in Virtual PC, select the Prepare For Use In Virtual PC option (shown in Figure 12-2), which ensures that the Windows Hardware Abstraction Layer (HAL) installed in the VHD is compatible with Virtual PC. This option is offered only when you run Disk2Vhd on Windows XP or Windows 2003.

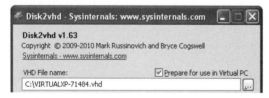

FIGURE 12-2 Disk2Vhd's Prepare For Use In Virtual PC option on Windows XP.

Disk2Vhd includes command-line options that enable you to script the creation of VHDs. The syntax is as follows:

```
disk2vhd [-h] drives vhdfile
```

The meanings of the command-line parameters are

- **–h**   When capturing Windows XP or Windows Server 2003 system volumes, **–h** fixes up the HAL in the VHD to be compatible with Virtual PC.

- *drives*   This is one or more drive letters with colons (for example, **c: d:**) indicating which volumes to convert. Or you can use "*****" to indicate all volumes.

- *vhdfile*   This is the full path to the VHD file to be created.

Here's an example:

```
disk2vhd c: e:\vhd\snapshot.vhd
```

Note that Microsoft Virtual PC supports a maximum virtual disk size of 127 GB. If you create a VHD from a larger disk, even if you include only data from a smaller volume on that disk, it will not be accessible from a Virtual PC VM.

Note also you should not attach a VHD to the same instance of Windows in which you created it if you plan to boot from that VHD. Windows assigns a unique signature to each mounted disk. If you attach the VHD to the system that includes the VHD's original source disk, Windows will assign the virtual disk a new disk signature to avoid a collision with the original. Windows references disks in the boot configuration database (BCD) by disk signature, so when the VHD is assigned a new one, Windows instances booted in a VM will fail to locate the boot disk identified in the BCD.

Note P2V Migration for Software Assurance uses the Microsoft Deployment Toolkit, Sysinternals Disk2VHD and, optionally, System Center Configuration Manager 2007 to convert a user's existing Windows XP or newer client environment to a virtual hard disk. Then it automates the delivery of an updated and personalized Windows 7 operating system containing a virtual machine with the user's previous Windows environment, applications, and Web browser. The user's previous virtual desktop retains its existing management components, domain membership, and policies. The process also publishes applications and the browser for the user to access them seamlessly within Windows 7's Start menu.

Diskmon

Diskmon is a GUI application that logs and displays all sector-level hard disk activity on a Windows system in real time. Unlike Process Monitor, which captures logical file events (including requests that are satisfied from cache or cached in memory for later writing to disk), Diskmon reports events that involve the physical disk. For every disk read and write, Diskmon identifies the disk and sector numbers, the amount of data read or written, and the duration of the operation. You can also run Diskmon as a taskbar notification area icon where it acts as a disk activity light, appearing as a green LED when there is disk read activity and as a red LED when there is disk write activity.

Diskmon requires administrative rights, and it works on all supported versions of Windows.

As you can see in Figure 12-3, Diskmon assigns a sequence number to each event and displays it in the first column. If Diskmon's internal buffers are overflowed during extremely heavy activity, this will be reflected with gaps in the sequence numbers.

FIGURE 12-3 Diskmon.

The Time column indicates the number of seconds elapsed between the start of the trace and when the request was initiated. This trace start is reset when you clear the results by pressing Ctrl+X or clicking the Clear toolbar button. You can choose to display clock time in this column instead (with or without milliseconds) from the Options menu. The Duration column indicates how long the requested read or write operation took to complete, in seconds.

Note that the Disk column reports the zero-based *disk* number, not a partition or volume number, and that a hard disk can have multiple volumes associated with it. The Length column indicates the number of sectors that were read or written. Most hard disk sectors are 512 bytes.

The menu and toolbar buttons work the same as in many other Sysinternals monitoring utilities. Press Ctrl+E to toggle data capture on and off. Choose Save or Save As from the File menu to write the displayed results to a tab-delimited text file. Toggle Autoscroll on to keep the most recently captured events displayed. Search for specific text in the results by pressing Ctrl+F, and repeat searches with F3. Limit how many events to retain and discard older events by setting the History Depth. Select one or more rows and copy their contents to the clipboard by pressing Ctrl+C, or delete them from the results by pressing Del. And change the font or keep Diskmon "always on top" via the Options menu.

To have Diskmon appear as a disk activity LED in your taskbar notification area, choose Minimize To Tray Disk Light from the Options menu, or start Diskmon with a **/l** (lowercase L) command-line parameter. The icon appears gray during disk inactivity, green during disk reads, and red during disk writes. Note that Diskmon does not capture event details for display in the main window when running in this mode. To display the full Diskmon window and resume capturing event data, double-click the Diskmon notification area icon.

Sync

Most UNIX systems come with a utility called *sync*, which is used to direct the operating system to flush all modified data in file system buffers to disk. This ensures that data in file system cache memory is not lost in case of system failure. I wrote an equivalent, also called *Sync*, that works on all versions of Windows. Sync requires Write permissions on the volume device being flushed. Write permissions are granted only to administrators in most cases. See the "Volume Permissions" sidebar in this chapter for more information.

> **Note** After writing to an NTFS-formatted removable drive, you should dismount the volume before removing the drive. Whenever possible, it is best to use the Safe Removal applet before you remove any external storage device from the system.

Sync's command-line syntax is

```
sync [-r | -e | drive_letters]
```

Without command-line options, Sync enumerates and flushes fixed drives. If you specify **–r** or **–e**, Sync enumerates and flushes removable drives in addition to fixed drives; with the **–e** option, Sync also ejects the removable drives. To flush specific drives, specify their drive letters. To flush drives C and E, for example, run **sync c e** as shown in Figure 12-4.

```
C:\>sync c e

Sync 2.2: Disk Flusher for Windows 9x/Me/NT/2K/XP
Copyright (C) 1997-2004 Mark Russinovich
Sysinternals - www.sysinternals.com

Flushing: C E

C:\>_
```

FIGURE 12-4 Sync used to flush drives C and E.

Volume Permissions

Several of the utilities in this chapter depend on the permissions on the target volume. For example, the command **sync e** requires that the caller have Write permissions on the E drive. Volume permissions are distinct from those on the volume's root directory, and these permissions can apply restrictions even on volumes with file systems such as FAT that do not support access control.

Write permissions are granted only to administrators for all volumes on Windows XP and all versions of Windows Server. Beginning with Windows Vista, interactively logged-on users are granted Write permissions for removable volumes such as flash drives.

Windows does not provide any utilities that show the permissions on volume objects. You can use AccessChk for this purpose, using the syntax **accesschk \\.\x:**, where *x* is the drive letter of the volume you want to inspect. See Chapter 8, "Security Utilities," for more information about AccessChk.

FIGURE 12-5 The effects of volume permissions.

Figure 12-5 shows Sync attempting to flush the disk caches for C and E while running as a standard user on Windows 7. Sync, which requires Write permissions, fails for C but succeeds for E. The example then shows AccessChk displaying the effective permissions for the two volumes. On C, standard users have only the Read permissions granted to Everyone, but on E interactive users (NT AUTHORITY\INTERACTIVE) are granted Read and Write permissions.

DiskView

DiskView shows you a cluster-oriented graphical map of an NTFS-formatted volume, allowing you to determine which clusters a file is located in and whether it is fragmented, or to determine what file occupies any particular sector. DiskView requires administrative privileges and works on all supported versions of Windows.

Run DiskView, select a volume from the Volume drop-down list in the lower left area of the DiskView window, and then click the Refresh button. DiskView scans the entire volume, filling in the two colored graphical regions as shown in Figure 12-6. The lower graphical area displays a horizontally-oriented, color-coded representation of the entire volume, with cluster 0 to the left. Choose Legend from the Help menu to see the meanings of the color codes. In the lower graph, blue indicates contiguous file clusters, red indicates fragmented file clusters, green indicates system file clusters, and white indicates free clusters.

FIGURE 12-6 DiskView.

The upper graph represents a portion of the volume, which you can select by clicking on the corresponding area in the lower graph or by scrolling it vertically. The portion shown in the upper graph is marked in the lower graph with black brackets. I suggest maximizing the DiskView window to see as large a portion of the volume as possible.

Note After scanning a volume, DiskView might display a File Errors dialog box listing objects that could not be accessed. Figure 12-7 shows a typical example, in which the pagefile cannot be accessed because it is in use, and the System Volume Information folder cannot be accessed because of permissions.

FIGURE 12-7 DiskView File Errors dialog box.

Each cell in the upper graph represents a volume cluster. (The default cluster size on NTFS volumes of 2 GB or more is 4096 bytes.) Clicking the Zoom up-arrow increases the cells' size, which makes it easier to distinguish individual clusters and to click on a specific cell. If you scroll to the top of the upper graph, the top row represents the first clusters on the disk, with cluster number zero represented in the upper left cell, and cluster 1 to its right. The second row represents the next set of clusters, and so on.

The default color coding in the upper graph shows the arrangement of files on the disk. A dark blue cell indicates the first of a set of clusters associated with a file, with the subsequent blue cells representing the clusters of the file that are contiguous with the first one. A red cell indicates the start of a file's second or later fragment, with the subsequent blue cells representing the other clusters in that fragment.

If you deselect Show Fragment Boundaries from the Options menu, these first-cluster markers are not displayed, and fragment cells show entirely in red. Although this is how defragmenters have historically displayed file fragmentation, it is an overly pessimistic view. Indeed, the defragmentation algorithm in Windows 7 does not attempt to coalesce fragments that are over 64 MB, because the benefits become insignificant while the costs of moving the fragment data increase.

If you click on a colored cell in the upper graph, DiskView displays the name of the file occupying that cluster in the text area at the top of the DiskView window and highlights all clusters belonging to the same file in yellow. Double-click the cell to display the Cluster Properties dialog box. In addition to showing the selected disk cluster number and the name of the file occupying that cluster, this lists the file fragments showing contiguous cluster numbers relative to the file, with file cluster 0 being the first cluster in the file, and the corresponding disk cluster numbers. In the example shown in Figure 12-8, the file occupies 568 clusters, of which the selected cluster is the 114th.

FIGURE 12-8 DiskView Cluster Properties.

To locate a particular file's clusters, click the ellipsis button to the right of the text area and select the file. The first fragment belonging to the file will be selected and visible in the upper graph. Click the Show Next button to select and move the display to view subsequent fragments. Note that very small files can be stored in the Master File Table (MFT) itself, and because DiskView does not analyze files in the MFT, if you select one of these files, DiskView will report "The specified file does not occupy any clusters."

Choose Statistics from the File menu to display the Volume Properties dialog box, shown in Figure 12-9. In this dialog box, Files shows the total number of files on the volume, including those in the MFT, while Fragments reports the number of file fragments belonging to files outside of the MFT.

FIGURE 12-9 DiskView Volume Properties.

The Export button dumps the scanned data to a text file, which you can import into a database for advanced analysis. Note that this file can be very large because it has a separate line of text for every file and for every cluster on the disk. The dump format is

- One line containing the number of files on the disk
- For each file, one space-delimited line containing the following:
- The number of clusters in the file
- The number of fragments in the file
- The file path

- One line containing the number of clusters on the disk

- For each cluster, one space-delimited line containing the following:

- The index of the file (in the preceding list) the cluster belongs to

- The index of the cluster within the file

- The type of cluster: 0=data, 1=directory, 2=metadata, 3=unused

Contig

Most disk-defragmentation solutions defragment an entire volume at a time. Contig is a console utility that lets you defragment one file or a set of files, as well as see file fragmentation levels. The ability to target a specific file can be helpful if you have one that continually becomes fragmented through frequent updates. You can also use Contig to create a new file that is guaranteed to be in one set of contiguous clusters.

Contig works on all versions of Windows. It uses the standard Windows defragmentation APIs, so it won't cause disk corruption, even if you terminate it while it is running. Contig requires Write permissions on the target volume to defragment a file; it requires only Read permissions to report the amount of fragmentation. Contig requires Write permissions in the target directory to create a new contiguous file. See the "Volume Permissions" sidebar earlier in this chapter for more information.

Note Defragmentation is not needed on solid state drives. In fact, they can reduce the usable lifetime of such drives.

To work with existing files, use Contig as follows:

```
contig [-v] [-q] [-s] [-a] filename
```

The *filename* parameter accepts wildcards. If you don't use the **–a** option and the target file is not in one contiguous block, Contig searches for a free disk block large enough to accommodate the entire file, and if it finds one, moves the file's fragments to that block. Files that are already contiguous are left alone. At the end of the defragmentation operation, Contig reports the number of files processed and the number of fragments per file before and after the defragmentation.

The **–a** option analyzes the file or files, reporting the number of fragments but not moving them. The **–v** (verbose) option displays additional detail while performing operations. The **–q** (quiet) option processes files in silent mode, displaying only the summary at the end. The **–s** option performs a recursive search of subdirectories when you specify a file name with wildcards. For example, the following command analyzes fragmentation of all .bin files in the ProgramData hierarchy:

```
contig -a -s C:\ProgramData\*.bin
```

To create a new file of a fixed size that is guaranteed to be in one contiguous block, use Contig as follows:

```
contig -n filename length
```

Figure 12-10 demonstrates the creation of a 1-GB contiguous file.

FIGURE 12-10 Contig creating a contiguous file.

PageDefrag

One of the limitations of the Windows defragmentation interface is that it is not possible to defragment files that are open for exclusive access. Thus, event logs, registry hives, and paging and hibernation files cannot be defragmented while Windows is running. PageDefrag (PageDfrg.exe) is a utility I wrote that overcomes this limitation. It shows the current amount of fragmentation for these files and enables you to schedule their defragmentation early in the Windows boot cycle.

> **Note** PageDefrag works only on the x86 editions of Windows XP and Server 2003, and it requires administrative rights.

When you run PageDefrag (shown in Figure 12-11), it presents a list of system files that cannot be defragmented while Windows is running and indicates how many clusters they occupy and in how many fragments. You can then choose to defragment these files the next time the system boots or every time the system boots by selecting the appropriate radio button and clicking OK. You can also configure a timeout period before the defragmentation begins, during which you can press any key to skip the defrag operations.

FIGURE 12-11 Configuring PageDefrag.

If you choose to defragment, PageDefrag registers a native executable to be launched by the Windows Session Manager process as a BootExecute program immediately after Autochk. The defragmentation status output appears on the Windows bootup screen as shown in Figure 12-12.

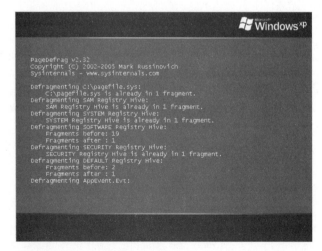

FIGURE 12-12 PageDefrag running.

You can also script PageDefrag with the following command-line syntax:

```
pagedfrg { -e | -o | -n }
```

where **–e** schedules defrag on every boot, **–o** schedules a one-time defrag on the next boot, and **–n** (never) cancels any scheduled defrags.

DiskExt

DiskExt is a console utility that displays information about what disks the partitions of a volume are located on and the physical locations of the partitions on a disk. (Volumes can span multiple disks.) Run DiskExt without parameters to enumerate and report on all volumes. Name one or more volumes on the DiskExt command line to report only on those volumes—for example:

```
diskext c e
```

Figure 12-13 shows the output from DiskExt (without parameters) on one of my laptops.

FIGURE 12-13 DiskExt.

Per MSDN, "A disk extent is a contiguous range of logical blocks exposed by the disk. For example, a disk extent can represent an entire volume, one portion of a spanned volume, one member of a striped volume, or one plex of a mirrored volume." Each extent begins at an offset measured in bytes from the beginning of the disk, and has a length, also measured in bytes.

DiskExt works on all supported versions of Windows and does not require administrative rights.

LDMDump

LDMDump is a console utility that displays detailed information about the contents of the Logical Disk Manager (LDM) database. Windows has the concept of *basic* and *dynamic* disks. Dynamic disks implement a more flexible partitioning scheme than that of basic disks. The dynamic scheme supports the creation of multipartition volumes that provide performance, sizing, and reliability features not supported by simple volumes. Multipartition volumes include mirrored volumes, striped arrays (RAID-0), and RAID-5 arrays. Dynamic disks are partitioned using LDM partitioning. The LDM maintains one unified database that stores partitioning information for all the dynamic disks on a system and that resides in a 1-MB reserved space at the end of each dynamic disk.

> **Note** See *Windows Internals: Including Windows Server 2008 and Windows Vista, 5th Edition* (Microsoft Press, 2009) for more information on volume management and the LDM database.

LDMDump takes a zero-based disk number with the **/d#** command-line switch like this:

```
ldmdump /d0
```

Note that there is no space between the **/d** and the disk number.

The following example shows excerpts of LDMDump output. The LDM database header displays first, followed by the LDM database records that describe a 12-GB volume with three 4-GB dynamic disks. The volume's database entry is listed as Volume1 (E:). At the end of the output, LDMDump lists the partitions and definitions of volumes stored in the database.

```
PRIVATE HEAD:
Signature          : PRIVHEAD
Version            : 2.12
Disk Id            : b5f4a801-758d-11dd-b7f0-000c297f0108
Host Id            : 1b77da20-c717-11d0-a5be-00a0c91db73c
Disk Group Id      : b5f4a7fd-758d-11dd-b7f0-000c297f0108
Disk Group Name    : WIN-SL5V78KD01W-Dg0
Logical disk start : 3F
Logical disk size  : 7FF7C1 (4094 MB)
Configuration start: 7FF800
Configuration size : 800 (1 MB)
Number of TOCs     : 2
TOC size           : 7FD (1022 KB)
Number of Configs  : 1
Config size        : 5C9 (740 KB)
Number of Logs     : 1
Log size           : E0 (112 KB)

TOC 1:
Signature          : TOCBLOCK
Sequence           : 0x1
Config bitmap start: 0x11
Config bitmap size : 0x5C9
Log bitmap start   : 0x5DA
Log bitmap size    : 0xE0
...
VBLK DATABASE:
0x000004: [000001] <DiskGroup>
          Name         : WIN-SL5V78KD01W-Dg0
          Object Id    : 0x0001
```

```
         GUID       : b5f4a7fd-758d-11dd-b7f0-000c297f010
0x000006: [000003] <Disk>
         Name       : Disk1
         Object Id  : 0x0002
         Disk Id    : b5f4a7fe-758d-11dd-b7f0-000c297f010


0x000007: [000005] <Disk>
         Name       : Disk2
         Object Id  : 0x0003
         Disk Id    : b5f4a801-758d-11dd-b7f0-000c297f010


0x000008: [000007] <Disk>
         Name       : Disk3
         Object Id  : 0x0004
         Disk Id    : b5f4a804-758d-11dd-b7f0-000c297f010


0x000009: [000009] <Component>
         Name       : Volume1-01
         Object Id  : 0x0006
         Parent Id  : 0x0005


0x00000A: [00000A] <Partition>
         Name       : Disk1-01
         Object Id  : 0x0007
         Parent Id  : 0x3157
         Disk Id    : 0x0000
         Start      : 0x7C100
         Size       : 0x0 (0 MB)
         Volume Off : 0x3 (0 MB)


0x00000B: [00000B] <Partition>
         Name       : Disk2-01
         Object Id  : 0x0008
         Parent Id  : 0x3157
         Disk Id    : 0x0000
         Start      : 0x7C100
         Size       : 0x0 (0 MB)
         Volume Off : 0x7FE80003 (1047808 MB)


0x00000C: [00000C] <Partition>
         Name       : Disk3-01
         Object Id  : 0x0009
         Parent Id  : 0x3157
         Disk Id    : 0x0000
         Start      : 0x7C100
         Size       : 0x0 (0 MB)
         Volume Off : 0xFFD00003 (2095616 MB)


0x00000D: [00000F] <Volume>
         Name       : Volume1
         Object Id  : 0x0005
         Volume state: ACTIVE
         Size       : 0x017FB800 (12279 MB)
         GUID       : b5f4a806-758d-11dd-b7f0-c297f0108
         Drive Hint : E:
```

VolumeID

While Windows provides numerous interfaces to change the label of a disk volume, it does not provide any means for changing the volume ID, which is the 8 hex digit value reported as the Volume Serial Number in directory listings:

```
C:\>dir
 Volume in drive C has no label.
 Volume Serial Number is 48A6-8C4B
[...]
```

VolumeID is a console utility that lets you change the ID number on FAT or NTFS drives, including flash drives. VolumeID works on all versions of Windows and uses the following syntax:

volumeid *d*: *xxxx-xxxx*

where *d* is the drive letter and *xxxx-xxxx* is the new 8 hex digit ID value. Figure 12-14 shows VolumeID changing the ID on drive E to DAD5-1337.

FIGURE 12-14 VolumeID.

Changes on FAT drives take effect immediately, but changes on NTFS drives require remounting the drive or rebooting. Note that VolumeID does not work on exFAT volumes.

VolumeID requires Write permissions on the target volume, which in many cases is granted only to administrators. See the "Volume Permissions" sidebar in this chapter for more information.

Chapter 13

Network and Communication Utilities

The utilities described in this chapter focus on network and device connectivity. TCPView is like a GUI version of the Windows Netstat utility, showing TCP and UDP endpoints on your system. Whois is a command-line utility for looking up Internet domain registration information or for performing reverse DNS lookups from IP addresses. And Portmon is a utility for monitoring serial and parallel port I/O in real time. This chapter does not cover Process Explorer or Process Monitor, although both include network monitoring functionality. They are covered in chapters 3 and 4, respectively.

TCPView

TCPView, shown in Figure 13-1, is a GUI program that shows up-to-date and detailed listings of all TCP and UDP endpoints on your system, including IPv4 and IPv6 endpoints. For each endpoint, it shows the owning process name and process ID (PID), the local and remote addresses and ports, and the states of TCP connections. When run with administrative rights, it also shows the numbers of packets sent and received via those endpoints. Click on any column header to sort the view by that column.

FIGURE 13-1 TCPView.

By default, TCPView automatically refreshes once per second. You can set the update speed to two or five seconds via the View menu or turn off automatic refreshing altogether. Press the space bar to toggle between automatic and manual refresh mode, and press F5 to refresh the view. New endpoints since the previous update are highlighted in green, and endpoints that have been removed since the previous update are highlighted in red. Endpoints that have changed state are highlighted in yellow.

TCPView's Resolve Addresses option is on by default, which has TCPView resolve the domain names of IP addresses and the service names of port numbers. For example, 445 is shown as "microsoft-ds" and 443 as "https". Turn the option off to display only IP addresses and port numbers. You can toggle Resolve Addresses by pressing Ctrl+R or clicking the "A" toolbar button. Toggling this option does not refresh the data.

TCPView shows all endpoints by default. To show only connected endpoints, deselect Show Unconnected Endpoints on the Options menu or click the corresponding toolbar button. Note that toggling this option refreshes the data.

If the remote address is a fully-qualified domain name, you can try to perform a "whois" lookup of the domain's registration information by right-clicking the connection and choosing Whois from the context menu. If its lookup is successful, TCPView displays the information in a dialog box as shown in Figure 13-2.

FIGURE 13-2 Results from TCPView's Whois lookup.

You can close an established TCP connection by right-clicking it and choosing Close Connection from the context menu. This option is available only for IPv4 TCP connections, not IPv6. You can also view additional information about a process by double-clicking on it or choosing Process Properties from its context menu, or you can terminate the process by choosing End Process from that menu.

Choose Save or Save As from the File menu to save the displayed data to a tab-delimited ASCII text file. You can also copy data from one or more rows to the Windows clipboard by selecting those rows and pressing Ctrl+C.

Whois

Unix installations typically include a *whois* command-line utility to look up domain registration information and to perform reverse DNS lookups of IP addresses. Because Windows doesn't include one, I created a Whois utility. The syntax is simple:

```
whois domainname [whois-server]
```

The **domainname** parameter can be either a DNS name such as sysinternals.com or an IPv4 address. You can optionally specify the particular whois lookup server to query. Otherwise, Whois starts by querying *tld*.whois-servers.net (for example, com.whois-servers.net for .com domains and uk.whois-servers.net for .uk domains) on the standard whois port (TCP 43) and following referrals to other whois servers. Whois lists all the servers queried before outputting the returned registration data.

Portmon

Portmon logs all serial and parallel port input/output control (IOCTL) commands and displays them in real-time along with interesting information regarding their associated parameters. For read and write requests, Portmon displays a portion of the data that was read or written. By default, this data is shown as ASCII characters, using "." to represent nonprintable characters, but you can choose to display the data in hexadecimal format instead.

Portmon works on all x86 versions of Windows and requires administrative rights.

> **Note** Portmon displays only "Error 2" if you run it on a 64-bit version of Windows.

Portmon works like many of the other Sysinternals real-time monitors. Start Portmon and it immediately begins capturing commands and data sent to all serial (COM*n*) and parallel (LPT*n*) ports defined on the system, as shown in Figure 13-3.

FIGURE 13-3 Portmon.

You can toggle data capture on and off by pressing Ctrl+E or clicking the Capture icon in the toolbar, and you can enable Autoscroll to scroll new events into the display as they arrive. Each event appears in the Portmon window as a separate row with resizable columns. If data in a particular column is wider than that column can accommodate, hover the cursor over the displayed text and Portmon will display the full column text in a tooltip.

The first column is a Portmon-assigned event counter that gets reset to zero when you clear the display. Gaps in this sequence can occur if the amount of incoming data exceeds Portmon's ability to keep up, or if filters (described later) exclude events from the display. The Time column shows how long the request took to complete. You can have this column display the time of day of the event instead by selecting Clock Time on the Options menu. Note that this change affects the display only for subsequently captured data. You can also hide the Time column by deselecting Show Time Column on the Options menu.

The Process column identifies the name of the process that made the request.

The Request column shows the symbolic name of the control code sent to the port. The names are mostly self-explanatory (assuming you know something about port communications). IOCTL stands for *input/output control*, and IRP stands for input/output request packet, with MJ used to define major functions. IOCTLs are for configuring the device's behavior, while IRPs typically request or contain data.

The Port column identifies the name of the port to which the request was sent. By default, Portmon monitors all serial ports listed in HKLM\Hardware\DeviceMap\SerialComm and all parallel ports listed in HKLM\Hardware\DeviceMap\Parallel Ports. You can selectively disable the monitoring of specific ports via the Ports submenu of the Capture menu, as shown in Figure 13-4. Portmon remembers your selections and reapplies them the next time it runs.

FIGURE 13-4 Portmon port selection.

The Result column shows the result of the request.

Finally, the Other column shows additional relevant data about the request. For example, for a "set baud rate" IOCTL, Portmon shows the requested baud rate in the Other column. For read and write operations, Portmon displays the data length and then at least some of the data. By default, Portmon displays up to 64 bytes of data in ASCII form, using "." to represent nonprintable characters. You can change the amount of data that is shown by choosing Max Output Bytes from the Options menu and setting a different number in the Max Bytes dialog box. You can also choose to show the data in hexadecimal form instead of ASCII by selecting Show Hex from the Options menu. Both of these options take effect on subsequently captured data. Portmon doesn't change the display of data that has already been captured.

Portmon monitors system memory usage and suspends its data capture if it detects that memory is running low, resuming capture only when the low-memory condition has eased. One way to limit Portmon's own memory consumption is to set the History Depth to a non-zero value. This setting, on the Options menu, limits the number of events Portmon displays, discarding older events.

You can increase the display space for output by selecting Hide Toolbar on the Options menu. You can also increase the number of visible rows by selecting a smaller font size. Choose Font from the Options menu to change the font.

Unlike most Sysinternals utilities, which store their settings under HKCU\Software\ Sysinternals, Portmon's settings are stored in HKCU\Software\Systems Internals\Portmon, except the *EulaAccepted* flag, which is in HKCU\Software\Sysinternals\Portmon.

Searching, Filtering, and Highlighting

If you want to search for a line containing text of interest, press Ctrl+F to display the Find dialog box. If the text you specify matches text in the output window, Portmon selects the next matching line and turns off the Autoscroll feature to keep the line in the window. Press F3 to repeat a successful search.

Another way to isolate output that you are interested in is to use Portmon's filtering capability. Click the Filter button in the Portmon toolbar to display the Filter dialog box, shown in Figure 13-5. Filter and Highlight rules are automatically saved on exit and can be reapplied the next time you run Portmon.

FIGURE 13-5 Portmon filter dialog box.

Enter expressions in the Include field to identify column content that you want Portmon to display, in the Exclude field to specify content that should cause a line not to be displayed, or in the Highlight field to identify content that should be emphasized with color coding. You can enter multiple expressions, separating each with a semicolon. Do not include spaces in the filter expression unless you want the spaces to be part of the filter. Note that the "*" character is interpreted as a wildcard, and that filters are interpreted in a case-insensitive manner. The default rules include everything ("*") and exclude nothing.

An expression must completely match a column value for the rule to apply. For example, if you want to match lines that contain the word "baud" in the middle of other text (such as IOCTL_SERIAL_GET_BAUD_RATE), you need to use "*****" to account for the text before and after the word "baud". Use ***baud*** as your filter expression.

As an example, say you want Portmon to display all events except those that have a field ending with "_WRITE" and to highlight events that include the word "baud". You would apply this filter:

```
Include:     *

Exclude:     *_write

Highlight:    *baud*
```

Filtering is applied only to new events as they are captured. New text lines that match the rules that are in effect are displayed; those that don't are dropped and cannot be "unhidden" by changing the filter rules after the fact. Also, changing the filter rules does not remove lines that are already displayed by Portmon.

Highlighting is applied when you set the highlighting rules. The default colors for highlighted rows are white text on a red background. You can change these colors by choosing Highlight Colors from the Filter menu.

If any Include or Exclude filter rules are in effect when you exit Portmon, Portmon will display them in a dialog box the next time you start it. Simply click OK to continue using those rules, or change them first. You can edit them in place, or click Reset to remove the filter.

Saving, Logging, and Printing

You can select one or more rows from the Portmon list and copy them as tab-delimited text to the Windows clipboard by pressing Ctrl+C. Note that the Time column is always included even if the Show Time Column option is deselected, while the sequence number column is not included. Portmon supports standard Windows methods of selecting multiple rows such as holding down Shift while pressing the Up or Down arrow keys to select consecutive rows, or holding down Ctrl while clicking nonconsecutive rows.

You can save the data captured by Portmon as a text file by choosing Save or Save As from the File menu. Portmon uses the .LOG extension by default. The file format is tab-delimited ASCII text and always includes the sequence number and Time columns.

To have Portmon log output to a file as it displays it, choose Log To File from the File menu. The first time you choose that menu item or click the Log To File button on the toolbar, Portmon displays the Log-To-File Settings dialog box shown in Figure 13-6, prompting you for a file location. From that point forward, the Log To File menu option and toolbar button toggle logging to that file on or off. To log to a different file or to change other log file settings, choose Log To File As from the File menu. (If log-to-file is currently enabled, choosing Log To File As has the same effect as toggling Log To File off.) The Settings dialog box also lets you configure a maximum size beyond which the log file will not grow, and whether to overwrite or append to an existing log file. After the log file grows beyond the max log size, Portmon disables logging to the file but continues to display new events as they come in. A max log size of 0 indicates no limit.

FIGURE 13-6 The Portmon Log-To-File Settings dialog box.

When logging to a file, Portmon writes two lines of output with the same sequence number for each event. The first line of each pair includes the process, request, port, and other information supplied by the process with the request. The second line includes the event duration (if the Clock Time option is not selected) and the result. Note that related lines may not be adjacent if an operation completes asynchronously and also that columns are separated by two spaces, not by tabs. Here is an example of data written to a Portmon log file:

```
0  0.00000000  spoolsv.exe  IRP_MJ_CREATE  Serial1  Options: OpenIf Sequential
0  0.00065288  SUCCESS
1  0.00000000  spoolsv.exe  IRP_MJ_SET_INFORMATION  Serial1  -1699359072
1  0.00000587  SUCCESS
2  0.00000000  spoolsv.exe  IRP_MJ_SET_INFORMATION  Serial1  -1699359044
2  0.00000223  SUCCESS
3  0.00000000  spoolsv.exe  IOCTL_SERIAL_GET_BAUD_RATE  Serial1
3  0.00000615  SUCCESS
4  0.00000000  spoolsv.exe  IOCTL_SERIAL_GET_LINE_CONTROL  Serial1
4  0.00000279  SUCCESS
```

Choose Print or Print Range from the File menu to print the captured data to a printer. Choose Print Range if you want to print only a subset of the sequence numbers displayed, or choose Print if you want to print all the output records. Note that capture must be disabled prior to printing.

The Print Range dialog box (shown in Figure 13-7) also lets you specify whether or not data from the sequence number and Time columns will be included in the output. Omitting these fields can save page space if they are not necessary. The settings you choose are used in all subsequent print operations.

FIGURE 13-7 The Portmon Print Range dialog box.

To prevent wrap-around when output lines are wider than a page, consider using landscape mode instead of portrait when printing.

Chapter 14

System Information Utilities

The utilities in this chapter show system information that doesn't fit into the categories of the earlier chapters in this book:

- **RAMMap** provides in-depth detail about the allocation of physical memory from several different perspectives.

- **CoreInfo** shows the mapping between logical processors and the physical processor, the NUMA node, and the socket on which they reside, the caches assigned to each logical processor, and internode access costs on NUMA systems.

- **ProcFeatures** reports whether the processor and Microsoft Windows support various features such as No-Execute memory pages.

- **WinObj** lets you navigate Windows' Object Manager namespace and view information about objects it contains.

- **LoadOrder** shows the approximate order in which Windows loads device drivers and starts services.

- **PipeList** lists the named pipes on the local computer.

- **ClockRes** displays the current resolution of the system clock.

RAMMap

RAMMap is an advanced physical memory usage analysis utility that shows how Windows allocates physical memory, also known as random access memory or RAM. RAMMap presents RAM usage information from different perspectives, including by usage type, page list, process, file, priority, and physical address. You can also use RAMMap to purge portions of RAM to test memory-management scenarios from a consistent start point. Finally, RAMMap provides support for saving and loading memory snapshots. RAMMap runs on Windows Vista and newer and requires administrative rights.

All user-mode processes, and most kernel-mode software, access code and data through virtual memory addresses. That code and data might be in physical memory or in a backing file on disk, but it must be mapped into the process' working set[1]—the physical memory that the memory manager assigns to the process—when the process actually reads, writes, or executes it. VMMap, described in Chapter 7, "Process and Diagnostic Utilities," shows memory from the perspective of one process' virtual address space: how much is consumed by

---

[1] This is usually but not always true: Address Windowing Extension (AWE) and large page memory is not part of the working set even while it is being accessed.

executables and other mapped files; how much is consumed by stacks, heaps, and other data regions; how much of its virtual memory is mapped in the process' working set; and how much is unused. RAMMap focuses on RAM as a systemwide resource shared by all processes. Process virtual memory that is not committed and paged in is not shown in RAMMap. Figure 14-1 shows RAMMap with the Use Counts tab selected.

RamMap - Sysinternals: www.sysinternals.com

File   Empty   Help

Use Counts | Processes | Priority Summary | Physical Pages | Physical Ranges | File Summary | File Details

Usage	Total	Active	Standby	Modi...	M...	Trans...	Zeroed	Free	Bad
Process Private	246,072 K	192,256 K	392 K	53,424 K					
Mapped File	357,292 K	74,392 K	282,900 K						
Shared Memory	24,136 K	17,328 K		6,808 K					
Page Table	11,052 K	11,044 K		8 K					
Paged Pool	79,164 K	43,252 K		35,912 K					
Nonpaged Pool	101,048 K	101,040 K					8 K		
System PTE	21,756 K	15,588 K	632 K	5,536 K					
Session Private	41,900 K	36,592 K		5,308 K					
Metafile	27,324 K	13,892 K	13,212 K		220 K				
AWE									
Driver Locked	612 K	612 K							
Kernel Stack	11,776 K	11,016 K		760 K					
Unused	1,174,564 K							906,268 K	268,296 K
Total	2,096,696 K	517,012 K	297,136 K	107,756 K	220 K		8 K	906,268 K	268,296 K

FIGURE 14-1 RAMMap's Use Counts tab.

RAMMap's seven tabs analyze RAM along different dimensions, including by allocation type and page list, by per-process usage, by priority, by mapped file, and more. Several of the tabs can contain a great deal of information. You can quickly find the next row containing specific text, such as a file or process name, by pressing Ctrl+F to open the Find dialog box, and you can repeat the previous search by pressing F3. You can refresh the data at any time by pressing F5.

For more information about the concepts described here, see the "Memory Management" and "Cache Manager" chapters of *Windows Internals: Including Windows Server 2008 and Windows Vista* (Microsoft Press, 2009).

Use Counts

The table and graphs in RAMMap's Use Counts tab, shown in Figure 14-1, display RAM usage by allocation type and by page list. The table columns and the summary graph above the table indicate how much RAM is in each of the memory manager's page lists. The table rows and the summary graph to the left of the table indicate RAM assignment by allocation type. The colored blocks in the row and column headers serve as keys to their respective graphs. You can reorder columns by dragging a header to a new position, and you can sort the table by a column's data by clicking the column's header. Clicking a column header multiple times toggles the items between ascending and descending order.

The page lists shown on the Use Counts tab are

- **Active**   Memory that is immediately available for use without incurring a fault. This includes memory that is in the working set of one or more processes or one of the system working sets (such as the system cache working set), as well as nonpageable memory such as nonpaged pool and Address Windowing Extension (AWE) allocations.

- **Standby**   Cached memory that has been removed from a working set but that can be soft-faulted back into active memory. It can be repurposed without incurring a disk I/O.

- **Modified**   Memory that has been removed from a working set and that was modified while in use but has not yet been written to disk. It can be soft-faulted back into the working set from which it had been removed, but it must otherwise be written to disk before it can be reused.

- **Modified no write**   The same as Modified, except that the page has been marked at the request of file system drivers not to be automatically written to disk—for example, with NTFS transaction logging.

- **Transition**   A temporary state for a page that has been locked into memory by a driver to perform an I/O to or from it.

- **Zeroed**   Memory that has been initialized to all zeros and that is available for allocation.

- **Free**   Memory that is not in use and has not been initialized to zeros. Free memory is available for kernel allocation or for user-mode allocation if initialized from a disk read. If necessary, the memory manager can zero pages from the free list before giving them to a user process. The zero page thread, which runs at lower priority than all other threads, fills free pages with zeros and moves them to the Zeroed list, which is why there are typically very few pages on this list.

- **Bad**   Memory that has generated parity or other hardware errors and cannot be used. The Bad list is also used by Windows for pages transitioning from one state to another or are on internal look-aside lists.

The memory allocation types shown in the table's rows are

- **Process Private**   Memory that can be used only by a single process.

- **Mapped File**   Shareable memory that represents a file on disk. Executable images and resource DLLs are examples of mapped files.

- **Shared Memory**   Memory that can be shared by multiple processes and that can be paged out to a paging file.

- **Page Table**   Kernel-mode memory that describes processes' virtual address spaces.

- **Paged Pool**   Kernel-allocated memory that can be paged out to disk.

- **Nonpaged Pool**   Kernel-allocated memory that must always remain in physical memory. Nonpaged pool is always represented only in the Active column.

- **System PTE**   Memory used by system page table entries (PTEs), which are used to dynamically map system pages such as I/O space, kernel stacks, and the mapping for memory descriptor lists.

- **Session Private**   Memory allocated by Win32k.sys or session drivers (for example, video, keyboard, or mouse) for use by a single terminal services session.

- **Metafile**   Memory used to represent file system metadata, including directories, paging files, and NTFS metadata files such as the MFT.

- **AWE**   Memory used by Address Windowing Extensions. AWE is a set of functions that programs can use to control the data kept in RAM.

- **Driver Locked**   Memory allocated by a driver, charged to system commit and always in active pages. Microsoft Hyper-V and Virtual PC make use of driver locked memory to provide RAM to virtual machines.

- **Kernel Stack**   Memory assigned to kernel thread stacks.

- **Unused**   Memory that is not in use. Unused memory is always in the Zeroed, Free, or Bad page lists.

Processes

The Processes tab (shown in Figure 14-2) shows the breakdown of physical memory pages that can be associated with a single process. These include each process' private user-mode allocations as well as the kernel memory containing the process' page tables. The Private, Standby, and Modified columns show the amount of process private RAM on the Active, Standby, and Modified page lists, respectively. The Page Table column shows the sum of page table kernel-mode allocation for the process on any of the page lists.

FIGURE 14-2 RAMMap's Processes tab.

Priority Summary

The Priority Summary tab (shown in Figure 14-3) lists the amount of RAM currently on each of the prioritized standby lists. The Repurposed column shows the amount of RAM that has been removed from each standby list to satisfy new allocation requests since system start, rather than being soft-faulted back into a working set. High repurpose counts for priorities 5 and higher are a possible sign that the system is or was under memory pressure and might benefit from having more RAM added.

FIGURE 14-3 RAMMap's Priority Summary tab.

Physical Pages

The Physical Pages tab breaks down memory to the individual page level. The columns in the Physical Pages tab are

- **Physical Address**   The page's physical address.
- **List**   The page list to which the page is assigned.
- **Use**   The allocation type, such as Process Private, Kernel Stack, or Unused.
- **Priority**   The memory priority currently associated with the page.
- **Image**   Marked "Yes" if the page contains all or part of a mapped image file.
- **Offset**   Identifies the offset within a page table or a mapped file that the page represents.
- **File Name**   Identifies the name of the mapped file backing the physical page.

- **Process**   Identifies the owning process if the memory is directly attributable to a single process.

- **Virtual Address**   For Process Private allocations, shows the corresponding virtual address in the process' address space. For kernel-mode allocations such as System PTE, it shows the corresponding virtual address in the system space.

- **Pool Tag**   For paged and nonpaged pool, shows the tag (if any) associated with the memory. The tag is shown only for pages that are entirely within a single allocation.

The two drop-down lists at the bottom of the Physical Pages tab allow you to filter which physical pages to display in the table. Select the column on which to filter in the first drop-down list and the value to show in the second. Note that you can simplify further analysis by clicking a column header to sort the filtered results. For example, to show only the pages that are at priority 7, select Priority in the first drop-down list and 7 from the second. Click on the Use column to make it easier to see what kinds of allocations are assigned priority 7, as demonstrated in Figure 14-4.

FIGURE 14-4 RAMMap's Physical Pages tab.

Physical Ranges

The Physical Ranges tab (shown in Figure 14-5) lists the valid ranges of physical memory addresses. Discontinuities in the sequences typically indicate physical addresses assigned to device memory.

FIGURE 14-5 RAMMap's Physical Ranges tab.

File Summary

The File Summary tab (shown in Figure 14-6) lists the path of every mapped file that has data in RAM. For each file, it shows the total amount of RAM the file occupies, and then how much of that amount is Active (in one or more working sets) and how much is on the Standby, Modified, and Modified No-Write page lists. As with other RAMMap tables, the columns can be sorted or reordered by clicking or dragging the column headers.

Windows can map files into memory for several reasons, including the following:

- Executables and DLLs are mapped by the loader when they are loaded for execution.
- An application can map a file explicitly using the *MapViewOfFile* API.
- The cache manager can map a file when an application performs cached I/O on it.
- The Superfetch service can prefetch executables and other files into the standby list.

FIGURE 14-6 RAMMap's File Summary tab.

File Details

Like the File Summary tab, the File Details tab (shown in Figure 14-7) lists the path of every mapped file that has data in RAM and the total amount of RAM each file occupies. Clicking the "plus" icon next to a file expands the entry to list every physical page the file occupies on a separate row. For each page, RAMMap shows the page's physical address, to what list the page is assigned, the allocation type (which is always Mapped File), the memory priority, whether it is loaded as an executable image, and the offset within the mapped file that the page represents.

FIGURE 14-7 RAMMap's File Details tab.

Purging Physical Memory

RAMMap gives you the ability to purge working sets and paging lists. This can be useful for measuring the memory usage of applications after they have started or when specific application features are exercised. For example, you can compare the physical memory impact of different features by emptying all working sets prior to exercising each feature and then capturing a new snapshot after exercising each one.

Choose one of the selections described in the following list from the Empty menu and RAMMap will immediately purge that portion of memory. Note that RAMMap does not automatically refresh its data, so you can purge multiple areas of memory before pressing F5 to update RAMMap's data.

- **Empty Working Sets**   Removes memory from all user-mode and system working sets to the Standby or Modified page lists. Note that by the time you refresh RAMMap's data, processes that run any code will necessarily populate their working sets to do so.

- **Empty System Working Set**   Removes memory from the system cache working set.

- **Empty Modified Page List**   Flushes memory from the Modified page list, writing unsaved data to disk and moving the pages to the Standby list.

- **Empty Standby List**   Discards pages from all Standby lists, and moves them to the Free list.

- **Empty Priority 0 Standby List**   Flushes pages from the lowest-priority Standby list to the Free list.

Saving and Loading Snapshots

You can save all the details of a RAMMap snapshot to a file for viewing at a later time and on a different computer by choosing Save from the File menu. By default, RAMMap uses the .RMP extension to signify a RAMMap file, but does not create an actual file association. The RAMMap snapshot file format is XML but with encoded portions. To view a saved snapshot, choose Open from the File menu and select the saved snapshot.

CoreInfo

CoreInfo is a command-line utility that shows you the mapping between logical processors and the physical processor, NUMA node, processor group (on Windows 7 and newer), and socket on which they reside, as well as the caches assigned to each logical processor. It uses the Windows *GetLogicalProcessorInformation* or *GetLogicalProcessorInformationEx* functions, depending on the operating system version, to obtain this information and prints it to the screen, representing a mapping to a logical processor with an asterisk. In addition to dumping NUMA topology information, CoreInfo measures and displays the internode access costs on NUMA systems. CoreInfo is useful for gaining insight into the processor and cache topology of your system.

CoreInfo runs on Windows XP Service Pack 3 and newer, and Windows Server 2003 and newer, including IA-64 systems. It does not require administrative rights.

Without command-line options, CoreInfo outputs all the information it gathers. To limit CoreInfo's output to only portions of that information, specify one or more of the following options on the CoreInfo command line:

- **−c** Dump information on cores.
- **−g** Dump information on groups.
- **−l** Dump information on caches.
- **−n** Dump information on NUMA nodes.
- **−s** Dump information on sockets.
- **−m** Dump the NUMA access cost.

The following output is from a two-socket, quad-core AMD Opteron system. Note how each socket corresponds to a NUMA node, and each CPU has its own L1 instruction and data cache, an L2 unified cache, and a shared L3 unified cache:

```
Coreinfo v2.11 - Dump information on system CPU and memory topology
Copyright (C) 2008-2010 Mark Russinovich
Sysinternals - www.sysinternals.com

Logical to Physical Processor Map:
*-------  Physical Processor 0
-*------  Physical Processor 1
--*-----  Physical Processor 2
---*----  Physical Processor 3
----*---  Physical Processor 4
-----*--  Physical Processor 5
------*-  Physical Processor 6
-------*  Physical Processor 7

Logical Processor to Socket Map:
****----  Socket 0
----****  Socket 1

Logical Processor to NUMA Node Map:
****----  NUMA Node 0
----****  NUMA Node 1

Approximate Cross-NUMA Node Access Cost (relative to fastest):
     00  01
00: 1.0 1.4
01: 1.5 1.2
```

```
Logical Processor to Cache Map:
*-------    Data Cache          0, Level 1,     64 KB, Assoc    2, LineSize  64
*-------    Instruction Cache   0, Level 1,     64 KB, Assoc    2, LineSize  64
*-------    Unified Cache       0, Level 2,    512 KB, Assoc   16, LineSize  64
-*------    Data Cache          1, Level 1,     64 KB, Assoc    2, LineSize  64
-*------    Instruction Cache   1, Level 1,     64 KB, Assoc    2, LineSize  64
-*------    Unified Cache       1, Level 2,    512 KB, Assoc   16, LineSize  64
--*-----    Data Cache          2, Level 1,     64 KB, Assoc    2, LineSize  64
--*-----    Instruction Cache   2, Level 1,     64 KB, Assoc    2, LineSize  64
--*-----    Unified Cache       2, Level 2,    512 KB, Assoc   16, LineSize  64
---*----    Data Cache          3, Level 1,     64 KB, Assoc    2, LineSize  64
---*----    Instruction Cache   3, Level 1,     64 KB, Assoc    2, LineSize  64
---*----    Unified Cache       3, Level 2,    512 KB, Assoc   16, LineSize  64
****----    Unified Cache       4, Level 3,      2 MB, Assoc    1, LineSize  64
----*---    Data Cache          4, Level 1,     64 KB, Assoc    2, LineSize  64
----*---    Instruction Cache   4, Level 1,     64 KB, Assoc    2, LineSize  64
----*---    Unified Cache       5, Level 2,    512 KB, Assoc   16, LineSize  64
-----*--    Data Cache          5, Level 1,     64 KB, Assoc    2, LineSize  64
-----*--    Instruction Cache   5, Level 1,     64 KB, Assoc    2, LineSize  64
-----*--    Unified Cache       6, Level 2,    512 KB, Assoc   16, LineSize  64
------*-    Data Cache          6, Level 1,     64 KB, Assoc    2, LineSize  64
------*-    Instruction Cache   6, Level 1,     64 KB, Assoc    2, LineSize  64
------*-    Unified Cache       7, Level 2,    512 KB, Assoc   16, LineSize  64
-------*    Data Cache          7, Level 1,     64 KB, Assoc    2, LineSize  64
-------*    Instruction Cache   7, Level 1,     64 KB, Assoc    2, LineSize  64
-------*    Unified Cache       8, Level 2,    512 KB, Assoc   16, LineSize  64
----****    Unified Cache       9, Level 3,      2 MB, Assoc    1, LineSize  64

Logical Processor to Group Map:
********    Group 0
```

ProcFeatures

ProcFeatures is a simple command-line utility that uses the Windows *IsProcessorFeaturePresent* function to determine whether the processor and Windows support various features such as No-Execute memory pages, Physical Address Extensions (PAE), and a real-time cycle counter. Its primary purpose is to identify systems running the PAE version of the kernel and that can support hardware-based Data Execution Prevention. ProcFeatures runs on all supported versions of Windows and does not require administrative rights.

Figure 14-8 shows example output from an Intel Core2 Duo system running on Windows 7 64-bit edition.

FIGURE 14-8 ProcFeatures.

WinObj

WinObj is a GUI utility that lets you navigate Windows' Object Manager namespace and view information about the objects it contains. The Object Manager provides a directory structure and a common, consistent interface for creating, deleting, securing, and accessing objects of many different types. For more information about the Windows Object Manager, see the "Object Manager" section of Chapter 3, "System Mechanisms," in *Windows Internals: Including Windows Server 2008 and Windows Vista Fifth Edition*.

WinObj runs on all versions of Windows and does not require administrative rights. However, WinObj can display more information when run with administrative rights, because several areas in the Object Manager namespace require administrative rights even to view. And because some objects grant access to the System account but not to Administrators, running WinObj as System generally provides the most complete view. (PsExec, described in Chapter 6, "PsTools," can help with this.) On Windows Vista and newer, you can restart WinObj with elevated rights by choosing File, Run As Administrator.As shown in Figure 14-9, WinObj shows the Object Manager directory hierarchy as an expandable tree structure in the left pane. The root directory is named with simply a backslash. When you select a directory in the left pane, the right pane lists the objects contained in that directory. When you select a directory in the left pane or an object in the right pane, the status bar shows the item's full path. You can refresh the view at any time by pressing F5.

FIGURE 14-9 WinObj.

The sortable table in the right pane lists each object's name and type; for symbolic links, the SymLink column identifies the link target. Click any column header to sort the object list by that column. Next to each object's name is an icon corresponding to the object type:

- Mutexes (mutants) are indicated with a padlock.

- Sections (Windows file-mapping objects) are shown as a memory chip.

- Events are shown as an exclamation point in a triangle.

- KeyedEvents have the same icon as Events with a key overlaid.

- Semaphores are indicated with an icon that resembles a traffic signal.

- Symbolic links are indicated with a curved arrow.

- Devices are represented with a desktop computer icon.

- Drivers are represented with gears on a page (like the standard icon for .sys files).

- Window Stations are represented with a video monitor icon.

- Timers are represented with a clock.

- Gears indicate other objects, such as ALPC ports and jobs.

To view more information about a directory or an object, right-click it and choose Properties. Double-clicking an object will also display its Properties dialog box (as shown in Figure 14-10), unless it is a Symbolic Link: double-clicking a symbolic link navigates to the link target.

FIGURE 14-10 A WinObj object property dialog box.

The Details tab of the WinObj Properties dialog box, shown in Figure 14-10, shows the following information for all object types:

■ The object's name and type.

■ Whether the object is "permanent"—an object that is not automatically deleted when it is no longer referenced.

■ Reference and handle counts. Because each handle includes a reference to the object, the reference count is never smaller than the handle count. The difference between the two figures is the number of direct references to the object structure from within kernel mode rather than indirectly through a handle.

■ Quota charges—how much paged and nonpaged pool is charged to the process' quota when it creates the object.

The bottom portion of the Details tab shows object-specific information, where possible. For example, a SymbolicLink shows its creation time and the directory path to its target object, while an Event object shows the event type and whether it is in a signaled state.

The Security tab of the Properties dialog box shows the generic permissions on the object. Note, however, that not all object types can be opened, and that permissions on a specific object might also prevent viewing its properties.

Some directories of interest within WinObj are

- **\BaseNamedObjects**   Objects such as events and semaphores created in the Global namespace appear in this object directory, as do objects created in a Local namespace by a process running in terminal services session 0.

- **\Sessions*n***   Contains data private to the terminal services or Fast User Switching session identified by the number *n*, where *n* is 1 or higher.

- **\Sessions*n*\BaseNamedObjects**   Objects such as events and semaphores created in the Local namespace of processes running in a terminal services or Fast User Switching session identified by the number *n*.

- **\Sessions\0\DosDevices*LUID***   Contains data private to an LSA logon session indicated by the locally-unique ID (LUID) in the directory name, including SMB connections, network drive letter mappings, and SUBST mappings.

- **\GLOBAL??**   This object directory contains symbolic links that map global names— including globally defined drive letters and other legacy MS-DOS device names such as AUX and NUL—to devices.

- **\KnownDLLs and \KnownDlls32**   Section names and paths for DLLs that are mapped by the system at startup. \KnownDlls32 exists only on 64-bit versions of Windows and lists 32-bit versions of known DLLs.

LoadOrder

LoadOrder (Loadord.exe) is a simple applet that shows the approximate order in which Windows loads device drivers and starts services. LoadOrder runs on all versions of Windows and does not require administrative rights.

LoadOrder determines load order for drivers and services based on start value, group name, tag ID, and dependencies. As shown in Figure 14-11, LoadOrder lists all those attributes except for dependencies. Boot start drivers are loaded first, then System start drivers, and then Automatic start drivers and services. Note that LoadOrder does not list demand start (also known as Manual start) drivers and services. Within a start phase, Windows loads drivers by group, and within a group sorted by Tag ID. Windows loads groups in the order they are listed in HKLM\System\CurrentControlSet\Control\ServiceGroupOrder, and it orders tags in the order listed for the respective group in HKLM\System\CurrentControlSet\Control\ GroupOrderList. Groups or tags that are not specified in those keys are ignored when determining load order, and LoadOrder marks those with an asterisk. In addition to Start value, Group Name, and Tag, LoadOrder shows the internal and display name and the image path for each driver or service.

FIGURE 14-11 LoadOrder.

Click the Copy button to copy LoadOrder's data to the clipboard as tab-delimited text.

Some drivers and services might load in a different order from that shown by LoadOrder. Plug-and-Play drivers are typically registered as demand-start and are therefore not listed, but they will load during device detection and enumeration. Also, LoadOrder does not distinguish between "Automatic" and "Automatic (Delayed Start)" services. Delayed-start services start after Automatic start services.

For more information on how Windows loads and starts drivers and services, see *Windows Internals: Including Windows Server 2008 and Windows Vista, Fifth Edition*.

PipeList

Named pipes are implemented on Windows by a file system driver called NPFS.sys, which stands for *Named Pipe File System*. PipeList is a console utility that lists all the named pipes on the local computer by performing a directory listing of that file system. As shown in Figure 14-12, PipeList also shows the number of instances that have been created for a name and the maximum number of instances allowed. A Max Instances value of –1 means that there is no upper limit on the number of instances allowed.

PipeList works on all versions of Windows and does not require administrative rights.

FIGURE 14-12 PipeList.

ClockRes

ClockRes is a simple command-line utility that displays the current resolution of the system clock, as well as the minimum and maximum interval between clock ticks. It does not require administrative rights.

The current resolution is typically higher than the maximum when a process, such as one hosting a multimedia application, increases the resolution to deliver audio or video. Use the Windows Powercfg.exe tool on Windows 7 with the **/energy** command to generate an HTML report that includes the names of processes that have changed the timer resolution.

FIGURE 14-13 ClockRes.

Chapter 15
Miscellaneous Utilities

The utilities in this chapter are not for diagnostic or troubleshooting purposes. They are simple utilities I wrote for my own needs or amusement and later published to the Sysinternals Web site.

- **RegJump** launches RegEdit and navigates to the registry path you specify.

- **Hex2Dec** converts numbers from hexadecimal to decimal and vice versa.

- **RegDelNull** searches for and deletes registry keys with embedded null characters in their names.

- **Bluescreen Screen Saver** is a screen saver that realistically simulates a "Blue Screen of Death."

- **Ctrl2Cap** is a keyboard filter driver that converts Caps Lock keypresses to Control keypresses for those of us who are used to keyboards where the Control key is located immediately to the left of the A key.

RegJump

RegJump is a command-line utility that takes a registry path, opens the Windows RegEdit applet, and navigates RegEdit to the path you specify. You can specify the root key in standard or abbreviated form, or even in Microsoft Windows PowerShell drive-specifier format. Note that it is not necessary to quote registry paths that contain spaces. The following commands are all equivalent:

```
regjump HKEY_LOCAL_MACHINE\SYSTEM\CurrentControlSet\Control
```

```
regjump HKLM\SYSTEM\CurrentControlSet\Control
```

```
regjump HKLM:\SYSTEM\CurrentControlSet\Control
```

RegJump works by programmatically sending keystrokes to RegEdit. This means that on Windows Vista and newer, RegJump must run with at least as high an integrity level as that of RegEdit. Also note that if you are a member of the Administrators group, RegEdit requires elevation, so RegJump must also run elevated. If you are logged on as a standard user, neither RegJump nor RegEdit require elevation.

Hex2Dec

If you spend a lot of time in a command prompt or Windows PowerShell console, Hex2Dec is a handy way to convert numbers from hexadecimal to decimal and vice versa without having to open the Windows Calculator. Simply enter the number you want to convert on the command line, using the prefix *x* or *0x* to indicate a hex number. Hex2Dec interprets input as 64-bit (qword) integers, treating decimal values as signed 64-bit integers. Figure 15-1 shows examples.

FIGURE 15-1 Hex2Dec.

RegDelNull

Because of the way that the Windows native APIs and the Windows kernel handle string values, the native APIs make it possible to create and access registry keys and values with embedded null characters in their names. Because the Win32 APIs use a null character to indicate the end of a string value, it is impossible to access or delete such keys or values using the Win32 APIs, or with standard registry-editing tools such as RegEdit that use those APIs.

RegDelNull searches for and allows you to delete registry keys that contain embedded null characters. Specify the key to search, and add –s to recurse into subkeys. If RegDelNull finds any keys with embedded nulls, it displays the path with an asterisk replacing the null, and it prompts you to specify whether to delete the key, as shown in Figure 15-2. Note that deleting registry keys might cause the applications that use those keys to fail.

```
C:\>regdelnull hklm\software -s

RegDelNull v1.10 - Delete Registry keys with embedded Nulls
Copyright (C) 2005-2006 Mark Russinovich
Sysinternals - www.sysinternals.com

Null-embedded key (Nulls are replaced by '*'):

HKLM\SOFTWARE\Systems Internals\Can't touch me!*

Delete? (y/n) y
Key successfully deleted.

Scan complete.

C:\>_
```

FIGURE 15-2 RegDelNull.

Bluescreen Screen Saver

This one is just for fun. The Bluescreen Screen Saver realistically simulates an endless cycle of "Blue Screen of Death" (BSOD) crashes and system restarts. For each simulated crash, Bluescreen randomly picks a bugcheck code and displays realistic data corresponding to that code. For the restarts, Bluescreen displays a Windows XP startup splash screen with a progress bar (it has not been updated to display a Windows Vista or Windows 7 splash screen), and then "crashes" again.

To install the Bluescreen Screen Saver, copy SysinternalsBluescreen.scr to your System32 folder and select it from the Windows screen saver dialog box. Alternately, copy it to any folder on your computer, right-click it in Windows Explorer and choose Install from the context menu. Note that the Bluescreen Screen Saver is not included in the Sysinternals Suite but can be downloaded separately from the Sysinternals Web site.

> **Note** The Bluescreen Screen Saver configuration dialog box offers a Fake Disk Activity check box, but this option has no effect when used on any operating system newer than Windows NT 4.0, after which BSOD screens underwent significant streamlining.

The Bluescreen Screen Saver works on all versions of Windows and does not require administrative rights. However, because it needs to change the display mode, Bluescreen will not work in a remote desktop session; and because it also requires DirectX, it might not work in a virtual machine.

Be careful when using the Bluescreen Screen Saver! We have heard stories of unwitting victims power-cycling their computers to "recover" from the endless simulated crashes. We also heard about one Bluescreen user whose screen saver appeared during a presentation. He nonchalantly pressed a key and resumed his demonstration, not realizing the effect on his audience. They ignored the rest of his presentation and reported to upper management, "We have a quick blue screen recovery mechanism! We'll make a fortune!"

Ctrl2Cap

Before I began working on Windows systems, I spent all my time on UNIX computers on which the Control key was located where the Caps Lock key is on standard PC keyboards. Rather than unlearn that muscle memory, I chose to learn about Windows' extensibility and built a kernel-mode driver that converts Caps Lock keypresses into Control keypresses. Ctrl2Cap was the first Sysinternals utility I wrote. I still use it to this day and have never missed having Caps Lock.

Ctrl2Cap works on all x86 and x64 versions of Windows. Installing or uninstalling Ctrl2Cap requires administrative privileges.

To install Ctrl2Cap, run the command **ctrl2cap /install** from the folder into which you have unzipped the Ctrl2Cap files. To uninstall it, run **ctrl2cap /uninstall**. Unlike every other Sysinternals utility that is packaged as a single executable file that can self-extract any additional files that it needs, the Ctrl2Cap download includes a Ctrl2Cap.exe file and several *.sys files. During installation, Ctrl2Cap.exe determines which of its *.sys files is the correct one for the current system, copies it into the System32\Drivers folder as Ctrl2Cap.sys, and registers it as a keyboard class filter.

Part III

Troubleshooting—"The Case of the Unexplained..."

Chapter 16
Error Messages

In this chapter, I'll demonstrate troubleshooting techniques using the Sysinternals utilities when the primary symptom is an error message. In this chapter, Procmon is the troubleshooting tool of choice in all but the first two cases:

- **The Case of the Locked Folder** highlights a common use case for Procexp.

- **The Case of the Failed AV Update** demonstrates Autoruns' Analyze Offline System feature to repair an unbootable computer.

- **The Case of the Failed Lotus Notes Backups** is interesting to me and will be useful to many readers because it shows what a search for a missing DLL looks like in Procmon.

- **The Case of the Failed Play-To** and **The Case of the Crashing Proksi Utility** highlight different ways in which "Access Denied errors can manifest.

- **The Case of the Installation Failure** turned out to be caused by ill-advised security guidance.

- **The Case of the Missing Folder Association** demonstrates comparing a Procmon trace from a problematic system to one from a working system.

- **The Case of the Temporary Registry Profiles** is especially interesting because it affected a large number of users and made use of one of Procmon's lesser-known features: boot logging.

The Case of the Locked Folder

While writing up "The Case of the IExplore-Pegged CPU" (in Chapter 17, "Hangs and Sluggish Performance"), I decided to rename the folder containing the files. However, I ran into an unexpected error (shown in Figure 16-1) because another program had an open handle to the folder or to something in it. After making sure I didn't have any files open or command prompts in that folder, I clicked Try Again, but the folder remained in use and could not be renamed.

FIGURE 16-1 File system folder or something in it is open in another program.

I pressed Ctrl+F in Procexp to open the Search dialog box, entered the current name of the folder, and clicked Search. Procexp pointed to Microsoft Outlook as the program with the open handle. (See Figure 16-2.)

FIGURE 16-2 Searching for processes with open handles to the IexplorePeggedCPU folder.

I then remembered that I had saved an attachment from an e-mail message into a subfolder of the folder I was trying to rename. I opened the Outlook.exe process' Properties dialog box in Procexp, and on the Image tab verified that the current directory was still set to that subfolder. (See Figure 16-3.) I could have made the problem go away by closing Outlook, but instead I simply saved a random e-mail attachment to a different folder, making it the current directory and releasing the handle that was preventing the rename. Problem solved.

FIGURE 16-3 Outlook's current directory preventing a rename in that folder hierarchy.

The Case of the Failed AV Update

After "The Case of the Process Killing Malware" was solved (as discussed in Chapter 18, "Malware"), Aaron's friend Paul went home and instructed his son to keep all his software patched and up to date. He then set a good example by doing the same on his own desktop. Unfortunately, the result was an unbootable computer.

Software must be kept up to date, so Paul updated the free antivirus software on his Microsoft Windows XP computer. When he rebooted, the computer displayed the Windows XP startup splash screen progress bar and then blue-screened. Subsequent restarts ended the same way.

Naturally, Paul called Aaron, who changed into his well-worn "No, I will not fix your computer" t-shirt and came over. Aaron could probably have solved the problem in Safe Mode or with System Restore, but those options must have seemed too easy for him. (Actually, he wanted to ensure that the failing software did not load.) Instead, he booted the computer with an old Windows Preinstallation Environment (WinPE) CD. He then ran Autoruns, chose File | Analyze Offline System, pointing Autoruns to the C:\Windows folder on the hard drive and to one of the profiles in the C:\Documents and Settings folder.

The old WinPE instance was not able to verify signatures, so Aaron chose to hide Microsoft and Windows entries without signature verification, simply trusting that in this case no modules on the system would falsely claim to be from Microsoft. In addition to the failing antivirus' Autostart Extensibility Points (ASEPs), Autoruns revealed several other services and drivers that were no longer needed and were out of date. Aaron disabled all of them, as shown in Figure 16-4, and restarted the computer.

FIGURE 16-4 Autoruns analyzing an offline system, disabling failing antivirus applications and other unneeded entries.

The computer restarted without incident. After logging in, Paul was hesitant about risking another failed update. So he took Aaron's recommendation to upgrade to another free antivirus solution (shown in Figure 16-5) and uninstalled his previous antivirus product. Case solved.

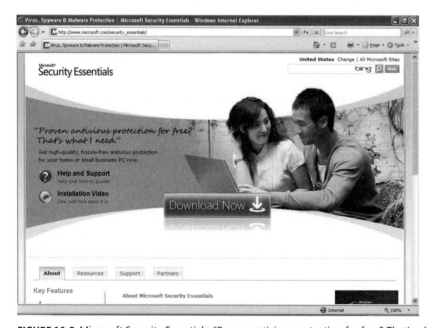

FIGURE 16-5 Microsoft Security Essentials: "Proven antivirus protection for free? That's what I need."

The Case of the Failed Lotus Notes Backups

A sysadmin reported that Lotus Notes backups began failing, displaying the error shown in Figure 16-6: "none of the files in the file list exist."

FIGURE 16-6 Lotus Notes backups failing.

He checked the backup application's log, which reported a DLL load failure for nnotes.dll. (See Figure 16-7.) He found it odd that the reported DLL file path was in a folder belonging to a completely different application.

```
datePath(): INF - Path updated with Lotus Program Dir 'd:\domino\data'
s_backup::V_VerifyLotus: INF - Lotus Notes INI PATH set to: d:\domino\notes.ini
s_backup::V_VerifyLotus: INF - Lotus Notes INI PATH set to: d:\domino\data with Lotus Notes:\d:\domino\data
s_backup::V_VerifyLotus: INF - Replaced: d:\domino\data with Lotus Notes:\d:\domino\data
nblnagent main() [ ERR - failed to load LN library: C:\PROGRA~1\BMCSOF-1\MASTER-1\server\bin\nnotes.dll: Errno:126 (nnotes.dll)
```

FIGURE 16-7 Backup application log showing DLL load failure for nnotes.dll.

He ran Procmon and tried to initiate the backup. Applying a filter for the backup application and all its child processes, he pressed Ctrl+F and searched for the first instances of "\nnotes.dll" in the trace. He found a sequence of QueryOpen calls (shown in Figure 16-8) trying to open the file in different folders, each failing with NAME NOT FOUND until it was finally found in C:\Program Files\BMC Software\MasterCell\server\bin. (The sysadmin says that some of these folders are in the PATH environment variable and that others are added by the backup application at runtime.)

FIGURE 16-8 Searching for nnotes.dll in several directories until found in the selected row.

Shortly after opening that copy of nnotes.dll, the process mapped the DLL into its virtual address space, as indicated by the *LoadImage* event shown in the first row of Figure 16-9. So why did the DLL load fail? As you can also see in Figure 16-9, immediately after loading nnotes.dll the process searched for but failed to find nxmlproc.dll.in a series of folders including all PATH locations in order.

FIGURE 16-9 Backup application successfully loads nnotes.dll and then can't find nxmlproc.dll.

The sysadmin ran the Microsoft Visual Studio utility "dumpbin" to view the DLL's import dependencies and verified that nnotes.dll statically depends on nxmlproc.dll. This explains why the search for nxmlproc.dll began immediately after nnotes.dll was loaded, and why the failure to find nxmlproc.dll resulted in a load failure for nnotes.dll.

He then searched the C and D drives for nxmlproc.dll, ultimately finding it in the D:\Domino folder (shown in Figure 16-10), which hadn't been searched. Interestingly, he also found a copy of nnotes.dll in the same folder. (See Figure 16-11.) He inserted "D:\Domino" into the PATH variable immediately following the default Windows folders and rebooted. Backups then worked without issue. Problem solved.

FIGURE 16-10 Searching C and D for nxmlproc.dll.

```
D:\>dir /s nnotes.dll
 Volume in drive D is Data
 Volume Serial Number is A4F8-810F

 Directory of D:\Domino

15.05.2007  11:40        14.282.752 nnotes.dll
               1 File(s)     14.282.752 bytes

    Total Files Listed:
               1 File(s)     14.282.752 bytes
               0 Dir(s)  251.235.536.896 bytes free
```

FIGURE 16-11 Searching for nnotes.dll.

The Case of the Failed Play-To

A user tried to use Windows 7's Play To feature to send a song to a media player but got the ambiguous error message shown in Figure 16-12: "Error occurred on your device." However, it would play other songs from the user's media library.

FIGURE 16-12 Play To fails with "Error occurred on your device."

The user then reproduced the error, this time while monitoring system activity with Procmon. Filtering on the song file, the trace showed successful operations from Wmplayer.exe and a single "ACCESS DENIED" result from Wmpnetwk.exe. (See Figure 16-13.)

Time	Process Name	PID	Operation	Path	Result
23:42...	wmplayer.exe	3672	ReadFile	C:\Users\erwynv\Documents\01-Chris Botti-Teacher's-Cubisn.wma	SUCCESS
23:42...	wmplayer.exe	3672	ReadFile	C:\Users\erwynv\Documents\01-Chris Botti-Teacher's-Cubisn.wma	SUCCESS
23:42...	wmplayer.exe	3672	QueryDirect...	C:\Users\erwynv\Documents\01-Chris Botti-Teacher's-Cubisn.wma	SUCCESS
23:42...	wmplayer.exe	3672	ReadFile	C:\Users\erwynv\Documents\01-Chris Botti-Teacher's-Cubisn.wma	SUCCESS
23:42...	wmplayer.exe	3672	ReadFile	C:\Users\erwynv\Documents\01-Chris Botti-Teacher's-Cubisn.wma	SUCCESS
23:42...	wmplayer.exe	3672	ReadFile	C:\Users\erwynv\Documents\01-Chris Botti-Teacher's-Cubisn.wma	SUCCESS
23:42...	wmplayer.exe	3672	ReadFile	C:\Users\erwynv\Documents\01-Chris Botti-Teacher's-Cubisn.wma	SUCCESS
23:43...	wmplayer.exe	3672	ReadFile	C:\Users\erwynv\Documents\01-Chris Botti-Teacher's-Cubisn.wma	SUCCESS
23:43...	wmplayer.exe	3672	ReadFile	C:\Users\erwynv\Documents\01-Chris Botti-Teacher's-Cubisn.wma	SUCCESS
23:43...	wmpnetwk.exe	4188	CreateFile	C:\Users\erwynv\Documents\01-Chris Botti-Teacher's-Cubisn.wma	ACCESS DENIED
23:43...	wmplayer.exe	3672	QueryDirect...	C:\Users\erwynv\Documents\01-Chris Botti-Teacher's-Cubisn.wma	SUCCESS
23:43...	wmplayer.exe	3672	ReadFile	C:\Users\erwynv\Documents\01-Chris Botti-Teacher's-Cubisn.wma	SUCCESS

Showing 25 of 6,450 events (0.38%)   Backed by logfile.PML

FIGURE 16-13 Successful operations from Wmplayer.exe, and failure from Wmpnetwk.exe.

He also noticed that other songs that played were in the default Music folder, while the one that failed was in his Documents folder. He compared the permissions between the songs that played and the one that failed, and he found that those that played granted "Read & execute" access to the WMPNetworkSvc service.[1] He added that permission to the file that had failed to play. (See Figure 16-14.) The song then played correctly. Problem solved.

FIGURE 16-14 Granting access to the WMPNetworkSvc service.

The Case of the Crashing Proksi Utility

The user had been using a utility called Proksi for over a year when it started crashing. To diagnose the issue, he ran Procmon while reproducing the issue. After the utility crashed, he stopped the trace. Scanning through the results (shown in Figure 16-15), he found an "ACCESS DENIED" result when attempting to open a file for Generic Write permissions.

Process ...	PID	Operation	Path	Result	Detail
doskey ...	3172	RegCloseKey	HKLM\System\CurrentControlSet\Services\WinSock2\Parameters	SUCCESS	
doskey ...	3172	CreateFile	D:\Ashutosh\NSE\Softwares\Network Programs\Proksi\doskey.log	ACCESS DENIED	Desired Access: Generic Write,...
doskey ...	3172	RegOpenKey	HKLM\Software\Microsoft\Windows NT\CurrentVersion\AeDebug	SUCCESS	Desired Access: Query Value
doskey ...	3172	RegQueryValue	HKLM\SOFTWARE\Microsoft\Windows NT\CurrentVersion\AeDeb...	SUCCESS	Type: REG_SZ, Length: 4, Dat...
doskey ...	3172	RegQueryValue	HKLM\SOFTWARE\Microsoft\Windows NT\CurrentVersion\AeDeb...	SUCCESS	Type: REG_SZ, Length: 52, Da...
doskey ...	3172	RegCloseKey	HKLM\SOFTWARE\Microsoft\Windows NT\CurrentVersion\AeDebug	SUCCESS	
doskey ...	3172	QueryOpen	C:\WINDOWS\system32\faultrep.dll	SUCCESS	CreationTime: 8/11/2004 04:00...
doskey ...	3172	CreateFile	C:\WINDOWS\system32\faultrep.dll	SUCCESS	Desired Access: Execute/Trav...
doskey ...	3172	CreateFileMapp...	C:\WINDOWS\system32\faultrep.dll	SUCCESS	SyncType: SyncTypeCreateSe...
doskey ...	3172	QueryStandardI...	C:\WINDOWS\system32\faultrep.dll	SUCCESS	AllocationSize: 81,920, EndOfFi...
doskey ...	3172	CreateFileMapp...	C:\WINDOWS\system32\faultrep.dll	SUCCESS	SyncType: SyncTypeOther
doskey ...	3172	CloseFile	C:\WINDOWS\system32\faultrep.dll	SUCCESS	

Showing 1,351 of 2,456 events (55%)   Backed by Logfile.PML

FIGURE 16-15 Procmon reports "ACCESS DENIED" right before AeDebug handles the crash.

---

[1] In Windows Vista and newer, services are assigned security identifiers (SIDs), and it becomes possible to grant or deny access to specific services.

He opened the Security tab of the file's Properties dialog box in Windows Explorer, but found nothing wrong. He then noticed that the Read-Only check box was selected on the General tab. (See Figure 16-16.) He cleared it, and the program began working correctly.

FIGURE 16-16 "ACCESS DENIED" caused by the Read-Only check box being selected.

The Case of the Installation Failure

A customer that my co-author Aaron was working with had Kodak scanners that came with CDs containing the required software. When the administrator inserted the CD, Windows Vista's Autorun didn't quite work correctly—the Autorun dialog box appeared but did not show the Autoplay option to install the software. So the administrator opened the folder in Explorer and started autorun.exe to start the installation. Shortly after approving the User Account Control elevation request, the administrator saw an error message with a strange title that looked like the installer was performing an incorrect operating system version check. (See Figure 16-17.)

FIGURE 16-17 Application installation error message.

The Troubleshooting

Aaron figured that the author of the installation program had believed that because Windows XP was so perfect Microsoft would never need to release another version of Windows, there was no reason to check for newer versions. He applied the Windows XP compatibility mode which, among other things, lies to the program about what the operating system version actually is and tried again. It failed in exactly the same way. Additionally, the installation worked perfectly well on freshly installed copies of Windows Vista that didn't have the organization's policies applied to it.

He started Procmon, ran the installation program again to the point of the error message and then stopped the Procmon trace. He dragged the Procmon crosshairs toolbar icon over the error message to apply a filter to show only events involving the window owner's process, Setup.exe. (See Figure 16-18.)

FIGURE 16-18 Procmon after filtering with "Include Process From Window."

Because of the "0" in the title in the error message, Aaron thought the problem might be due to the program searching for something and not finding it, so he right-clicked on items in the Result column and excluded events with result codes he figured would not be interesting: SUCCESS, FAST IO DISALLOWED, FILE LOCKED WITH ONLY READERS, REPARSE, BUFFER OVERFLOW, and END OF FILE. (Aaron usually excludes "known-good" result codes rather than including potentially bad results because it is easy to miss some and filter out important entries.)

When he looked at the remaining entries, one thing that quickly stood out was the name "DoesNotExist" appearing in path names near the end of the results. He used Procmon's highlighting feature to make them stand out in the context of surrounding events. (See Figure 16-19.)

FIGURE 16-19 Highlighting "DoesNotExist" in the filtered results.

Because the surrounding context didn't give him an idea of what had happened immediately prior to these failed searches, he took advantage of Procmon's nondestructive filtering and removed the filter rule that excluded SUCCESS results. As you can see in Figure 16-20, there had been a bunch of file accesses to D:\setup.ini and then a few to D:\autorun.inf before the attempted registry access to HKLM\Software\DoesNotExist\Info.

FIGURE 16-20 Unhiding the SUCCESS results prior to the failed registry opening.

He opened the event properties for the first *RegOpenKey* event and looked at the call stack (shown in Figure 16-21) to get an idea of how and why Setup.exe was trying to open that key. Line 12 of the stack showed that the randomly-named component of the setup program was calling into *GetPrivateProfileStringA*, which led (in line 7) to an attempt to open a registry key.

FIGURE 16-21 Call stack of a failed attempt to open HKLM\Software\DoesNotExist\Info.

GetPrivateProfileString is one of the APIs Windows programmers can use to read from files that are formatted like the old .ini files from 16-bit Windows. And as its documentation points out, those accesses can be redirected to the registry with an IniFileMapping. Aaron located the IniFileMapping that redirected autorun.inf to "DoesNotExist" (shown in Figure 16-22), deleted it, and rebooted—the installation then worked correctly.

FIGURE 16-22 IniFileMapping entry redirecting Autorun.inf to a nonexistent registry key.

The Analysis

Aaron found the technical reason for the installation failure, but he wanted to understand the root cause and why the IniFileMapping had been configured.

What Is IniFileMapping?

IniFileMapping has been part of Windows since NT 3.1. When programs use the ini-file APIs to access files, an IniFileMapping entry can redirect the access to the machine or user registry (HKLM or HKCU). IniFileMapping was designed to help older applications that used .ini files to use the registry instead, to take advantage of the scalability benefits and to enable multiple users to have their own copies of settings instead of sharing a single ini file.

What Is Autorun.inf?

When a removable disk, such as a CD or a USB drive, is inserted and Windows detects the new disk, Windows Explorer checks for an Autorun.inf file in the root folder of the drive. The Autorun.inf is a text file formatted as an .ini file (that is, section names are in square brackets, and there are *name=value* pairs within each section). It can include entries that tell Explorer what icon to display for the drive and a default Autoplay action to offer to the user, or in some cases, the program can just begin running. This is the mechanism that allows a program installation to automatically start just by inserting a CD. There are registry settings and group policies that can control whether and how Autorun and Autoplay work. (Microsoft Knowledge Base article 967715 (*http://support.microsoft.com/kb/967715*) describes the distinction between Autorun and Autoplay.)

A problem with Autoplay is that by default it has also been applied to writable drives such as thumb drives. Worms such as Conficker were able to propagate through such devices by writing an Autorun.inf and a copy of itself to the drive. The malware could then infect other computers simply by inserting the drive. That was compounded by a bug in the implementation of the settings that were supposed to disable Autoplay. That bug has since been fixed. Furthermore, updated Windows systems now have Autoplay disabled by default for writable drives, as described in KB article 971029 (*http://support.microsoft.com/kb/971029*). Autorun and Autoplay still work for CDs and DVDs, because the threat of worm propagation through that avenue is much smaller and (at this time) does not outweigh the benefits.

Why Did This Computer Have an IniFileMapping for Autorun.inf?

A couple of years ago, a blog post described a clever trick to disable Autoplay for all drives. The trick leveraged the fact that Autorun.inf is formatted as an ini file and that Explorer uses the ini file APIs to read it. By creating an IniFileMapping for Autorun.inf that redirects access to a nonexistent registry key, Autoplay entries cannot be read. The author asserted that the only negative effect was that users must browse for the file to execute. As more malware began using writable removable drives as a propagation mechanism, Carnegie Mellon University's Computer Emergency Response Team (CERT) and other security-conscious organizations began recommending this trick, adding the assertion that "This setting appears to disable Autorun behaviors without causing other negative side effects." Since then, the setting has been mandated as part of the standard image for many organizations.

Why Did This Application Install Fail?

It turns out that the Autorun.inf on Kodak's installation CD contained much more than just Autoplay entries:

```
[autorun]
open=autorun.exe

[Info]
Dialog=Kodak i610/i620/i640/i660 Scanner
Model=600
ModelDir=kds_i600
ProgramGroup=i610,i620,i640,i660

[Versions]
CD=04040000
FIRMWARE=04000300
ISISDRIVER=2.0.10711.12001
ISISTOOLKIT=57.0.260.2124
KDSMM=01090000
PKG=02010000
SVT=06100000
TWAIN=09250500

[Install]

[SUPPORTEDOSES]
WIN=WINVISTA WINXP WIN2K

[REQUIREDSPS]
WINXP=1
WIN2K=3
```

Kodak and other vendors use the Autorun.inf not only for Autoplay but as a general-purpose ini file containing configuration settings for their installation programs. The installation program of course uses standard APIs to read the file, but the IniFileMapping redirects to a nonexistent registry location, causing the installer to fail. It needs to be said here that what Kodak is doing is perfectly legitimate. There are no guidelines that say that the Autorun.inf cannot contain other application-specific settings.

Could the customer have worked around the problem by copying the CD content to the hard drive and running it from there? No. The IniFileMapping setting applies to any file called "Autorun.inf" no matter where it is.

The bottom line is that the installation failed because the assurances of no "negative side effects" were not backed with extensive compatibility testing, and it denied legitimate usage scenarios. Because the new Autoplay defaults and already-available policy settings largely mitigate the threat of viruses automatically propagating through USB drives, unsupported hacks such as this IniFileMapping are not warranted. Aaron advised the customer to remove the registry setting from their systems and rely on the new default behavior.

The Case of the Missing Folder Association

The user found that any attempt to open any folder in Windows Explorer resulted in an error message like that shown in Figure 16-23: "This file does not have a program associated with it for performing this action." This happened whenever he double-clicked a folder on his desktop or clicked the Computer, Control Panel, Documents, Pictures, or other folders in his Start menu.

FIGURE 16-23 Error message displayed on any attempt to open a folder.

Program associations are stored in the HKEY_CLASSES_ROOT hive in the registry, so he assumed that something was missing or corrupted there. He decided that the best course of action to identify the problem would be to compare Procmon results on the system exhibiting the problem and a similar computer without the problem.

Procmon can capture a lot of data in a short amount of time, so he knew it was important to narrow down the data set as much as possible. He started Procmon with the **/noconnect** option in order not to begin capturing events until he was ready to reproduce the problem. He then pressed Ctrl+E to begin capture, double-clicked on a folder, and pressed Ctrl+E to stop the capture as soon as the error message appeared. Next, he dragged the crosshairs icon from the Procmon toolbar over the error message to apply a filter limiting the display only to events from that process. Because Explorer.exe also manages the entire desktop— including the taskbar, notification area, and more—he decided to narrow down the display just to the thread that had displayed the error message. He right-clicked on the column headers, enabled the Thread ID (TID) column, and dragged it next to the PID column. Guessing that the thread with the most activity was the one he wanted, he used the Count Occurrences tool to identify the thread (shown in Figure 16-24) and added it to the filter. Then he saved that trace, selecting the save option that includes only the events displayed with the current filter.

FIGURE 16-24 Identifying the thread with the most activity.

Then he reproduced the steps on a computer that didn't exhibit the problem. Because there was no error message, he stopped the capture when the folder window appeared, dragging the crosshairs toolbar icon to filter on the Explorer.exe process that owned the folder window and saving the results to a file.

He opened the two result files side by side, adding the TID column to both. The results on the "good" system had many more events. Assuming that the problem lay in the registry, he used the event class toggle filters in the toolbar to hide all other event classes. Then he began looking for patterns in the "good" trace that looked like the events in the "bad" trace to match up a corresponding thread. He found one and set a filter on that thread in the "good" trace. When he found the beginning of a series of identical events, he right-clicked the event in each and chose Exclude Events Before in both so that both traces had a common starting point. (See Figure 16-25.)

FIGURE 16-25 Side-by-side comparison of Procmon traces.

Paging through the results to find differences, he soon saw a *RegOpenKey* operation on HKCR\Folder\shell\open\command that resulted in NAME NOT FOUND in the "bad" trace and SUCCESS in the "good" trace. (See Figure 16-26.) Using Regedit, he exported that key from the good machine and imported it into the registry on the bad machine. That simple fix solved the problem.

FIGURE 16-26 Identifying differences between Procmon traces.

Visually comparing traces side by side is sometimes necessary when there are enough differences between them that a tool like WinDiff wouldn't be helpful, but in this case WinDiff could have sped up the investigation. In each instance of Procmon, he would have first disabled the column display for Time of Day, PID, and TID, because these would always be different between traces. After saving the displayed events (without profiling events) to Comma-Separated Values (CSV) files, he could have compared the files with WinDiff and immediately zeroed in on the missing registry key. (See Figure 16-27.)

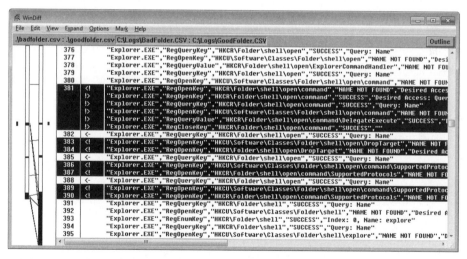

FIGURE 16-27 Comparing Procmon traces with WinDiff.

The Case of the Temporary Registry Profiles

The case opened when a customer contacted Microsoft support reporting that several of their users would occasionally get the "User Environment" error message shown in Figure 16-28 when logging on to their systems. This error caused Windows to create a temporary profile for the user's logon session.

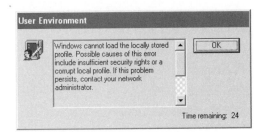

FIGURE 16-28 User profile load error at logon.

A user profile consists of a file system folder, %UserProfile%, into which applications save user-specific configuration and data files, as well as a registry hive file stored in that folder, %UserProfile%\Ntuser.dat, that the Winlogon process loads when the user logs in. Applications store user settings in the registry hive by calling registry functions that refer to the HKEY_CURRENT_USER (HKCU) root key. The users' loss of access to their profile made the problem critical because whenever that happened, users would appear to lose all their settings and access to files stored in their profiles. In most cases, users contacted the company's support desk, which would ask the user to try rebooting and logging in until the problem resolved itself.

As with all cases, Microsoft support began by asking about the system configuration, inventory of installed software, and any recent changes the company had made to their systems. In this case, the fact that stood out was that all the systems on which the problem had occurred had recently been upgraded to a new version of Citrix Corporation's ICA client, a remote desktop application. Microsoft contacted Citrix support to see if they knew of any issues with the new client. They didn't, but said they would investigate.

Unsure whether the ICA client upgrade was responsible for the profile problem, Microsoft support instructed the customer to enable profile logging, which you can do by configuring a registry key as described in Microsoft Knowledge Base article 221833 (*http://support.microsoft.com/221833*), "How to enable user environment debug logging in retail builds of Windows." The customer pushed a script out to their systems to make the required registry changes and, shortly after, got another call from a user with the profile problem. They grabbed a copy of the profile log off the system from %SystemRoot%\Debug\UserMode\Userenv.log and sent it into Microsoft. The log was inconclusive, but it did provide an important clue: it indicated that the user's profile had failed to load because of error 32, which is ERROR_SHARING_VIOLATION. See (Figure 16-29.)

```
USERENV(2dc.a6c) 16:23:14:599 GetGPOInfo:  Local GPO's gpt.ini is not
USERENV(2dc.c14) 16:23:14:678 PolicyChangedThread: UpdateUser failed w
USERENV(2dc.2e0) 16:33:04:565 MyRegLoadKey:  Failed to load subkey
<S-1-5-21-1292428093-343818398-839522115-49106>, error =32
USERENV(2dc.2e0) 16:33:04:565 ReportError: Impersonating user.
```

FIGURE 16-29 Userenv.log indicating a profile load failure due to a sharing violation.

When a process opens a file, it specifies what kinds of sharing it allows for the file. If it is writing to the file, it might allow other processes to read from the file, for example, but not also to write to the file. The sharing violation in the log file meant that another process had opened the user's registry hive in a way that was incompatible with the way that the logon process wanted to open the file.

In the meantime, more customers around the world began contacting Microsoft and Citrix with the same issue, all of whom had also deployed the new ICA client. Citrix support then reported that they suspected the sharing violation might be caused by one of the ICA client's processes, Ssonvr.exe. During installation, the ICA client registers a Network Provider DLL (Pnsson.dll) that the Windows Multiple Provider Notification Application (%SystemRoot%\System32\Mpnotify.exe) calls when the system boots. Mpnotify.exe is itself launched at logon by the Winlogon process. The Citrix notification DLL launches the Ssonvr.exe process asynchronous to the user's logon, as shown in Figure 16-30. The only problem with the theory was that Citrix developers insisted that the process did not attempt to load any user registry profile or even read any keys or values from one. Both Microsoft and Citrix were stumped.

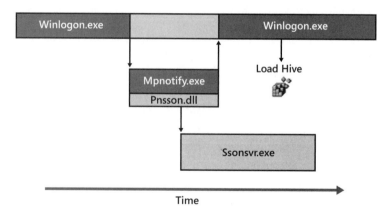

FIGURE 16-30 Asynchronous launch of Ssonsvr.exe during user logon.

Microsoft created a version of Winlogon and the kernel with additional diagnostic information and tried to reproduce the problem on lab systems configured identically to the client's, but without success. The customer couldn't even reproduce the problem with the modified Windows images, presumably because the images changed the timing of the system enough to avoid the problem. At this point, a Microsoft support engineer suggested that the customer capture a trace of logon activity with Procmon.

There are a couple of ways to configure Procmon to record logon operations: one is to use Sysinternals PsExec to launch it in a noninteractive window station in session 0[2] so that it survives the logoff and subsequent logon, and another is to use the boot logging feature to capture activity from early in the boot, including the logon. The engineer chose the latter, so he told the customer to run Process Monitor on one of the systems that regularly exhibited the problem, select Enable Boot Logging from the Process Monitor Options menu, and reboot, repeating the steps until the problem reproduced. This procedure configures the Process Monitor driver to load early in the boot process and log activity to %SystemRoot%\Procmon.pmb. When the customer next encountered the issue, they were to run Process Monitor again, at which point the driver would stop logging and Process Monitor would offer to convert the boot log into a standard Process Monitor log file.

After a couple of attempts, the user captured a boot log file and submitted it to Microsoft. Microsoft support engineers scanned through the log and came across the sharing violation error when Winlogon tried to load the user's registry hive. (See Figure 16-31.) It was obvious from operations immediately preceding the error that Ssonsvr.exe was the process that had the hive opened. The question was, why was Ssonsvr.exe opening the registry hive?

ssonsvr.exe	3976	CreateFileMapp...	C:\Documents and Settings\a700373\NTUSER.DAT	SUCCESS
ssonsvr.exe	3976	QueryStandardI...	C:\Documents and Settings\a700373\NTUSER.DAT	SUCCESS
ssonsvr.exe	3976	CreateFileMapp...	C:\Documents and Settings\a700373\NTUSER.DAT	SUCCESS
winlogon.exe	684	QueryOpen	C:\Documents and Settings\a700373\NTUSER.DAT	SUCCESS
winlogon.exe	684	CreateFile	C:\Documents and Settings\a700373\NTUSER.DAT	SHARING VIOLATION
ssonsvr.exe	3976	CloseFile	C:\Documents and Settings\a700373\NTUSER.DAT	SUCCESS
winlogon.exe	684	CreateFile	C:\Documents and Settings\TEMP\NTUSER.DAT	NAME NOT FOUND
winlogon.exe	684	CreateFile	C:\Documents and Settings\Default User\NTUSER.D...	SUCCESS

FIGURE 16-31 SSonsvr.exe opening Ntuser.dat, leading to a sharing violation when opened by Winlogon.exe.

To answer that question, the engineers turned to Process Monitor's stack trace functionality. Process Monitor captures a call stack for every operation, which represents the function call nesting responsible for the operation. By looking at a call stack, you can often determine an operation's root cause when it might not be obvious just from the process that executed it. For example, the stack shows you if a DLL loaded into the process executed the operation, and if you have symbols configured and the call originates in a Windows image or other image for which you have symbols, it will even show you the names of the responsible functions.

The stack for Ssonsvr.exe's open of the Ntuser.dat file (shown in Figure 16-32) showed that Ssonsvr.exe wasn't actually responsible for the operation: the Windows Logical Prefetcher was.

---

[2] See Chapter 2, Windows Core Concepts," for more information about window stations and session 0 and Chapter 4, "Process Monitor," for more information about launching it with PsExec.

```
 8  ntkrnlpa.exe   nt!IopfCallDriver+0x31
 9  ntkrnlpa.exe   nt!ObpLookupObjectName+0x53c
10  ntkrnlpa.exe   nt!ObOpenObjectByName+0xea
11  ntkrnlpa.exe   nt!IopCreateFile+0x407
12  ntkrnlpa.exe   nt!IoCreateFile+0x8e
13  ntkrnlpa.exe   nt!CcPfGetSectionObject+0x91
14  ntkrnlpa.exe   nt!CcPfPrefetchSections+0x2b7
15  ntkrnlpa.exe   nt!CcPfPrefetchScenario+0x7b
16  ntkrnlpa.exe   nt!CcPfBeginAppLaunch+0x158
17  ntkrnlpa.exe   nt!PspUserThreadStartup+0xeb
18  ntkrnlpa.exe   nt!KiThreadStartup+0x16
```

FIGURE 16-32 Highlighted Prefetcher code invoking *IoCreateFile* to open Ntuser.dat.

Introduced in Windows XP, the Logical Prefetcher is a kernel component that monitors the first 10 seconds of a process launch, recording the directories and portions of files accessed by the process during that time to a file it stores in %SystemRoot%\Prefetch. So that multiple executables with the same name but in different folder get their own prefetch files, the Logical Prefetcher gives the file a name that's a concatenation of the executable image name and the hash of the path in which the image is stored—for example, NOTEPAD.EXE-D8414F97.pf. You can actually see the files and folders the Logical Prefetcher saw in an application reference the last time it launched by using the Sysinternals Strings utility to scan a prefetch file like this:

```
strings prefetch-file
```

The next time the application launches, the Logical Prefetcher, executing in the context of the process's first thread, looks for a prefetch file. If one exists, it opens each directory it lists to bring the folder's metadata into memory if it's not already present. The Logical Prefetcher then maps each file listed in the prefetch file and references the portions accessed the last time the application ran so that they also get brought into memory. The Logical Prefetcher can speed up an application launch because it generates large, sequential I/Os instead of issuing small random accesses to file data as the application would typically do during startup.

The implication of the Logical Prefetcher in the profile problem only raised more questions, however. Why was it prefetching the user's hive file in the context of Ssonsvr.exe when Ssonsvr.exe itself never accesses registry profiles? Microsoft support contacted the Logical Prefetcher's development team for the answer. The developers first noted that the registry on Windows XP is read into memory using cached file I/O operations, which means that the Cache Manager's read-ahead thread will proactively read portions of the hive. Because the read-ahead thread executes in the System process, and the Logical Prefetcher associates System process activity with the currently launching process, a specific timing sequence of process launches and activity during the boot and log on could cause hive accesses to be seen by the Logical Prefetcher as being part of the Ssonsvr.exe launch. If the order was slightly different during the next boot and log on, Winlogon might collide with the Logical Prefetcher, as seen in the captured boot log.

The Logical Prefetcher is supposed to execute transparently to other activities on a system, but its file references can lead to sharing violations like this on Windows XP systems. (On server systems, the Logical Prefetcher prefetches only boot activity, and it does so synchronously before the boot process proceeds.) For that reason, on Windows Vista and Windows 7 systems, the Logical Prefetcher makes use of a file system minifilter driver, Fileinfo (%SystemRoot%\System32\Drivers\Fileinfo.sys) to watch for potential sharing violation collisions and prevent them by stalling a second open operation on a file being accessed by the Logical Prefetcher until the Logical Prefetcher closes the file.

Now that the problem was understood, Microsoft and Citrix brainstormed on workarounds customers could apply while Citrix worked on an update to the ICA Client that would prevent the sharing violation. One workaround was to disable application prefetching and another was to write a logoff script that deletes the Ssonsvr.exe prefetch files. Citrix published the workarounds in a Citrix Knowledge Base article[3] and Microsoft published one in Microsoft Knowledge Base article 969100 (*http://support.microsoft.com/kb/969100*). The update to the ICA Client, which was made available a few days later, changed the network provider DLL to 10 seconds after Ssonsvr.exe launches before returning control to Mpnotify.exe. Because Winlogon waits for Mpnotify to exit before logging on a user, the Logical Prefetcher won't associate Winlogon's accesses of the user's hive with Ssonsvr.exe's startup.

As I said in the introduction, I find this case particularly interesting because it demonstrates a little-known Procmon feature, boot logging, and the power of stack traces for root cause analysis—two key tools for everyone's troubleshooting arsenal. It also shows how successful troubleshooting sometimes means coming up with a workaround when there is no fix or when you must wait until a vendor provides one. Another case successfully closed with Procmon!

---

3   *http://support.citrix.com/article/CTX118226*

Chapter 17
Hangs and Sluggish Performance

The cases in this chapter involve application hangs and slow system performance. Call-stack analysis features prominently in these cases, using Procexp, Procmon, and ProcDump.

- **The Case of the IExplore-Pegged CPU** demonstrates the use of thread stacks in Procexp to identify a root cause.

- **The Case of the Excessive ReadyBoost** uses Procexp to establish a hypothesis and Procmon to confirm it.

- **The Case of the Slow Keynote Demo** proves that what can go wrong, will go wrong, and that the probability of demo failure tends to be proportional with the size of the audience. It identifies long gaps between events captured by Procmon, which leads to a diagnosis.

- **The Case of the Slow Project File Opens** demonstrates Procmon's File Summary dialog box, which can help you quickly identify the files being accessed the most and the ones consuming the most time. Call-stack analysis then helps you identify the module causing the performance issues.

- **The Compound Case of the Outlook Hangs** describes a pair of related cases from Microsoft support services and highlights the use of ProcDump, which I specifically wrote for their use.

The Case of the IExplore-Pegged CPU

One day after installing Adobe Reader and closing Internet Explorer, I noticed from the Procexp icon in my notification area ("the tray") that CPU usage was abnormally high. When I hovered my mouse over the icon, the tooltip shown in Figure 17-1 informed me that an Iexplore.exe process was consuming an even 50 percent. Because I was using a two-processor system, I hypothesized that one thread in the Iexplore.exe process was caught in an infinite loop.

FIGURE 17-1 Procexp notification area icon and tooltip reporting high CPU usage in Iexplore.exe.

I opened Procexp, found the Iexplore.exe process, opened its Properties dialog box, and clicked on the Threads tab. As I expected, a single thread was CPU-bound, as you can see in Figure 17-2. This demonstrates one of the benefits of multi-CPU systems: a runaway thread can consume only the equivalent of one CPU—a maximum of 50 percent on this system—leaving plenty of CPU available for other work, including your troubleshooting efforts. On a single-CPU system, a runaway thread tends to completely bog down the entire system.

FIGURE 17-2 A runaway thread hogging the equivalent of one CPU on a dual-core system.

The start address of the runaway thread didn't provide any clues—it was just the standard thread entry point in the Windows C runtime DLL. To get a better idea of what code it was running, I selected it in the thread list and clicked the Stack button. The call stack showed code originating in gp.ocx, as shown in frames 21–25 in Figure 17-3.

FIGURE 17-3 Code in the runaway thread originating in gp.ocx.

I had never heard of gp.ocx, so I opened DLL view and searched for it in the Iexplore.exe process. It describes itself as "getPlus(R) ActiveX Control", from NOS Microsystems Ltd. (See Figure 17-4.)

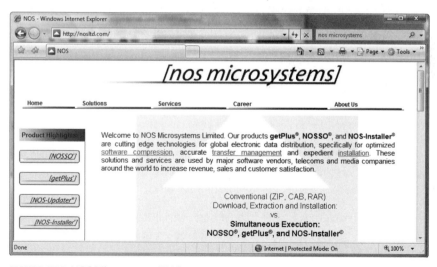

FIGURE 17-4 Finding out about gp.ocx in DLL View.

I Bing-searched for "NOS Microsystems" and found its Web page. (See Figure 17-5.) It looked like a legitimate downloader, and I vaguely recalled seeing the name "getPlus" on the Adobe Reader download program. I then ran Autoruns and verified that gp.ocx was not configured to auto-start and that it would get loaded again only if a Web page specifically invoked it, which I considered unlikely. I terminated Iexplore.exe in Procexp and restarted Internet Explorer. After verifying that it hadn't loaded gp.ocx again, I closed the case.

FIGURE 17-5 NOS Microsystems' Web page.

The Case of the Excessive ReadyBoost

The user had been running Windows 7 on his laptop for over a year with no issues at all, often leaving the laptop running for weeks at a time. However, he had recently begun having problems when bringing the laptop out of sleep mode. Performance was sluggish and the hard disk light stayed on solid for at least five minutes.

He started Procexp to see what process or processes were consuming CPU cycles and found the System process consuming about 35 percent, which is a lot for a dual-processor system. Double-clicking on the System process to open its Properties and clicking on the Threads tab, he saw that the culprit had a start address in Rdyboost.sys, the ReadyBoost driver. (See Figure 17-6.)

FIGURE 17-6 A System thread starting in Rdyboost.sys consuming 35 percent of available CPU.

ReadyBoost is a feature of Windows Vista and Windows 7 that offers performance advantages by using a solid state drive such as an SD card or USB thumb drive as memory cache. Such drives are typically faster than traditional disks.

To confirm that the problem was with ReadyBoost, he captured a Procmon trace. At first, he didn't see anything interesting, but then he remembered to remove the default filter that hides System process activity. (See Figure 17-7.)

FIGURE 17-7 Un-hiding System process activity in Procmon by deselecting the Exclude filter.

As shown in Figure 17-8, the trace showed long sequences of reads from the H drive, an 8-GB flash card he had configured for use with ReadyBoost.

FIGURE 17-8 Long sequences of reads from the ReadyBoost cache file on drive H.

Finally, he looked at the File Summary from the Procmon Tools menu and found that a great deal of CPU time was spent reading from the ReadyBoost drive. (See Figure 17-9.) Satisfied that he knew where the root cause of the performance problems lay, he removed the flash card and the computer immediately settled down. Problems with ReadyBoost like this are rare; he guessed that something specific in his configuration or the flash card triggered this anomalous behavior, which was probably due to a bug.

FIGURE 17-9 Procmon File Summary shows a lot of time spent reading from the ReadyBoost cache.

The Case of the Slow Keynote Demo

In 2009, I participated in the keynote at Microsoft's TechEd US conference to a room of over 5000 attendees.[1] Bill Veghte, Senior Vice President of Windows marketing, led the keynote and gave a tour of the user-focused features of Windows 7, Iain McDonald, General Manager for Windows Server, demonstrated new functionality in Hyper-V and Windows Server 2008 R2, and I demonstrated IT Pro–oriented enhancements in Windows 7 and the Microsoft Desktop Optimization Pack (MDOP).

I showed features like BitLocker-To-Go Group Policy settings, Windows PowerShell version 2's remoting capabilities, PowerShell's ability to script Group Policy objects, Microsoft Enterprise Desktop Virtualization (MED-V), and how the combination of App-V, roaming user profiles, and folder redirection enable a replaceable PC scenario with minimal downtime. One point I reinforced was the fact that we made every effort to ensure that application-compatibility fixes (called *shims*) that IT Pros have developed for Windows Vista applications work on Windows 7. I also demonstrated Windows 7's new AppLocker feature, which allows IT Pros to restrict the software that users can run on enterprise desktops with flexible rules for identifying software.

In the weeks leading up to the keynote, I worked with Jason Leznek, the owner of the IT Pro portion of the keynote, to identify the features I would showcase and to design the demos. We used dry runs to walk through the script, tweaking the demos and creating transitions, trimming content to fit the time allotted to my segment and tightening my narration to focus on the benefits of the new technologies. For the application-compatibility demo, we decided to use a sample program called StockViewer that my friend Chris Jackson (The App Compat Guy) created to demonstrate common bugs that cause compatibility problems on Windows Vista and Windows 7. (StockViewer is now the demo application that comes with

---

[1] The keynote is available for viewing online at *http://www.msteched.com/2009/NorthAmerica/KEY01*. My part begins at around 42:20.

the Microsoft Application Compatibility Toolkit.) In my demo, I would launch StockViewer on Windows 7 and show how its Trends function fails with an obscure error message caused by a compatibility bug. (See Figure 17-10.) Then I would show how I could deploy an application-compatibility shim that enables the application to work correctly on Windows Vista and then rerun the application successfully.

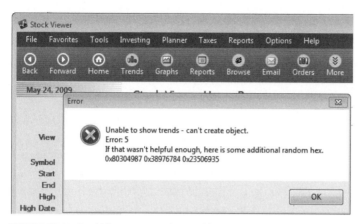

FIGURE 17-10 StockViewer error triggered by a compatibility bug.

We also wanted to show how AppLocker's Rule Creation wizard makes it easy to allow software to run based on the publisher or version if the software is digitally signed. Originally, we planned on showing AppLocker after the application-compatibility demo and enabling Adobe Acrobat Reader, an application commonly used in enterprises. We rehearsed this flow a couple of times but found the transitions a little awkward, so I suggested that we sign the StockViewer executable and move the AppLocker demo before the shim demo. I'd be able to enable StockViewer to run with an AppLocker rule and then show how the shim helps it run correctly, using it for both demos.

I went back to my office, signed StockViewer with the Sysinternals signing certificate and sent it to Jason. A few hours later he e-mailed me that something was wrong with the demo system because StockViewer, which had previously launched instantly, now took over a minute to start. We were counting down to TechEd and he was panicking because we needed to nail down the demos. I had heard at some point in the past that .NET performs Authenticode signature checks when it loads digitally signed assemblies, so my first suspicion was that it was related to that. I asked Jason to capture a Process Monitor trace, and he e-mailed it back a few minutes later.

After opening the log, the first thing I did was filter events for StockViewer.exe by finding its first operation and right-clicking to set a quick filter, as shown in Figure 17-11.

FIGURE 17-11 Setting a filter for StockViewer.exe with a quick filter.

Then I looked at the time stamps on the first item (2:27:20) and the last item (2:28:32), which correlated with the one-minute delay Jason had observed. As I scrolled through the trace, I saw many references to cryptography (crypto) registry keys and file system folders, as well as references to TCP/IP settings, but I knew that there had to be at least one major gap in the time stamps to account for the long delay. I scanned the log from the beginning and found a gap of roughly 10 seconds at 2:27:22. (See Figure 17-12.)

Time of Day	Process Name	Operation	Path	Result
2:27:21.1500415 PM	StockViewer.exe	CloseFile	C:\Windows\System32\rasadhlp.dll	SUCCESS
2:27:21.1501741 PM	StockViewer.exe	CreateFile	C:\Windows\System32\rasadhlp.dll	SUCCESS
2:27:21.1503016 PM	StockViewer.exe	CreateFileMa...	C:\Windows\System32\rasadhlp.dll	FILE LOCKED WI...
2:27:21.1503485 PM	StockViewer.exe	CreateFileMa...	C:\Windows\System32\rasadhlp.dll	SUCCESS
2:27:21.1505176 PM	StockViewer.exe	Load Image	C:\Windows\System32\rasadhlp.dll	SUCCESS
2:27:21.1505375 PM	StockViewer.exe	CloseFile	C:\Windows\System32\rasadhlp.dll	SUCCESS
2:27:22.0634600 PM	StockViewer.exe	Thread Create		SUCCESS
2:27:32.3219796 PM	StockViewer.exe	CreateFile	C:\Windows\System32\en-US\winhttp.dll.mui	SUCCESS
2:27:32.3220001 PM	StockViewer.exe	CreateFileMa...	C:\Windows\System32\en-US\winhttp.dll.mui	FILE LOCKED WI...
2:27:32.3220976 PM	StockViewer.exe	QueryStanda...	C:\Windows\System32\en-US\winhttp.dll.mui	SUCCESS
2:27:32.3221374 PM	StockViewer.exe	CreateFileMa...	C:\Windows\System32\en-US\winhttp.dll.mui	SUCCESS
2:27:32.3224601 PM	StockViewer.exe	RegOpenKey	HKLM\SYSTEM\CurrentControlSet\Services\crypt32	REPARSE
2:27:32.3225041 PM	StockViewer.exe	RegOpenKey	HKLM\System\CurrentControlSet\Services\crypt32	SUCCESS
2:27:32.3225577 PM	StockViewer.exe	RegQueryVa...	HKLM\System\CurrentControlSet\Services\crypt32\Debu...	NAME NOT FOUND

FIGURE 17-12 A 10-second gap between StockViewer events.

The operations immediately before were references to the Rasadhlp.dll, a networking-related DLL, and a little earlier there were lots of references to Winsock registry keys, with accesses to crypto registry keys immediately after the 10-second delay. It appeared that the system was not connected to the Internet and that the application was held up by some networking timeout of roughly 10 seconds. I looked further down to find the next gap and came across a 12-second interval. (See Figure 17-13.)

Time of Day	Process Name	Operation	Path	Result
2:27:32.4735745 PM	StockViewer.exe	RegCloseKey	HKCU	SUCCESS
2:27:32.4735906 PM	StockViewer.exe	RegCloseKey	HKCU\Software\Microsoft\Windows\CurrentVersion\Inter...	SUCCESS
2:27:32.4741019 PM	StockViewer.exe	RegQueryVa...	HKLM\System\CurrentControlSet\Services\WinSock2\P...	SUCCESS
2:27:32.4741331 PM	StockViewer.exe	RegOpenKey	HKLM\System\CurrentControlSet\Services\WinSock2\P...	NAME NOT FOUND
2:27:44.3248702 PM	StockViewer.exe	RegOpenKey	HKLM\SYSTEM\CurrentControlSet\Services\crypt32	REPARSE
2:27:44.3249124 PM	StockViewer.exe	RegOpenKey	HKLM\System\CurrentControlSet\Services\crypt32	SUCCESS
2:27:44.3249669 PM	StockViewer.exe	RegQueryVa...	HKLM\System\CurrentControlSet\Services\crypt32\Debu...	NAME NOT FOUND
2:27:44.3249930 PM	StockViewer.exe	Thread Exit		SUCCESS
2:27:44.3249967 PM	StockViewer.exe	RegCloseKey	HKLM\System\CurrentControlSet\Services\crypt32	SUCCESS
2:27:44.3252962 PM	StockViewer.exe	RegOpenKey	HKLM\SYSTEM\CurrentControlSet\Services\crypt32	REPARSE
2:27:44.3253251 PM	StockViewer.exe	RegOpenKey	HKLM\System\CurrentControlSet\Services\crypt32	SUCCESS

FIGURE 17-13 A 12-second gap between StockViewer events.

Again, there was network-related activity before and crypto-related activity after the gap. The subsequent gap, also of 12 seconds, was identical. (See Figure 17-14.)

Time of Day	Process Name	Operation	Path	Result
2:27:44.4206750 PM	StockViewer.exe	RegCloseKey	HKCU\Software\Classes	SUCCESS
2:27:44.4208480 PM	StockViewer.exe	RegCloseKey	HKCU\Software\Microsoft\\Windows\CurrentVersion\Inter...	SUCCESS
2:27:44.4208788 PM	StockViewer.exe	RegCloseKey	HKCU	SUCCESS
2:27:44.4208920 PM	StockViewer.exe	RegCloseKey	HKCU\Software\Microsoft\\Windows\CurrentVersion\Inter...	SUCCESS
2:27:50.9861369 PM	StockViewer.exe	Thread Exit		SUCCESS
2:27:56.3482524 PM	StockViewer.exe	RegOpenKey	HKLM\SYSTEM\CurrentControlSet\Services\crypt32	REPARSE
2:27:56.3482970 PM	StockViewer.exe	RegOpenKey	HKLM\System\CurrentControlSet\Services\crypt32	SUCCESS
2:27:56.3483472 PM	StockViewer.exe	Thread Exit		SUCCESS
2:27:56.3483529 PM	StockViewer.exe	RegQueryVa...	HKLM\System\CurrentControlSet\Services\crypt32\Debu...	NAME NOT FOUND

FIGURE 17-14 Another 12-second gap between events.

In fact, the next few gaps looked virtually identical. In each case, there was a reference to HKCU\Software\Microsoft\Windows\CurrentVersion\Internet Settings\Connections immediately before the pause, so I set a filter for that path and for the *RegOpenKey* operation and, sure enough, could easily see five gaps of exactly 12 seconds each. (See Figure 17-15.)

Time of Day	Process Name	Operation	Path	Result
2:27:21.0764339 PM	StockViewer.exe	RegOpenKey	HKCU\Software\Microsoft\windows\CurrentVersion\Inter...	SUCCESS
2:27:21.1212746 PM	StockViewer.exe	RegOpenKey	HKCU\Software\Microsoft\windows\CurrentVersion\Inter...	SUCCESS
2:27:32.3539308 PM	StockViewer.exe	RegOpenKey	HKCU\Software\Microsoft\windows\CurrentVersion\Inter...	SUCCESS
2:27:32.4215307 PM	StockViewer.exe	RegOpenKey	HKCU\Software\Microsoft\windows\CurrentVersion\Inter...	SUCCESS
2:27:44.3402017 PM	StockViewer.exe	RegOpenKey	HKCU\Software\Microsoft\windows\CurrentVersion\Inter...	SUCCESS
2:27:44.3970143 PM	StockViewer.exe	RegOpenKey	HKCU\Software\Microsoft\windows\CurrentVersion\Inter...	SUCCESS
2:27:56.4164436 PM	StockViewer.exe	RegOpenKey	HKCU\Software\Microsoft\windows\CurrentVersion\Inter...	SUCCESS
2:27:56.4816304 PM	StockViewer.exe	RegOpenKey	HKCU\Software\Microsoft\windows\CurrentVersion\Inter...	SUCCESS
2:28:08.3923185 PM	StockViewer.exe	RegOpenKey	HKCU\Software\Microsoft\windows\CurrentVersion\Inter...	SUCCESS
2:28:08.4287594 PM	StockViewer.exe	RegOpenKey	HKCU\Software\Microsoft\windows\CurrentVersion\Inter...	SUCCESS
2:28:20.3860900 PM	StockViewer.exe	RegOpenKey	HKCU\Software\Microsoft\windows\CurrentVersion\Inter...	SUCCESS
2:28:20.4268362 PM	StockViewer.exe	RegOpenKey	HKCU\Software\Microsoft\windows\CurrentVersion\Inter...	SUCCESS

FIGURE 17-15 Five gaps of 12 seconds each.

The sum of the gaps—12 times 5—equaled the delay Jason was seeing. Next, I wanted to verify that the repeated attempts to access the network were caused by signing verification, so I started looking at the call stacks of various events by selecting them and pressing Ctrl+K to open the Stack Properties dialog box. The stack for events related to the Internet connection settings revealed that crypto was the reason. (See Figure 17-16.)

U 9	KernelBase.dll	RegCloseKey + 0x7d
U 10	winhttp.dll	CRegBlob::~CRegBlob + 0x17
U 11	winhttp.dll	WinHttpGetIEProxyConfigForCurrentUser + 0xc9
U 12	cryptnet.dll	InetGetProxy + 0xcf
U 13	cryptnet.dll	InetSendReceiveUrlRequest + 0x26f
U 14	cryptnet.dll	CInetSynchronousRetriever::RetrieveObjectByUrl + 0x5f
U 15	cryptnet.dll	InetRetrieveEncodedObject + 0x64
U 16	cryptnet.dll	CObjectRetrievalManager::RetrieveObjectByUrl + 0xbb
U 17	cryptnet.dll	CryptRetrieveObjectByUrlWithTimeoutThreadProc + 0x67
U 18	kernel32.dll	BaseThreadInitThunk + 0xe
U 19	ntdll.dll	__RtlUserThreadStart + 0x70
U 20	ntdll.dll	_RtlUserThreadStart + 0x1b

FIGURE 17-16 Call stack reveals involvement of cryptographic operations.

One final piece of evidence I wanted to check for was that .NET was ultimately responsible for these checks. I rescanned the log, and I saw events in the trace that confirmed that StockViewer is a .NET application. (See Figure 17-17.)

StockViewer.exe	CreateFileMapping	C:\Program Files\StockViewer\StockViewer.exe
StockViewer.exe	CreateFileMapping	C:\Windows\Microsoft.NET\Framework\v2.0.50727\mscorwks.dll
StockViewer.exe	CreateFileMapping	C:\Windows\Microsoft.NET\Framework\v2.0.50727\mscorwks.dll
StockViewer.exe	CreateFileMapping	C:\Windows\winsxs\x86_microsoft.vc80.crt_1fc8b3b9a1e18e3b_8.0.50727.3521_none...
StockViewer.exe	CreateFileMapping	C:\Windows\winsxs\x86_microsoft.vc80.crt_1fc8b3b9a1e18e3b_8.0.50727.3521_none...
StockViewer.exe	CreateFileMapping	C:\Windows\assembly\NativeImages_v2.0.50727_32\mscorlib\3ff595610f8be0c50733...
StockViewer.exe	CreateFileMapping	C:\Windows\assembly\NativeImages_v2.0.50727_32\mscorlib\3ff595610f8be0c50733...
StockViewer.exe	CreateFileMapping	C:\Windows\Microsoft.NET\Framework\v2.0.50727\mscorsec.dll
StockViewer.exe	CreateFileMapping	C:\Windows\Microsoft.NET\Framework\v2.0.50727\mscorsec.dll
StockViewer.exe	CreateFileMapping	C:\Windows\winsxs\x86_microsoft.windows.common-controls_6595b64144ccf1df_5.82...
StockViewer.exe	CreateFileMapping	C:\Windows\winsxs\x86_microsoft.windows.common-controls_6595b64144ccf1df_5.82...

FIGURE 17-17 Evidence that .NET is involved.

I also looked at the stacks of some of the early events referencing crypto registry keys and saw that it was the .NET runtime invoking the call to *WinVerifyTrust*, the Windows function for checking the digital signature on a file, that started the cascade of attempted Internet accesses. (See Figure 17-18.)

FIGURE 17-18 .NET Framework invoking *WinVerifyTrust*.

Confident now that the cause of the startup delay was due to .NET seeing that Stockviewer. exe was signed and then checking to see if the signing certificate had been revoked, I entered Web searches looking for a way to make .NET skip the check, because I knew that the keynote machines probably wouldn't be connected to the Internet during the actual keynote. After a couple of minutes of reading through articles by others with similar experiences, I found Knowledge Base article 936707, "FIX: A .NET Framework 2.0 managed application that has an Authenticode signature takes longer than usual to start" (available at *http://support.microsoft.com/kb/936707*) The article describes exactly the symptoms we were seeing and notes that .NET 2.0, which is the version of .NET I could see StockViewer was using based on the paths of the .NET DLLs it accessed during the trace, supports a way to turn off its obligatory checking of assembly digital signatures: create a configuration file in the executable's directory with the same name as the executable except with ".config" appended (for example, StockViewer.exe.config) containing the following XML:

```xml
<?xml version="1.0" encoding="utf-8"?>
<configuration>
      <runtime>
              <generatePublisherEvidence enabled="false"/>
      </runtime>
</configuration>
```

About 15 minutes after I had received Jason's e-mail, I sent him a reply explaining my conclusion with the configuration file attached. Shortly after, he wrote back confirming the delays were gone and expressing amazement that I had figured out the problem and solution so quickly. It might have seemed like magic to him, but I had simply used basic Procmon troubleshooting techniques and the Web to solve the case. Needless to say, the revised demo flow and transition between AppLocker and application compatibility came off great.

The Case of the Slow Project File Opens

The case opened when the customer, a network administrator, contacted Microsoft support because a user reported that Microsoft Project files located on a network share were taking up to a minute to open and about once every 10 times the open resulted in the error shown in Figure 17-19.

FIGURE 17-19 Error that occurred on Project file opens one time in 10.

The administrator verified the issue and checked networking settings and latency to the file server, but he could not find anything that would explain the problem. The Microsoft support engineer assigned to the case asked the administrator to capture Procmon and Network Monitor traces of a slow file open. After receiving the logs a short time later, he opened the Procmon log and set a filter to include only operations issued by the Project process and then another filter to include paths that referenced the target file share. The File Summary dialog box, which he opened from Procmon's Tools menu, showed significant time spent in file operations accessing files on the share, shown in the File Time column in Figure 17-20.

FIGURE 17-20 File Summary dialog box showing time spent in file operations (domain name obscured).

The paths in the trace revealed that the user profiles were stored on the file server and that the launch of Project caused heavy access of the profile's AppData subdirectory. If many users had their profiles stored on the same server via folder redirection and were running similar applications that used stored data in AppData, that would surely account for at least some of the delays the user was experiencing. It is well known that redirecting the AppData directory can result ihbn performance problems, so based on this, the support engineer arrived at his first recommendation: for the company to configure its roaming user profiles not to redirect AppData and to sync the AppData directory only at logon and logoff per the guidance found in this Microsoft blog post[2]:

> *Special considerations for AppData\Roaming folder:*
>
> *If the AppData folder is redirected, some applications may experience performance issues because they will be accessing this folder over the network. If that is the case, it is recommended that you configure the following Group Policy setting to sync the AppData\Roaming folder only at logon and logoff and use the local cache while the user is logged on. While this may have an impact on logon/logoff speeds, the user experience may be better since applications will not freeze due to network latency.*
>
> *User configuration>Administrative Templates>System>User Profiles>Network directories to sync at Logon/Logoff.*
>
> *If applications continue to experience issues, you should consider excluding AppData from Folder Redirection – the downside of doing so is that it may increase your logon/logoff time.*

Next, the engineer examined the trace to see if Project was responsible for all the traffic to files such as Global.MPT or if an add-in was responsible. This is where the stack trace was indispensible. After setting a filter to show just accesses to Global.MPT, the file that accounted for most of the I/O time as shown by the summary dialog box, he noticed that it was opened and had been read multiple times. First, he saw five or six long runs of small, random reads. (See Figure 17-21.)

FIGURE 17-21 Long runs of small, random reads over the network.

---

2   User Profiles on Windows Server 2008 R2 Remote Desktop Services, *http://blogs.msdn.com/b/rds/ archive/2009/06/02/user-profiles-on-windows-server-2008-r2-remote-desktop-services.aspx*

The stacks for these operations showed that Project itself was responsible, however. In Figure 17-22, frame 25 shows WINPROJ.EXE invoking code in Ole32.dll, which eventually calls into Kernel32.dll (frame 15), which calls the *ReadFile* API in Kernelbase.dll—all of which are Windows DLLs.

Frame	Module	Location
U 6	wow64cpu.dll	CpupSyscallStub + 0x9
U 7	wow64cpu.dll	ReadWriteFileFault + 0x31
U 8	wow64.dll	RunCpuSimulation + 0xa
U 9	wow64.dll	Wow64LdrpInitialize + 0x429
U 10	ntdll.dll	LdrpInitializeProcess + 0x17e2, d:\
U 11	ntdll.dll	_LdrpInitialize + 0x14533
U 12	ntdll.dll	LdrInitializeThunk + 0xe, d:\w7rtm
U 13	ntdll.dll	ZwReadFile + 0x15, o:\w7rtm.obj.
U 14	KERNELBASE.dll	ReadFile + 0x118
U 15	kernel32.dll	ReadFileImplementation + 0xf0
U 16	ole32.dll	CFileStream::ReadAt_FromFile + 0
U 17	ole32.dll	CFileStream::ReadAt + 0xb1, d:\w
U 18	ole32.dll	CDirectStream::ReadAt + 0x222, c
U 19	ole32.dll	CDirectStream::ReadAt + 0x1e7, c
U 20	ole32.dll	PSStream::ReadAt + 0x46, d:\w7r
U 21	ole32.dll	CTransactedStream::ReadAt + 0x:
U 22	ole32.dll	PSStream::ReadAt + 0x3f, d:\w7rt
U 23	ole32.dll	CPubStream::ReadAt + 0x56, d:\w
U 24	ole32.dll	CExposedStream::Read + 0x7d, d
U 25	WINPROJ.EXE	WINPROJ.EXE + 0x123663
U 26	WINPROJ.EXE	WINPROJ.EXE + 0x126528

FIGURE 17-22 Winproj.exe invokes Windows code to read a file.

He also saw sequences of large, noncached reads. (See Figure 17-23.) The small reads he had looked at first were cached, so there would be no network access after the first read caused the data to cache locally. But noncached reads would go to the server every time, making them much more likely to impact performance:

Operation	Path	Result	Detail
ReadFile	\\........COM\LON-...	SUCCESS	Offset: 0, Length: 4,096, I/O Flags: Non-cached, Paging I/O, Priority: Normal
ReadFile	\\........COM\LON-...	SUCCESS	Offset: 524,288, Length: 3,584, I/O Flags: Non-cached, Paging I/O, Priority: Normal
ReadFile	\\........COM\LON-...	SUCCESS	Offset: 516,096, Length: 4,096, I/O Flags: Non-cached, Paging I/O, Priority: Normal
ReadFile	\\........COM\LON-...	SUCCESS	Offset: 520,192, Length: 4,096, I/O Flags: Non-cached, Paging I/O, Priority: Normal
ReadFile	\\........COM\LON-...	SUCCESS	Offset: 4,096, Length: 4,096, I/O Flags: Non-cached, Paging I/O, Priority: Normal
ReadFile	\\........COM\LON-...	SUCCESS	Offset: 61,440, Length: 4,096, I/O Flags: Non-cached, Paging I/O, Priority: Normal
ReadFile	\\........COM\LON-...	SUCCESS	Offset: 122,880, Length: 4,096, I/O Flags: Non-cached, Paging I/O, Priority: Normal
ReadFile	\\........COM\LON-...	SUCCESS	Offset: 323,584, Length: 4,096, I/O Flags: Non-cached, Paging I/O, Priority: Normal
ReadFile	\\........COM\LON-...	SUCCESS	Offset: 458,752, Length: 4,096, I/O Flags: Non-cached, Paging I/O, Priority: Normal
ReadFile	\\........COM\LON-...	SUCCESS	Offset: 131,072, Length: 4,096, I/O Flags: Non-cached, Paging I/O, Priority: Normal
ReadFile	\\........COM\LON-...	SUCCESS	Offset: 196,608, Length: 4,096, I/O Flags: Non-cached, Paging I/O, Priority: Normal
ReadFile	\\........COM\LON-...	SUCCESS	Offset: 450,560, Length: 4,096, I/O Flags: Non-cached, Paging I/O, Priority: Normal
ReadFile	\\........COM\LON-...	SUCCESS	Offset: 495,616, Length: 4,096, I/O Flags: Non-cached, Paging I/O, Priority: Normal
ReadFile	\\........COM\LON-...	SUCCESS	Offset: 253,952, Length: 4,096, I/O Flags: Non-cached, Paging I/O, Priority: Normal
ReadFile	\\........COM\LON-...	SUCCESS	Offset: 466,944, Length: 4,096, I/O Flags: Non-cached, Paging I/O, Priority: Normal
ReadFile	\\........COM\LON-...	SUCCESS	Offset: 499,712, Length: 4,096, I/O Flags: Non-cached, Paging I/O, Priority: Normal
ReadFile	\\........COM\LON-...	SUCCESS	Offset: 512,000, Length: 4,096, I/O Flags: Non-cached, Paging I/O, Priority: Normal
ReadFile	\\........COM\LON-...	SUCCESS	Offset: 507,904, Length: 4,096, I/O Flags: Non-cached, Paging I/O, Priority: Normal
ReadFile	\\........COM\LON-...	SUCCESS	Offset: 483,328, Length: 8,192, I/O Flags: Non-cached, Paging I/O, Priority: Normal
ReadFile	\\........COM\LON-...	SUCCESS	Offset: 471,040, Length: 8,192, I/O Flags: Non-cached, Paging I/O, Priority: Normal
ReadFile	\\........COM\LON-...	SUCCESS	Offset: 479,232, Length: 4,096, I/O Flags: Non-cached, Paging I/O, Priority: Normal
ReadFile	\\........COM\LON-...	SUCCESS	Offset: 106,496, Length: 4,096, I/O Flags: Non-cached, Paging I/O, Priority: Normal
ReadFile	\\........COM\LON-...	SUCCESS	Offset: 110,592, Length: 4,096, I/O Flags: Non-cached, Paging I/O, Priority: Normal
ReadFile	\\........COM\LON-...	SUCCESS	Offset: 454,656, Length: 4,096, I/O Flags: Non-cached, Paging I/O, Priority: Normal

FIGURE 17-23 Sequences of large, noncached reads over the network.

To make matters worse, he saw the same file being re-read over the network multiple times in the trace. The trace shown in Figure 17-24 is filtered to show the initial file reads, where the file offset in the Detail column is set to 0.

FIGURE 17-24 Files being re-read over the network; file offset 0 indicates reading from the beginning of the file.

The stacks for these reads revealed them to be the result of a third-party driver, SRTSP64.SYS. The first hint that it is a third-party driver is visible in frames 18–21 in the stack trace dialog box shown in Figure 17-25. With Procmon configured to obtain symbols from Microsoft's symbol servers, SRTSP64.SYS has no symbol information and invokes *FltReadFile* (frame 17).

Frame	Module	Location	Path
K 0	fltmgr.sys	FltpPerformPreCallbacks + ...	C:\Windows\system32\drivers\fltmgr.sys
K 1	fltmgr.sys	FltpPassThrough + 0x2d9	C:\Windows\system32\drivers\fltmgr.sys
K 2	fltmgr.sys	FltpDispatch + 0xb7	C:\Windows\system32\drivers\fltmgr.sys
K 3	ntoskrnl.exe	IoPageRead + 0x252	C:\Windows\system32\ntoskrnl.exe
K 4	ntoskrnl.exe	MiPfExecuteReadList + 0xff	C:\Windows\system32\ntoskrnl.exe
K 5	ntoskrnl.exe	MmPrefetchForCacheMan...	C:\Windows\system32\ntoskrnl.exe
K 6	ntoskrnl.exe	CcFetchDataForRead + 0x...	C:\Windows\system32\ntoskrnl.exe
K 7	ntoskrnl.exe	CcCopyRead + 0x16b	C:\Windows\system32\ntoskrnl.exe
K 8	rdbss.sys	RxCommonRead + 0xdb1, ...	C:\Windows\system32\DRIVERS\rdbss.sys
K 9	rdbss.sys	RxFsdCommonDispatch + ...	C:\Windows\system32\DRIVERS\rdbss.sys
K 10	rdbss.sys	RxFsdDispatch + 0x224, d...	C:\Windows\system32\DRIVERS\rdbss.sys
K 11	mrxsmb.sys	MRxSmbFsdDispatch + 0x...	C:\Windows\system32\DRIVERS\mrxsmb.sys
K 12	mup.sys	MupiCallUncProvider + 0x...	C:\Windows\System32\Drivers\mup.sys
K 13	mup.sys	MupStateMachine + 0x12...	C:\Windows\System32\Drivers\mup.sys
K 14	mup.sys	MupFsdIrpPassThrough + ...	C:\Windows\System32\Drivers\mup.sys
K 15	fltmgr.sys	FltpLegacyProcessingAfter...	C:\Windows\system32\drivers\fltmgr.sys
K 16	fltmgr.sys	FltPerformSynchronousIo +...	C:\Windows\system32\drivers\fltmgr.sys
K 17	fltmgr.sys	FltReadFile + 0x334	C:\Windows\system32\drivers\fltmgr.sys
K 18	SRTSP64.SYS	SRTSP64.SYS + 0x2b11b	C:\Windows\System32\Drivers\SRTSP64.SYS
K 19	SRTSP64.SYS	SRTSP64.SYS + 0x3c49f	C:\Windows\System32\Drivers\SRTSP64.SYS
K 20	SRTSP64.SYS	SRTSP64.SYS + 0x691b6	C:\Windows\System32\Drivers\SRTSP64.SYS
K 21	SRTSP64.SYS	SRTSP64.SYS + 0x69241	C:\Windows\System32\Drivers\SRTSP64.SYS

FIGURE 17-25 Srtsp64.sys in the call stacks of initial file reads.

Further, the stack frames higher up the same stack (shown in Figure 17-26) showed that the sequence of SRTSP64.SYS reads were being performed within the context of filter manager callbacks (frame 31) performed when Project opened the file with the *CreateFileW* call in frame 50. This behavior is common to on-access virus scanners.

Frame	Module	Location	Path
K 30	SRTSP64.SYS	SRTSP64.SYS + 0x2052e	C:\Windows\System32\Drivers\SRTSP64.SYS
K 31	fltmgr.sys	FltpPerformPostCallbacks ...	C:\Windows\system32\drivers\fltmgr.sys
K 32	fltmgr.sys	FltLegacyProcessingAfter...	C:\Windows\system32\drivers\fltmgr.sys
K 33	fltmgr.sys	FltpCreate + 0x2a9	C:\Windows\system32\drivers\fltmgr.sys
K 34	ntoskrnl.exe	IopParseDevice + 0x5a7	C:\Windows\system32\ntoskrnl.exe
K 35	ntoskrnl.exe	ObpLookupObjectName + ...	C:\Windows\system32\ntoskrnl.exe
K 36	ntoskrnl.exe	ObOpenObjectByName + ...	C:\Windows\system32\ntoskrnl.exe
K 37	ntoskrnl.exe	IopCreateFile + 0x2b7	C:\Windows\system32\ntoskrnl.exe
K 38	ntoskrnl.exe	NtCreateFile + 0x78	C:\Windows\system32\ntoskrnl.exe
K 39	ntoskrnl.exe	KiSystemServiceCopyEnd ...	C:\Windows\system32\ntoskrnl.exe
U 40	ntdll.dll	ZwCreateFile + 0xa, o:\w7...	C:\Windows\System32\ntdll.dll
U 41	wow64.dll	whNtCreateFile + 0x10f	C:\Windows\System32\wow64.dll
U 42	wow64.dll	Wow64SystemServiceEx ...	C:\Windows\System32\wow64.dll
U 43	wow64cpu.dll	TurboDispatchJumpAddre...	C:\Windows\System32\wow64cpu.dll
U 44	wow64.dll	RunCpuSimulation + 0xa	C:\Windows\System32\wow64.dll
U 45	wow64.dll	Wow64LdrpInitialize + 0x429	C:\Windows\System32\wow64.dll
U 46	ntdll.dll	LdrpInitializeProcess + 0x1...	C:\Windows\System32\ntdll.dll
U 47	ntdll.dll	_LdrpInitialize + 0x14533	C:\Windows\System32\ntdll.dll
U 48	ntdll.dll	LdrInitializeThunk + 0xe, d:...	C:\Windows\System32\ntdll.dll
U 49	ntdll.dll	NtCreateFile + 0x12, o:\w7...	C:\Windows\SysWOW64\ntdll.dll
U 50	KernelBase.dll	CreateFileW + 0x35e	C:\Windows\SysWOW64\KernelBase.dll

FIGURE 17-26 File open indicated by *CreateFileW* in frame 50 results in file reads from SRTSP64.SYS.

Sure enough, double-clicking on one of the SRTSP64.SYS lines in the stack displayed the module's properties. The dialog box shown in Figure 17-27 confirmed that it was Symantec AutoProtect that was repeatedly performing on-access virus detection each time Project opened the file with certain parameters.

FIGURE 17-27 Module Properties dialog box for SRTSP64.SYS.

Typically, administrators configure antivirus on file servers, so there's no need for clients to scan files they reference on servers because client-side scanning simply results in duplicative scans. This led to the support engineer's second recommendation, which was for the administrator to set an exclusion filter on their client antivirus deployment for the file share hosting user profiles.

In less than 15 minutes, the engineer had written up his analysis and recommendations and sent them back to the customer. The network monitor trace merely served as confirmation of what he observed in the Procmon trace. The administrator proceeded to implement the suggestions and, a few days later, confirmed that the user was no longer experiencing long file loads nor the errors he had reported. Another case closed with Procmon and thread stacks.

The Compound Case of the Outlook Hangs

This case was shared with me by a friend of mine, Andrew Richards, a Microsoft Exchange Server Escalation Engineer. It's a really interesting case because it highlights the use of a Sysinternals utility I specifically wrote for use by Microsoft support services and it's actually two cases in one.

The case unfolds with a systems administrator at a corporation contacting Microsoft support to report that users across the company's network were complaining of Outlook hangs lasting up to 15 minutes. The fact that multiple users were experiencing the problem pointed at an Exchange issue, so the call was routed to Exchange Server support services.

The Exchange team has developed a Performance Monitor data collector set that includes several hundred counters that have proven useful for troubleshooting Exchange issues, including LDAP, RPC, and SMTP message activity; Exchange connection counts; memory usage, and processor usage. Exchange support had the administrator collect a log of the server's activity with 12-hour log cycles, the first from 9 p.m. until 9 a.m. the next morning. When Exchange support engineers viewed the log, two patterns were clear despite the heavy density of the plots: first and as expected, the Exchange server's load increased during the morning when users came into work and started using Outlook; and second, the counter graphs showed a difference in behavior between about 8:05 and 8:20 a.m., a duration that corresponded exactly to the long delays users were reporting.

The support engineers zoomed in and puzzled over the counters in the timeframe and could see Exchange's CPU usage drop, the active connection count go down, and outbound response latency drastically increase, but they were unable to identify a cause. (See Figure 17-28.)

They escalated the case to the next level of support, and it was assigned to Andrew. Andrew studied the logs and concluded that he needed additional information about what Exchange was doing during an outage. Specifically, he wanted a process memory dump of Exchange when it was in the unresponsive state. This would contain the contents of the process address space, including its data and code, as well as the register state of the process' threads. Dump files of the Exchange process would allow Andrew to look at Exchange's threads to see what was causing them to stall.

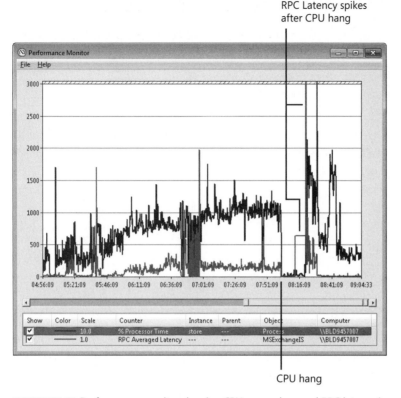

FIGURE 17-28 Performance monitor showing CPU usage drop and RPC latency increase.

One way to obtain a dump is to "attach" to the process with a debugger like Windbg from the Debugging Tools for Windows package (included with the Windows Software Development Kit) and execute the **.dump** command; however, downloading and installing the tools, launching the debugger, attaching to the right process, and saving dumps is an involved procedure. Instead, Andrew directed the administrator to download ProcDump. ProcDump makes it easy to obtain dumps of a process and includes options that create multiple dumps at a specified interval. Andrew asked the administrator to run ProcDump the next time the server's CPU usage dropped so that it would generate five dumps of the Exchange Server engine process, Store.exe, spaced three seconds apart:

```
procdump -n 5 -s 3 store.exe c:\dumps\store_mini.dmp
```

The next day, the problem was reproduced and the administrator sent Andrew the dump files ProcDump had generated. When a process temporarily hangs, it is often because one thread in the process acquires a lock protecting data that other threads need to access and holds the lock while performing some long-running operation. Andrew's first step, therefore, was to check for held locks. The most commonly used intraprocess synchronization lock is a critical section, and the **!locks debugger** command lists the critical sections in a dump that are locked, the thread ID of the thread owning the lock, and the number of threads waiting to acquire it. Andrew used a similar command, **!critlist** from the Sieext.dll debugger extension[3]. The output showed that multiple threads were piled up waiting for thread 223 to release a critical section:

```
0:000> !sieext.critlist
CritSec at 608e244c.  Owned by thread 223.
  Waiting Threads: 43 218 219 220 221 222 224 226 227 228 230 231 232 233
```

His next step was to see what the owning thread was doing, which might point at the code responsible for the long delays. He switched to the owning thread's register context using the ~ command and then dumped the thread's stack with the **k** command:

```
0:000> ~223s
eax=61192840 ebx=00000080 ecx=0000000f edx=00000074 esi=7c829e37 edi=40100080
eip=7c82860c esp=61191c40 ebp=61191cdc icpl=0          nv up ei pl nz na po nc
cs=001b  ss=0023  ds=0023  es=0023  fs=003b  gs=0000             efl=00000202
ntdll!KiFastSystemCallRet:
7c82860c c3              ret

0:223> knL
 # ChildEBP RetAddr
00 61191c3c 7c826e09 ntdll!KiFastSystemCallRet
01 61191c40 77e649ff ntdll!ZwCreateFile+0xc
02 61191cdc 608c6b70 kernel32!CreateFileW+0x377
WARNING: Stack unwind information not available. Following frames may be wrong.
03 61191cfc 7527e1a6 SAVFMSEVSAPI+0x6b70
04 00000000 00000000 0x7527e1a6
```

As sometimes happens, the debugger was unsure how to interpret the stack when it came across a stack frame pointing into Savfmsevsapi, an image for which it couldn't obtain symbols. Most Windows images have their symbols posted on the Microsoft symbol server, so this was likely a third-party DLL loaded into Exchange's Store.exe process and was therefore a suspect in the hangs. The list modules (**lm**) command dumps version information for loaded images, and the path of the image made it obvious that Savfmsevsapi was part of Symantec's mail security product:

```
0:000> lmvm SAVFMSEVSAPI
start    end           module name
608c0000 608e9000   SAVFMSEVSAPI T (no symbols)
    Loaded symbol image file: SAVFMSEVSAPI.dll
    Image path: C:\Program Files\Symantec\SMSMSE\6.0\Server\SAVFMSEVSAPI.dll
    Image name: SAVFMSEVSAPI.dll
    Timestamp:        Wed Jul 08 03:09:42 2009 (4A547066)
    CheckSum:         00033066
    ImageSize:        00029000
    File version:     6.0.9.286
    Product version:  6.0.9.286
```

---

[3] The public version, SieExtPub.dll, can be downloaded from microsoft.com.

```
File flags:      0 (Mask 0)
File OS:         10001 DOS Win16
File type:       1.0 App
File date:       00000000.00000000
Translations:    0000.04b0 0000.04e4 0409.04b0 0409.04e4
```

Andrew checked the other dumps, and they all had similar stack traces. With the anecdotal evidence seeming to point at a Symantec issue, Andrew forwarded the dumps and his analysis, with the administrator's permission, to Symantec technical support. Several hours later, they reported that the dumps indeed revealed a problem with the mail application's latest antivirus signature distribution and forwarded a patch to the administrator that would fix the bug. He applied it and continued to monitor the server to verify the fix. Sure enough, the server's performance established fairly regular activity levels and the long delays disappeared.

However, over the subsequent days, the administrator started to receive, albeit at a lower rate, complaints from several users that Outlook was sporadically hanging for up to a minute. Andrew asked the administrator to send a correlating 12-hour Performance Monitor capture with the Exchange data collection set, but this time there was no obvious anomaly.

Wondering whether the hangs would be visible in the CPU usage history of Store.exe, he removed all the counters except for Store's processor usage counter. When he zoomed in on the morning hours when users began to log in and the load on the server increased, he noticed three spikes around 8:30 a.m. (See Figure 17-29.)

FIGURE 17-29 CPU spikes in Store.exe around 8:30 a.m.

Because the server has eight cores, the processor usage counter for an individual process has a possible range between 0 and 800, so the spikes were far from taxing the system, but they were definitely higher than Exchange's typical range on that system. Zooming in further and setting the graph's vertical scale to make the spikes more distinct, he observed that average CPU usage was always below about 75 percent of a single core and the spikes were 15–30 seconds long. (See Figure 17-30.)

FIGURE 17-30 Zooming in on CPU spikes.

What was Exchange doing during the spikes? They were too short-lived and random for the administrator to run ProcDump like he had before and reliably capture dumps when they occurred. Fortunately, I designed ProcDump with this precise scenario in mind. It supports several trigger conditions that, when met, cause it to generate a dump. For example, you can configure ProcDump to generate a dump of a process when the process terminates or when its private memory usage exceeds a certain value, or even to generate one based on the value of a performance counter you specify. Its most basic trigger, though, is the CPU usage of the process exceeding a specified threshold for a specified length of time.

The Performance Monitor log gave Andrew the information he needed to craft a ProcDump command line that would capture dumps for future CPU spikes:

```
procdump.exe -n 20 -s 10 -c 75 -u store.exe c:\dumps\store_75pc_10sec.dmp
```

The arguments configure ProcDump to generate a dump of the Store.exe process when Store's CPU usage exceeds 75 percent (**–c 75**) relative to a single core (**–u**) for 10 seconds (**–s 10**), to generate up to 20 dumps (**–n 20**) and then exit, and to save the dumps in the C:\Dumps directory with names that begin with **store_75pc_10sec**. The administrator executed the command before leaving work, and when he checked on its progress the next morning it had finished creating 20 dump files. He e-mailed them to Andrew, who proceeded to study them in the Windbg debugger one by one.

When ProcDump generates a dump because the CPU usage trigger is met, it sets the thread context in the dump file to the thread that was consuming the most CPU at the time of the dump. Because the debugger's stack-dumping commands are relative to the current thread context, simply entering the stack dumping command shows the stack of the thread most likely to have caused a CPU spike. Over half the dumps were inconclusive, apparently captured after the spike that triggered the dump had already ended, or with threads that were executing code that obviously wasn't directly related to a spike. However, several of the dumps had stack traces similar to the one in Figure 17-31.

```
0:145> knL
 # ChildEBP RetAddr
00 5c2be9bc 00405df7 store!JetRetrieveColumnFn+0xd
01 5c2bea10 0040604f store!JTAB_BASE::EcRetrieveColumnByPtagid+0x152
02 5c2bea3c 00425919 store!JTAB_BASE::EcRetrieveColumn+0x28
03 5c2bea70 00411828 store!MINIMSG::PfidContainingFolder+0x5b
04 5c2beabc 00420663 store!UNK::EcCheckRights+0x1f3
05 5c2bead0 00420e58 store!MINIMSG::EcCheckRights+0x72
0                                                        0x134

08 5c2bedd4 00425ea5 store!MFTWIR::EcGetProp+0x376
09 5c2bee24 0041f1b7 store!TWIR::EcRestrictProperty+0x163
0a 5c2bee54 0041f218 store!TWIR::EcRestrictHier+0x1f3
0b 5c2bee84 0044aafa store!TWIR::EcRestrictHier+0x6d
0c 5c2beea8 0044aa12 store!TWIR::EcFindRow+0xae
0d 5c2bf0d8 0044a5ae store!VMSG::EcSlowFindRow+0x1ed
0e 5c2bf228 0044a24a store!VMSG::EcFindRow+0x511
0f 5c2bf26c 0044a103 store!EcFindRowOp+0xf9
10 5c2bf5a4 0040f0cc store!EcFindRow+0x168
11 5c2bf83c 0040ffda store!EcRpc+0xf4a
12 5c2bf8b8 004ffdf1 store!EcRpcExt+0x196
13 5c2bf90c 77c80193 store!EcDoRpcExt+0x8d
```

store!TWIR::EcFindRow+0xae

FIGURE 17-31 Store.exe stack trace with *store!TWIR::EcFindRow+0xae*.

The stack frame that stuck out listed Store's *EcFindRow* function, which implied that the spikes were caused by lengthy database queries, the kind that execute when Outlook accesses a mailbox folder with thousands of entries. With this clue in hand, Andrew suggested the administrator create an inventory of large mailboxes and pointed him to an article the Exchange support team had written that describes how to do this for each version of Exchange ("Finding High Item Count Folders Using the Exchange Management Shell," available at *http://msexchangeteam.com/archive/2009/12/07/453450.aspx*).

Sure enough, the script identified several users with folders containing tens of thousands of items. The administrator asked the users to reduce their item count to well below 5000 (the Exchange 2003 recommendation—this has been increased in each version, with a recommendation of 100,000 in Exchange 2010) by archiving the items, deleting them, or organizing them into subfolders. Within a couple of days, they had reorganized the problematic folders and user complaints ceased entirely. Ongoing monitoring of the Exchange server over the following week confirmed that the problem was gone.

With the help of ProcDump, the compound case of the Outlook hangs was successfully closed.

Chapter 18
Malware

Malware causes more than its fair share of computer problems. Of course, by definition it always performs actions that are not in your best interest. Sometimes it tries to do so quietly without your noticing its presence. Other times, it makes itself unavoidably obvious, such as with the scareware described in "The Case of the Process-Killing Malware" in this chapter. Like a lot of legitimate software, sometimes malware is just poorly written. Unlike most legitimate software, though, malware often *actively* tries to prevent its discovery or removal.

- **The Case of the Sysinternals-Blocking Malware** is interesting because it involves malware that specifically tried to prevent Sysinternals utilities from running. The case was solved with Sysinternals utilities, of course.

- **The Case of the Process-Killing Malware** happened as we were finishing up this book. A friend of Aaron's brought his son's infected laptop over to be cleaned. The malware did not want to go quietly. It didn't count on Autoruns in Safe Mode.

- **The Case of the Fake System Component** demonstrates the use of the Strings utility to diagnose malware.

- **The Case of the Mysterious ASEP** revealed malware creating its own Auto-start Extensibility Point (ASEP). It was solved with ListDLLs, Procmon, Procexp, and Autoruns.

The Case of the Sysinternals-Blocking Malware

A friend asked a Sysinternals user to take a look at a system that the friend believed was infected with malware. Startup and logon took a long time, and malware scans with Microsoft Security Essentials would never complete. The user looked for unusual processes in Task Manager, but nothing jumped out at him.

He then turned to Sysinternals, trying AutoRuns, Procmon, Procexp, and RootkitRevealer[1], but each one exited immediately after starting. As an experiment, he tried opening a text file named "Process Explorer" with Notepad, and it too terminated right away. At this point, he had plenty of reason to believe that the system was infected, but he didn't know how to identify the cause, let alone remove it.

Looking through the rest of the Sysinternals Suite, he noticed the Desktops utility. His experiment with Notepad suggested to him that the malware was monitoring window titles

---

[1] RootkitRevealer is a rootkit detection utility I created several years ago when rootkits were still relatively unknown and the major anti-malware vendors had not yet taken on the challenge of detecting or removing them. RootkitRevealer has since been retired.

for programs it didn't like. Because window enumeration returns only the windows on the same desktop as the caller, he surmised that the malware author probably hadn't considered the possibility of programs running on non-default desktops. Sure enough, after running Desktops and switching to the second desktop, he was able to launch Procmon and other utilities. (See Figure 18-1.) (For more information about these concepts, see "Sessions, Window Stations, Desktops, and Window Messages" in Chapter 2, "Windows Core Concepts.")

FIGURE 18-1 Running Sysinternals utilities on a different desktop.

First he looked at Procexp. All the process names looked legitimate, so he enabled the Verify Signers option and the Verified Signer column. He was able to ascertain that all of the process' main executable image files appeared valid.

Next he ran Procmon. He noticed a lot of activity in the Winlogon process. He set a filter to show only Winlogon.exe activity (shown in Figure 18-2) and saw that it was checking a strange registry key once every second:

```
HKLM\Software\Microsoft\Windows NT\CurrentVersion\Winlogon\Notify\acdcacaeaacbafbeaa
```

Process Name	PID	Operation	Path
winlogon.exe	728	RegCreateKey	HKLM\Software\Microsoft\Windows NT\CurrentVersion\Winlogon\Notify\acdcacaeaacbafbeaa
winlogon.exe	728	RegOpenKey	Software\Microsoft\Windows NT\CurrentVersion\Winlogon\Notify\acdcacaeaacbafbeaa
winlogon.exe	728	RegQueryValue	HKLM\SOFTWARE\Microsoft\Windows NT\CurrentVersion\Winlogon\Notify\acdcacaeaacbafbeaa\DllName
winlogon.exe	728	RegQueryValue	HKLM\SOFTWARE\Microsoft\Windows NT\CurrentVersion\Winlogon\Notify\acdcacaeaacbafbeaa\DllName
winlogon.exe	728	RegQueryValue	HKLM\SOFTWARE\Microsoft\Windows NT\CurrentVersion\Winlogon\Notify\acdcacaeaacbafbeaa\Impersona
winlogon.exe	728	RegQueryValue	HKLM\SOFTWARE\Microsoft\Windows NT\CurrentVersion\Winlogon\Notify\acdcacaeaacbafbeaa\Impersona
winlogon.exe	728	RegQueryValue	HKLM\SOFTWARE\Microsoft\Windows NT\CurrentVersion\Winlogon\Notify\acdcacaeaacbafbeaa\Asynchro
winlogon.exe	728	RegQueryValue	HKLM\SOFTWARE\Microsoft\Windows NT\CurrentVersion\Winlogon\Notify\acdcacaeaacbafbeaa\Asynchro

FIGURE 18-2 Procmon displaying unusual registry activity from Winlogon.exe.

Now he ran Autoruns, opting to verify image signatures and to hide Microsoft and Windows entries. With only third-party and unsigned entries displayed, he quickly found the culprit: an unsigned DLL with a random-looking name registered as a Winlogon notification package that loads a DLL into the Winlogon process. (See Figure 18-3.) He deleted the entry in Autoruns, but found that it was back when he rescanned.

FIGURE 18-3 Autoruns identifying malware registered as a Winlogon notification package.

At this point, he went back to Microsoft Security Essentials and directed it to scan just the random-named DLL. (See Figure 18-4.) After cleaning, he was able to delete the entry. The system returned to normal.

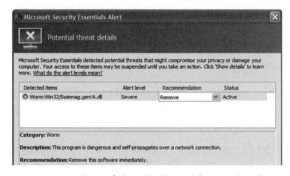

FIGURE 18-4 Microsoft Security Essentials removing the specific threat identified by Sysinternals utilities.

The Case of the Process-Killing Malware

Aaron's friend Paul called and said that his son's laptop had recently begun displaying a message that the computer was infected and demanding credit card payment to clean it. Aaron suggested that it might just be a misleading popup from a dishonest Web page ad and that logging off could make it go away. "No, already tried that." "Oh. Can you bring it over?" "Be right there."

When Paul started the laptop and entered his son's password, a full-screen, always-on-top window took over the screen. It claimed it was an anti-malware program and listed what it said were numerous types of malware infecting the computer. It then demanded valid credit card information before it could remove the "malware" that it had found. However, this program was not the reputable anti-malware brand that Paul had purchased and installed (yet had allowed this particular piece of malware to run).

Aaron popped in a CD containing the Sysinternals utilities and tried to run Procexp, Autoruns, and others. None would start. Thinking about the "Case of the Sysinternals-Blocking Malware" (earlier in this chapter), he tried running Desktops, but that failed to launch also. The malware allowed no new process to run, including Command Prompt, Windows PowerShell, or Task Manager. At most, the frame of a window would begin to appear, and then immediately disappear.

Aaron restarted the computer in Safe Mode with Command Prompt, which loads a minimal set of drivers and runs Cmd.exe instead of Windows Explorer. It also processes very few ASEPs (described in Chapter 5, "Autoruns"). The malware did not launch at this point, indicating that it depended on one of those ASEPs. Aaron ran Autoruns, opting to verify signatures and to hide Microsoft and Windows entries. He found a number of suspicious items, including several file-sharing programs, Internet Explorer toolbars, and browser helper objects, each of which he disabled rather than deleted (shown in Figure 18-5), in case he changed his mind later. The dates on the folder locations where these items were installed indicated that they had been there for a long time and were therefore not the likely cause of the current problem.

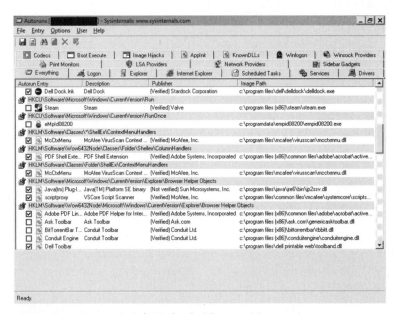

FIGURE 18-5 Autoruns in Safe Mode, disabling suspicious entries.

The culprit was easy to identify: it had no description or publisher, had the nondescriptive name "eMpId08200", launched from the HKCU RunOnce key, was installed under the C:\ProgramData folder, and to top it all off it had the same icon that the fake anti-malware displayed. Aaron deleted the ASEP in Autoruns and deleted its files in Cmd.exe. (See Figure 18-6.) For good measure, he left the unnecessary file-sharing programs and Internet Explorer extensions disabled. He restarted the computer, which ran without issue.

It is interesting to note that the malware in this case never appears to have used administrative rights. It installed itself to a user-writable folder and ensured that it would run again by hooking one of the user's ASEPs instead of a global ASEP. In fact, the same malware infected Aaron's mother-in-law's Windows XP computer a few weeks later. Because Aaron had made sure that she always logged on with a standard user account, Aaron was able to clean the infection easily by logging on to the administrative account, which the malware had not been able to infect. From there, he ran Autoruns, selected the infected account from the User menu, and deleted the offending ASEP entry. (Unfortunately, he failed to capture any screen shots.) The two lessons here are that malware is increasingly able to cause harm without requiring administrative rights, and that such malware is much easier to clean than malware that is able to subvert the integrity of the operating system.

FIGURE 18-6 Deleting the malware from Cmd.exe in Safe Mode.

The Case of the Fake System Component

The next two cases were brought to me by Greg Cottingham, a Senior Support Escalation Engineer at Microsoft. In September 2010, Greg's team began receiving reports from several companies of a new worm that was eventually called Win32/Visal.b. Greg was assigned one such case and began his investigation of a suspected infected work station by pressing Ctrl+Shift+Esc to start Task Manager. At first glance, none of the processes shown in Task Manager in Figure 18-7 might appear suspicious to an untrained observer. However, when Show Processes From All Users is not selected, there should be only one Csrss.exe listed, but Task Manager showed two. (Task Manager's Show Processes From All Users option actually determines whether Task Manager shows processes only from the current *terminal services session* or from all TS sessions. See Chapter 2 for more information about TS sessions.)

FIGURE 18-7 Task Manager showing two instances of Csrss.exe in one terminal session.

One of the limitations of Task Manager is that it does not show the full path of executable images. Malware often hides itself behind legitimate names such as Svchost.exe and Csrss.exe but is installed in other locations such as %windir% instead of %windir%\System32, where the actual Windows files are. Procexp overcomes this limitation by showing the executable's full path in the tooltip (shown in Figure 18-8) or in a column.

FIGURE 18-8 Procexp establishing the path to the "extra" Csrss.exe.

After establishing that the "extra" Csrss.exe was in %windir% and did not pass signature verification, Greg ran Strings on it to get an idea of what it was up to. (See Figure 18-9.) Strings revealed evidence of several malware behaviors, including text for the creation of an Autorun.inf to copy to a removable drive and trick a user into running malware when the drive was inserted into another computer, enumeration of computers and file shares, and copying malware to file shares with misleading file names and extensions.

FIGURE 18-9 Strings revealing malware in the fake Csrss.exe.

Greg has also diagnosed malware files with Strings by discovering text such as "UPX0" (indicating that the file was packed) or references to "non-professional" PDB symbol file paths such as "d:\hack.86" or "c:\mystuff".

Having confirmed that this fake Windows component was indeed malicious, Greg and his team worked with the Microsoft Malware Protection Center to document its behaviors and recovery steps and to provide an anti-malware solution.

The Case of the Mysterious ASEP

Greg was assigned a case from a customer representing a large US hospital network that reported it had been hit with an infestation of the Marioforever virus. The customer had discovered the virus when its printers started getting barraged with giant print jobs of garbage text, causing its network to slow and the printers to run out of paper. Their antivirus software identified a file named Marioforever.exe in the %SystemRoot% folder of one of the machines spewing files to the printers as suspicious, but deleting the file just resulted in it reappearing at the subsequent reboot. Other antivirus programs failed to flag the file at all.

Greg started looking for clues by seeing if there were additional suspicious files in the %SystemRoot% directory of one of the infected systems. One file, a DLL named Nvrsma.dll, had a recent time stamp, and although it was named similarly to Nvidia display driver components, the computer in question didn't have an Nvidia display adapter. When he tried to delete or rename the file, he got a sharing violation error, which meant that some process had the file open and was preventing others from opening it. There are several Sysinternals tools that will list the processes that have a file open or a DLL loaded, including Process Explorer and Handle. Because the file was a DLL, though, Greg decided on the Sysinternals Listdlls utility, which showed that the DLL was loaded by one process, Winlogon:

```
C:\>listdlls -d nvrsma.dll

ListDLLs v2.25 - DLL lister for Win9x/NT
Copyright (C) 1997-2004 Mark Russinovich
Sysinternals - www.sysinternals.com


---------------------------------------------------------------------------
winlogon.exe pid: 416
Command line: winlogon.exe

   Base      Size      Version         Path
   0x10000000 0x34000                  C:\WINDOWS\system32\nvrsma.dll
```

Winlogon is the core system process responsible for managing interactive logon sessions, and in this case it was also the host for a malicious DLL. The next step was to determine how the DLL was configured to load into Winlogon. It had to be via an autostart location, so he ran both Autoruns and the console-mode AutorunsC. However, there was no sign of Nvrsma. dll, and all the autostart entries were either Windows components or legitimate third-party components. That appeared to be a dead end, so he turned to Procmon.

Winlogon starts during the boot process, so Greg enabled Procmon's boot-logging feature, rebooted the system, ran Procmon, and loaded the boot log. He then pressed Ctrl+F and searched for "nvrsma". Figure 18-10 shows what he found: the first reference occurred when Winlogon.exe had queried the registry value HKLM\SOFTWARE\Microsoft\Windows NT\ CurrentVersion\Windows\dzpInit_DLLs, which returned the text value "nvrsma". Several events later, Winlogon.exe opened and then mapped nvrsma.dll into memory.

FIGURE 18-10 Procmon showing why Winlogon.exe loaded nvrsma.dll.

Greg then looked at the call stack for that first registry event. As you can see in Figure 18-11, the registry read was apparently initiated from User32.dll. Greg knew that the name "dzpInit_DLLs" is very similar to that of the well-known and widely-abused "AppInit_DLLs" ASEP defined in the same registry key and which is also initiated from User32.dll[2]. But this wasn't AppInit_DLLs. Was dzpInit_DLLs a new ASEP that Greg (and Autoruns) had never heard of?

FIGURE 18-11 Call stack showing a registry event initiated within User32.dll.

Greg now turned his attention to User32.dll. He noticed that on infected machines, the last-modified date for User32.dll in both the System32 and DllCache folders was the date of the initial infection. Taking a closer look at the Autoruns results, Greg found that User32.dll failed signature verification (shown in Figure 18-12) and had therefore either been modified or completely replaced.

Greg ran Procexp on a known-good Windows XP machine and on an infected one. On both, he selected the Winlogon.exe process, opened DLL View, double-clicked User32.dll in the lower pane to open its Properties dialog box, and clicked on the Strings tab. He then compared the text strings found in each. All but one were completely the same. The difference was that AppInit_DLLs in the known-good one was replaced with dzpInit_DLLs in the modified one. (See Figure 18-13.) Performing a binary comparison of the good and bad User32.dll files with the Windows command **fc /b**, Greg found that those two bytes were the only differences between the two files. The malware had created its own ASEP by changing two bytes in User32.dll so that it loaded DLLs listed in the dzpInit_DLLs registry value instead of in AppInit_DLLs.

---

[2] When a process on Windows XP and earlier loads User32.dll, it also loads any DLLs named in the AppInit_DLLs registry value. Autoruns lists these DLLs on its AppInit tab.

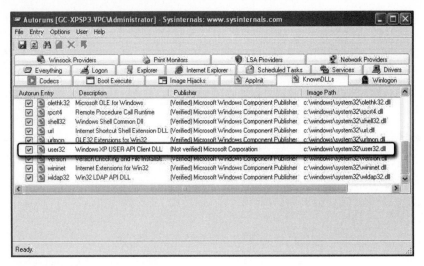

FIGURE 18-12 Autoruns showing User32 failing signature verification.

FIGURE 18-13 Comparing text strings in a known-good User32.dll (left) and an infected one (right)

With the knowledge of exactly how the malware's primary DLL activated, Greg set out to clean the malware off the system. Because User32.dll would be locked by the malware whenever Windows was online, he booted the Windows Preinstallation Environment (WinPE) from a CD-ROM and, from there, copied a clean User32.dll over the malicious version. Then he deleted the associated malware files he had discovered in his investigation. When he was done, he rebooted the system and verified that it was clean. He closed the case by giving the hospital network administrators the cleaning steps he had followed and submitted the malware to the Microsoft antimalware team so that they could incorporate automated cleaning into Forefront and the Malicious Software Removal Toolkit. He had solved a seemingly impossible case by applying several Sysinternals utilities and helped the hospital get back to normal operation.

Index

Symbols

paging files, defragmenting, 345–346

paging lists, purging, 367

paging metrics, 94

parent-child relationships, viewing, 189

parent processes, 21

partitioning, LDM, 348

partitions, location information, 347

passwords, for domain and local user accounts, 196–197

PATH environment changes to, 177

Path system environment variable, launching utilities from, 7–8

paths
cross-references to, 140
of dump files, 229–230
file and folder operations, listing by, 136
spaces in, 176
types of, 105

pause command, 202

PDB extension, 26

PendMoves, 333–334

per-user ASEPs, 145, 151
Internet Explorer ASEPs, 157–158
logon ASEPs, 154
modification of, 151
Windows Explorer ASEPs, 156

performance, system, troubleshooting, 405–426

performance counters
counter names, 232
process dump files triggered by, 232

performance metrics, viewing, 79–80

permissions
actual vs. effective, 268
editing, 276
Everyone Full Control, 277
on file shares, 277–278
misconfiguration of, identifying, 275–277
on objects, 295, 372
reporting, 267–275

on services, 87

troubleshooting errors with, 390

volume permissions, 340

Permissions button, 84, 87

Physical Address Extensions (PAE), processor support of, 369–370

physical disks
capturing images of, 335–337
event logging on, 338–339

physical memory
analyzing, 211–227
graphs of, 65, 93–94
metrics on, 94
purging, 367
releasing, 220
usage analysis, 359–367

physical memory addresses, valid ranges, 364–365

physical processors, mapping to logical processors, 367–369

PID 0 pseudo-process, 190

PIDs. See process IDs (PIDs)

PipeList, 374–375

Play To feature errors, 389–390

Plug-and-Play drivers, load order, 374

PML file format, 124

port monitors, 164

Portmon, 353–358
administrative rights for, 353
display options, 354
event counter, 354
filtering capabilities, 355–356
highlighting, 356
logging data, 357
Log-To-File Settings dialog box, 357
printing data, 358
Print Range dialog box, 358
saving data, 357
search capabilities, 355
settings, storage of, 355

ports, input/output control commands, 353–357

post-logoff logging, 128–129

postmortem debuggers, ProcDump as, 236

post-reboot file operation utilities, 333–334

PowerShell remoting capabilities, 410

prefetch files, 403–404

print spooler, troubleshooting problems with, 164

printer shares, enumerating, 277–278

prioritized standby lists, 363

private bytes, 215
graph of, 81

private I/O counts, 61–62

private memory, 216, 217

private symbol files, 27

private virtual address spaces, 21

privileges
disabled, 84
removing, 183
reporting on, 272
user privileges, 16

ProcDump, 211, 227–237
administrative rights for, 229
call-stack analysis features, 405–426
command-line syntax, 228–229
commit charges dumps, 232
crash dumps, 236–237
default thread context, 237
dump criteria, specifying, 230–232
dump file path, specifying, 229–230, 236
dump files, 421, 424–425
dump files, series of, 231
dump options, 232–233
exceptions, dumps on, 231
hung windows, dumps on, 231, 235
list modules command, 422
Miniplus (–mp) dumps, 233–235
as postmortem debugger, 236
process_PID notation, 232
process reflection and, 233
processes to monitor, specifying, 229
running noninteractively, 235

About the Authors

Mark Russinovich is a Technical Fellow in the Windows Azure group at Microsoft, working on Microsoft's datacenter operating system. He is a widely recognized expert in Windows operating system internals as well as operating system security and design. He is the author of the recently published cyberthriller Zero Day and co-author of the Microsoft Press Windows Internals books. Russinovich joined Microsoft in 2006 when Microsoft acquired Winternals Software, the company he cofounded in 1996, as well as Sysinternals, where he authors and publishes dozens of popular Windows administration and diagnostic utilities. He is a featured speaker at major industry conferences, including Microsoft's TechEd, WinHEC, and Professional Developers Conference.

You can contact Mark at *markruss@microsoft.com* and follow him on Twitter at *http://www.twitter.com/markrussinovich*.

Aaron Margosis is a Principal Consultant with Microsoft Public Sector Services where he has worked primarily with U.S. federal government customers since 1999. He specializes in application development on Microsoft platforms with an emphasis on security and application compatibility in locked-down environments, and is a highly-regarded speaker at Microsoft conferences. He is well known for having evangelized running Windows XP as a non-admin and for publishing utilities and guidance to make doing so more feasible. His MakeMeAdmin script pioneered the concept of a single user account running in both administrative and non-admin contexts, influencing the design of User Account Control. Aaron's several security utilities can be downloaded through his blog (*http://blogs.msdn.com/aaron_margosis*) and his team's blog (*http://blogs.technet.com/fdcc*).

You can contact Aaron at *aaronmar@microsoft.com*.

SIT DOWN WITH THE EXPERTS
who literally wrote the book on Windows internals!

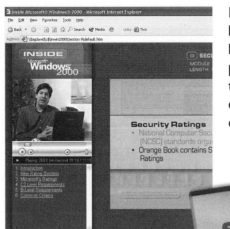

If you liked their book, you'll love hearing them in person. Get one of their video tutorials or come to a live class.

LIVE, INSTRUCTOR LED CLASSES

If you're an IT professional deploying and supporting Windows servers and workstations, you need to be able to dig beneath the surface when things go wrong. In our classes, you'll gain a deep understanding of the internals of the operating system and how to leverage advanced troubleshooting tools to solve system and application problems and understand performance issues more effectively. Attend a public class or schedule a private on site seminar at your location. For dates, course details, pricing, and registration information, see www.solsem.com.

INTERACTIVE DVD TUTORIAL

Sit down with the experts who literally wrote the book on Windows internals. Windows Internals COMPLETE consists of 12 hours of interactive training taking you under the hood of the operating system to learn how the kernel components work. As the ultimate compliment, Microsoft Corporation licensed these videos for their corporate training worldwide.

The Sysinternals Video Library (also 12 hours) covers essential Windows troubleshooting topics such as crash dump analysis and memory trouble-shooting as well as how to leverage key Sysinternals tools.

To view video samples or for a detailed outline, visit www.solsem.com or email videos@solsem.com

Get Certified—Windows® 7

Desktop support technicians and administrators—demonstrate your expertise with Windows 7 by earning a Microsoft® Certification focusing on core technical (MCTS) or professional (MCITP) skills. With our 2-in-1 *Self-Paced Training Kits*, you get a comprehensive, cost-effective way to prepare for the certification exams. Combining official exam-prep guides + practice tests, these kits are designed to maximize the impact of your study time.

EXAM 70-680
MCTS Self-Paced Training Kit: Configuring Windows 7
Ian McLean and Orin Thomas
ISBN 9780735627086

EXAM 70-685
MCITP Self-Paced Training Kit: Windows 7 Enterprise Desktop Support Technician
Tony Northrup and J.C. Mackin
ISBN 9780735627093

EXAM 70-686
MCITP Self-Paced Training Kit: Windows 7, Enterprise Desktop Administrator
Craig Zacker and Orin Thomas
ISBN 9780735627178

GREAT FOR ON THE JOB

Windows 7 Resource Kit
Mitch Tulloch, Tony Northrup, Jerry Honeycutt, Ed Wilson, and the Windows 7 Team at Microsoft
ISBN 9780735627000

Windows 7 Inside Out
Ed Bott, Carl Siechert, Craig Stinson
ISBN 9780735626652

Windows 7 Administrator's Pocket Consultant
William R. Stanek
ISBN 9780735626997

What do you think of this book?

We want to hear from you!
To participate in a brief online survey, please visit:

microsoft.com/learning/booksurvey

Tell us how well this book meets your needs—what works effectively, and what we can do better. Your feedback will help us continually improve our books and learning resources for you.

Thank you in advance for your input!